PEDAGOGIES AND POLICIES FOR PUBLISHING RESEARCH IN ENGLISH

Offering a nuanced examination of the complex landscape that international scholars who publish their research in English must navigate, this edited volume details 17 perspectives on scholarly writing for publication across seven geolinguistic regions. This innovative volume includes first-hand accounts and analyses written by local scholars and pedagogues living and working outside Anglophone centres of global knowledge production. The book provides an in-depth look into the deeply contextualized pedagogical activities that support English-language publishing. It also brings much-needed insight to discussions of policies and practices of global scholarly research writing. Bookended by the editors' introductory overview of this burgeoning field and an envoi by the eminent applied linguist John M. Swales, the diverse contributions in this volume will appeal to scholars who use English as an additional language, as well as to researchers, instructors, and policymakers involved in the production, support, and adjudication of global scholars' research writing.

James N. Corcoran is an Assistant Professor of Applied Language Studies and English Language Studies at Renison University College/University of Waterloo, Canada.

Karen Englander is an applied linguist and former professor at the Universidad Autónoma de Baja California, Mexico, and York University, Canada.

Laura-Mihaela Muresan is a Professor of English at the Bucharest University of Economic Studies, Romania.

ESL & Applied Linguistics Professional Series
Eli Hinkel, Series Editor

The Politics of English Second Language Writing Assessment in Global Contexts
Edited by Todd Ruecker and Deborah Crusan

Transnational Writing Education
Theory, History, and Practice
Edited by Xiaoye You

Understanding and Teaching English Spelling
A Strategic Guide
Adam Brown

Teaching Essential Units of Language
Beyond Single-word Vocabulary
Edited by Eli Hinkel

What English Language Teachers Need to Know Volume I
Understanding Learning, 2nd Edition
Denise E. Murray and MarryAnn Christison

Pedagogies and Policies for Publishing Research in English
Local Initiatives Supporting International Scholars
James N. Corcoran, Karen Englander, and Laura-Mihaela Muresan

For more information about this series, please visit: www.routledge.com/ESL--Applied-Linguistics-Professional-Series/book-series/LEAESLALP

PEDAGOGIES AND POLICIES FOR PUBLISHING RESEARCH IN ENGLISH

Local Initiatives Supporting International Scholars

Edited by
James N. Corcoran, Karen Englander, and Laura-Mihaela Muresan

NEW YORK AND LONDON

First published 2019
by Routledge
52 Vanderbilt Avenue, New York, NY 10017

and by Routledge
2 Park Square, Milton Park, Abingdon, Oxon, OX14 4RN

Routledge is an imprint of the Taylor & Francis Group, an informa business

© 2019 Taylor & Francis

The right of James N. Corcoran, Karen Englander and Laura-Mihaela Muresan to be identified as the authors of the editorial material, and of the authors for their individual chapters, has been asserted in accordance with sections 77 and 78 of the Copyright, Designs and Patents Act 1988.

All rights reserved. No part of this book may be reprinted or reproduced or utilised in any form or by any electronic, mechanical, or other means, now known or hereafter invented, including photocopying and recording, or in any information storage or retrieval system, without permission in writing from the publishers.

Trademark notice: Product or corporate names may be trademarks or registered trademarks, and are used only for identification and explanation without intent to infringe.

Library of Congress Cataloging-in-Publication Data
A catalog record for this title has been requested

ISBN: 978-1-138-55808-3 (hbk)
ISBN: 978-1-138-55809-0 (pbk)
ISBN: 978-1-315-15122-9 (ebk)

Typeset in Bembo
by Swales & Willis Ltd, Exeter, Devon, UK

CONTENTS

Acknowledgements   *viii*

1 Diverse Global Perspectives on Scholarly
  Writing for Publication   1
  James N. Corcoran, Karen Englander, and Laura-Mihaela Muresan

REGION 1
Latin America   17

2 A Utilization-Focused Program Evaluation
  of an ERPP Tutoring Service at One Colombian
  University   19
  Gerriet Janssen and Silvia Restrepo

3 Trajectories Towards Authorship: Eight
  Mexican English Language Teaching Professionals   36
  Fátima Encinas-Prudencio, Verónica Sánchez-Hernández, Maria Thomas-Ruzic, Gicela Cuatlapantzi-Pichón, and Georgina Aguilar-González

4 Writing for Publication in English: Some
  Institutional Initiatives at the Universidad
  Nacional de Entre Ríos   56
  Diana Waigandt, Alicia Noceti, and Raquel María Teresa Lothringer

REGION 2
Northern Europe   75

5 Supporting Nordic Scholars Who Write
   in English for Research Publication Purposes   77
   Birna Arnbjörnsdóttir

6 The Unreal and the Real: English for Research
   Purposes in Norway   91
   Tom Muir and Kristin Solli

REGION 3
Eastern and Southern Europe   107

7 Research Writing in English in a Romanian
   Academic Ecosystem: A Case Study of an
   Experienced Multiliterate Researcher   109
   Laura-Mihaela Muresan and Carmen Pérez-Llantada

8 English or Spanish for Research Publication Purposes?
   Reflections on a Critical Pragmatic Pedagogy   128
   Sally Burgess, Pedro Martín, and Diana Balasanyan

REGION 4
East Asia   141

9 Observing and Reflecting in an ERPP "Master
   Class": Learning and Thinking About Application   143
   Yongyan Li and Margaret Cargill

10 Publishing Research in English for
   Chinese Multilingual Scholars in Language-Related
   Disciplines: Towards a Biliteracy Approach   161
   Yongyan Zheng and Yuan Cao

REGION 5
South Asia   177

11 The Impact of English Language Teaching Reforms
   on Pakistani Scholars' Language and Research Skills   179
   Sarwat Nauman

REGION 6
Africa   193

12 Teaching the Craft: From Thesis Writing to Writing
    Research for Publication   195
    Hayat Messekher and Mohamed Miliani

13 Scholarly Publishing in Nigeria: The Enduring
    Effects of Colonization   215
    *Ayokunle Olumuyiwa Omobowale, Olayinka Akanle, and
    Charles Akinsete*

REGION 7
Persian Gulf   233

14 Examining the Status Quo of Publication in Iranian
    Higher Education: Perceptions and Strategies   235
    Hesamoddin Shahriari and Behzad Ghonsooly

15 Writing Louder? Coping With the Push to Publish
    in English at an Iranian University   252
    Seyyed-Abdolhamid Mirhosseini and Zahra Shafiee

16 "Holistic Argumentation Creation": Integrated
    Principles for Helping Graduate Students Create
    a Journal Paper   266
    Roger Nunn and Tanju Deveci

17 Envoi   284
    John M. Swales

Contributor Biographies   291
Index   294

ACKNOWLEDGEMENTS

This book would not have been possible without the diligence, dedication, and hard work of the contributing authors. The many author groups responsible for the diverse perspectives included in the volume were highly professional, negotiating respectfully with their colleagues and editors, submitting and re-submitting in a timely manner, allowing for this project to stay its course and ultimately come to fruition. We would like to acknowledge the diligent and caring mentorship of more established authors during manuscript revisions; this certainly contributed to the overall quality of the chapters within, not to mention, potentially, the longer-term publishing processes and practices of the less experienced authors. Further, we thank John Swales for his Envoi contribution. As a towering figure in our field, and a personal mentor to Karen, his participation in this book is welcomed as an endorsement of the work we have undertaken. Finally, we are grateful for the support and guidance of Karen Adler, Eli Hinkel, Emmalee Ortega, Siobhan Murphy, Colin Morgan, Victoria Hattersley, and the entire editorial and production team at Routledge; their flexibility in adapting to our rather "non-standard" positioning vis-a-vis "Englishes" is admirable, leading to a rich volume of diverse global voices.

1
DIVERSE GLOBAL PERSPECTIVES ON SCHOLARLY WRITING FOR PUBLICATION

James N. Corcoran
RENISON UNIVERSITY COLLEGE/UNIVERSITY OF WATERLOO, CANADA

Karen Englander
YORK UNIVERSITY, CANADA

Laura-Mihaela Muresan
THE BUCHAREST UNIVERSITY OF ECONOMIC STUDIES, ROMANIA

Introduction

This edited volume details 17 perspectives on scholarly writing for publication pedagogies and policies aimed at plurilingual scholars who use English as an additional language (EAL) across seven distinct geolinguistic regions. More than simply a collection of program and workshop descriptions, this volume includes first-hand accounts and analyses written by local scholars and pedagogues working in global regions outside traditional centres of knowledge production. Importantly, although some contributors are well known scholars, the majority of the authors are themselves rarely heard in the mainstream ERPP literature. Thus, this book provides a scholarly look into deeply contextualized activities that promote English-language publishing, written by those who teach and research these programs.

The primary audiences for this book are research writing pedagogues working in global locales who are attempting to effectively and equitably provide support to plurilingual EALs as well as researchers investigating these scholars' perceptions, practices, and processes. Such a readership can expect to expand their knowledge of global and regional policy and pedagogy aimed at preparing scholars for achieving publication of research in English. The significance of this collection is enhanced by the Envoi, written by John Swales, one of the foundational voices in this field. Ultimately, this volume should be of acute interest to those researchers, scientists, academics, instructors, and policymakers involved in the production, support, and adjudication of global scholars' research writing.

Words Matter: Terminology, Normativity and the Privileging of English(es)

In order to make this volume as accessible as possible, we feel it is important to clarify particular concepts, discipline-specific jargon, and acronyms before proceeding any further. Throughout this volume, you will see varying ways of referring to those who use English as an additional language (EAL). As editors, we prefer to use the term plurilingual users of EAL, or plurilingual EALs, when referring to this diverse group of scholars. This choice reflects the apparent preference of those in the field who self-identify as such, challenging problematic, deficit terminologies such as "non-native" speakers of English. As defined by Grommes and Hu (2014), plurilingualism focuses on "the individual's ability to make use of two or more languages... at varying levels of competence and in varying contexts" (p. 2). Given the multiple languages that scholars access and the policies that privilege English for publication, plurilingualism seems to be the best term to capture the complexities of language, pedagogy, publishing and academic knowledge creation. We also mindfully employ the term plurilingual when describing our collective orientation towards knowledge production, one that challenges monolingual ideologies and resulting practices that privilege English in a diverse, asymmetrical knowledge production landscape (Englander & Corcoran, 2019; Kubota, 2014; Marshall & Moore, 2018).

In line with other recent edited collections (Bennett, 2014; Cargill & Burgess, 2017; Curry & Lillis, 2017; Habibie & Hyland, in press), this volume is focused on describing perspectives, pedagogies and policies for scholarly writing for publication, at times referred to in this volume as English for research publication purposes (ERPP). Though this acronym may sound like a belch(!), we have chosen to use this term as it most accurately reflects research and writing activities conducted with the express intent of fostering *English* language publication. There is a valid argument to be made that doing so promotes and privileges the use of English over other languages (Curry & Lillis, 2017); we do not dispute this claim. Nonetheless, we aim to provide a space to describe and analyze phenomena related to global knowledge production, something happening increasingly in English. Indeed, we do so with a keen eye on challenging the global hegemony of English and promoting plurilingual perspectives, discourses, and epistemologies (Englander & Corcoran, 2019).

Throughout this volume, we also describe ERPP policies and pedagogies in terms of the geolinguistic locale where this knowledge is being produced, employing terms such as *centre*, *periphery*, and *semi-periphery* of knowledge production (Bennett, 2015; Galtung, 1980; Lillis & Curry, 2010; Wallerstein, 1991). Though these categories can be somewhat limiting given some scholars' transnational fluidity, our objective is to situate scholarly writing support taking place from locales outside traditional Anglophone centres of knowledge production, something we view as essential to understanding the differentiated, specific, and grounded needs, practices, and processes employed by plurilingual EAL scholars—and those who support their research writing—in these locales.

Finally, we acknowledge that choosing particular lexical items, stylistic elements, rhetorical patterns, etc. highlights not only our personal preferences but also our particular ideologies of English-language research writing. In our gatekeeping duties as language literacy brokers (Lillis & Curry, 2010), we are deliberately flexible regarding non-dominant/non-standard forms of English(es) throughout this volume. We contend that this approach does not result in sub-standard academic products; rather we argue it provides space for contributors to extend the traditional constraints of scholarly texts. Drawing on work from the sub-fields of World Englishes (Kachru, 2001; Matsuda & Matsuda, 2010), English as a lingua franca (Jenkins, 2014; Seidlhofer, 2011), translanguaging (Canagarajah, 2013; Garcia & Leiva, 2013), and plurilingualism (Coste, Moore & Zarate, 2009; Marshall & Moore, 2018; Piccardo, 2013), we adopt a pluralistic approach (Heng-Hartse & Kubota, 2014; Lin, 2016) to editing that stretches the traditional boundaries of academic Englishes. In doing so, we challenge the field to free itself of preconceived and prescriptive notions of *standard* English language use (Jenkins, 2014; Swales, 2017).

Editorial Positioning

The genesis of this work emerged from our shared pedagogical experiences. Englander taught in Mexico's Universidad Autonoma de Baja California for more than a decade (2004–2010), and it was there she was first invited by a science research institution to help their scientists improve their specialized writing in English. This led to pursuing a doctorate where she examined the writing processes and challenges of Mexican scientists. While she worked in her second language Spanish, she experienced the frustrations of lack of material resources, institutional constraints and curricular dilemmas that inhibit supporting scientists in publishing their research in English. Likewise, Corcoran has been a scholarly writing for publication instructor across global contexts. When working with plurilingual EAL scientists in Mexico, he was struck by both the lack of robust institutional support for emerging scholars' research writing as well as a widespread perception among these scholars of inequity in scientific publishing (Corcoran, 2017; Corcoran, forthcoming). These experiences led to a doctoral research project investigating the experiences of these health and life scientists, culminating in recommendations for modification of policy and pedagogy at Mexico University (a pseudonym). Muresan comes to this field with experience of more than a decade of coordinating a masters' programme initiated specifically for supporting both emerging and experienced plurilingual Romanian scholars in their research and writing for publication endeavors. In addition, she has also been involved in supporting novice scholars to develop academic and research writing skills in both English and German, an area opening up multiple opportunities for cross-linguistic and rhetorical transfers of expertise.

English and Research Publication Across Global Contexts

Claims abound that "English is currently the global language of science" (Thomson Reuters, 2014, p. 12). The motivation to publish one's research in English is driven by many factors, including the desire to reach a specialist audience that largely exists overseas and who can best be reached through relevant, specialized journals which publish in English; or conversely, to reach the broadest possible readership; to gain prestige; or to fulfill institutional requirements (Baldauf & Jernudd, 1983; Hanauer & Englander, 2013; López-Navarro, Moreno, Quintanilla, & Rey-Rocha, 2015; Muresan & Pérez-Llantada, this volume; Salager-Meyer, 2014). Thus a scholar's desire to communicate with an audience outside of his or her dominant language motivates many to embrace English-language publishing. Participation in the English-language world of scholarship creates opportunities for funding, conference presentations and advancement within international disciplinary associations. All these activities bestow prestige and international disciplinary interaction, which are highly sought (Lillis & Curry, 2010; Englander, 2014). Recognizing this advantage, Omobowale, Akanle and Akinsete (this volume) characterize this as "coming to wisdom" for Nigerian academics.

As globalization has taken hold among the nations and higher education institutions of the world, expectations for publishing in English have become enshrined in institutional and/national policies. While this pressure is not necessarily in conflict with the motivations above, complying with new policy demands has sometimes brought new pressures to plurilingual EAL scholars, especially those located outside the centre or *Anglosphere*, to publish in English-language journals (Salager-Meyer, 2014; Shahriari & Gonsooly, this volume; Sheridan, 2015; Zheng & Gao, 2016). Policies that drive these scholars' participation in English-medium versus local/regional journals have been somewhat documented (e.g. see special issue of *Language Policy*, 2013). In some cases, national and institutional bodies provide incentives (such as bonus pay or reduced teaching load) for publishing specifically in English-medium journals (Uzuner-Smith & Englander, 2015); in other cases, there are threats of demotion made for not producing a minimum number of publications (Lee & Lee, 2013; Li, 2014). Very often, prestige is conferred upon those who comply with prioritizing English (Burgess, 2017; Corcoran, 2015; Flowerdew & Li, 2009; Lillis & Curry, 2010; Muir & Solli, this volume; Salager-Meyer, 2014). However, often this line of research has focused on scholars' individual responses to these pressures as opposed to organized national, regional or institutional policy or pedagogical responses (Curry & Lillis, 2017; Flowerdew, 2015; Hyland, 2015).

Despite the dominance of English, academic work has been and continues to be carried out in languages other than English (Curry & Lillis, 2017; Hamel, 2013). In fact, the vast volume of scholarly work in non-English languages is often overlooked, and far less than 25% of the international, peer reviewed journals is indexed in the prestigious Web of Science (Lillis & Curry, 2010). Many plurilingual scholars balance their scholarly production among multiple languages. Publishing in other languages is often seen as a "responsibility" to connect with regional and local audiences about issues of deep, shared concern (Altbach, 2009; Muresan & Pérez-Llantada, this volume; Sibahi, 2015; Waigandt et al., this volume). Indeed, we (the editors) have all published in languages other than English (e.g. Avalos-Rivera & Corcoran, 2017; Englander, 2009; Englander et al., 2009; Muresan & Calciu, 2009). However, even for the scholars who maintain plurilingual writing practices, English increasingly occupies the more prestigious and dominant position in this writing for publication hierarchy (Burgess, Martín, & Balasanyan, this volume; Gentil, 2011; Hamel, 2007; Lillis & Curry, 2010; Pérez-Llantada, 2015).

Targeted Policies and Pedagogies

During the processes of delivering writing for publication courses or workshops in differing global locales, each of us has been struck by both the magnitude of challenges facing plurilingual scholars across disciplines in achieving publication of research in English as well as their resilience in persevering in order to achieve their (or their institutions') publishing objectives. We have all heard first-hand from these scholars regarding the trials and tribulations associated with writing for publication in an additional language, particularly from global locales such as Latin America and Eastern Europe which are outside traditional centres of knowledge production. This is not to say that there is a neat binary between *plurilingual* vs. *monolingual* or *native* vs. *non-native* English users; there most certainly is not (Habibie, 2019; Hyland, 2016; Salö, 2017). In fact, we acknowledge that there is currently heated debate about how much advantage is bestowed upon those who use English as their first language (see recent debate in the *Journal of Second Language Writing* between Hyland and Pohlitzer-Ahles et al.). We contend, however, that there is strong evidence of the burden of writing research in an additional language (Hanauer, Sheridan & Englander, 2019; Hanauer & Englander, 2011; Pérez-Llantada, Plo & Ferguson, 2011). Further, there now appears to be consensus among many applied linguists and English for Academic Purposes (EAP) practitioners that there are distinct obstacles for plurilingual EAL scholars (Englander & Hanauer, 2011; Curry & Lillis, 2017; Flowerdew, 2015; Politzer-Ahles et al., 2016), challenges potentially exacerbated when authors write from the geolinguistic regions in the global periphery or semi-periphery (Ingvardsdottir & Arnbjornsdottir, 2018; Bennett, 2014; Canagarajah, 2002; Corcoran, 2017; Lillis & Curry, 2010; Pérez-Llantada, 2012; Muresan & Pérez-Llantada, 2014).

Consequently, a foundational element of this volume is the recognition of the distinct challenges facing these plurilingual scholars in an asymmetrical market of knowledge production that favours English over other languages. As is clear throughout the chapters from different geolinguistic regions in this volume (Mirhosseini & Shafiee, this volume; Zheng & Cao, this volume), there is little agreement—even among those using English as an additional language—about the impact these characteristics have on plurilingual EAL scholars' publication outcomes, individually or collectively.

The plurilingual EAL scholar is immersed in a domain where policy concerning language production deeply affects their professional lives. The English language publishing efforts of these scholars may be affected by the networks they can access and the daily work pressures they experience (Encinas et al., this volume). Pedagogical initiatives to support the scholars who perform English-language research writing necessarily occur within policy contexts (Janssen & Restrepo, this volume). Thus, an area that calls for greater description and analysis is the intersection of writing for publication "policy" and "pedagogy" as they affect scholars in periphery and semi-periphery contexts. This volume looks to provide a much-needed mobilization of knowledge. We recognize that global, plurilingual scholars are likely to be both the recipients and future shapers of efforts aimed at supporting English language writing for publication. Yet there is still little documentation or discussion in the extant literature about efforts that are institutionally funded and aim to support global scholars in publishing in English, with only a few exceptions (Bardi & Muresan, 2014; Bazerman et al., 2012; Cargill & O'Connor, 2013; Corcoran, 2017; Englander & Corcoran, 2019; Kwan, 2010; Paltridge, 2018). This volume aims to address this gap by i) describing and analyzing pedagogical initiatives from diverse global locales; and ii) framing these pedagogies within the institutional, national or international policies and pressures that lead to such classroom work.

English for Research Publication Purposes: Pedagogical Responses and Orientations

Surprisingly, applied linguistics has been slow to take up the task of researching pedagogies aimed at supporting advanced research writing (Hyland, 2015; Flowerdew, 2015). However, the past decade has seen an increasing number of publications addressing research writing pedagogies, with evidence of differing orientations and approaches across global contexts (e.g. Bardi, 2015; Cargill & Burgess, 2017; Casanave, 2014; Corcoran, 2017; Curry & Lillis, 2013; Day & Gastel, 2006; Ferreira, 2016; Hanauer & Englander, 2013; Kwan, 2010; Paltridge & Starfield, 2016). In this volume, researchers document what policymakers, pedagogues, and individual plurilingual scholars have experienced when engaging with advanced research writing. Many of the contributors focus on pedagogical interventions that respond to the increased national and/or institutional push for publishing in English (e.g. Arnbjornsdottir, this volume; Burgess et al., this volume; Li & Cargill, this volume; Muir & Solli, this volume; Nunn & Deveci, this volume; Waigandt et al, this volume). These chapters describe the rationale for particular pedagogical orientations and content, discussing what can be achieved via these grounded, targeted research writing interventions.

In examining the literature, one common content design for such pedagogies appears to be predicated upon instrumentalist understandings of language as a tool for disseminating content knowledge as being inherently separate from the language itself. Such approaches suggest lexico-grammatical knowledge and accuracy are keys to achieving effective writing, something highlighted in several writing for publication handbooks (e.g. Day & Gastel, 2006; Glasman-Deal, 2010) and echoed by Nauman (this volume).

Another content design focuses on increasing scholars' knowledge of the structural, rhetorical, and broader discoursal patterns of research writing. This awareness-raising has been forefronted in a number of different approaches, including corpus, intercultural rhetoric, and genre. Empirical knowledge from corpus linguistics has been shown to help EAL scholars to identify and use the collocations and formulaic expressions that are typical of scientific communication (Gledhill, 2000; Harwood, 2005; Lee & Swales, 2006). Intercultural rhetorical approaches to writing for publication have been used to identify first-language discursive elements in texts (Connor & Rozicki, 2013; Pérez-Llantada, 2012) and provide evidence for their modification or elimination in order to increase the likelihood of manuscript acceptance by gatekeepers (Moreno, 2010; Sheldon, 2011). Genre-based approaches, it is argued, may allow scholars to identify and adhere to the normative patterns common in their field-specific writing while, potentially, opening up space for innovation (e.g. Cargill & O'Connor, 2013; Swales & Feak, 2012; Swales, 2017; Tardy, 2016). Pedagogies that take advantage of these kinds of linguistic knowledge in their pragmatic content seem to support plurilingual EAL scholars' confidence in participating in ERPP.

Another content design, somewhat differently oriented, is one that forefronts the social practices associated with research writing, emphasizing the importance of developing practices and processes that lead to effective writing for publication outcomes. Such practices include developing networks of literacy brokers, attending to the particular communicative demands of navigating the submission and review process, as well as forming effective writing processes that suggest the potential of sustainability in achieving writing for publication (e.g. Curry & Lillis, 2013; Paltridge & Starfield, 2016). Several contributions in this volume attest to the importance of these design features when supporting both emerging and established scholars' research writing (Encinas et al., this volume; Shahriari & Gonsooly, this volume; Waignadt et al., this volume).

Some have argued that a "pragmatic" orientation should be adopted, in which plurilingual scholars are helped to understand and fulfill English scholarly writing discoursal norms (e.g. Cargill & O'Connor, 2013). Such an approach typically examines the lexico-grammatical features of the language, but more importantly, focuses instruction on identifying and following the field-broad and/or field-specific genre expectations of academic writing. A pragmatic approach could also include building awareness of the demands associated with identifying appropriate journals, and developing the skills needed to navigate the norms suggested by the journal and its gatekeepers. In what has been described as more "critical" approaches to writing for publication, the focus is on analyzing normative discourses and epistemologies, challenging inequitable structures/policies, and developing a plurilingual authorial identity alongside genre awareness (e.g. Corcoran & Englander, 2016; Englander & Corcoran, 2019). Such approaches are predicated on the understanding that teaching particular literacies—in this case scholarly writing for publication—must necessarily include a critical orientation that holds central notions of equality/equity, identity, social relations of power, and the potential of language (use) to create, maintain, or resist particular inequitable relations. Though not evidence of "criticality" in and of itself, one aspect of such approaches is the fostering of plurilingual scholars' bi- or pluriliteracies rather than solely English language research writing, something emphasized by several researchers in this volume (Arnbjornsdottir, this volume; Burgess et al., this volume; Encinas et al., this volume; Muir & Solli, this volume; Muresan & Perez-Llantada, this volume; Mirhosseini & Shafiee, this volume; Waigandt et al., this volume; Zheng & Cao, this volume).

As the variety of contributions in our volume indicates, there is considerable disagreement as to the primacy of English language proficiency in achieving research publication (see Messekher & Miliani, this volume; Nauman, this volume; Waigandt et al., this volume). Certainly, scholars require a particular level of language proficiency in order to take on the monumental task of producing a "publishable" piece. However, one wonders at the threshold of proficiency required in order to fully benefit from ERPP instruction. Relatedly, if there is low English language proficiency, could these courses not be offered in the national language? If so, those with high levels of bi- or pluriliteracy in the national language *and* English would be better positioned to offer such instruction (see Li & Cargill, this volume). Further, how much disciplinary focus should there be in such courses, workshops or programs? What may become clear in reading this volume is that there can be no "one size fits all" approach to ERPP interventions aimed at plurilingual EAL scholars; there is a need for consideration of local scholars' experiences and needs as they navigate the challenging task(s) associated with scholarly writing for publication in an era of increasing English language hegemony for the dissemination of research.

Elucidation on and discussion of *local* writing for publication policies and pedagogies are sorely needed. Empirical evidence as to the efficacy of such pedagogical initiatives could provide a welcome addition to the growing body of literature in the field as many questions remain:

- What motivates the institution to invest in this area of pedagogy and are those investments sufficient?
- Which pedagogical approaches or orientations are employed for such research writing support?
- Who teaches these courses/workshops?

- How much should such research writing instruction be catered to scholars' different career stages (emerging vs. established)?
- How effective are they in improving plurilingual scholars' confidence with English language research writing?
- How do these interventions address the social practices of scholarly writing? How is effectiveness demonstrated?
- How are pedagogies and policies in different global regions impacted by neoliberal models of knowledge production driving institutional evaluation schemes?

While this volume certainly does not provide all the answers to these questions, there is undoubtedly great benefit for scholars and practitioners in our field (and related fields) to engage with the many contributions detailing such pedagogical responses across (often underrepresented) geolinguistic contexts.

Organization of This Book

To date, Anglophone scholars (or those located in Anglo-dominant research locales) have dominated the discussion of ERPP policies and pedagogies (Flowerdew, 2015; Swales, 2015). This is a limitation that this edited volume (and other recent volumes to some extent, e.g. Bennett, 2015; Plo Alastrué & Pérez-Llantada, 2015) attempts to address, forefronting voices from underrepresented regions and scholars. While this volume includes several chapters from more recognized voices, we have sought out chapters from scholars with deep contextual knowledge from various regions of the world: Latin America; Northern Europe; Eastern and Southern Europe; East Asia; South Asia; Africa, and the Persian Gulf. Contributions examine writing programs, courses or interventions held outside the Anglophone countries whose aim is to enhance the scholarly English-language research writing success of plurilingual scholars. Many of the chapters are descriptive of particular programs, but are also analytical in terms of the pedagogies and policies that underpin the programs. Many of the chapters also provide a national or regional perspective in regard to the (perceived) dominance of English and the subsequent policy and pedagogical responses—at both the individual and collective levels—to the increasing pressures brought to bear by this dominance. Following our introductory chapter, this volume contains contributions from seven geolinguistic regions:

Region 1: Latin America

In Chapter 2, Janssen and Restrepo describe a Colombian university's burgeoning tutoring service seeking to support the academic research production needs of emerging and established plurilingual scholars' English language research writing. In Chapter 3, Encinas-Prudencío, Sánchez-Hernández, Thomas-Ruzic, Cuatlapantzi-Pichón, and Aguilar-González conduct a longitudinal study to determine the characteristics which seem to foster or undermine EFL language teachers' efforts at scholarly publication while conducting their professional lives, revealing the impact of collaboration, mentoring networks, and workplace demands. In Chapter 4, the final contribution from Latin America, Waigandt, Noceti and Lothringer describe and reflect upon the impact and evolution of four initiatives aimed at supporting both emerging and established Argentine scholars' research writing in English and Spanish, including cross-disciplinary collaboration.

Region 2: Northern Europe

In Chapter 5, Arnbjörnsdóttir describes a research-driven, critical-pragmatic oriented English writing for publication purposes initiative aimed at supporting the research writing of experienced scholars at the University of Iceland. In Chapter 6, Muir and Solli highlight a socially-situated framework for addressing curriculum development aimed at supporting emerging scholars, while encouraging new ways of thinking about and approaching scholarly research writing support.

Region 3: Eastern and Southern Europe

In Chapter 7, Muresan and Pérez-Llantada take an ecosystem approach to describe the publishing life of a highly proficient senior social scientist whose experiences encompass overcoming both linguistic and non-linguistic challenges in achieving international visibility. In Chapter 8, Burgess, Martín and Balasanyan describe a critical pragmatic approach to research writing instruction aimed at emerging arts and humanities scholars at the University of Zaragosa that problematizes an uncritical acceptance of English for publication purposes and encourages advanced biliteracies.

Region 4: East Asia

As Chinese scholars face immense pressure to produce research articles in English, in Chapter 9, Li and Cargill present a "master-class" methodology for English as a Foreign Language teachers to become teachers of Writing for Publication, responding to a nation-wide emphasis on ERPP being taught by those whose training is not always sufficient. In Chapter 10, Zheng and Cao explore the views of plurilingual Chinese scholars from six important Chinese universities regarding language choice, outlining a widespread preference for maintenance of bilingual publishing practices.

Region 5: South Asia

In the lone contribution from this region, Chapter 11 sees Nauman critique Pakistan's Higher Education Commission's commitment to increasing its national research profile through the improvement of researchers' English language proficiency, culminating with suggestions on how to address the needs of Pakistani scholars throughout their educational trajectories.

Region 6: Africa

In Chapter 12, Messekher and Miliani reflect upon the challenges facing emerging scholars looking to publish their dissertation work in the form of research articles, suggesting a grounded approach to research writing instruction for graduate students at Algerian universities. In Chapter 13, Omobowale, Akanle and Akinsete analyze the colonial imposition of English and characterize how Nigerian-English formal speech, somewhat paradoxically, both supports and undermines the efforts of Nigerian scholars to publish internationally.

Region 7: Persian Gulf

In Chapter 14, Shariari and Ghonsooly critically reflect upon findings from a study investigating the perceptions of emerging and established Iranian scholars to increasing expectations for "visible" research production, suggesting the need for greater research writing support for Iranian scholars amid international political tensions. In Chapter 15, Mirhosseini and Shafiee reflect upon the hegemony of English in global scientific knowledge production and the resulting pressures facing experienced scholars based at an Iranian university of medical sciences. In Chapter 16, Nunn and Deveci describe a pedagogical approach they term "holistic argumentation creation" to support emerging scientists' and engineers' awareness of research writing conventions.

Envoi

In a sage Envoi, Swales positions this volume within the EAP/ESP/ERPP literature, hinting at how its content focus may be emblematic of a shift from describing plurilingual EAL scholars' problems with ERPP to potential solutions. He goes on to problematize the assumption that scholars from the Anglophone centre are all equally prepared and supported, highlighting the fact that there exist semiperipheral zones and institutions in the North American research landscape as well, something we would do well to remember when painting with overly large brushstrokes in describing the politics of global knowledge production.

References

Altbach, P. G. (2009). Peripheries and centers: research universities in developing countries. *Asia Pacific Education Review, 10*(15), 27.
Avalos-Rivera, A. D., & Corcoran, J. (2017). Ser o no ser como un hablante nativo del inglés: Creencias ambivalentes e ideología en el imaginario de los profesores de inglés en Brasil y México [Be like a native speaker of English? Brazilian and Mexican English

language teachers' ambivalent beliefs and language ideologies]. *Revista Mexicana de Investigación Educativa, 22*(75), 1117–1141.

Baldauf, R. B., & Jernudd, B. H. (1983). Language of publications as a variable in scientific communication. *Australian review of applied linguistics, 6*(1), 97–108.

Bardi, M. (2015). Learning the practice of scholarly publication in English—A Romanian perspective. *English for Specific Purposes, 37,* 98–111.

Bardi, M., & Muresan, L.-M. (2014). Changing Research Writing Practices in Romania: Perceptions and Attitudes. In K. Bennett (Ed.). *The Semi-Periphery of Academic Writing: Discourses, communities and practices* (pp. 121–147). Basingstoke: Palgrave Macmillan.

Bazerman, C., Keranen, N., & Encinas Prudencio, F. (2012). Facilitated immersion at a distance in second language scientific writing. In M. Castelló & C. Donahue (Eds.). *University writing: Selves and texts in academic societies* (pp. 235–248). Bingley, UK: Emerald.

Bennett, K. (2014). Introduction: The political and economic infrastructure of academic practice: The 'semiperiphery' as a category for social and linguistic analysis. In K. Bennett (Ed). *The semiperiphery of academic writing: discourses, communities, and practices* (pp. 1–9). London: Palgrave Macmillan.

Bennett, K. (2015). Towards an epistemological monoculture: Mechanisms of epistemicide in European research publication. In R. Plo Alastrué & C. Pérez-Llantada (Eds.). *English as a scientific and research language: Debates and discourses* (pp. 9–36). Berlin, Germany: de Gruyter.

Burgess, S. (2017). Accept or contest: A life-history study of humanities scholars' responses to research publication policies in Spain. In M. Cargill & S. Burgess (Eds.). *Publishing research in English as an additional language: Practices, pathways and potentials* (pp. 13–33). Adelaide, Australia: University of Adelaide Press.

Canagarajah, A. S. (2002). *A geopolitics of academic writing.* Pittsburgh, PA: University of Pittsburgh Press.

Canagarajah, A. S. (2013). Negotiating translingual literacy: An enactment. *Research in the Teaching of English, 48*(1), 40–67.

Cargill, M. & Burgess, S. (Eds.). (2017). *Publishing research in English as an additional language: Practices, pathways and potentials.* Adelaide, Australia: University of Adelaide Press.

Cargill, M., & O'Connor, P. (2013). *Writing scientific research articles (2nd edition).* West Sussex, UK: Wiley-Blackwell.

Casanave, C. P. (2014). *Before the dissertation: A textual mentor for doctoral students at early stages of a research project.* Ann Arbor, MI: University of Michigan Press.

Corcoran, J. N. (forthcoming). Competing perceptions of bias in scientific adjudication: Addressing "the bias gap". *Written Communication.*

Corcoran, J. N. (2017). The potential and limitations of an English for research publication purposes course for Mexican scholars. In M. J. Curry & T. Lillis (Eds.) *Global academic publishing: Policies, practices, and pedagogies* (pp. 233–248) Bristol, UK: Multilingual Matters.

Corcoran, J., & Englander, K. (2016). A proposal for critical-pragmatic pedagogical approaches to English for research publication purposes. *Publications 4*(1) 6.

Corcoran, J. N. (2015). English as the international language of science: A case study of Mexican scientists' academic writing for publication. Unpublished dissertation, University of Toronto.

Coste, D., Moore, D., & Zarate, G. (2009). Plurilingual and pluricultural competence. *Language Policy Division. Strasbourg: Council of Europe.*

Curry, M. J., & Lillis, T. (2017). Problematizing English as the privileged language of global academic publishing. In M. J. Curry & T. Lillis (Eds.). *Global academic publishing: Policies, practices, and pedagogies* (pp. 1–22). Clevedon, UK: Multilingual Matters.

Curry, M. J., & Lillis, T. (2013). *A scholar's guide to getting published in English: Critical choices and practical strategies.* Bristol, UK: Multilingual Matters.
Curry, M. J., & Lillis, T. (2017). *Global academic publishing: Policies, perspectives and pedagogies.* Clevedon, UK: Multilingual Matters.
Day, R. A., & Gastel, B. (2006). *How to write and publish a scientific paper, Sixth edition.* Westport, CN: Greenwood Press.
Englander, K. (2009). El mundo globalizado de las publicaciones científicas en inglés: Un enfoque analítico para comprender a los científicos multilingües. *Discurso y Sociedad* 3(1), 90–118.
Englander, K. (2014). *Writing and publishing scientific papers in English: A global perspective.* Amsterdam, The Netherlands: Springer.
Englander, K., & Corcoran, J. N. (2019). *English for research publication purposes: Critical plurilingual pedagogies.* London: Routledge.
Englander, K., Tinajero, G., González, M., & Valdivia, O. (2009). *Los Docentes como Sujetos y Objetos en Relación a las Practicas de Literacidad—en ingles y español—el caso de México* [Teachers as subjects and objects in relation to literacy practices—in English and Spanish—the case of Mexico]. *Proceedings, UNESCO Conference on Reading and Writing in Higher Education.* Caracas, Venezuela: UNESCO.
Ferreira, M. M. (2016). Challenges for Brazilian post/graduate students writing in the academy: Insights for future pedagogical interventions. In C. Badenhorst and C. Guerin (eds.) *Research Literacies and Writing Pedagogies for Masters and Doctoral Writers* (pp. 93–112). Leiden, Netherlands: Brill.
Flowerdew, J. (2015). Some thoughts on English for research publication purposes (ERPP) and related issues. *Language Teaching* 48(2), 250–262. doi: 10.1017/S0261444812000523
Flowerdew, J., & Li, Y. (2009). English or Chinese? The trade-off between local and international publication among Chinese academics in the humanities and social sciences. *Journal of Second Language Writing*, 18(1), 1–16.
Galtung, J. (1980). *The true worlds: A transnational perspective.* New York: The Free Press.
Garcia, O., & Leiva, C. (2013). Theorizing and enacting translanguaging for social justice. In A. Blackledge and A. Cleese (Eds.). *Heteroglossia as practice and pedagogy* (pp. 199–216). Dordrecht, the Netherlands: Springer.
Gentil, G. (2011). A biliteracy agenda for genre research. *Journal of Second Language Writing*, 20(1), 6–23.
Glasman-Deal, H. (2010). *Science research writing for non-native speakers of English.* London, UK: World Scientific.
Gledhill, C. (2000). The discourse function of collocation in research article introductions. *English for Specific Purposes*, 19(2), 115–135.
Grommes, P., & Hu, A. (2014). *Plurilingual education policies—practices—language development.* Amsterdam: John Benjamins Publishing Company.
Habibie, P. (2019). To be native or not to be native: That is not the question. In P. Habibie and K. Hyland (Eds.). *Novice writers and scholarly publication: Authors, mentors, gatekeepers* (pp. 35–52). London: Palgrave MacMillan.
Hamel, R. E. (2007). The dominance of English in the international scientific periodical literature and the future of language use in science. *AILA Review, 20,* 53–71.
Hamel, R. E. (2013). El campo de las ciencias y la educación superior entre el monopolio del inglés y el plurilingüismo: Elementos para una política del lenguaje en América Latina. *Trabalhos em Linguística Aplicada, 52*(2), 321–384.

Hanauer, D. I., & Englander, K. (2013). *Scientific writing in a second language.* Anderson, SC: Parlor Press.

Hanauer, D.I. and Englander, K. (2011). Quantifying the burden of writing research articles in a second language: Data from Mexican scientists. *Written Communication, 28*(4), 403–416. doi: 10.1177/0741088311420056

Hanauer, D. I., Sheridan, C. L., & Englander, K. (2019). Linguistic injustice in the writing of research articles in English as a second language: Data from Taiwanese and Mexican researchers. *Written Communication,* 36(1), 136–154.

Harwood, N. (2005). 'Nowhere has anyone attempted. . . In this article I aim to do just that': A corpus-based study of self-promotional I and we in academic writing across four disciplines. *Journal of Pragmatics, 37*(8), 1207–1231.

Heng-Hartse, J., & Kubota, R. (2014). Pluralizing English? Variation in high-stakes academic texts and challenges of copyediting. *Journal of Second Language Writing, 24,* 71–82.

Hyland, K. (2015) *Academic publishing: Issues and challenges in the construction of knowledge.* Oxford, UK: Oxford University Press.

Hyland, K. (2016). Academic publishing and the myth of linguistic injustice. *Journal of Second Language Writing, 31,* 58–69.

Hyland, K. (2017). Language myths and publishing mysteries: A response to Pohlizer-Ahles et al. *Journal of Second Language Writing, 34,* 9–11.

Ingvarsdóttir, H., & Arnbjörnsdóttir, B. (2018). Writing English for research and publication purposes (ERPP): Personal identity and professional voice. In B. Arnbjörnsdóttir & H. Ingvarsdóttir (Eds.). *Language development across the life span: The impact of English on education and work in Iceland* (pp. 197–214). Cham, Switzerland: Springer International Publishing.

Jenkins, J. (2014). *English as a lingua franca in the international university: The politics of academic English language policy.* London: Routledge.

Kachru, B. (2001). NES Englishes. *Concise encyclopedia of sociolinguistics,* 519–524.

Kubota, R. (2014). The multi/plural turn, postcolonial theory, and neoliberal multiculturalism: Complicities and implications for applied linguistics. *Applied Linguistics, 37*(4), 474–494.

Kwan, B. S. C. (2010). An investigation of instruction in research publishing offered in doctoral programs: The Hong Kong case. *Higher Education, 59*(1), 55–68.

Lee, H., & Lee, K. (2013). Publish (in international indexed journals) or perish: Neoliberal ideology in a Korean university. *Language Policy, 12*(3), 215–230.

Lee, D., & Swales, J. (2006). A corpus-based EAP course for NNS doctoral students: Moving from available specialized corpora to self-compiled corpora. *English for Specific Purposes, 25*(1), 56–75.

Li, Y. (2014). Seeking entry to the North American market: Chinese management academics publishing internationally. *Journal of English for Academic Purposes, 13,* 41–52.

Lin, A. M. (2016). Critical perspectives. In A. M. Lin (Ed.). *Language across the curriculum and CLIL in English-as-an-additional language (EAL) contexts: Theory and practice* (pp. 159–172). Singapore: Springer.

Lillis, T., & Curry, M. J. (2010). *Academic writing in a global context: The politics and practices of publishing in English.* London, UK: Routledge.

López-Navarro, I., Moreno, A. I., Quintanilla, M. Á., & Rey-Rocha, J. (2015). Why do I publish research articles in English instead of my own language? Differences in Spanish researchers' motivations across scientific domains. *Scientometrics, 103*(3), 939–976.

Marshall, S., & Moore, D. (2018). Plurilingualism amid the panoply of lingualisms: Addressing critiques and misconceptions in education. *International Journal of Multilingualism, 15*(1), 19–34.

Matsuda, A., & Matsuda, P. K. (2010). World Englishes and the teaching of writing. *TESOL Quarterly, 44*(2), 369–374.

Moreno, A. I. (2010). Researching into English for research publication purposes from an applied intercultural perspective. *English for Professional and Academic Purposes, 22*, 59–73.

Muresan, L. M., & Calciu, R. B. (2009). Selbstevaluation und Europäisches Sprachenportfolio in Aktion—zur Förderung der Mehrsprachigkeit und der Qualitätssicherung. *IDV Magazin des Internationalen Deutschlehrerverbandes 81*, 540–548.

Muresan, L. M., & Pérez-Llantada, C. (2014). English for research publication and dissemination in bi-/multiliterate environments: The case of Romanian academics. *Journal of English for Academic Purposes, 13*, 53–64.

Paltridge, B. (2018). Writing for publication. In L. Woodrow (Ed.). *Introducing course design in English for specific purposes* (pp. 228–233). London: Routledge.

Paltridge, B., & Starfield, S. (2016). *Getting published in academic journals: Navigating the publication process*. Ann Arbor: MI: University of Michigan Press.

Pérez-Llantada, C., Plo, R., & Ferguson, G. R. (2011). "You don't say what you know, only what you can": The perceptions and practices of senior Spanish academics regarding research dissemination in English. *English for Specific Purposes, 30*, 18–30.

Pérez-Llantada, C. (2012). *Scientific discourse and the rhetoric of globalization: The impact of culture and language*. London, UK: A&C Black.

Pérez-Llantada, C. (2015). Teasing out the tensions between English monolingualism vs. plurilingualism in European academic and research settings. In R. Plo Alastrué & C. Pérez-Llantada (Eds.). *English as a scientific and research language*, (pp. 353–361). Berlin: deGruyter.

Piccardo, E. (2013). Plurilingualism and curriculum design: Toward a synergic vision. *Tesol Quarterly, 47*(3), 600–614.

Plo Alastrué, R. & Pérez-Llantada, C. (eds.) (2015). *English as a scientific and research language*. Berlin: deGruyter.

Politzer-Ahles, S., Holliday, J. J., Girolamo, T., Spychalska, M., & Harper Berkson, K. (2016). Is linguistic injustice a myth? A response to Hyland (2016). *Journal of Second Language Writing, 34*, 3–8.

Salager-Meyer, F. (2014). Writing and publishing in peripheral scholarly journals: How to enhance the global influence of multilingual scholars? *Journal of English for Academic Purposes, 13*, 78–82.

Salö, L. (2017). *The sociolinguistics of academic publishing: Language and the practices of homo academicus*. London: Palgrave Macmillan.

Seidlhofer, B. (2011). *Understanding English as a lingua franca*. Oxford: Oxford University Press.

Sheldon, E. (2011). Rhetorical differences in RA introductions written by English L1 and L2 and Castilian Spanish L1 writers. *Journal of English for Academic Purposes, 10*(4), 238–251.

Sheridan, C. L. (2015). National journals and centering institutions: A historiography of an English language teaching journal in Taiwan. *English for Specific Purposes, 38*, 70–84.

Sibahi, R. (2015). English triumphalism in academic writing: The price of global visibility. *Arab World English Journal, 6*(3), 205–218.

Swales, J. M. (2015). Review of "The semiperiphery of academic writing: Discourses, communities and practices." *English for Specific Purposes, 39*, 80–82.

Swales, J. (2017). Standardization and its discontents. In M. Cargill and S. Burgess (Eds.). *Publishing research in English as an additional language: Practices, pathways and potentials* (pp. 239–254). Adelaide: University of Adelaide Press.

Swales, J., & Feak, C. B., (2012). *Academic writing for graduate students: Essential tasks and skills., 3rd edition*. Ann Arbor, MI: University of Michigan Press.

Tardy, C. M. (2016). *Beyond convention. Genre innovation in academic writing*. Ann Arbor: University of Michigan Press.

Thomson Reuters. (2014). *Connecting the dots across the research ecosystem: A white paper*. New York, NY: Thomson Reuters.

Uzuner-Smith, S., & Englander, K. (2015). Exposing ideology within university policies: A critical discourse analysis of faculty hiring, promotion and remuneration practices. *Journal of Education Policy, 30*(1), 62–85.

Wallerstein, I. (1991). *Geopolitics and geoculture*. Cambridge: Cambridge University Press.

Zheng, Y., & Gao, A. X. (2016). Chinese humanities and social sciences scholars' language choices in international scholarly publishing: A ten-year survey. *Journal of Scholarly Publishing, 48*(1), 1–16.

REGION 1
Latin America

2

A UTILIZATION-FOCUSED PROGRAM EVALUATION OF AN ERPP TUTORING SERVICE AT ONE COLOMBIAN UNIVERSITY

Gerriet Janssen

UNIVERSIDAD DE LOS ANDES—COLOMBIA

Silvia Restrepo

UNIVERSIDAD DE LOS ANDES—COLOMBIA

Introduction

Today, reports on English language publication by scholars located in underrepresented regions of the world (Africa; Central, South, and West Asia; Latin America) are gaining some deserved spotlight. In the Latin American context, Fortes and Lomnitz (1994) presented a book-length treatise describing three bio-med cohorts from the 1970s and the challenges they faced as they became members of their scientific community; these challenges included effectively dealing with pressures to disseminate knowledge in English. More recent coverage of these concerns in Latin America has been increasingly thorough, with local long-term projects focusing on this topic (Carrasco & Kent, 2011; Carrasco, Kent, & Keranan, 2012; Hanauer & Englander 2011, 2013), edited volumes with chapters concerning this region (Bazerman et al., 2012; Curry & Lillis, 2017; Thaiss, Bräuer, Carlino, Ganobcsik-Williams, & Sinha, 2012; this volume), and international conferences being held in this region (e.g., the 2017 Writing Research Across Borders conference, held in Bogotá, Colombia). Additionally, some Latin American universities have developed programs to help their scholars publish in English-medium journals. This support includes university coursework for engineering students in Argentina (Baldi, Lothringer, & Waigandt, 2003, 2005), English for research publication purposes (ERPP) workshops at one university in Mexico (Corcoran, 2015, 2017), and a writing center supporting scholarly writing for publication in Brazil (Martínez & Figueiredo, 2017). To this body of literature, we add our description of an ERPP tutoring service at one Colombian university, describing how cycles of program evaluation helped this program better respond to local needs.

While our findings should not be generalized beyond the local context, our hope is that this program model and framework for program evaluation might be considered in other contexts where scholars need institutionalized support for the dissemination of their research.

Setting

The ERPP tutoring service we report on is located at a large private university in Colombia that in recent years has consistently ranked among the top 10 universities in Latin America (Times Higher Education, 2017). This positioning is extremely important to the university, and its leaders carefully monitor and strategically invest in improving the quality of the school's academic and research production with an eye on improving this ranking position. Investments include three-year grants for new assistant professors of approximately US $10,000 per year, a library system with access to major journal systems, and incentives for academic production, including bonuses for publication in highly ranked journals. Since 2009, the university has also invested in teaching the practices of English-language publication with the creation and implementation of a specific English curriculum for PhD students (see Janssen, 2016).

In the second semester of 2015 (in local nomenclature, 2015–2; the first semester of 2016 being written 2016–1, and so on), the university developed an ERPP tutoring service. Here, we use tutoring to refer to the concept of one-on-one meetings between a relative expert writer and a relative novice; these meetings have also been referred to as writing conferences in the literature (see Hyland & Hyland, 2006). This process began when this chapter's authors Silvia Restrepo—the university's vice-chancellor of research—and Gerriet Janssen—the coordinator of the PhD student English program at that time—met to discuss different avenues for supporting the publication and presentation efforts of PhD students in all areas of study. Ideas included increases in required English coursework, the provision of research publication workshops, and an individualized writing conference style tutoring service. We hypothesized that a tutoring service would best respond to differentiated student needs and thus help students best improve the quality of their publications, and hopefully, their publishing outcomes.

This chapter reports on the ongoing utilization-focused program evaluation conducted after the first three iterations of this tutoring service. In utilization-focused evaluation, evaluators provide the evaluation's primary intended users with the information that is "needed and wanted... that will actually be used for program improvement and decision making" (Patton, 2012, p. 187). This is a program-level framework that leaders in other contexts can use to assess or review their own services or programs. This program evaluation asks these evaluation questions posited by Patton (2012, pp. 184–185):

i) To what extent was the service implemented as designed? In our setting, this can be interpreted as: to what degree were each semester's pre-conditions for participation useful? To what degree was the tutoring process appropriate?
ii) What issues surfaced during implementation that need attention in the future? In our setting, this can be interpreted as: what conclusions can be drawn and which recommendations can be made for future iterations of this service?

By responding to these questions, this chapter illustrates the step-by-step logic of conducting an on-going utilization-focused program evaluation aimed at assessing the efficacy of a tutoring service. The chapter documents how a service can change, explaining how and why its developers—using evaluation findings—shifted initial conditions and goals across program iterations. The chapter concludes by identifying both ways in which the tutoring service is meeting (or not) the needs of its users as well as threats to this service's sustainability, thus providing potential guidance for those currently providing or considering provision of such support in other global contexts.

Theoretical Frameworks

Program Evaluation

This investigation is framed within the theory of program evaluation, a term that is used almost interchangeably with two other terms, program review and assessment. Craven posits an early definition of program review, calling it "the process of defining, collecting, and analyzing information about an existing program or noninstructional unit to arrive at a judgment about the continuation, modification, enhancement, or termination of the program or unit" (1980b, p. 434, in Conrad & Wilson, 1985, p. 10). Later, Fournier defines evaluation as "an applied inquiry process for collecting and synthesizing evidence that culminates in conclusions about the state of affairs, value, merit . . . of a program, product, person, policy, proposal, or plan" (2005, p. 140). Salient in these definitions is the applied nature of this process, that evaluators collect and then synthesize or analyze information, from which they draw conclusions or judgments. Banta and Palomba (2015) add that the collection of information is systematic, and that the information should be used to make improvements. These characteristics of program review and evaluation can also be seen in Leskes and Wright's (2005) four-step assessment cycle, which depicts assessment as first setting goals and asking questions; next, gathering evidence; then, interpreting the findings; afterwards, using these findings to make improvements; to finally—and critically—begin this cycle again with new goals and questions. Patton (2008, 2012) prioritizes the use of an evaluation's findings (i.e., starting the assessment or evaluative cycle anew) through the development of utilization-focused evaluation, the specific evaluation framework that informs this chapter.

Patton presents three essential questions in his framework for program evaluation. These are concerned with implementation, outcomes, and attribution, and are respectively: "What happens in the program? What results from the program? Can what results be attributed to what is implemented?" (2012, p. 192). These first two questions are visible in our evaluation questions; we do not address the third question, as we did not collect empirical data to establish causality (attribution). While a complete program evaluation in this context would consider the program, tutees, and tutors, in this study, the information that was important to the evaluation's intended users (the authors) included reflecting about (question 1) the adequacy of the program's structure and (question 2) the issues that arose in this tutoring framework. With this in mind, we determined how to make future program improvements.

Tutoring Framework: Social Theories of Learning

The tutoring process used within this ERPP service is based on social theories of learning, especially the community of practice theory of learning (Lave & Wenger, 1991). A community of practice viewpoint on learning to write for research and publication purposes broadly suggests that expert members (e.g., senior academics, doctoral supervisors) help novice scholars (PhD students) to identify publishable topics and appropriate publication venues (Lei & Hu, 2015); shape the manuscript, strengthening its position within disciplinary conversations (Li, 2006; Lillis & Curry, 2006); provide apprenticeship opportunities concerning the collective research and writing activities developed in laboratories (Carrasco et al., 2012; Curry, 2014); and gain access to both local and transnational networks of scholars, oftentimes important in terms of providing publication opportunities (Curry & Lillis, 2010). Literacy brokers (Lillis & Curry, 2006)—the people in this chapter we call tutors—can signal for writers the "specific cultural traditions and ways of constructing knowledge" (Lillis & Curry, 2006, p. 7).

Learning to write for publication purposes within a community of practice has its challenges and has been critiqued. Scholars are differently adept at making and maintaining the interpersonal bonds involved with being a community member (Curry & Lillis, 2010, p. 293). Furthermore, not all advisors mentor their students about the linguistic and symbolic knowledge related to publication: some PhD writers receive minimal or no publication writing support from advisors (Kwan, 2009), while others feel dominated by their advisors, ceding responsibility for their manuscripts to them (Huang, 2010). Critiques have been made concerning advisor impact—that it is "overestimated" (Zappa-Hollman & Duff, 2015, p. 358; see also Ferenz, 2005)—and concerning the unidirectional flow of information (expert to novice), especially when advanced field specialists (PhD students) work with language experts (tutors) on a publication draft (Merkel, 2018; Tardy, 2006).

Methodology

Participants and Recruitment

Before the first semester of tutoring (2015–2), Restrepo's office sent all PhD students at the university an email describing the tutoring service, its goals, and the requirements for participation. Of the 12 PhD students who participated in the tutoring service in 2015–2, we consider data from the nine who signed the informed consent form. These nine students, from five of the university's 15 PhD programs, may not fully represent this context's population of PhD students; nevertheless, we believe that their voluntary use of this service indicates that their experiences represent well the population of students at our university interested in being supported in their publication efforts by a tutoring service.

Data Collection and Analysis

First, Janssen developed a research archive for each writer. There, he kept research notes including information about the writer profile (MA student, PhD student, professor, other), number of hours and sessions attended, the topics discussed, and any homework assigned. Supporting data were collected for all nine PhD tutees in video-recorded, semi-structured interviews, conducted in both English and Spanish two months after the semester was over. By comparing these data with the service's stipulated preconditions (a fixed, 10-hour per semester tutee commitment; a nearly complete manuscript draft; supervisor confirmation of the draft being nearly complete; confirmation of having an active supervisor for content questions) and procedures (moving from social and political elements of publishing to organization to linguistic choices), we made interpretations about the usefulness of the service's preconditions and appropriateness of the tutoring procedure (question one), and we formed conclusions about the broad structural issues that required attention in the next iteration of the program (question two).

Procedures: The Tutoring Plan

For administrative purposes, the tutoring service was conceived of as being an informal, ungraded, one-on-one writing laboratory course with the tutor. To comply with this course framework, participating students were required to agree to four pre-conditions: (a) meet one-on-one with the tutor for 10 one-hour sessions throughout the 15-week semester; (b) bring a complete draft of a research article; (c) demonstrate supervisor confirmation that the article was nearly ready for publication; and (d) that the supervisor would be available to help with content and structure questions. Supervisors were to provide guidance on the content of the writer's developing text, including navigating the submission and review process, while the tutor would work with the tutee on the manuscripts' organizational and language-related issues.

The three steps of the tutoring service were informed by post-process pedagogies (see Russell, Lea, Parker, Street, & Donahue, 2009), discussions about the teaching of writing (Ferris & Hedgcock, 2014; Reynolds, 2009) and writing for publication (Curry & Lillis, 2013; Paltridge & Starfield, 2016). Initial discussions considered the social and political contexts of writing for publication (Casanave, 2004). Practically speaking, this meant that tutees evaluated what we called the fit and contribution of their research in view of current conversations in their academic community. This was superficially assessed by comparing the aims and scopes of potential target journals to the writer's concern and by comparing the bibliography of the draft article to what the writer identified as being prominent field voices (see Curry & Lillis, 2013; Paltridge & Starfield, 2016). The tutor—while providing broad reflections about the fit and contribution—was not assumed to have disciplinary knowledge; instead, he presented writers with questions they could answer themselves or with their supervisor.

Next, to understand broadly the structural dimensions of articles in target journals, writers were asked to characterize the organization of an article in a target journal (Hyland, 2011). When writers did not have a clear concept of this, the tutor suggested a variety of analyses using the website countwordsworth.com, which enabled writers to gauge article length, article section length, and sentence length, based on number of words, to provide a basis of comparison to the writer's own text. Then, drawing on Ferris (2002), Ferris and Hedgcock (2014), and Reynolds (2009), the tutor and writers considered the text's global features: its organization and cohesion, what Gosden (1995) and Swales (1990) refer to as rhetorical machining. As a final step, specific, repeated grammatical and lexical issues were addressed, what Gosden (1995) calls polishing. The tutor suggested beginning with the article sections that were least likely to change (methods, then results), then turning to the introduction and conclusion respectively. For 10 to 15 minutes, the tutor would read through the indicated section, first marking the text for global features of the writing (organization, cohesion) and then specific, repeated grammatical issues. The time invested in each step depended on what the tutor and writer deemed necessary at each stage.

Findings and Discussion

Evaluation of the Preconditions, 2015–2

During 2015–2, there was immediate evidence that two preconditions—completing 10 one-hour sessions and having a completed research article—were not being met by the tutees. Discussing this situation, we decided to consider 2015–2 as a pilot experience; we used it to explore the actual contexts and needs of the PhD students who were interested in using a tutoring service, rather than insist upon the original four pre-conditions. In terms of these pre-conditions, five of nine drafts were incomplete, and the different writers invested very different amounts of time in the tutoring program (see Table 2.1). Indeed, Ana (all tutee names are pseudonyms) and Berna's initial drafts included introductions and theoretical frameworks, but did not include any other section (e.g., methodology, findings, conclusions). Lina's initial draft only included an outline for an introduction. Leah had a draft that was nearly complete except for one paragraph of confirmatory data to be written by a co-author. In sharp contrast, only three tutees (Amy, Dino, Eli) arrived with a complete article. It is worth highlighting that these three writers were ready to submit their article for publication after one or several sessions, while the other authors used the tutoring service throughout the semester and were not ready to submit their articles at the end of the semester.

In considering these findings, we suggest that individual writers sought assistance from the tutoring service at distinctly different moments of writing and with different intensities. Indeed, Ferris and Hedgcock describe how early on, writers will be "discovering, generating, focusing, and organizing" (2014, p. 249) and that feedback should focus on the content; later, writers edit and proofread, which tutor or teacher feedback could support. More forcefully, Gosden describes the importance of all stages of writing, that "developing awareness of the social-constructionist nature of the hard, norm-developing processes of drafting,

TABLE 2.1 ERPP tutoring participation and focuses, 2015–2

Writer (pseudonym)	Hours	Days	Genre	Complete initial draft?	Submitted (Published?)
Andrea	15.25	14	Lit review	yes	yes (−)
Elaine	12.75	13	Theoretical paper	no	no
Ana	11.25	12	Empirical paper	no	no
Berna	9.25	10	Lit review	no	no
Lina	8.00	8	Lit review	no	no
Leah	5.50	6	Empirical paper	almost	no
Eli	3.50	3	Empirical paper	yes	yes (− ; +)*
Dino	2.50	3	Application	yes	yes (+)
Amy	2.00	1	Empirical paper	yes	yes (− ; −)*

Notes. Here, writers are ordered in terms of decreasing hours spent in the tutoring program. * Eli and Amy were rejected from their first choice journal (−) and submitted to a second journal.

feedback, negotiation, and redrafting is of primary importance to 'success' in research publication" (1995, pp. 46). Thus, if this tutoring service hopes to promote successful writing for publication, it should provide an as-needed service, instead of having a structured class framework (one hour per week for 10 weeks). Indeed, this flexibility should be a hallmark of an effective tutoring service, as it "contribute[s] more to the development of [a writer's] writing abilities than any of the activities that we plan for them because [it is] personalized and responsive to individual needs" (Reynolds, 2009, p. vii).

The writing projects the tutees were interested in advancing also differed qualitatively from what was postulated. Though four writers were working on empirical articles, a stipulated precondition, the other five were working on different academic genres such as literature reviews, theoretical articles, and scholarship applications (see Table 2.1). These data indicate that PhD writers have different academic and professional projects for which they may require assistance; research publication is not the single purpose of academic writing as participating members of a community of practice. Thus, we recommended that the tutoring service support writers in the diverse writing genres related to being a PhD student or an academic. In terms of these supporting or occluded genres, Swales and Feak note their complexity, for their lack of quality examples and for their use of nuanced language; as an example in cover letters, one must simultaneously express being "a serious scholar, research, or instructor . . . [and] a collegial but objective person" (2011, p. xiii). Elsewhere, Pérez-Llantada, Plo, and Ferguson (2011) highlight that conference presentations require special focus by language learners. In short, by being flexible in supporting diverse genres—both written and spoken—we follow Brent (2017) and focus on the plural nature of academic literacies, in which writers

> continually code-switch as they move between sets of disciplinary conventions. . . Learning to navigate these boundaries is not just key to becoming a successful student; it is also key to engaging with a diverse set of epistemological stances as instantiated in those varying conventions.
>
> *(pp. 337–338)*

The last pre-condition for the tutoring service was that the supervisors sign a form declaring that the draft was complete, that it was a research article, and that the supervisor would work with the writer on the content of the article. Four of nine supervisors (for Ana, Berna, Elaine, Lina) declared this to be so without it being the case. This may signal gaps between some supervisors and their PhD students, something that can happen in any community of practice (see Kwan, 2009). Additional evidence of this gap was provided by the writers during the post-tutoring interviews; though unsolicited, four writers remarked on their supervisors' unavailability. Indeed, in her interview, Ana commented:

Ana	I didn't got help from my advisor. And, I remember she wrote you an email saying that she was going to . . . [be the content supervisor]
Gerriet	sure, sure
Ana	so she just allowed me to do this [tutoring] but she never really check my article—she's very busy . . . she only told me "take a look at this book" and no more. And that was a pre-requisite for the tutoring, but after all it was never done. So right now, I ask another professor, a professor from my master to take a look at it.

(February, 2016, file 1, 20:46–21:42; square brackets = clarifying information)

Andrea, in her final interview, reported:

Andrea	the [tutoring] process was thought in that way that I should have an advisor that would, eh, give me feedback, but it was not so.
Gerriet	right
Andrea	when I sent you my documents I sent to him, eh, the document too but he never gave me, eh, feedback. [It] was another tutor or professor whom I show my document . . .
Gerriet	yeah, so there should be someone helping with the content part, yeah
Andrea	someone who is critical and about the content or who say you should read that document, but it's very hard with the advisor. He is very kind, he will always say "yes, I can support you," but he doesn't have time enough, or he's busy, or he is not so important for him because he know it's just an exercise or something, so, so I was alone with you, this works, our work.

(February, 2016, file 2, 20:45–21:57; square brackets = clarifying information)

These unprompted comments illustrate that some supervisors may not have close working relationships with their PhD students (see Kwan, 2009). This type of relationship may be problematic for PhD students, as one "crucial aspect of the response cycle . . . [is] *follow-up*" (Ferris & Hedgcock, 2014, p. 249, emphasis in the original). Without follow-up, the cycle of novice learners learning within a community of practice from old-timer experts deteriorates, as "expertise can only be developed gradually under the guidance of individuals who are in that particular discourse community" (Bourelle, 2012, p. 187). This gap between supervisor and PhD student may also negatively affect the strength of the student's research network, which has been linked to the opportunities one has to publish (Curry & Lillis, 2010).

Despite having busy supervisors, it is noteworthy that both of these PhD students sought outside assistance for their writing projects. Indeed, Ana worked with her MA supervisor and used the tutoring service, while Andrea used the tutoring service to develop "this works (sic), our work." Here, we suggest that writers may use tutoring to build a surrogate community of practice, especially when the writer is not heavily connected to other members of their research community, as seemed to be the case for Ana and Andrea. By having this available resource, the condition existed for "students to perceive themselves as active players in the production of knowledge and to understand how, in fact, knowledge is produced so that they can continue active participation in it" (Hutchins, Fister, & MacPherson, 2002, p. 15, in Brent, 2017, p. 337).

This possible gap between some advisors and PhD students may also signal that some advisors may not know how to support the development of their PhD student's writing in English. Indeed, Zhu (2004) documents faculty opinions about writing in the disciplines and indicates that many faculty members consider themselves as "providers of writing opportunities and as providers of content-related feedback on student writing . . . [whose feedback] was largely summative than formative" (2004, p. 43). We predicted that some faculty supervisors might also benefit from access to the tutoring service, to develop their own texts, and by virtue of this, to help them in their own understanding of research writing and associated sub-genres. Accordingly, we opened the tutoring service to all graduate students and professors working on professional documents, irrespective of the completeness of their draft. We postulated that this investment could be especially important as these professors could then share with their students what they had noticed from tutoring, amplifying the impact of the service.

Evaluation of the Process, 2015–2

Several trends emerged concerning the tutoring process itself; indeed, it evolved unexpectedly to include a much greater focus on the final step (linguistic polishing) than the earlier steps (identifying social and political elements of publishing/navigating submission and review; considering organization and cohesion). Some writers could describe in a sentence or two who their audience was and the contribution their article was making. For instance, Leah described how her DNA analysis of a specific population of animal species revealed information that had not been presented before. Interestingly, these writers were the same ones who completed their drafts and submitted their articles for publication. Others (Ana, Andrea, Berna) were less clear on their text's contribution. Andrea thought that a literature review by its nature would be publishable, and the tutor and Andrea discussed on several occasions the degree to which a published literature review should develop a new focus or make some other contribution. In cases such as these, the tutoring focus often shifted towards linguistic polishing—ideally a latter concern to be addressed—leaving these social or organizational issues unresolved. These shifts to a linguistic focus were made to avoid undermining the overall tutoring process.

We interpreted the occurrence of differing tutoring processes as additional evidence that writers seek tutoring at very different moments of writing. We concluded that writers require and should be provided with individualized and flexible support at each of these different moments. Indeed, this evidence gave us further reason to offer the writing service as a "personalized, individualized support . . . that allows [writers] immediate and continual access when and where they need it" (Hanauer & Englander, 2013, p. 138).

After the 2015–2 semester, based on our evaluation, we reformulated the tutoring service to:

a) be conceived of an "as-needed" service, not as a writing lab class;
b) support diverse written genres (e.g., statements of purposes, grant applications, research summaries, PowerPoints, posters);
c) include the tutoring of oral genres (presentations);
d) continue to implement the same tutoring process;
e) provide tutoring for all levels of graduate students and university professors;
f) include additional tutors to help meet this increased work load.

In a meeting following the 2015–2 semester, we proposed these changes to the department directors. They were implemented during the next semester the tutoring service was offered, 2016–2.

Evaluation of 2016–2 and 2017–1

During these semesters, about 65% of the tutoring sessions focused on research article support, 25% on other types of written documents, and approximately 10% on oral presentations. A similar distribution of interests was found by Gea-Valor, Rey-Rocha, and Moreno (2014) in their analysis of the writing support needed by Spanish scholars. Based on this distribution, we concluded that research articles are an important focus in the tutoring service at our university, but that there is also value in attending to other scholarly genres. As there is currently no other comparable service offered by the university concerning the use of English for scholarly/professional purposes, our tutoring service provides an important resource for these university community members. Ultimately, the tutoring service was supporting "a continuum of understanding of and engagement in the research community" (Brent, 2017, p. 341) in all of its written and spoken forms.

In terms of its use, the tutoring service was utilized consistently across semesters by different university groups. As shown in Table 2.2, MA students used about 25–30% of the service's hours; PhD students used between 25–40% of the service's hours; and professors used between 10–20% of the tutoring hours (N.B. these figures are ranges across several semesters, thus they do not add up to 100%). These data indicate the potential value of this service throughout our university,

TABLE 2.2 Program hours invested (2015–2–2017–1)

	2015–2	2016–1	2016–2	2017–1
Meetings	–	–	6.25 (3%)	–
PhD students	72.5 (100%)	–	65.50 (40%)	19.25 (26%)
MA students	–	–	58.00 (29%)	26.75 (36%)
BA students	–	–	13.00 (7%)	2.25 (3%)
Post-docs	–	–	12.75 (6%)	9.50 (13%)
Professors	–	–	43.25 (22%)	8.00 (11%)
Employees	–	–	–	9.25 (12%)
Total	72.5	0	198.75	75.00
Tutees	12	0	42	26
Tutors	1	0	5*	6

and our recommendation for future semesters is that the service remain open to all interested in working on these types of academic projects. Table 2.2 also shows wide variations in total hours offered in tutoring across different semesters, something of potential concern, as is discussed below.

Lessons Learned and Future Directions

In this program evaluation, we asked whether the tutoring service was being implemented as planned "to inform decisions . . . identify improvements . . . and provide information" (Patton, 2008, p. 40). As our first recommendation, we find that tutoring services benefit from flexibility, in terms of foci, tutee populations, and hours. Our initial conceptualization of the tutoring program was quite inflexible: an informal lab-class, working explicitly on research articles, only with PhD students, on a relatively strict schedule. While this initial structure was an attempt to locate the service within an established framework—one oriented by parameters including teaching duties, contact hours, and filling seats—based on the evidence we presented in this chapter, we felt that we had no choice but to recommend a more flexible structure during the service's second semester.

The second iteration of the tutoring service confirmed that increased flexibility was useful to the people who used the service. Along with PhD students, MA students and professors also took advantage of having support when developing a variety of academic and professional genres, including research articles and presentations, at the moment of the development process for which they sought support. Brent (2017) writes how "an important part of a liberal education is precisely to participate in and understand th[e] knowledge-making system, at least at a novice level" (p. 352), and we believe that this tutoring service does vitally important work helping both emerging and established scholars approach these systems of knowledge-making, in all of their manifestations, at all of their different moments. Following Luo and Hyland (2016), "if properly nurtured by institutional support, this resource may help more authors to turn their submissions into published papers in quality journals" (p. 45), not to mention produce other genres related to being a field professional.

Looking towards the future, we have two concerns that should be addressed through continued cycles of program evaluation. These include developing a resilient structure backing this service and demonstrating to university leaders how this service produces value for our university community. Currently, this service is threatened most by its informal structure. Indeed, all tutors—including the program coordinator—currently work in the service for extra money after completing their other full-time academic duties. As shown in Table 2.2, there are large fluctuations of availability, and potential tutees may be turned away. As this chapter goes to press, we are negotiating with the university leaders and are formalizing a tutoring coordinator position with defined hours and that tutors can have a reduced class hour load in exchange for a certain amount of tutoring. Without this sort of formalized institutional structure, this service could disappear when tutoring service leadership and tutors are directed to carry out other tasks.

The program coordinator position should include ongoing program development and evaluation centered on the tutors and the tutees, two evaluation foci left aside in this chapter focused on program structure. For example, although tutors have a minimum of a Master's degree in TESOL or Applied Linguistics, they should also have opportunities for ongoing professional development, something lacking in the current model. While some may assume that these tutors are suited to edit text drafts by virtue of their "nativeness" in English, it is deeply worrisome that only one has authored publications. This leads to questioning the tutors' understanding of the social and political elements of publications, or even the rhetorical machining (Gosden, 1995) that may be involved in moving a draft towards publication. Regular group reflections by the tutors about a recorded tutoring session could help highlight important elements of tutoring processes. There are also possibilities for additional professional development by increasing contact between the tutors and researchers at the university, building a mutual awareness of the different research tasks and their linguistic and content components, something which may carry high value (Willey & Tanimoto, 2013). These professional development experiences should be subsequently assessed in evaluations with either a formative or empowerment focus (Patton, 2012).

The tutoring service coordinator should also work with alongside tutors to conduct different outreach activities related to research publication at the university, ideally highlighting the value this service brings the university. Calls for these types of activities in Latin America have been made by Corcoran and Englander (2016), who argue that there should be "critical ERPP support in courses and workshops in order to attend more fully to the concerns of multilingual scholars" (p. 7). Gea-Valor et al. (2014) describe how such support could also include "translation and editing services, practical workshops and computer-based resources" (p. 55). During the 2017–1 and 2017–2 semesters, a series of additional workshops on writing research abstracts, building cohesion in writing, and summarizing and paraphrasing were delivered. Though implemented during finals week, over 40 people attended the workshops, an attendance rate that indicates relevance. Finally, the tutoring service and the service overseeing the English-language coursework currently offered throughout the university should work to complement each other. In this way, the tutoring service can amplify its reach by working together with the university's professors to include conversations about the practices related to publication in their different courses. The above projects should be assessed in evaluations with a monitoring focus (Patton, 2012).

In terms of a program evaluation of the tutees, we anecdotally documented that some tutees do not have active supervisors, and that these tutees may be seeking tutoring as a surrogate research or support network to get the "levels of experience, support and networking" (Swales, 2004, p. 58) necessary for successful publication. Future research should focus on the degree to which the tutees are impacted by their supervisors and co-authors. This is of vital importance as the social process of discussing a text could help writers establish what is "recognised and valued by readers in their disciplines" (Hyland, 2013, p. 251). If the tutoring service is being used as a surrogate research network, then the service should consider further actions as part of its protocol to help tutees socially situate themselves within their research context and "to align the vision of the researcher to that of the potential readership and peer-reviewers" (Bardi, 2015, ppp. 103). This is admittedly challenging given the limits of language tutors' disciplinary knowledge and suggests the need for improved collaboration between content and language experts.

Despite recent pedagogical developments in Latin America, resources such as this ERPP tutoring service are still uncommon. As such, this service—the opportunity to discuss one's written and spoken professional projects with a language expert in private consultations—represents an innovation and a value-added component within this university context. However, care must be taken in the design and delivery of this service to ensure that scholars continue to enjoy and benefit from this resource.

References

Baldi, M., Lothringer, R., & Waigandt, D. (2003). Gris de ausencia: Los géneros académicos en la formación docente de grado en profesorados de inglés [The grey of absence: Academic genre in English professorship university degrees]. In *Enseñanza de lenguas extranjeras en el nivel superior: Balances y perspectivas en investigación y docencia* [Advanced foreign language teaching: Balances and perspectives in research and teaching] (pp.177–179). Buenos Aires, AR: Araucaria Editora.

Baldi, M., Lothringer, R., & Waigandt, D. (2005). Academic genres in teacher education. In L. Anglada, M. Barrios, & J. Williams (Eds.). *Towards the knowledge society: Making EFL education relevant. Conference proceedings from the 2005 Federación Argentina de Asociaciones de Profesores de Inglés* (pp. 442–448). Córdoba, AR: Comunicarte Editorial.

Banta, T., & Palomba, C. (2015). *Assessment essentials: Planning, implementing, and improving assessment in higher education*, (2nd ed.). San Francisco, CA: Jossey-Bass.

Bardi, M. (2015). Learning the practice of scholarly publication in English: A Romanian perspective. *English for Specific Purposes, 37*, 98–111. http://dx.doi.org/10.1016/j.esp.2014.08.002

Bazerman, C., Dean, C., Early, J., Lunsford, K., Null, S., Rogers, P., & Stansell, A. (Eds.) (2012). *International advances in writing research: Cultures, places, measures*. Fort Collins, CO: WAC Clearinghouse.

Bourelle, T. (2012). Bridging the gap between the technical communication classroom and the internship: Teaching social consciousness and real-world writing. *Journal of Technical Writing and Communication, 42*, 183–197.

Brent, D. (2017). Senior students' perceptions of entering a research community. *Written Communication, 34*(3), 333–355.

Carrasco, A., & Kent, R. (2011). Leer y escribir en el doctorado y el reto de formarse como autor de ciencias [Reading and writing in a PhD and the challenge of forming oneself as an author in the sciences]. *Revista Mexicana de Investigación Educativa, 16*(51), 1227–1251.

Carrasco, A., Kent, R., & Keranen, N. (2012). Learning careers and enculturation: Production of scientific papers by PhD students in a Mexican physiology laboratory: An exploratory case study. In C. Bazerman, C. Dean, J. Early, K. Lunsford, S. Null, P. Rogers, & A. Stansell (Eds.), *International advances in writing research: Cultures, places, measures* (pp. 335–351). Fort Collins, CO: WAC Clearinghouse.

Casanave, C. P. (2004). *Controversies in second language writing: Dilemmas and decisions in research and instruction*. Ann Arbor, MI: The University of Michigan Press.

Conrad, C. F., & Wilson, R. F. (1985). *Academic program reviews: Institutional approaches, expectations, and controversies* (No. ASHE-ERIC Higher Education Report No. 5). Washington, DC: Association for the Study of Higher Education.

Corcoran, J. N. (2015). *English as the international language of science: A case study of Mexican scientists' writing for publication*. PhD dissertation, University of Toronto.

Corcoran, J. N. (2017). The potential and limitations of an intensive English for Research Publication Purposes course for Mexican scholars. In M.J. Curry & T. Lillis (Eds.), *Global academic publishing: Policies, perspectives, and pedagogies* (pp. 242–255). Clevedon, UK: Multilingual Matters.

Corcoran, J., & Englander, K. (2016). A proposal for critical pragmatic approaches to English for Research Publication Purposes. *API Publications, 4*(6), 1–10.

Curry, M. J., & Lillis, T. (2004). Multilingual scholars and the imperative to publish in English: Negotiating interests, demands, and rewards. *TESOL Quarterly, 38*(4), 663–688.

Curry, M. J., & Lillis, T. (2010). Academic research networks: Accessing resources for English-medium publishing. *English for Specific Purposes, 29*, 281–295. doi:10.1016/j.esp.2010.06.002

Curry, M. J. & Lillis, T. (2013). *A scholar's guide to getting published in English: Critical choices and practical strategies*. Clevedon, UK: Multilingual Matters.

Curry, M. J. & Lillis, T. (Eds.). (2017). *Global academic publishing: Policies, perspectives, and pedagogies*. Bristol, UK: Multilingual Matters.

Ferenz, O. (2005). EFL writers' social networks: Impact on advanced academic literacy development. *Journal of English for Academic Purposes, 4*(4), 339–351.

Ferris, D. (2002). *Treatment of error in second language student writing*. Ann Arbor, MI: The University of Michigan Press.

Ferris, D., & Hedgcock, J. (2014). *Teaching L2 composition*. New York, NY: Routledge.
Fournier, D. (2005). Evaluation. In S. Mathison (Ed.). *Encyclopedia of evaluation* (pp. 139–140). Thousand Oaks, CA: Sage.
Fortes, J., & Lomnitz, L. (1994). *Becoming a scientist in Mexico: The challenge of creating a scientific community in an underdeveloped country*. University Park, PA: Penn State University Press.
Gea-Valor, M.-Ll., Rey-Rocha, J., & Moreno, A. (2014). Publishing research in the international context: An analysis of Spanish scholars' academic writing needs in the social sciences. *English for Specific Purposes, 36*, 47–59.
Gosden, H. (1995). Success in research article writing and revision: A social-constructionist perspective. *English for Specific Purposes, 14*(1), 37–57.
Hanauer, D. I., & Englander, K. (2011). Quantifying the burden of writing research articles in a second language: Data from Mexican scientists. *Written Communication, 28*(4), 403–416. doi:10.1177/074108831142005
Hanauer, D. I., & Englander, K. (2013). *Scientific writing in a second language*. Anderson, SC: Parlor Press.
Huang, J. C. (2010). Publishing and learning writing for publication in English: Perspectives of NNES PhD students in science. *Journal of English for Academic Purposes, 9*(1), 33–44.
Hyland, K. (2011). Welcome to the machine: Thoughts on writing for scholarly publication. *Journal of Second Language Teaching and Research, 1*(1), 58–68.
Hyland, K. (2013). Faculty feedback: Perceptions and practices in L2 disciplinary writing. *Journal of Second Language Writing, 22*, 240–253. doi:10.1016/j.jslw.2013.03.003
Hyland, K., & Hyland, F. (Eds.). (2006). *Feedback in second language writing: Contexts and issues*. Cambridge, MA: Cambridge University Press.
Janssen, G. (2016). "Inglés para doctorados": A case study in program development. In B. Forero and A. Merlo (Eds.). *Entre lenguas y culturas* [Between languages and cultures] (Vol. 1). Bogotá: Ediciones Uniandes.
Kwan, B. S. C. (2009). An investigation of instruction in research publishing offered in doctoral programs: The Hong Kong case. *Higher Education, 59*(1), 55–68. doi:10.1007/s10734-009-9233-x
Lave, J. & Wenger, E. (1991). *Situated learning: Legitimate peripheral participation*. New York, NY: Cambridge University Press.
Lei, J., & Hu, G. (2015). Apprenticeship in scholarly publishing: A student perspective on doctoral supervisors' roles. *Publications, 3*(1), 27–42. doi:10.3390/publications301002
Leskes, A., & Wright, B. D. (2005). *The art and science of assessing general education outcomes*. Washington, DC: Association of American Colleges and Universities.
Li, Y. (2006). A doctoral student of physics writing for publication: A sociopolitically-oriented case study. *English for Specific Purposes, 25*(4), 456–478. doi: 0.1016/j.esp.2005.12.002
Lillis, T., & Curry, M. J. (2006). Professional academic writing by multilingual scholars: Interactions with literacy brokers in the production of English-medium texts. *Written Communication, 23*(1), 3–35. doi:10.1177/0741088305283754
Luo, N., & Hyland, K. (2016). Chinese academics writing for publication: English teachers as text mediators. *Journal of Second Language Writing, 33*, 43–55.
Martínez, R., & Figueiredo, E. (2017). *Supporting academic publication in a Brazilian university: Reducing the English 'ecological footprint'*. Presentation at the 18th World Congress of Applied Linguistics (AILA), July 23–28, Rio de Janeiro, Brazil.
Merkel, W. (2018). Role reversals: A case study of dialogic interactions and feedback on L2 writing. *Journal of Second Language Writing, 39*, 16–28.
Paltridge, B., & Starfield, S. (2016). *Getting published in academic journals: Navigating the publication process*. Ann Arbor, MI: The University of Michigan Press.

Patton, M. (2008). *Utilization-focused evaluation* (4th ed.). Thousand Oaks, CA: Sage Publications.

Patton, M. (2012). *Essentials of utilization-focused evaluation*. Thousand Oaks, CA: Sage Publications.

Pérez-Llantada, C., Plo, R., & Ferguson, G. (2011). "You don't say what you know, only what you can": The perceptions and practices of senior Spanish academics regarding research dissemination in English. *English for Specific Purposes, 30,* 18–30.

Reynolds, D. (2009). *One on one with second language writers: A guide for writing tutors, teachers, and consultants*. Ann Arbor, MI: The University of Michigan Press.

Russell, D., Lea, M., Parker, J., Street, B., & Donahue, T. (2009). Exploring notions of genre in "academic literacies" and "writing across the curriculum": Approaches across countries and contexts. In C. Bazerman, A. Bonini, & D. Figueiredo (Eds.). *Genre in a changing world* (pp. 395–423). Fort Collins, CO: The WAC Clearinghouse/ West Lafayette, IN: Parlor Press.

Swales, J. (1990). *Genre analysis: English in academic and research settings*. Cambridge, UK: Cambridge University Press.

Swales, J. (2004). *Research genres: Explorations and applications*. Cambridge, UK: Cambridge University Press.

Swales, J., & Feak, C. (2011). *Navigating academia: Writing supporting genres*. Ann Arbor, MI: The University of Michigan Press.

Tardy, C. (2006). Appropriation, ownership, and agency: Negotiating teacher feedback in academic settings. In K. Hyland & F. Hyland (Eds.). *Feedback in second language writing: Contexts and issues*. Cambridge, MA: Cambridge University Press.

Thaiss, C., Bräuer, G., Carlino, P., Ganobcsik-Williams, L., & Sinha, A. (Eds.). (2012). *Writing programs worldwide: Profiles of academic writing in many places*. Fort Collins, CO: The WAC Clearinghouse; Anderson, SC: Parlos Press.

Times Higher Education. (2017). *Latin American university rankings 2017*. Retrieved from: https://www.timeshighereducation.com/world-university-rankings/2017/latin-america-university-rankings#!/page/0/length/25/sort_by/rank/sort_order/asc/cols/stats

Willey, I., & Tanimoto, K. (2013). "Convenience editors" as legitimate participants in the practice of scientific editing: An interview study. *Journal of English for Academic Purposes, 12,* 23–32. doi:10.1016/j.jeap.2012.10.007

Zappa-Hollman, S., & Duff, P. (2015). Academic English socialization through individual networks of practice. *TESOL Quarterly, 49*(2), 333–368.

Zhu, W. (2004). Faculty views on the importance of writing, the nature of academic writing, and the teaching and responding to writing in the disciplines. *Journal of Second Language Writing, 13*(1), 29–48.

3
TRAJECTORIES TOWARDS AUTHORSHIP

Eight Mexican English Language Teaching Professionals

Fátima Encinas-Prudencio
BENEMÉRITA UNIVERSIDAD AUTÓNOMA DE PUEBLA

Verónica Sánchez-Hernández
BENEMÉRITA UNIVERSIDAD AUTÓNOMA DE PUEBLA

Maria Thomas-Ruzic
UNIVERSITY OF COLORADO

Gicela Cuatlapantzi-Pichón
BENEMÉRITA UNIVERSIDAD AUTÓNOMA DE PUEBLA

Georgina Aguilar-González
BENEMÉRITA UNIVERSIDAD AUTÓNOMA DE PUEBLA

Introduction

Latin American scholars are gradually "going more global," presenting and publishing more widely in English than ever before, particularly in certain fields and countries (Colina, 2011; Huggett, 2012). The dominance of publication in English is certainly a major challenge for most scholars. The need for international English in academic and professional multilingual and multicultural settings—driven by each country's priorities, higher education policies and grants—entails rigorous research and also the English competence required to meet editors' and reviewers' academic writing standards in English. In many Latin American universities, there are writing and publication resources such as onsite and online courses and workshops which have been introduced to support scholars in the processes of publishing in English. However, the effectiveness of such resources have also been questioned (Bazerman, Keranen, & Encinas, 2012; Corcoran & Englander, 2016; Curry & Lillis, 2017) mainly because often they tend not to address the particular practices of the different disciplines and the complexities of publication politics that multilingual scholars require throughout the entire writing and publication processes.

The thrust of the current chapter comes from a recognition that traditional resources for writing scholars fall short, and that the key to being able to provide the relevant supports is to better understand ELT and other professionals' trajectories towards authorship, including research and writing apprenticeship processes. Understanding these processes could allow ELT scholar-mentors with research and publication experience to provide the support that advanced level writers who want to publish internationally in English require.

Developments in ELT in the Mexican Context

In Mexico as elsewhere, ELT has been developing steadily over the past 40 years. Most Mexican public and private universities have departments or centers dedicated to the teaching of English and other foreign languages. As for teacher education and development, nationally, there are 180 undergraduate (ANUIES, 2016) and 12 graduate programs in ELT or related fields such as Applied Linguistics. Higher education institutions view internationalization and the learning of English as crucial to gaining and maintaining their competitive position in the future.

Despite the advances, ELT in higher education is still viewed as being in a stage of development (Ramírez & Dzul, 2013). One critique that persists is that students' English results fall short of expectations (González, Vivaldo, & Castillo, 2004; Davies, 2009). Another common acknowledgement is that a number of academic, social and political factors have complicated the implementation of national and institutional policies for English teaching and learning. For Ramírez and Dzul (2013), advancing the field would imply raising the level of professionalization of the ELT community.

This chapter reports on a two-year-long study of eight Mexican ELT professionals working in higher education contexts. We were able to study their professional careers over the 8 to 10 years that followed their graduation as Master's students. Findings from our investigation into these alumni's professional paths allowed us to identify characteristics and conditions that shaped each person's authorship trajectory.

This study contributes to the understanding that relevant, meaningful support for ELT professionals must go beyond the emphasis of traditional pre-service training (Pickering & Gunashekar, 2015) and in-service professional development (Cheung, 2013) to include research regarding issues that emerge from their teaching practice.

Theoretical Framework

This study adopts the concept of Legitimate Peripheral Participation (LPP) (Lave & Wenger, 1991) related to communities of practice to explore eight ELT professionals in their trajectories towards authorship. LPP belongs to a social theory of learning which refers to the process a newcomer undergoes to become a full member of a community of practice depending on his/her participation. In this process, the newcomer learns through social interaction and collaboration with old timers as well as the use of tools inherent to the community.

However, driven by the complexity of social systems today, the idea of community of practice has been explored further by Wenger (1998) and Wenger-Trayner, Fenton-O'Creevy, Hutchinson, Kubiak, and Wenger-Trayner (2015). This theory uses the concept of learning in landscapes of practice which is "defined by practice, not by institutional affiliation; . . . the landscape so defined is a weaving of both boundaries and peripheries" (Wenger, 1998, p. 118). This theory can illuminate how the participants in this study configure their authorship through their participation in different communities (often ELT, applied linguistics, education and others) as well as other activities they engage in.

These processes of becoming full members of any community, however, are not absent of significant tensions and conflictive negotiations. Gaining legitimacy in a community could imply considerable time and some may fail to overcome these situations. Trajectories to authorship are not lineal and are facilitated or affected by numerous personal, social factors and contexts.

Authoring and *authorship* have often been used interchangeably. For the purposes of this paper, we will take authoring as the writing of an electronic text or software program and authorship as the researcher's production in the broader sense, for example, conference presentations or workshops and publishing (articles, chapters and books on line or paper).

The challenges to authorship in English by multilingual researchers have received increasing attention over the last decades (e.g. Flowerdew, 1999, 2001; Lillis & Curry, 2014; Englander, 2014). Bazerman and Paradis (1991) and Swales (1998) among others, discuss the intricacies of varieties of scientific texts in different disciplines. Some recent case studies have looked at practices and issues related to both authorship and publication in English in specific discourse communities (Curry & Lillis, 2010; Lillis & Curry, 2014). In Mexico, Carrasco and Kent (2012) explore the enculturation processes of science PhD students. Additionally, Bazerman et al. (2012) discuss facilitating immersion at a distance in a Physics Department in Mexico.

Publication in ELT by plurilingual scholars in Mexico has been far less studied (Perales-Escudero, 2010; Crawford, 2010). Roux, Mora, and Trejo (2011) uncovered the processes of a Mexican undergraduate student becoming an author, while Trujeque, Encinas, and Ruzic (2015) related the authorship development of experienced ELT Mexican scholars directly to their literacy development. There are, however, very few longitudinal studies at the initial stages of trajectories towards authorship and none in ELT.

Methodology

As mentioned before, the study reported in this chapter is a longitudinal multiple case study (Yin, 2003) that seeks to understand ELT professional's trajectories toward authorship. It combined a sequential mixed methods approach. We used a convenience sample of eight Mexican ELT professionals in public universities who were graduates from one of two Master's cohorts (2005–2007 or 2007–2009) of an ELT program in a public university in central Mexico. Table 3.1 gives information about the eight participants.

TABLE 3.1 Participants' information

Participants	Faculty position	Work location	Administrative experience	Degrees
Elsa	Fulltime professor	Language Center English teacher	No	MA
Graciela	Fulltime professor	ELT undergraduate program	No	MA
Joaquin	Fulltime professor-researcher	Research Center	No	PhD student
Juan	Fulltime professor	ELT undergraduate program	Yes	PhD student
Lina	Fulltime professor	ELT undergraduate program	Yes	MA
Melia	Hour class professor	ELT undergraduate program	No	MA
Roberto	Hour class professor	Language Center English teacher	No	PhD student
Vania	Fulltime professor	ELT undergraduate program	No	PhD student

Over an 18-month period, August 2015 to January 2017, three data collection strategies were used for this study: the participants' CVs, interviews based on their CVs, and "talk around the text" (Lillis & Curry, 2010) interviews based on four texts selected by the participants (see Figure 3.1).

	1st & 2nd Stage		3rd Stage
DATA COLLECTION STRATEGY	CVs	Modified Subject-Object interview about their professional development based on CVs	Talk around the text interview (four texts: one in Spanish and 3 in English)
CATEGORIES	1. An inventory of working relationships & authorship	2. Context awareness, collaboration and networking	3. Literacy practices & publication
	4. AGENCY		
	FINDINGS		

FIGURE 3.1 Data collection and analysis

Participants who agreed to be part of the study sent their updated CVs to the authors. The CVs were then reviewed and notes were made for later discussion during the follow-up interviews.

The revision of the participants' CVs gave a panorama of their academic production. These products were categorized according to their role as: 1) presenters 2) authors in publications, 3) thesis readers and thesis supervisors (see Table 3.2).

The first interviews were modified subject-object (S-O) interviews (Lahey, Souvaine, Kegan, Goodman, & Felix, 1988). These were one-on-one, open-ended interviews lasting about one hour in which participants were invited to select events or developments in their academic and professional lives from their CVs. As part of the subject-object protocol the interviewer provided the eight participants ten index cards containing a prompt: angry, anxious, successful, standing up for your beliefs, confused, sad, moved, surprised, change, important to me. Then they were asked to choose one or two cards and discuss how the cards they chose were related to events or developments in their CVs. Interviews took place via Skype or in person and were recorded and transcribed. Both interviewees and interviewers were known to each other, having been in past relationships as student-professor/mentor or current relationships as colleagues. Interviewers probed with questions asking participants about relevant entries in their CVs and asking them to reflect further on how these were meaningful and relevant to them.

The second interviews were based on "talk around text", and involved a dialogue between the participant and the researcher in search of an in-depth understanding of the participants' literacy practices. The participants were asked to send four texts—one in Spanish and three in English—that they considered relevant for their professional development for whatever reasons. They were asked to talk about their texts in an open-ended interview that lasted approximately one hour. Thus, although literacy practices themselves are unobservable and constantly changing (Barton & Hamilton, 2000), the talk around the text approach used in the second interview and mediated by participants' own texts provided windows into their literacy practices.

The analysis of the data from the CVs and the S-O interviews were interwoven with the analysis of the data collected by the "talk around text" interview and based on the LPP framework and on the question that guided our study: Which characteristics and conditions shaped each one of these participants' authorship development? The objective was to obtain categories, which explained these participants' processes in becoming more expert members of the community and parallelly develop their authorship.

There were five coders in this project. We were organized in two groups and each group analyzed four participants' data collected in the CVs, the S-O and the "talk around text" interviews. Each group proposed certain categories. The two groups compared and contrasted them. Then, after discussing the framework (Wenger-Trayner, et al., 2015) we again went back to review the literature on

TABLE 3.2 Participants' production

	2007	2008	2009	2010	2011	2012	2013	2014	2015
Elsa			1	4 3 1	1 1 2	2 2 1 1 5	2 4	2 3	2 1 6
Graciela				6 1	1 2	7 2 8	3 4	3 7 1 3	1 1 3 6
Joaquín	4	4	3	2		3 4	3 1	3 4	2
Juan	5	3	4	4	5	4 5	5 3 1 1	4 1 2 6 1	1 2 7 3
Lina							1 2	2 5 3	2 4 1
Melia						1		1 1	2
Roberto	1			2 1	2	2			4
Vania	1			3	4	6	1 2 1	1 2 6 1 1	2 2 1

PR = Presentations   TR = Thesis Reader
PU = Publications   TS = Thesis Supervisor

issues we had detected in the data such as the relationship between networking and publication (Lillis & Curry, 2010) and agency (Holland Lachicotte, Skinner, & Cain, 2001). That is, the groups identified characteristics of belonging to a community and defined first categories of the analysis.

Findings and Discussion

Finally, the following four categories emerged: 1) Context Awareness in Higher Education and ELT Communities, 2) Collaboration and Networking, 3) Publication Practices, and 4) Agency.

Context Awareness: Higher Education and the ELT Communities

The participants in this study worked in public higher education and, therefore, knew that participation in professional communities and publication was imperative not only for securing or keeping an academic position but also for their professional development. However, their workplaces and positions varied; one worked in a Research Center, five worked in an undergraduate ELT program and two worked in a Language Center (general language courses). Thus, they disclosed varying levels of awareness regarding the Mexican higher education policies, their institution and the ELT community depending on their workplace and faculty position. Those working in a Research Center and the undergraduate ELT program tended to display more understanding of the institution, the ELT community as well as other interrelated communities. Furthermore, each participant's awareness tended to be directly related to his/her engagement in teaching, management and research activities.

Juan understood that in order to obtain a Federal Faculty recognition [PRODEP], he had to publish an article as one of the requirements. He needed that recognition to obtain financial support. "I needed an article before my application. Then, when my application came, I had everything . . . I got the PRODEP recognition, and then I had the, the financial support to get my equipment and the PhD."

Since federal Mexican policies request faculty collaborative work for PRODEP and individual publication for the National Research System; Joaquín who worked in a Research Center showed a realistic awareness of expectations. He was expected to work individually but at the same time connect across disciplines with other researchers and stay consistent with his coordinator's guidance and approvals. He reported: "In theory, we are working individually on a project. . .but it always implies working with other people from other areas, and institutions as well."

Two participants had administrative positions in the undergraduate ELT program. Their understanding of institutions as complex and constantly changing systems helped Juan and Lina navigate and participate in the context of higher education policies. Juan reflected on his new position: "I had some support but, you always have to learn this by yourself. . . I had to learn how to be aware of how the system worked. . ."

Another participant discussed how working in another state university allowed her to visualize new opportunities. Vania explained how her perspective changed when she returned to her home university. She saw opportunities in the university she had not seen before.

> We have a lot of opportunities to grow in the university but since we're in getting money [working in different institutions at the same time] we don't see the opportunities. . .If I hadn't gone probably I would be teaching 45 hours of classes (a week).

Two participants from the Language Center, however, had a dim understanding of the higher education policies. Elsa blamed workloads explicitly in the context of the recent loss of a colleague. "A teacher passed away. She started taking up jobs, responsibilities, she was given coordinator positions. She got ill . . . She wouldn't say "no" to anything. . . It makes me sad that jobs are taking people's lives."

As elsewhere in the world, a major concern for educators in higher education is obtaining full-time faculty positions. Roberto noted that his PhD credentials alone would not secure him a position, and that connections would also come into play:

> I feel a little bit anxious. . . job opportunities in Mexico are not very good, things are changing. . . with a lot of academic work we can get something, but there are many people ready for a position, so we also need, not just academic work but also connections.

These two last participants from the Language Center had an unclear understanding of higher education systems as well as of the ELT community probably due to their limited participation in both. Instead of feeling challenged and spurred on by the policies they were encountering, they felt discouraged or anxious and tended to see higher education policies in isolation and not as part of systems. As Lave and Wenger (1991, p. 53) state:

> Learning. . . implies becoming able to be involved in new activities, to perform new tasks and functions, to master new understandings. Activities, functions, and understandings do not exist in isolation; they are part of broader systems of relations in which they have meaning. . . Learning thus implies becoming a different person with respect to the possibilities enabled by these systems of relations.

As explained above, the directions the participants took after the MA reflected their participation in certain areas related to teaching, administrative positions, curriculum development, research or enrollment in a PhD program. Tables 3.2 and 3.3

TABLE 3.3 Publications and co-authoring

Participants	Single author journal articles	Co-authored journal articles	Single author book chapter	Co-authored book chapter	Co-authored books	Conference proceedings	Type of collaboration
	Indexed	Indexed					
Elsa Lang. Center	3(2E&1S)	1(E)		1(S)		1(E)	Peers (3)
Graciela ELT program				5(3E&2S)		3(2E&1S)	SFM (5) Peers (2)
Joaquín Research Center PhD student		4(3E&1S)		1(S)	1(S)		SFM (5) Peers (1)
Juan ELT program PhD student		2(2E)		1(E)			SFM (1) Peers (2)

Lina ELT program		5(2E&3S)	1(1S)	1(E)	TSup (1) SFM (2) Peers (4)
Melia ELT program		1(E)		1(E)	TSup (1)
Roberto Lang. Center PhD student	1(E)				
Vania ELT program PhD student	1(E)	2(2S)		1(E)	SFM (2) Peers (1)

E = English   SFM = Senior Faculty Member
S = Spanish   TSup = Thesis Supervisor

show these eight participants' diverse trajectories towards authorship. Most initiated their trajectories presenting in conferences and then started publishing. Similarly, most started as thesis readers and later became thesis supervisors. Those who participated more actively in these activities, Graciela, Juan, Joaquín, and Vania, gained understandings which enabled them to enhance their work in the university and comprehend the communities in which they worked. Each of these participants in diverse ways and at different stages of their development embraced their challenges and through engagement in their workplace context and disciplinary communities tended to have a clearer perspective of the situation. Therefore, those who understood the context took more strategic decisions regarding their professional development because through their engagement they acquired an increasingly clearer understanding of the whole picture and "the rules of the game". Whereas those who felt more limited and thwarted by the challenges tended to feel anxious and in some cases overwhelmed mainly because of the limited understanding of their context.

Collaboration and Networking Practices

Another emerging theme from the data analysis in both interviews and the CVs was the relationship between networking and publication. This theme clearly resonated with the findings of Englander (2014) in the hard sciences and Curry and Lillis (2010) in the social sciences.

Table 3.3 presents a more detailed analysis of participants' publications. Five of the participants published in both languages (24 publications in English and 15 in Spanish). Similarly to findings in China by Zheng and Cao (in this volume), participants' language choice for publication generally depended on the purpose, audience or the disciplinary community. Issues related to ELT or applied linguistics were regularly published in English whereas more general education themes were often published in Spanish, especially if related to local matters.

The data also exposed diverse co-authorship relationships for publication. Fifteen publications were co-authored. Most of them were indexed articles and book chapters, which seems to be the case for social sciences in general (Lillis & Curry, 2010). Two participants co-authored with their thesis supervisor, five with a more senior colleague and six co-authored with peers. Interestingly, almost all the articles published in indexed journals were co-authored.

The data revealed research and writing apprenticeship experiences through LPP. When discussing one of his co-authored articles, Joaquin acknowledges the guidance from his more experienced colleague and coauthor as a literacy broker (Curry & Lillis, 2010).

> She's been a great help. She asks questions. In many cases. . . I don't have answers. And they pinpoint the gaps in my research project or . . .the gaps in the interviews and then I go back into the field and fill those gaps . . . don't

> feel she's judging me . . . She used to say, "that's a good point", "but . . ..go back. . . get a holistic understanding".

> There is something else Maria helped me understand, she suggested and selected the specific journal we would send the document to. . . it was a different process. It was not only writing the document but editing according to the journal specifications, the line of discussion they have and the kind of articles they publish. . . she helped me to figure that out.

Another participant, Graciela, explained how her mentors were both her network and literacy brokers who facilitated her participation in national research networks and co-authored publications.

> I consider Anna my mentor and also Berenice, my thesis advisor. Anna introduced me to some other people. I was invited to work on another project, a big project. . . she introduced me to one of the best researchers in this area in Mexico. . .

Juan distinguished types of collaborative work. He viewed two of his more senior colleagues as a kind of network brokers. "I didn't think of Ann or Emma as my superiors but my mentors and friends and people who believed in me. . . that was the first circle of collaboration and the second one was my colleagues, my friends."

A participant from the Language Center reported less productive experiences largely due to her partial understanding of the system. Elsa states, "Yes. I did many things on my own. Later, the school would say "you also have to do things, with somebody else". Then, I looked for other people. Now, I find it very hard. . . to do things with other people.

Even though all the participants acknowledged the importance that collaborative research and writing had for their authorship development, three emphasized the challenges they had when negotiating with co-authors. Their experiences varied not only in the types of networks they engaged in but also in the degrees of productivity. The participants who were more open to collaboration were the ones who had articles in indexed journals (see Table 3.3). This is probably because they had a better understanding of the complexities of collaboration and networking practices during publication processes.

Networking and literacy development are interrelated and shaped by opportunities which often emerge from writing for publication (Curry & Lillis, 2010; Englander, 2014) mainly because writing for publication implies other social practices, which are related to participating in the discourse community such as researching, attending conferences, participating in research networks and supervising and reading theses (see Table 3.2). Publishing a paper, also, implies deciding where to submit the paper and later how to negotiate reviewers' feedback (Curry & Lillis, 2014). These social practices are learned through practice and interaction with other colleagues—often facilitated by network and literacy brokers—in other words through immersion in their disciplinary communities as Wenger, et al. (2015) clearly argue in their theory of learning in the landscapes of practice.

Publication Practices

Participants presented different stages of literacy awareness in the "talk around the text" interviews when reflecting about their writing—whether in English or Spanish. As expected, most participants claimed they had had more experience writing in English than in Spanish mainly due to their undergraduate and graduate studies in English. Joaquín was one of three of the participants working in a Spanish medium PhD program: "I've been writing mostly in Spanish recently. At first, it was very difficult because I used to write in English; I was not familiarized with the style in Spanish. . . the structure and the kind of writing for different audiences."

Three participants, Joaquin, Lina, and Vania, thought that their research on writing and genre awareness helped them cope with their challenges of writing both in English or Spanish. They implied they could write in either language because of their genre awareness.

Even though the MA program in which these participants studied did not propose a genre-based pedagogy, in the interviews, all the participants discussed genre either overtly or implicitly. Joaquín, for example, talked about an assignment for one of his PhD subjects and discussed genre differences depending on purpose. "I chose that particular document [to talk about with you]; of *'discusión de temas culturales' [discussion of cultural issues]* because. . .this one is particularly different in terms of the genre and linguistic resources used to create, to construct an argument. . ."

Graciela discussed how she wrote a chapter based on her thesis.

> It was my thesis and had to write it as a chapter . . . it took a long time because it was not only a summary. In a chapter, we couldn't. . . include all the participants. It implied reanalyzing, reorganizing information, rewriting.

Lina explained how she used her genre awareness and analysis skills to write a proposal: "I was not sure about how to write a proposal for *Tutorias* (Tutoring) then I checked the page from the *Facultad* to look at the moves professor Rodolfo used. [Note: 'Moves' refers to Swales' 1990 analysis of genres].

Even though all the participants acknowledged publication requirements and their connection to faculty promotion or compliance with PhD scholarship requirements, only two of the current PhD students showed an awareness of English medium publishing policies. With the support of a senior researcher, Joaquin gained insights into how a specific genre fulfills a rhetorical purpose, and how the writer, the intended reader, and the text itself, are informed by purpose. Joaquin said:

> With Maria's feedback, at that moment my ideas were more or less clear in terms of content, analysis, etc.. . . . but it was necessary to familiarize with the procedures and patterns for publishing. Even if I was familiar with academic writing and I felt I was ready for publishing, there were things I missed. . . For example writing [references] in alphabetical order, appropriate vocabulary, citation, generalization. Her feedback was hard and strict, but the changes were deeper from the previous article which was for a school paper, this was a more scholarly document.

As part of exploring participants' literacy development, the interviewers posed questions about the roles of their literacy brokers (supervisors, or journal reviewers) and their feedback. Those with more publication experience mainly discussed the journals reviewers' comments. Vania, for example, reflects on the benefits as well as the challenges.

> I learned that we write for ourselves, but I think it is a good exercise that somebody else reads us and gives feedback. That helped me to improve a lot. . .

> I had to revise the literature and organize the method section and explain more. . . it was terrible (laughs). I wanted to cry. . . Writing takes time, good writing takes more time.

Roberto discussed the feedback from PhD professors and how explicit, critical feedback questioned his background knowledge and paralyzed his research for a period of time.

> I chose this text [to discuss with you]. . . because it was negative. . . Actually, I think my professor tried to give some good feedback just to make me feel better. . . I stopped doing research because first I needed to understand the field, the different topics, the different methods, and then I continued working with my research, at the end I considered her feedback has been one of the best I got.

At least four participants were very critical about the limited feedback they received in the MA program. Some viewed their thesis supervisor's role as a literacy and/or network broker who promoted their engagement in the professional community, yet others perceived tensions and difficult negotiations which limited their participation. Most recognized feeling frustrated after receiving reviewers' feedback. However, overall, they seemed to perceive feedback as constructive and valued how it contributed to their work.

Participants revealed their genre awareness, in the second interviews, both overtly and implicitly. Their awareness varied from an awareness of academic texts in general to a very in-depth and sophisticated understanding of the discourse complexity and the various genres used in different disciplines and settings. Heightened awareness was displayed by those participants who had more experience in co-authoring processes probably because they were more habituated to discussing their research as well as their writing and rewriting. Vania, Graciela and especially Joaquin displayed a more sophisticated understanding of genres and valued explicit critical and even harsh feedback. They also displayed awareness that publication included often harsh interactions among authors, editors, journal editors, and critical reviewers. Those with little experience publishing in more scholarly publications tended not to mention these interactions probably because they had not lived these experiences.

As Casanave and Vandrick (2003, p. 7) state:

> …learning takes place via participation, and there may be no way to shorten this process. The greater ease of transition comes about as novice writers come to understand and thus not summarily reject the lengthy social, political, and sociolinguistic processes that lie hidden behind the polished product that we finally see in print.

Authorship development, then, necessarily implies enculturation processes and immersion in the disciplinary community (among others Canagarajah, 2002; Casanave & Vandrick, 2003) or interrelated communities of practice which happen through participation and support from different kinds of mentors especially professors and more experienced colleagues. These enculturation processes are very challenging and often generate both negative emotions such as frustration, anxiety as well as very positive emotions such as "flow", satisfaction and self-worth.

Agency

The data also revealed that some of the participants took strategic decisions about their development as professionals and authors. In other words, they had developed a sense of agency. Hernandez-Zamora (2017) defines agency as crucial to understanding how a person does not only depend on norms and regulations but can also become an actor or agent who takes strategic decisions about his life especially those related to his most valued aspirations. This sense of agency also led them to "make choices, take control, self-regulate, and thereby pursue their goals as individuals leading, potentially, to personal or social transformation" (Duff, 2012, p. 414).

Joaquin, for example, reflected on the challenge of dealing with "tough" feedback on a draft in order to pursue his goal which was publishing an article.

Her feedback was tough and strict. . . at first I was not satisfied 'cause I spent some time on it, but when I read the final version I understood I had to make those changes, to make it better, a more scholarly document.

Another participant, Lina, wanted to take control of her professional development by participating actively and belonging to an academic group. "I tried to participate in committees and belong to an "academia". . . my main purpose was to keep on learning and to get at least a change or promotion in my job."

The participants' agency was revealed in decisive and critical moments in their development and how they dealt with their emotional crisis. For example, Joaquin sees anxiety as part of his own learning:

. . . anxiety may have two different results. It can limit people; it can block them, or motivate them. Most of the time, I use anxiety as a trigger. . . At times I feel frustrated, at other I feel really excited to see that everything is going on relatively well.

Vania described a decisive moment when deciding to leave or stay in a new position in a different university: "I realized I didn't want to be there, because of many things. I said no good opportunity is going to hold me back if I don't feel comfortable, so I'm going back [to her home university]."

The examples above indicate how three participants evaluated their own value systems and managed conflict adequately. The decisions these teachers made in these situations were actions and displays of agency defining participants' identity as writers and authors (Duff, 2012).

Conclusions and Pedagogical Implications

This study's main finding revealed that the participants' trajectories towards authorship were not linear but complex enculturation processes. These were clearly permeated, shaped, and sometimes transformed by the awareness participants acquired of their working context through engaged participation, by collaboration, networking and publication practices, and the sense of agency each participant developed in and across all these practices.

Joaquin who during this study displayed a balanced equilibrium of the four practices, was the one who clearly showed more authorship development whereas others who had only developed in one or two of these had a lower authorship development. Elsa, Melia and Roberto, for example, displayed less collaboration, networking and publication practices which affected their awareness of their context and in Melia's and Roberto's cases their sense of agency. Elsa was the first to publish yet later her interpretation of higher education policies and particularly her difficulty to establish collaboration and networking relationships hindered her authorship development.

This study's findings also have implications for the understanding of professors' authorship and professional development in general, as detailed above. These results could guide professors in the evaluation and reflection of their own trajectories. Additionally, they could inform graduate programs which often struggle to initiate their students in their trajectories towards authorship.

First, graduate programs in the social sciences generally promote individual work and rarely provide opportunities for collaboration and networking as part of their curriculum which in this study are at the center of the participants' trajectories. Interestingly, collaboration and networking linked to writing and publication practices triggered participants' awareness of their decisions and actions to become authors, and very importantly, to become part of and be recognized by their professional communities. It is through practice that newcomers develop the insider knowledge and support to become full participants in the discourse community or communities. It is also evident that participation in the graduate program as well as collaboration with colleagues or with more experienced professionals is the response to workplace demands or a need to belong to a community. This study proposes that the main motivating factor in the road to authorship is engaged participation in the profession. Thus, teacher education programs need to create opportunities where ELT professionals have authentic access to the practices of the ELT community or related communities to understand their discourses and practices (Canagarajah, 2002). These graduate programs should also encourage students to publish in their mother tongue and English.

Second, as suggested by the participants, the guidance of more experienced colleagues had valuable implications in their trajectories as writers, which fits precisely in the legitimate peripheral participation understanding of developing expertise. Hargreaves and Fullan (2012) suggest that high-quality teacher professional development built on collegiality and collaboration in and among institutions contributes to teacher-researchers' development. This collegiality and collaboration can be expressed in the form of mentoring. Encinas and Sánchez-Hernández (2015) suggest teacher education programs need to explore diverse mentoring relationships to understand participants' future personal and professional development stages as well as how mentoring enhances or could enhance education in specific contexts in order to promote quality in education in general.

Finally, participants' authorship identity is permeated by the extent to which they become aware of contextual demands, collaboration/networking requirements and publishing policies as well as their internal motivation to take strategic decisions (Hernandez, 2017). As stated by Lasky (2005, p. 900), "agency is not inherent in the individual but, rather, inextricably linked to the social context and the cultural tools that shape the development of human beliefs, values, and actions". That is, the amalgamation of the external and internal resources developed in the participants a sense of agency defining their identities as writers and authors. Thus, graduate programs need strategies enhancing students' awareness of higher education and professional communities' policies and practices but also promote awareness/reflection of their own decisions to facilitate their trajectories towards authorship. Furthermore, our results indicate that only ELT scholar-mentors with research and publication experience will be able to provide the pertinent and relevant support to other multilingual researchers interested in publishing in English.

References

ANUIES. *Anuario Estadístico Población Escolar en la Educación Superior 2016–2017* (Annual Education Statistics in Higher Education 2016–2017). Mexico City: México: ANUIES.

Barton, D., & Hamilton, D. (2000). Literacy practices. In D. Barton, et al. (Eds.) *Situated literacies: Reading and writing in context*. London: Routledge.

Bazerman, C. & Paradis, J. (Eds.) (1991). *Textual dynamics of the professions*. Madison: University of Wisconsin Press.

Bazerman, C., Keranen, N., & Encinas, F. (2012). Facilitated immersion at a distance in second language scientific writing. In M. Castello, & C. Donahue (Eds.). *University writing: Selves and texts in academic societies*. Bradford, UK: Emerald.

Canagarajah. S. (2002). Multilingual writers and the academic community: Towards a critical relationship. *Journal of English for Academic Purposes, 1*, 29–44.

Carrasco, A., Kent, R., & Keranen, N. (2012). Learning careers and enculturation: Production of scientific papers by PhD students in a Mexican physiology laboratory: An exploratory case study. In C. Bazerman, C. Dean, J. Early, K. Lunsford, S. Null, P. Rogers, & A. Stansell (Eds.), *International advances in writing research: Cultures, places, measures*. Fort Collins, CO: The WAC Clearinghouse and Parlor Press.

Casanave, C, .& Vandrick, S. (Eds.) (2003). *Writing for scholarly publication*. Mahwah, NJ: Earlbaum.

Cheung, Y. L. (2013). The Impact of an in-service professional development course on writing teacher attitudes and pedagogy. *Journal of Pedagogy Development, 3*(1). Retrieved in May 25, 2017 https://www.beds.ac.uk/jpd/volume-3-issue-1/the-impact-of-an-in-service-professional-development-course-on-writing-teacher-attitudes-and-pedagogy

Colina-Escalante, A. (2011). *El crecimiento del campo de la investigación educativa en México. Un análisis a través de sus agentes* (The growth of educational research in Mexico: An analysis through its agents). *Perfiles Educativos, 33*(132), pp. 10–28. México: Universidad Nacional Autónoma de México.

Corcoran, J., & Englander, K. (2016). A proposal for critical pragmatic approaches to English for research publication purposes. *Publication, 4*(1), 1–10.

Crawford, T. (2010). *ESL writing in the University of Guanajuato: The struggle to enter a discourse community*. Guanajuato, Mx: Universidad de Guanajuato.

Curry, M. J., & Lillis, T. M. (2010). Academic research networks: Assessing resources for English-medium publishing. *English for Specific Purposes 29*, 281–95.

Curry, M.J., & Lillis, T.M. (2014). Strategies and tactics in academic knowledge production by multilingual scholars. *Education Policy Analysis Archives, 22*(32), 1–29.

Curry, M. J., & Lillis, T. (Eds.) (2017). *Global academic publishing: Policies, perspectives and pedagogies*. Studies in knowledge production and participation. Clevedon, OH: Multilingual Matters.

Davies, P. (2009). Strategic management of ELT in public education systems: Trying to reduce failure, increase success. *The Electronic Journal for English as a Second Language, 13*(3), 1–22.

Duff, P. A. (2012). Identity, agency and second language acquisition. In A. Mackey, & S. M. Gas (Eds.). *Handbook of Second Language Acquisition*. London: Routledge.

Encinas, F., & Sánchez, V. (2015). Constructing an interdisciplinary mentoring framework for ELT teacher education and teacher development. *International Journal of Educational Investigations*, 2(4),47–69.

Englander, K., & López-Bonilla, G. (2011). Acknowledging or denying membership: Reviewer's responses to non-anglophone scientist's manuscripts. *Discourse Studies*, 134(4), 395–416.

Englander, K. (2014). *Writing and publishing science research papers in English: A global perspective*. New York, NY: Springer.

Flowerdew, J. (1999). Writing for scholarly publication in English: The case of Hong Kong. *Journal of Second Language Writing*, 8(2), 123–145.

Flowerdew, J. (2001). Attitudes of journal editors to nonnative speaker contributions. *TESOL Quarterly*, 35(1), 121–50.

González, R. O., Vivaldo, J., & Castillo, A. (2004). *Competencia lingüística en Inglés de estudiantes de primer ingreso a instituciones de educación superior del Área Metropolitana de la Ciudad de México* (First entry students' English linguistic competence in higher education institutions of the Metropolitan area in Mexico City). México: ANUIES-UAM-Iztapalapa.

Hargreaves, A., & Fullan, M. (2012). *Professional capital: Transforming teaching in every school*. New York: Teachers College Press.

Hernandez-Zamora, G. (2017). *Agencia, voz y ethos en conflicto: La escritura académica como experiencia de silenciamiento* (Agency, voice and ethos in conflict: Academic writing as a silencing experience). In Espinoza Datsira, S. & Barrón Tirado, C (Coord.). *La lectura y la escritura en la educación en México. Aproximaciones teóricas, experiencias aplicadas y perspectivas de futuro* (Reading and writing in education in Mexico. Theoretical approximations, applied experiences and future perspectives). México: Universidad Nacional Autónoma de México Instituto de Investigaciones sobre la Universidad y la Educación.

Holland, D., Lachicotte, W., Skinner, D., & Cain. C. (2001). *Identity and agency in cultural worlds*. Cambridge, MA: Harvard University Press.

Huggett, S. (2012). The rise of Latin American science. *Research Trends Issue*, 31, 15–18.

Jurasaite-Harbison, E., & Rex, L (2005). Talking on researchers' identity: Teacher learning in and through research participation. *Linguistics and Education*, 16, 425–454.

Lahey, L., Souvaine, E., Kegan, R., Goodman, R., & Felix, S. (1988). *A guide to the subject-object interview: Its administration and interpretation*. Unpublished manuscript.

Lasky, S. (2005). A sociocultural approach to understanding teacher identity, agency and professional vulnerability in a context of secondary school reform. *Teaching and Teacher Education*, 21(8), 899–916.

Lave, J., & Wenger, E. (1991). *Situated learning: Legitimate peripheral participation*. Cambridge, UK: Cambridge University Press.

Lillis, T., & Curry, M. J. (2006). Professional academic writing by multilingual scholars: Interactions with literacy brokers in the production of English medium texts. *Written Communication* 23(1), 3–35.

Lillis, T., & Curry, M. J. (2010). *Academic writing in a global context: The politics and practices of publishing in English*. London: Routledge.

Mora, A., Trejo, N., & Roux, R. (2010). A small scale investigation into Mexican university students language learning motivation. *Actualidades Investigativas en Educación*, 10(1), 1–15.

Onwuegbuzie, A. J., & Combs, J. P. (2010). Emergent data analysis techniques in mixed methods research: a synthesis. In A. Tashakkori & C. Teddlie (Eds.). *Handbook of mixed methods in social and behavioral research* (2nd ed., pp. 397–430). Thousand Oaks, CA: Sage.

Perales-Escudero, M. (Ed.). (2010). *Literacy in Mexican higher education: Texts and contexts*. Puebla: Benemérita Universidad Autónoma de Puebla.
Pickering, G, & Gunashekar, P. (Eds.) (2015). *Ensuring quality in English language teacher education. Selected Papers from the Fifth International Teacher Educators Conference*. Hyderabad, India.
Ramírez, J. L., & Dzul, M. (2013). *Panorama general de la situación nacional* (General panorama of the national situation). In J. L. Ramírez (Ed). *Una década de búsqueda: Las investigaciones sobre enseñanza y aprendizaje y el aprendizaje de Lenguas Extranjeras en México* (A decade of research: the studies about teaching and learning in Mexico). DF, México: Pearson.
Roux, R., Mora, A., & Trejo, N. P. (2011). Exploring writers' identity in Mexican EFL students' academic writing. *Íkala, Revista de Lenguaje y Cultura 16*(2), 93–115.
Stake, R. E. (1995). *The art of case study research*. Thousand Oaks: Sage Publications.
Swales, J. M. (1998). *Other floors, other voices: A textography of a small university building*. Mahwah, NJ: Laurence Erlbaum.
Trujeque, E., Encinas, F., & Thomas Ruzic, M. (2015). Exploring authorship development (AD) among Mexican EFL teacher-researchers. *PROFILE Issues in Teacher' Professional Development, 17*(2), 43–62.
Wenger, E. (1998). *Communities of practice: Learning, meaning, and identity*. Cambridge: Cambridge University Press.
Wenger-Trayner, E., Fenton-O'Creevy, M., Hutchinson, S., Kubiak, C., & Wenger-Trayner, B. (2015). *Learning in landscapes of practice: Boundaries, identity, and knowledgeability in practice based learning*. London: Routledge.
Yin, R. K. (2003). *Case study research: Design and methods*. Thousand Oaks, CA: Sage Publications.

4

WRITING FOR PUBLICATION IN ENGLISH

Some Institutional Initiatives at the Universidad Nacional de Entre Ríos

Diana Waigandt

UNIVERSIDAD NACIONAL DE ENTRE RÍOS, ARGENTINA

Alicia Noceti

UNIVERSIDAD NACIONAL DE ENTRE RÍOS, ARGENTINA

Raquel María Teresa Lothringer

UNIVERSIDAD NACIONAL DE ENTRE RÍOS, ARGENTINA

Contextual Demands

English has become the main language for scientific research and academic publishing worldwide and its predominance as the global language for communication in academic settings is unquestioned (Bennett, 2013; Drubin & Kellogg, 2012; Mauranen, Pérez-Llantada, & Swales, 2010). This ongoing science *Englishization* (Swales, 2004, p. 52) is the result of the confluence of socio-historic and economic factors that have allowed the dominance of scientific research in the United States and other Anglophone countries.

As a consequence, international English-medium publications are increasingly part of official evaluation criteria in a range of institutional contexts, i.e., of individual scholars, their departments and institutions, and research grant awards (Lillis & Curry, 2010). These publications are typically produced in Anglophone contexts and distributed worldwide. Furthermore, they are often perceived as having a global value and enjoy greater prestige than journals published in other parts of the world and/or in other languages, as indicated by their inclusion in high status indexes and their high impact factors. These facts have resulted in growing pressure on scholars around the world to publish in English—especially in the top-ranked journals included in the Thomson Reuters' Web of Science, i.e. *Nature, Science*, and *Cell* for those doing research in the exact and natural sciences, and the *Journal of Memory and*

Language, Cognitive Psychology, and *Cognition* for those concerned with the language and linguistics areas.

The need to publish research papers in English often presents scholars working outside of English-dominant contexts with considerable challenges in terms of sustaining knowledge production in local languages and in securing publishing in prestigious (English-medium) publishing venues. In this sense, Latin America in general, and Argentina in particular, are no exceptions to these requirements.

In our country several institutions demand and value highly successful research and publication. The National Scientific and Technical Research Council (CONICET[1] in Spanish), whose mission is to carry out the promotion and execution of scientific and technological activities throughout the national territory and in the different areas of knowledge, has a specially designed evaluation system that has been implemented since its origins and which has been updated according to accumulated international experience. This participatory and rigorous evaluation system contemplates and ponders the quality of the research projects presented, the productivity derived from them, as well as the trajectory of individuals and research groups.

Besides, in the early 90s, within an "international agenda for the modernization of higher education systems" (Marginson & Mollis, 2001), a controversial Higher Education Law (N° 24,521) was passed in Argentina. It extended the reach of reform to all institutions of higher education, including university and non-university tertiary level institutions, and created central bodies to evaluate and accredit university institutions (i.e. the University Policies Secretariat (SPU in Spanish) and the National Commission for University Evaluation and Accreditation (CONEAU in Spanish)). The latter's mission is to ensure and improve the quality of university institutions belonging to the Argentine university system through the evaluation and accreditation of the quality of university education. Evaluation criteria for both the institutions and the individual scholars include, among other issues, engagement in research activities, participation in international research networks, and publication in high-status English-medium international journals.

These increasing demands have raised great interest in courses of English for research publication purposes (ERPP) in higher education settings in Argentina. The purpose of this chapter is to describe some institutional initiatives undertaken at the Universidad Nacional de Entre Ríos over the last decade to help undergraduate students, scholars, and researchers to write, in "acceptable" English, instantiations of the complex networks of genres that occur in academic and research settings and to navigate the article production, submission, and revision processes.

Theoretical Background

Literacy is a highly complex multidimensional construct that reflects notions of multiplicity of practices, contexts, genres, identities, and meanings (Gee, 1990; Street, 1993). From this point of view, literacy is best understood as a set of purposeful sociocultural practices that can be inferred from events mediated b texts. These practices are patterned by social institutions and power relationships. Moreover, literacy is historically situated, which brings about change in visibility, dominance and influence.

Academic literacy development plays a key role in academic settings worldwide. In our country, the pioneering work of Elvira Arnoux and Paula Carlino have paved the way for the advancement of reading and writing in higher education. In this sense, the creation of workshops aimed at helping school leavers enter tertiary education (Arnoux, et al., 1998), the publication of manuals (Narvaja de Arnoux, Di Stefano, & Pereira, 2002) and reflection upon the teaching-learning process involved in academic writing (Arnoux, 2006; Arnoux, Alvarado, Balmayor, Di Stéfano, Pereira, & Silvestri, 1996) helped to cope with the massification of higher education in our region. On the other hand, Carlino's work led to the establishment of the field, provided the scholarly community with fresh insight into the concept of academic literacy, and stimulated the advancement of a variety of actions in leading Argentinean universities that sought for the democratization of knowledge, inclusivity and social respect (Carlino, 2003, 2005, 2013).

Since then, the field has accumulated a growing body of literature, and multiple teaching and research initiatives have flourished. According to Ávila-Reyes (2017), Latin American scholars in this developing field are mainly influenced by Anglophone and European theoretical orientations and research traditions. This author also identifies the co-existence of seemingly conflicting traditions, such as cognitive and social orientations, which represent a unique local development. This particular theoretical configuration is rooted in reading comprehension and discourse analysis research that have been strong in the region thanks to the work of local influential scholars (Arnoux, 1998, 2006, 2008, Carlino, 2003, 2005, 2013, Marucco, 2001, 2004 in Argentina, Motta-Roth, 2001 in Brazil; and Parodi, 2005 in Chile).

In our country, scholars working in the academic literacy field have mixed backgrounds. Although linguistics (Arnoux, 1998, 2006, 2008) and educational/developmental psychology (Carlino, 2003, 2005, 2013) seem to be the main theoretical orientation of the top influencers, foreign language teachers have also encompassed investigative and practical efforts (Klett, 2007; Pipkin Embón, & Reynoso, 2010; Reynoso, Sforza, Rosa, Waigandt, & Leiva, 2009). Mainly English, French and German courses have been offered for over half a century in the formal Argentinean higher education system. Their implementation has been generally based on theoretical orientations and research related to the teaching of languages for specific purposes (LSP). Mainly influenced by Anglophone and European traditions, university teachers have gradually designed in-house materials and developed specific approaches for their courses. LSP teachers have shown interest and have become involved in the study of different aspects of the reading comprehension process, in translation matters, in the relationship between reading in L2 and writing in L1, in the writing process itself, and in the development of academic literacies.

The writing for publication initiatives described in section 3 are deeply grounded in sociocultural perspectives on literacy (Gee, 2000; Lewis,

Enciso, & Moje, 2007; Tracey & Morrow, 2006). According to Lillis and Curry (2014), writing for publication, viewed as a social practice, is influenced by the evolving expectations of particular social contexts, and inevitably entails the power dynamics of the institutional and governmental apparatus that support and regulate knowledge production. From this perspective, writers are not considered isolated individuals, but are rather seen as scholars working within social contexts and contending with the power relations of these contexts.

In her attempt to describe the concept of literacy from a sociocultural point of view, Perry (2012) refers to the theory of multiliteracies (Cope & Kalantzis, 2000) that engages with the multiplicity of communication channels and media, or what Kress (2000a, 2000b) calls "multimodality". This theoretical position widens the definition of text, as it conceives it as a variety of forms and semiotic systems instead of focusing exclusively on practices that surround print literacy. Perry (2012) then moves on to explain that critical theories emphasize both power and empowerment, and that they have recently expanded to include issues of agency and identity (Alvermann & Hagood, 2000; Hagood, 2002; Lewis, Enciso, & Moje, 2007; Moje & Luke, 2009). This is in line with Freire's (2001) idea of literacy as he defines it as the process of becoming conscious through taking the printed word, connecting it to the world, and then using it for purposes of empowerment.

Our initiatives are targeted at advanced students and scholars who regularly work, research, and publish in two or more languages. They can be categorized as plurilingual users of English as an additional language (EAL). To attend more fully to the needs of our audience, we have chosen an eclectic genre-centered approach which draws upon Swales' analysis of rhetorical moves (1990, 2004), and the most salient representatives of the North American New Rhetoric (Bazerman, Little, Bethel, Chavkin, Fouquette, & Garufis, 2005; Freedman & Medway, 1994; Miller, 1984).

In furtherance of the development of linguistic, grammatical, discourse and strategic competence of our audience, we focus on the analysis and critique of specific genres and explore the complex relations between textual features, rhetorical situations, and power. Moreover, we cater for the enculturation of emerging scholars into discipline-specific discourses and genres, together with a critical examination of institutional practices, rules and dominant discourses of the academy. In other words, we believe that English for research publication purposes (ERPP) instruction must aim to aid scholars not only in achieving genre-based expectations and/or navigating the submission and review process, but also in addressing the politics of English-language knowledge production, on a par with Corcoran and Englander's (2016) critical pragmatic approach.

Four Initiatives

In this section we provide an overview of four initiatives carried out at the Universidad Nacional de Entre Ríos (UNER), in Argentina, to guide undergraduate students and scholars on their way to publish in high-status English-medium international journals: first we describe two teaching experiences, then we focus on research activities and discuss some pedagogical implications, and lastly we refer to a language and "literacy brokering" (Lillis & Curry, 2006) service to help faculty members overcome writing problems in EAL.

Founded on May 10 1973, the Universidad Nacional de Entre Ríos (UNER) is a relatively young national university that is made up of nine colleges situated in different towns of the Entre Ríos Province[2]. One initiative was carried out at the Facultad de Ciencias de la Alimentación, located in Concordia, on the east coast of the Entre Ríos Province. Two initiatives are carried out at the Facultad de Ingeniería, located in Oro Verde, a small town on the west coast, at about 10 km from Paraná, the capital of the Province, while the other is carried out online.

Undergraduate Education: Seminar "Writing for Academic and Professional Purposes"

In line with the sociocultural perspectives on literacy described in section 2, and bearing in mind Swales's conceptualization of discourse community (1990, pp. 24–27), we firmly believe that novice members should be guided by experts on their way to discoursal expertise. In educational settings, the concept that best suits this process and allows for this guidance is that of communities of practice (Lave & Wenger, 1991). The notion of such a community creates a social fabric for learning within a common ground inspiring members to participate, guiding their learning and giving meaning to their action. Through legitimate peripheral participation (Lave & Wenger, 1991), students become experienced members, initially by participating in simple and low-risk tasks that are nonetheless productive and necessary to further the goals of the community as they become acquainted with the tasks, the genres, and the organizing principles of their target discourse community.

To this end, since 2003, a "Writing for Academic and Professional Purposes" seminar has been conducted at the Facultad de Ingeniería aimed at advanced undergraduate students. The objectives of the seminar are:

- To discuss preconceptions related to academic and professional reading and writing.
- To explore academic and professional genres.
- To strengthen students' reading competence as a means to develop scholarly writing.
- To start writing some of the many occluded genres that make up the constellation of genres produced in higher education and professional settings (scholarship forms & the personal statement, letters—of application, of inquiry, of complaint, of invitation—academic e-mails, *curriculum vitae*, and research article abstracts).

During the 25-hour face-to-face seminar (plus a similar amount of time allotted to text production), students work on the essential elements of genre-based and pragmatic instruction, as well as on the implications of language choice(s), positioning and author agency, from a critical point of view, in order to gradually raise their awareness to an increasing global English hegemony in the academia (Corcoran & Englander, 2016).

Postgraduate Education: Online Seminar for Scholarly Publication

As early as 2003, within the framework of an in-service professional development programme, the Faculty of Engineering (FIUNER) organized a face-to-face course on academic writing for its faculty, entitled *"Comunicar la ciencia: La producción del texto académico escrito en inglés"*. Its central objectives were to raise awareness about the complex process involved in writing for academic purposes and to provide opportunities to explore abstracts, reviews and research articles. The participants were asked to attend four two-hour classes and to complete a series of writing activities at home. In the classroom, Spanish was the language of communication.

In 2005, the UNER virtual campus began operating, so the course on academic writing turned online, was opened to professionals from national as well as foreign institutions[3], and has been offered yearly to date. Since then the ever increasing institutional pressures have ushered in new professional needs which, in turn, have prompted a series of changes to meet the new demands. In order to provide a description of the current postgraduate academic offering we will characterize the target audience, will account for choice of course type, purposes, materials selection and design, and will refer to the type and function of the activities chosen. In Figure 4.1 the most significant changes introduced through time are summarized.

Class format was not a minor decision as it implied the adoption of a pedagogical stance which would impact on the way participants relate to the object of study and to other participants. In this respect the seminar approach was the best option to foster research, encourage collaborative practices and favour symmetrical relationships (Pérez Porto & Merino, 2013).

A brief description of the heterogeneous target audience will help explain the challenges involved in the design of this online seminar. All the participants are users of EAL that belong to different discourse communities and with significant differences in writing proficiency; some of them are experienced or "senior" researchers, some others are "junior" ones[4]. When asked if they had taken courses on academic writing before, only 17% of the informants answered affirmatively and 100% expressed their interest in participating in new seminars hinging on writing for academic and professional purposes[5].

We fully agree with Hyland (2017) when he asserts that the conventions of academic communication differ considerably across disciplines and that teachers, therefore, have to devise courses around the principle of "specificity". Nevertheless, due to budget and administrative restrictions it is impossible to offer courses for a variety of specific disciplines and for different proficiency levels. As shown in Figure 4.1, only two options concerning both level and specificity are available. To compensate for this shortcoming, right at the beginning of each seminar, participants are asked to select an open access online journal in their field of specialization, to choose one of the journal volumes, to share its URL and to justify their choices. This material is then used by the selector as reading and exemplification material, and by the teacher to design tailor-made activities.

The overall purpose of the seminar is to raise academics' confidence in their ability to write for publication in English. This is not an easy task as we generally have heterogeneous groups in terms of English language background knowledge. While some have reached elementary or pre-intermediate levels, others have

The Initiative through time	
2003	2017
Course type	
In service face to face course →	Online seminar (Moodle)
Participants provenance	
Universidad Nacional de Entre Ríos →	National and foreign institutions
Proficiency Levels	
Level I →	Level I and Level II
Disciplinary Communities	
Natural and Hard Sciences →	Natural and Hard Sciences Humanities and Social Sciences
Activities	
Individual activities →	Individual and collaborative tasks
Assessment	
Tutor assessment →	Tutor, peer and self assessment
Material Selection	
Tutor as material selector →	Tutor and participants as material selectors

FIGURE 4.1 Changes introduced through time in the online postgraduate seminar for scholarly publication

benefited from a great exposure to English during their primary and secondary education. Moreover, some have had the opportunity to study and/or work abroad and are members of international networks. In keeping with our central purpose and as a result of the feedback from different cohorts and insights derived from our work, it has become necessary to prioritize another purpose: to raise awareness of the difficulties arising from being a non-Anglophone scholar writing from the (semi) periphery and of the complex process involved in writing for publication. Its contents privilege discussion about inequality in academic communication and the study of professional genres. In Figure 4.2 we present the list of topics grouped by level. This enumeration does not indicate either hierarchy or presentation sequence.

The seminar teaching materials are evenly distributed in a series of lessons[6], which are under a Creative Commons licence. Each lesson lasts two weeks, is uploaded according to calendar, displays the same internal and external layout and consists of three perfectly distinct parts. The first provides an overview that includes a synoptical presentation of the central topic and the lesson aims. In the second, the lesson proper, a selection of didacticized reading materials alternate with a set of instructions aimed at triggering different types of activities. Finally, at the end of each lesson, an assignment for tutor assessment and references are included. In order to make instructions clear and reduce the cognitive load, a number of icons are used. Grammar notes, self-assessment activities, guidelines and disclaimers, as well as documents that unveil the rationale underlying classroom activities such as forums, wikis and glossaries complete the set of materials.

Assessment is not regarded as a discrete, final action but as a continuous process which allows visualization of participants' achievements and the efficacy of the teaching proposal. To successfully complete the course, participants have to make meaningful contributions to the activities proposed throughout the course and to write a text in accordance with their needs and interests. This text should be an instantiation of one of the genres explored during the course and respond to the participants' interests, to the data they have gathered and to their personal objectives. Besides, they are asked to complete a questionnaire to evaluate the seminar and the data collected, so as to provide valuable feedback for future action.

At the moment of assessing the participants, priority is given to performance over achievement. Since the seminars are task-based, we are particularly interested in the potentialities of interaction, symmetrical relationships, peer assessment and collaborative work. To this effect, we have designed different types of activities: 1) activating prior knowledge activities; 2) tutor-assessment activities; 3) self-assessment activities. Concerning those of the third type, we have prepared dossiers entitled "Self-assessment activities" (one for each lesson), which include a set of tasks with their corresponding keys, so that each participant can assess his/her own production.

On the whole, the initiative has shown good results all the way back to its beginnings in 2003, as can be seen from the surveys administered to the participants of the

	Seminar Contents
Level I	Speech community and discourse community. Genre sets and genre chains. Paratextual elements. Titles and keywords. Intertextual relationships. Patterns of text organization. Cohesion. Autobiographical academic genres. Slide presentations. Electronic mails. Posters. Visual displays. Conference guidelines. Abstracts.
Level II	Occluded and supporting genres. Register. Intertextual relationships. Citation patterns. Hedging and metadiscourse. Academic malpractices. Plagiarism. Journal guidelines. Abstracts. Reviews. Literature reviews. Conference Papers. Cover letters. (Grant) Proposals

FIGURE 4.2 Topics grouped by level corresponding to the online postgraduate seminar for scholarly publication

different cohorts. The answers to three questions in the questionnaire administered in 2016 indicate the value attributed to this type of initiative and the favourable evaluation of the seminar. All the participants expressed their interest in taking new seminars on the topic and 100% indicated that in their opinion the aims had been fulfilled and the seminar contents had met their expectations.

Linking Research and Teaching at the Facultad de Ciencias de la Alimentación

English has been taught to Food Engineering undergraduates since the Facultad de Ciencias de la Alimentación was created. Academic genres, their access and production are the purposes of pedagogical actions. The research article is explored in detail in the English II Course, since it is the prototypical genre used to circulate new knowledge in the academic world.

In this section we describe two research experiences. The first one, carried out in 1998, was triggered by the fact that characteristics of research papers published in Food Science required further exploration in order to cater for researchers' needs. Several studies have revealed that rhetorical choices vary significantly across disciplines because they express very different epistemological and social practices (Hyland & Bondi, 2006; Swales, 2004; Hyland, 2017).

The English Department carried out a study of research papers published in English in the Food Science field[7]. A corpus of 30 research articles from high-impact journals were analyzed from a genre analysis perspective following Swales' framework (1990). Results of the aforementioned analysis suggested that knowledge of the generic structure, as well as the characterization of the corresponding moves, metadiscourse and intertextual resources might provide researchers with the rhetorical engineering strategies necessary to produce this genre efficiently for publication purposes.

The second research project aimed at overcoming difficulties undergraduates face while writing academic genres, such as their Final Project. Actions were performed within the Writing Across the Curriculum and Writing in the Disciplines framework (Bazerman, 2005).

Previous Final Project titles included very little information about the actual content, thus revealing that senior students lacked awareness of readership expectations and of the potential visibility their work may have when available on the Web. This genre, which is associated with graduation as Food Engineers, is dealt with in the Project Design and Assessment (PD&A) course, taught by Engineering specialists and written in Spanish. English professors have always been in charge of teaching discourse features in their classes and comparing them with those in Spanish. Therefore, the engineers and the English teachers decided to work together in an attempt to optimize the students' written production. Different actions, described below, were implemented to familiarize students with the characteristics of this genre and to facilitate its production: the specialists focused on content and the linguists on discourse. Due to time constraints, our actions targeted title and abstract production, as the importance of both is paramount due to the *distillatation* (Swales, 1990) of the information scientists perform to encapsulate their work and communicate their findings on the Internet.

Titles of research articles have been widely explored (Busch-Lauer, 2000; Soler, 2007; Noceti, 2012). However, titles produced by undergraduates required further studies. The objective of this study[8] was to explore whether interdisciplinary actions could optimize their writing. All Final Project titles, produced since the first Food Engineer graduated, were collected into two corpora: Corpus A and Corpus B. The former consisted of those written before the aforementioned interdisciplinary actions were performed, and the latter included all titles produced after our joint actions. Every fifth title was selected from Corpus A to constitute a 25-title sample. Results of the analysis showed 5.04 as the average number of words.

The joint activities, designed and implemented as from 2012, involved seminars dealing with the discourse aspect of the Final Project and implementation of writing seminars in Spanish. Both engineers and linguists worked together in workshops to activate previous knowledge, focusing on discourse and working with sample texts and the prototypical language characteristics used. Different concepts that had been dealt with during English I and II were activated in Spanish. Topics included disciplinary culture (Hyland, 2000; Swales, 1990, 2004), academic genres characteristics (Swales, 1990), disciplinary discourse (Hyland, 2004, 2008), generic structure and similarities/differences between the Final Project and the Research Article. A Discourse Analysis specialist was invited to deliver seminars in Spanish to deal with issues at the micro and macro writing levels.

Furthermore, students attended tutorials with the engineers and interviews with the linguists to discuss titles and abstracts in Spanish and English. An unexpected outcome of this study was a tutoring space spontaneously generated by the English teacher-students' interactions that enabled students to clarify doubts, design slides and rehearse their final oral presentation.

Corpus B analysis, including all titles produced after our joint actions, indicated that students were able to pack relevant information. Results showed an average of 17 words, showing that students had become aware of the importance of including more words in the title, in keeping with science writing conventions. This fact also suggested that students had understood the role of language in knowledge distribution.

The engineering specialists teaching the PD&A course realized the importance of mastering good communication skills and the need to work with linguists in a collaborative manner. Conversely, linguists need engineers to provide specialists' comments on the content of the Final Project. Collaboration between department chairs fostered collaborative work among students. A highly significant production during the writing seminar in Spanish (2015) was a set of instructions on how to write the final project. This document has been included in the digital classroom to be used freely. Feedback collected after graduation by means of a survey demonstrated that interdisciplinary activities focusing on language as a cross-disciplinary content contributed to the adequate production of academic genres. Results of this study may affect curricular design and decisions at the macro level, since implementation of writing seminars along undergraduates' trajectories has been positioned as a top priority.

Language and Literacy Brokering

Research is not considered complete until it is made available to the wider research community. Further, publication is the major route to tenure, promotion, scholarship awards, and research grants for scholars, while it has a significant effect on national and institutional prestige. As we have already discussed in previous sections, the widespread choice of English for academic communication resulting from "the pressures of globalization and the marketization of the academy" (Flowerdew, 2007, p. 14) confronts plurilingual users of (EAL) with several challenges.

Similar to what happens in other Latin American countries, professors and researchers working at the Universidad Nacional de Entre Ríos are Spanish-speaking L1 scholars who must take additional time out of their academic and research careers if they wish to acquire and maintain high-level English language competences. This is a crucial decision they are bound to make and, in many cases, despite its recognition in the shape of demands for "more academic English courses", many scholars cannot take action on their own initiatives due to work and family constraints. On the other hand, if they want to get published in English-medium international journals, they must face not only the challenge of producing rigorous scientific data, but also the complex task of writing articles that meet the English-language expectations of journal gatekeepers.

This situation has presented many Argentinean teachers of English as a foreign language (EFL) working in higher education settings with the challenge of assisting plurilingual scholars who use English as an additional language (EAL). Scholars need guidance not only to navigate the complexities involved in shaping a manuscript prior to submission, but also to understand and appropriately respond to issues involved in the post-submission process such as communication with editors and reviewers. In addition, besides writing journal articles, for a variety of reasons, scholars also produce other genres—conference proceedings, chapters in edited books, and books—for which they use multiple languages (Curry & Lillis, 2004, 2013; Lillis & Curry, 2010). Moreover, they need help to design posters and slide presentations to accompany their conference presentations in English when attending international conferences or symposia.

At the Universidad Nacional de Entre Ríos we have taken up this challenge as an opportunity for EFL teachers' professional development. In this sense, and because we are aware of the fact that individual competence in (academic) English is neither a prerequisite for, nor a guarantee of, publishing success, as EFL teachers we have, following Swales' advice, for many years "walked the long way round to the bathroom" (2009, p. 180). This has allowed us to engage in enriching conversations with scholars from a variety of scientific disciplines that led to a council directive enacted at the Facultad de Ingeniería in 2003. It establishes a general framework for assistance in text mediation, i.e. translating and reviewing manuscripts for scholarly publication in English-medium journals.

As *language and literacy brokers* (Lillis & Curry, 2010), we have a role in helping shape manuscripts prior to submission, and, in some cases, we become involved in the post-submission process, for example handling reviewer comments. We have surmounted the obstacle of lack of disciplinary knowledge in transforming the problem-laden texts into publishable papers by closely communicating and working with the authors both face-to-face and online. This can be seen as a symbiotic relationship as we have drawn upon our knowledge and experience as writers, presenters, and reviewers to help colleagues with their manuscripts, while we have gained insights into the shaping of discipline-specific knowledge through collaboration with scientists from a variety of fields. Scholars seem to trust our goodwill, knowledge and expertise unquestioningly, and avoid submitting a manuscript without our revision.

Along this two-way street we have not only become aware of the needs and common mistakes committed by less proficient users of English, but have also transformed our teaching practice to meet those needs. Valuable insights into the complex nature of academic and research literacies have led us to informed pedagogical practices to facilitate visibility and participation of local scholars in global scholarship. We have gradually moved from a one-size-fits-all grammar-centered approach in our courses and seminars to a community-specific one, as academic literacies, community-specific norms, and discipline-specific conventions seem to pose more serious problems than grammar, especially to novice writers. Manuscripts produced by well established scholars, on the other hand, generally require modifications concerning spelling, morphology, and syntax.

As a result of our actions, the work of several scholars from our university has been published in international English-medium journals or included in the proceedings of international conferences, and our work as language and literacy brokers has been referred to in the acknowledgement section of the articles[9]. Moreover, some authors have even included our name(s) in the list of authors as a method of crediting our contribution to the publication of their research[10].

Revisiting Our Initiatives and Looking to the Future

In this chapter we have revisited some initiatives and told the story of our experience teaching ERPP at the Universidad Nacional de Entre Ríos (Argentina). The actions described are aimed at responding to the needs of heterogeneous groups of multilingual undergraduates and scholars who face the ever increasing personal, institutional and governmental demands to meet genre-based expectations and navigate the submission and review process to get their work published in English-medium international journals.

Though diverse in target audience, purposes, modality, and duration, the four initiatives tap into an eclectic genre-centered approach which draws upon Swales' analysis of rhetorical moves and the most salient representatives of the North American New Rhetoric. They all focus on the analysis and critique of specific genres and explore the complex relations between textual features, rhetorical situations, and power. Besides, and in order to prevent our scholars from succumbing to conformity, we have taken a critical stance towards the politics of English-language knowledge production in accord with critical pragmatic approaches to ERPP (Corcoran & Englander, 2016). Such an approach advocates for attending to the particular practices and politics surrounding multilingual scholars' writing for publication within an asymmetrical market of global knowledge production without disregarding the normative codes and conventions of academic research genres.

These tailor-made courses, research activities, and language and literacy brokering services have been developed, carried out, and sustained by teachers of English belonging to the EFL departments of the different colleges that make up our University. The institutional support received, both in terms of encouragement and financial aid (especially in the case of research activities) has led us to commit ourselves to our professional development in this particular field of EFL. In this sense, and because we are aware of the fact that individual competence in (academic) English is neither a prerequisite for, nor a guarantee of, publishing success, as EFL teachers we have engaged in enriching conversations with scholars from a variety of scientific disciplines. Close communication as well as face-to-face and online work have helped us surmount the obstacle of lack of disciplinary knowledge and enabled the co-transformation of problem-laden texts into publishable papers. Furthermore, we have not only become aware of the needs and common mistakes committed by less proficient users of English, but have also transformed our teaching practice to meet those needs. In this sense, we have gradually moved from a one-size-fits-all grammar-centered approach in our courses and seminars to a community-specific one.

Experience has made us aware of the fact that writing, despite disciplinary specificities, operates in a similar fashion at all the levels and fields of academia. In other words, being a successful writer, both in the mother tongue (whichever it may be) and in English, is the key to graduation for students, and to academic and professional prestige for scholars. This is why we stress the importance of fostering initiatives to support the development of writing across the curriculum in both undergraduate and graduate programs, as well as for research purposes. In other words, we believe that both the scholars' and the literacy brokers' commitment to knowledge mobilisation should be institutionalized.

We feel that revisiting our initiatives has presented us with both a challenge and an opportunity. The challenge is to be ready to meet the local needs of our students and scholars so that we can prepare them, accordingly, to be active participants in their global scientific community. The opportunity is to build an Argentinean, Latin American, and/or Spanish-users' field of ERPP, based on shared experience and research findings through cross-disciplinary and international networks, and to join an international critical conversation on academic literacies and ERPP in higher education settings. This would allow for the democratization of knowledge, inclusivity and growing international respect. After all, we have a voice, we have something to say, and we want to be heard.

Notes

1. CONICET was created in 1958. It is an autarchic entity within the jurisdiction of the Ministry of Science, Technology and Productive Innovation.
2. Facultad de Ciencias de la Salud, Facultad de Bromatología, Facultad de Ciencias de la Administración, Facultad de Ciencias de la Alimentación, Facultad de Ciencias de la Educación, Facultad de Trabajo Social, Facultad de Ciencias Económicas, Facultad de Ciencias Agropecuarias, and Facultad de Ingeniería. www.uner.edu.ar
3. To date, participants from 13 universities (11 national and 2 foreign ones), from INTA (Instituto Nacional de Tecnología Agropecuaria) and teachers of English graduated from tertiary level institutions have taken the seminar.
4. We follow Swales (2004, 56–57) in this distinction.
5. The data were collected at the end of the 2016 seminar.
6. Seven lessons for Level I and 5 for Level II.
7. PID 206/98: El Inglés en la Comunicación Científica en las Ciencias de la Alimentación: Implicancias Pragmáticas de un Enfoque Basado en el Análisis de Género. Directora: Prof. Marta L. Benedetti. Integrante: Prof. Alicia M. Noceti.
8. PID NOVEL N° 8072 - Resolución CS N° 267/14: Optimización de la Producción de Títulos de Géneros Académicos mediante la Toma de Conciencia de su Función Retórica. Directora: Alicia M. Noceti. Integrantes: Chacón C.; Chiarella, C. y Erbetta, E.
9. https://www.ncbi.nlm.nih.gov/pmc/articles/PMC5097364/ http://www.mdpi.com/2313-433X/3/1/7/htm
10. http://www.scielo.br/scielo.php?script=sci_arttext&pid=S0103-84782017000400752

References

Alvermann, D. E., & Hagood, M. C. (2000). Critical media literacy: Research, theory, and practice in "New Times". *The Journal of Educational Research*, 93, 193–205.

Arnoux, E., Alvarado, M., Balmayor, E., Di Stéfano, M., Pereira, C., & Silvestri, A. (1996). El aprendizaje de la escritura en el ciclo superior [Learning writing in higher education]. In Z. Solana (Comp.). *Adquisición de la escritura* [The acquisition of writing], pp. 199–234. Rosario: Ediciones Juglaría.

Arnoux, E., Alvarado, M., Balmayor, E., Di Stéfano, M., Pereira, C., & Silvestri, A. (1998). *Talleres de lectura y escritura* [Reading and writing workshops]. Buenos Aires: Eudeba.

Arnoux, E. (2006). Incidencia de la lectura de pares y expertos en la reescritura del trabajo de tesis [*The impact of peer and expert reading on thesis rewriting*]. *Revista de Lingüística Teórica y Aplicada*, 44(1). Retrieved from http://selloeditorial.udec.cl/rla-44-1/

Arnoux, E. (2008). Lectura y escritura en el primer año universitario: investigaciones y orientaciones pedagógicas [*Reading and writing in freshman year: Research and pedagogical orientations*]. In M. del R. Badano, N. Bearzotti & S. Berger (Eds.). *Políticas, prácticas y saberes sobre el ingreso a la universidad* [Policies, practices and knowledge about entering college]. Paraná: Universidad Autónoma de Entre Ríos & Universidad Nacional de Entre Ríos.

Ávila-Reyes, N. (2017). Postsecondary writing studies in Hispanic Latin America: Intertextual dynamics and intellectual influence. *London Review of Education*, 15(1), 21–37.

Bazerman, C, Little, J., Lisa Bethel, L, Chavkin, T, Fouquette, D, & Garufis, J. (2005). *Reference guide to writing across the curriculum*. Lafayette, IN: Parlor Press.

Bennett, K. (2013). English as a lingua franca in academia: Combating epistemicide through translator training. *The Interpreter and Translator Trainer*, 7(2), 169–173.

Busch-Lauer, I. (2000). Titles in English and German research papers in medicine and linguistics. A. Trosborg (Ed.). *Analysing Professional Genres*, pp. 77–97. Amsterdam: John Benjamins.

Carlino, P. (2003). Alfabetización académica: Un cambio necesario, algunas alternativas posibles [*Academic literacy: A necessary change, Some possible alternatives*]. *Educere*, 6(20), 409–20.

Carlino, P. (2005). Escribir, leer y aprender en la universidad: Una introducción a la alfabetización académica [*Writing, reading and learning in college: An introduction to academic literacy*]. Buenos Aires: FCE.

Carlino, P. (2013). Alfabetización académica diez años después [*Academic Literacy Ten Years Later*]. *RMIE*, 18(57), 355–81.

Cope, B., & Kalantzis, M. (2000). *Multiliteracies: Literacy learning and the design of social futures*. London: Routledge.

Corcoran, J., & Englander, K. (2016). Proposal for critical-pragmatic pedagogical approaches to English for research publication purposes. *Publications*, 4, 6.

Curry, M. J., & Lillis, T. M. (2004). Multilingual scholars and the imperative to publish in English: Negotiating interests, demands, and rewards. *TESOL Quarterly*, 38(4), 663–688. http://dx.doi.org/10.2307/3588284

Curry, M. J., & Lillis, T. M. (2013) *A Scholar's guide to publishing journal articles in English: Critical choices and practical strategies*. Clevedon, UK: Multilingual Matters.

Curry, M. J., & Lillis, T. M. (2014). Strategies and tactics in academic knowledge production by multilingual scholars. *Education Policy Analysis Archives*, 22(32), 1–28.

Drubin, D. G., & Kellogg, D. R. (2012). English as the universal language of science: Opportunities and challenges. *Molecular Biology of the Cell*, 23(8), 1399. http://doi.org/10.1091/mbc.E12-02-0108

Englander, K. (2006). Revision of scientific manuscripts by non-native English-speaking scientists in response to journal editors' language critiques. *Journal of Applied Linguistics and Professional Practice*, 3(2), 129–161.

Flowerdew, J. (2007). The non-Anglophone scholar on the periphery of scholarly publication. *AILA Review*, 20(1), 14–27. doi: 10.1075/aila.20.04flo

Freedman, A., & Medway, P. (Eds.) (1994). *Genre and the new rhetoric*. London: Taylor and Francis.

Freire, P. (2001). *The Paulo Freire reader*. In A. Freire, & D. Macedo, (Eds.). New York: Continuum.

Gee, J. (1990). *Social linguistics and literacies: Ideology in discourses*. Brighton, UK: Falmer Press.

Gee, J. (2000). Discourse and sociocultural studies in reading. In M.L. Kamil, P.B. Mosenthal, P.D. Pearson, & R. Barr (Eds.). *Handbook on reading research, volume III*, pp. 195–208. London: Routledge.

Hagood, M.C. (2002). Critical literacy for whom? *Reading Research and Instruction*, 41, 247–266.
Hyland, K. (2000). *Disciplinary discourses: Social interactions in academic writing*. London: Longman.
Hyland, K. (2004) *Disciplinary discourses*. Ann Arbor, MI: University of Michigan Press.
Hyland, K. (2004). *Genre and second language writing*. Ann Arbor, MI: University of Michigan Press.
Hyland, K. (2005). *Metadiscourse: exploring interaction in writing*. London & New York: Continuum.
Hyland, K., & Bondi, M. (Eds.) (2006). *Academic discourse across disciplines*. Frankfurt, Germany: Peter Lang.
Hyland, K. (2007). English for professional academic purposes: Writing for scholarly publication. In D. Belcher (Ed.). *Teaching language purposefully: English for specific purposes in theory and practice*. New York: Cambridge University Press.
Hyland, K. (2008). As can be seen: Lexical bundles and disciplinary variation. *English for Specific Purposes*, 27(1), 4–21. doi:10.1016/j.esp.2007.06.001.
Hyland, K. (2008). *English for academic purposes. An advanced resource book*. In C. Candlin, & R. Carter (Eds.). London & New York: Routledge Applied Linguistics.
Hyland, K. (2017). English in the disciplines: Arguments for specificity. *ESP Today*, (1) 5–23. e-ISSN:2334–9050. https://doi.org/10.18485/esptoday. 2017.5.1.1.
Klett, E. (Ed.) (2007). *Recorridos en didáctica de las lenguas extranjeras* [Paths in Foreign Language Teaching]. Buenos Aires: Araucaria Editora.
Kress, G. (2000a). Design and transformation: New theories of meaning. In B. Cope & M. Kalantzis (Eds.). *Multiliteracies: Literacy learning and the design of social futures*, pp. 153–161. London: Routledge.
Kress, G. (2000b). Multimodality. In B. Cope & M. Kalantzis (Eds.). *Multiliteracies: Literacy learning and the design of social futures*, pp. 182–202. London: Routledge.
Lave, J., & Wenger, E. (1991). *Situated learning: Legitimate peripheral participation*. Cambridge: Cambridge University Press.
Lewis, C., Enciso, P., & Moje, E. B. (2007). *Reframing sociocultural research on literacy: Identity, agency, and power*. Mahwah, NJ: Lawrence Erlbaum Associates.
Lillis, T., & Curry, M. (2006). Professional academic writing by multilingual scholars. Interactions with literacy brokers in the production of English-medium texts. *Written Communication*, 23(1) January 2006, 3–35.
Lillis, T., & Curry, M. (2010). *Academic writing in a global context: The politics and practices of publishing in English*. London, New York: Routledge.
Marginson, S., & Mollis, M. (2001). The door opens and the tiger leaps. Theories and reflexivities of comparative education for a global millennium. *Comparative Education Review* (Chicago University Press), 45(4), 581–615.
Marucco, M. (2001). "La enseñanza de la lectura y la escritura en el aula universitaria" [Teaching Reading and Writing in the University Classroom]. Luján, Argentina: Universidad Nacional de Luján.
Marucco, M. (2004). Aprender a enseñar a escribir en la universidad [*Learning to teach writing at university*]. In P. Carlino (Coord.), *Leer y escribir en la universidad* [*Reading and writing at university*]. Buenos Aires: Lectura y Vida.
Mauranen, A., Pérez-Llantada, C., & Swales, J. M. (2010). Academic Englishes: A standardized knowledge?. In A. Kirkpatrick (Ed.). *The Routledge handbook of world Englishes* (pp. 634–652). New York: Routledge.

Miller, C. (1984). Genre as social action. *Quarterly Journal of Speech*, 70, 151–167.
Moje, E. B., & Luke, A. (2009). Literacy and identity: Examining the metaphors in history and contemporary research. *Reading Research Quarterly*, 44, 415–437.
Motta-Roth, D. (2001). *Redação acadêmica: Princípios básicos* [Academic writing: The basic principles]. Santa Maria: Imprensa Universitária.
Narvaja de Arnoux, E., Di Stefano, M., & Pereira, C. (2002). *La lectura y la escritura en la universidad* [Reading and writing at university]. Buenos Aires: Eudeba.
Noceti, A. (2012): Los títulos de artículos de investigación en la ingeniería en alimentos: Un estudio exploratorio desde la perspectiva del análisis de género [*Food engineering research articles titles: An exploratory study from a genre analysis perspective*]. In N. Gigena, & D. Waigandt (Comp.). *Aprender y enseñar en tiempos posparentéticos* [Learning and teaching in the post-parenthetical age]. Retrieved from http://www.bioingenieria.edu.ar/referencia/eventos/ingles-libro/
Parodi, G. (Ed.) (2005). *Discurso especializado e instituciones formadoras* [Specialized Discourse and Training Institutions]. Valparaíso: Ediciones Universitarias de Valparaíso.
Pérez Porto, J., & Merino, M. (2013). *Definición de Seminario* [Definition of Seminar]. Retrieved from: http://definicion.de/seminario/
Perry, K.H. (2012). What is literacy? A critical overview of sociocultural perspectives. *Journal of Language and Literacy Education*, 8 (1), 50–71.
Pipkin Embón, M., & Reynoso, M. (2010). *Prácticas de lectura y escritura académicas* [Academic Reading and Writing Practices]. Córdoba: Editorial Comunicarte.
Reynoso, M., Sforza, M., Rosa, B., Waigandt, D. M., & Leiva, G. (2009). Argumentación y didaxis. [*Argumentation and Didaxis*]. *Ciencia, Docencia y Tecnología*, 39(20), 13–47.
Soler, V. (2007): Writing titles in science: An exploratory study. *English for Specific Purposes* 26 (2007) 90–102.
Street, B. (1993). The new literacy studies. *Journal of Research in Reading*, 16(2), 81–97.
Swales, J. (1990). *Genre analysis: English in academic and research settings*. Cambridge: Cambridge University Press.
Swales, J. (2004). *Research genres. Explorations and applications*. Cambridge: Cambridge University Press.
Swales, J. (2009). *Incidents in and educational life. A memoir (of sorts)*. Ann Arbor, MI: The University of Michigan Press.
Tracey, D. H., & Morrow, L.M. (2006). *Lenses on reading: An introduction to theories and models*. New York: Guilford.

REGION 2
Northern Europe

5

SUPPORTING NORDIC SCHOLARS WHO WRITE IN ENGLISH FOR RESEARCH PUBLICATION PURPOSES

Birna Arnbjörnsdóttir

UNIVERSITY OF ICELAND, ICELAND

Introduction

Many recent studies have outlined the challenges faced by scholars writing in English for research publication purposes (ERPP) (Bennett, 2014; Dimova, Hultgren, & Jensen, 2015; Flowerdew, 2015; Ingvarsdóttir & Arnbjörnsdóttir, 2017b; Lillis & Curry, 2010). They describe the stigma associated with research reported in languages and contexts outside of English "center" countries and describe the lexical, grammatical and structural characteristics of texts written in English as an additional language (Connor, 1996; Flowerdew, 1999, 2000, 2015; Lillis & Curry, 2006, 2010; Swales, 1990). Other challenges faced by English as an additional language (EAL) writers are also beginning to emerge, particularly those related to agency and authorial voice (Flowerdew, 2013), access to resources and research networks (Bennett, 2015) and the subsequent effects on EAL scholars' participation in knowledge creation (Englander & Uzuner-Smith, 2013).

The focus of much of the research cited above has been on the use of EAL in academic pursuits in countries with traditionally limited access to English, such as in some countries of Eastern and Southern Europe (Lillis & Curry, 2010). The assumption has been that these challenges do not apply to countries with massive daily exposure to English language and culture, specifically the Nordic countries (Arnbjörnsdóttir, 2011, Arnbjörnsdóttir & Ingvarsdóttir, 2017) where the notion of "Parallel Language Use" is "a firmly established ideology" (Hultgren, 2016). This ideology is expressed in the common 2006 Nordic Language Policy (Deklaration, 2007), and reflected in educational policies and practices at Nordic universities (Hultgren, 2016). The assumption is that Nordic peoples' linguistic repertoires comprise levels of English proficiency to the point that they can choose which language to use in different domains and for different functions. The policy of "Parallel Language" use, although not binding, has been espoused enthusiastically by Nordic Universities where it seems to be taken for granted that Nordic scientists have adequate skills for writing in English for research publication purposes (ERPP), and have access to information on par with English center scientists in the competition for international publications (Bennett, 2015; Gregersen, 2014; Hultgren, Gregersen, & Thögersen, 2014; Ingvarsdóttir & Arnbjörnsdóttir, 2013, 2015). This pervasive ideology helps drive pressure on Nordic scientists to publish in English language journals and is used as a requirement for research funding and professional advancement (Hultgren, et al., 2014).

Publications in English in the Nordic countries have proliferated over the past decades (Gregerson, 2014). In 2011, about 70% of scholarly publications at the University of Iceland were written in English and 92% at Reykjavík University, as were 84% of all PhD dissertations (Gregersen, 2014). A 2013 study revealed that younger scientists at the University of Iceland write almost all of their papers in English, while older scholars write up to 75% of their papers in English, suggesting that publications in English are increasing in this context (Ingvarsdóttir & Arnbjörnsdóttir, 2013). The numbers above seem to reinforce the ideology that Icelandic scholars are not challenged by writing in English and, as a result, no official systematic support for writing ERPP is offered at the University of Iceland. However, despite an increase in publications in English, Nordic scientists' confidence with English writing for publication skills is not supported empirically. The disparity between ideology and practice in relation to the use of English in academic settings in the Nordic countries is beginning to be recognized (Hultgren, et al., 2014), including in Iceland (Arnbjörnsdóttir & Ingvarsdóttir, 2017a, 2017b).

This chapter presents the findings from a mixed methods study which explores the views of faculty from across disciplines at the University of Iceland regarding writing for publication in English, followed by description of the development of a pedagogical intervention aimed at meeting the specific writing needs of researchers in the humanities and social sciences identified in the study. The motivation of this study was the frequent complaints among faculty about changes in the University advancement system that increasingly favors publications in English over local or even regional (Nordic) publications. A survey was therefore launched that included questions on instructors' own English proficiency and preparedness to use English in academia (Ingvarsdóttir & Arnbjörnsdóttir, 2010), how much they wrote in English for publication purposes, as well as if and where they sought English writing support (Ingvarsdóttir & Arnbjörnsdóttir, 2013, 2015). One part of the survey gauged the views of instructors specifically on the process of writing and publishing academic papers in English. The survey was followed-up with two sets of interviews that gave a better view of the numerous challenges experienced by Icelandic scholars when writing English academic papers. The main themes that emerged were the lack of support, the extra work-load, time and energy, as well as inadequate skills to make a strong enough claim for their research and the conflict they experience when forced to present research in journals that may not be accessible to the people affected by their research findings. These findings have been described in previous publications (Ingvarsdóttir & Arnbjörnsdóttir, 2017a). The next section provides a brief overview of the findings of the mixed method study described above. The study, a needs assessment if you will, revealed challenges that became an impetus for establishing organized assistance in writing ERPP at the University of Iceland. After a brief description of the aims, methodology and findings of the study—with a focus on their pedagogical implications—this chapter outlines an intensive, genre based, individualized writing workshop designed to meet the identified needs of faculty with research degrees in the humanities at the University of Iceland.

The Study

The study of how ERPP affects Icelandic scientists and their work reported here is based on data that was collected over a three-year period using a cross-sectional, mixed method approach that included a survey and two sets of follow-up interviews. The focus in this chapter is on the aspects of the survey and interviews that have direct pedagogical implications and have not been reported previously. The research questions that guided the study were how academics view their own preparedness for writing academic papers in English, whether and where they received assistance, and whether this varied between disciplines. The same survey questions also guided the first set of interviews. Based on the findings of the first interviews, follow-up questions were developed for the second round of interviews. They were: What kind of challenges do informants encounter while reporting their research in English? Do concerns differ depending on English proficiency levels, and if so, in what ways?

Participants and Data Collection

A survey was sent out to everyone registered on the University of Iceland's faculty Listserv. The 258 survey responses accounted for 17% of the faculty. The participants, who represented all five Schools at the University, were between the ages of 22 and 72. Fifty-two percent were men and 48% were women. This reflects the approximate distribution of age and gender of the faculty. The survey was analyzed using a simple percentage and correlation calculation (Ingvarsdóttir & Arnbjörnsdóttir, 2010, 2015). The interviews were conducted two years after the survey in two phases with different participants using a purposeful random sampling method (Patton, 1990). First, in 2014, a general interview that followed up on the survey results was conducted with ten faculty members, five men and five women, two from each of the five Schools at the University. The second set of more in-depth, critical interviews (Patton, 1990) were conducted with a further ten men and women a year later, in 2015. Interviewees were between the ages of 40 and 60. The same participant model was used for all 20 interviews. The interviews were conducted in Icelandic, with representative extracts translated into English by the authors. An interpretative approach of content analysis using an inductive method was used to identify main themes (Patton, 1990).

The survey revealed that Icelandic scholars seemed quite confident in their English and felt prepared to use English in academic pursuits (Ingvarsdóttir & Arnbjörnsdóttir, 2010), they receive no official writing support despite official pressures to publish in English (Ingvarsdóttir & Arnbjörnsdóttir, 2015), and report difficulty in expressing their own voice while writing in English (Arnbjörnsdóttir & Ingvarsdóttir, 2017a,b; Flowerdew & Wang, 2015). Other themes emerged such as the nature of participants' English skills, specifically their limited awareness of their own language skills; experiences encountered in the publication process; whether they felt they needed writing support and if so, what kind of support. These themes are examined below in relation to their pedagogical implications.

Theme 1: The nature of participants' English skills. While the main finding of the survey was the contradiction that emerged between the confidence respondents expressed in their English and the struggles they encounter while writing ERPP, interviews also revealed a lack of awareness of the nature of their English proficiency and the functions it could serve, specifically that their general English skills did not suffice when writing for publication.

More than two thirds of the participants (N=208) reported that their English was very good or good. The younger the respondent, the better they rated their English. Men tended to be more confident in their English skills than women and respondents in the natural sciences more so than those in humanities and social sciences (Arnbjörnsdóttir & Ingvarsdóttir, 2017b; Ingvarsdóttir & Arnbjörnsdóttir, 2010).

Initial questions during the interviews about the professional use of English were, more often than not, met with answers that interviewees had no problem using English; however, many respondents seemed unaware of the nature of different registers and genres. Two respondents mentioned how well they did at foreign languages in secondary school, and another said that English had been a lingua franca at home as they spoke other languages natively but English was the only language they had in common. Another interviewee suggested that his English was good but that the greatest challenge in writing academic papers was tackling the differences between British and American English. An interviewee in the sciences reported that he had excellent English skills, but when probed about whether he found it equally easy to read novels and write academic papers, he did not seem to understand the question at first and then only reluctantly acknowledged that there might be a difference. Two respondents in the social sciences didn't see this as an issue at all as their colleagues simply write their papers in Icelandic and then have them translated by professional translation services. They did not seem to question whether a translation service could deliver papers written in the appropriate discourse or genre of the discipline accepted by journal editors.

The fact that participants lack awareness of the different functions of language make theirs a "hidden challenge" which has clear pedagogical implications. These findings suggest that preceding actual ERPP writing coaching or text composition, instruction should focus on the development of awareness of the functions of language, the characteristics of academic genres and the specific characteristics of genres in the disciplines (Corcoran & Englander, 2016; Flöttum, Dahl, & Kinn, 2006).

Theme 2: The publication process. Many of the plurilingual interviewees had strong publication records in other languages than English. The "hidden challenge" is seen in the trepidations expressed about their own role in the publication process; their lack of agency while writing in English, as reported below. Most of the participants in the study, although critical of the pressure to publish, seemed to believe that this was a personal challenge rather than a collective one to be addressed at the level of the University.

All participants mention feeling the pressure from the University, their department, and their peers to publish. One interviewee from education expressed his views this way: ". . . but one knows how the system works and one hears like you know in the back rooms 'yes, well she hasn't published anything', you know". Another interviewee said that if they don't publish, they end up being a financial burden on their unit.

With one exception, participants seem unaware of any systematic funding or support for writing ERPP. It was simply not available and most respondents pay out of pocket, or from their research funds, for language services, which reduces the amount they have available for actual research. A few called for financial support to pay for proofreader or translation services. Even a senior researcher seemed unaware of the challenges faced by writers of ERPP. He is regularly involved in international research networks and suggested that others might have problems and therefore they might benefit from courses that "help people deal with plagiarism and citations", as he put it, and called for a proofreading service that ensures the quality of the English, largely for students.

When asked whether there had ever been any demands made by faculty for writing support, the answer is negative from all interviewees. A common thread throughout the interviews was the lack of reference to the right to any type of official writing support or critical examination of the rationale behind the pressure to publish in English. No reference was made to a collective sense that others might be in the same situation regarding ERPP. Two respondents mentioned how unfair and unrealistic it is to publish in and maintain fluency in two languages. One interviewee from social science believed that there should not have to be any systematic pressure or policy to publish in English. He stated: "This is just how it is."

Interviewees seemed to agree that difficulties in English are due to their own shortcomings rather than a result of unrealistic expectations. No one questioned the requirement that they write in a different language than the one they have had their academic training in and is the official language of their university.

Those who have had their academic training in an Anglophone university, and thus are supposedly better at academic English, were more forthcoming about the challenges they faced than their colleagues educated in English non-center countries. They only mentioned official support when asked whether they think there should be such support.

In terms of the pedagogical implications of these responses, clearly any writing support should include a critical examination of writer's own role, their agency, and an examination of the responsibility of the institution to provide support so scientists can meet the institution's demand for international publication. Further, findings suggest a potential need for explicit reflection upon the politics of language choice and consequences for knowledge production. Finally, a pedagogical intervention should include ways to use research articles as a means of communicating with particular discourse communities (Englander, 2014; Corcoran & Englander, 2016).

Theme 3: The need for writing assistance. When asked in the survey about whether they felt that they needed writing assistance with ERPP, participant responses were almost equally divided as a third said they never need assistance, another third said they sometimes need assistance, and a third respond that they often or always needed help from an English expert. There are expected differences between the five academic Schools. Faculty from engineering and the natural sciences seemed to think they needed the least help (63% said they did not require writing help). In the humanities and education, the pattern is different as 33% and 28% respectively claimed they always needed help. Scholars from health sciences and social sciences seemed to be similar in their need for assistance and position themselves between the three when asked about whether they needed help writing ERPP (Ingvarsdóttir & Arnbjörnsdóttir, 2010). Despite being probed by the interviewer, a professor in medicine not educated in an English academic setting never acknowledged difficulty using English other than it requires "a little more work". While recognizing having received comments on her English in the publishing process the same professor felt that the process would have been much easier and her English much better if she had not lived so long in a non-English speaking country. Again, those who have had their academic training in an English-speaking university, to some extent, are more forthcoming about the challenges they face than their colleagues educated in non-Anglophone countries.

Almost all, or 82% (N=238) said they were well or rather well prepared to write academic papers in English with the highest confidence expressed by engineering and natural sciences faculty (94%). Education faculties were less confident, with 68% responding that they were well or rather well prepared. Men were much more confident than women and those educated in English as a medium of instruction universities are more confident than those who had their academic training elsewhere, although this confidence was not evident when discussing the specific drawbacks associated with writing in English.

A variety of responses were given to open ended survey questions about where writers seek assistance. The majority pay English "experts" to proofread or translate papers, or they get help from colleagues who are either native speakers or have spent a number of years in an English-speaking country (no mention of having spent time in academia). Sometimes they ask friends and family and only seek professional assistance if it is "a very important paper". One senior professor talked about writing his thesis in English with the aid of how-to books, as in "How to write a PhD", "a quick fix" and confessed to using Google as a tool to find appropriate language. The key finding here seems to be that scholars try to find someone who is a "good English speaker", which was the most frequent response, in order to give the paper "the native touch", as expressed by one senior faculty member. No one mentioned struggling with academic language specifically, or that school English or living in an English-speaking environment might not be sufficient preparation for writing for publication.

Some respondents seem to have a sense of where the challenges lie, especially in the humanities and education. An education professor with a degree from a non-Anglophone country said: "I would say that it was probably the greatest hurdle (of) of my academic career to master writing about my field in English." A natural scientist acknowledged that it was not always easy to write in English despite knowing the terminology of his field. To him, it was the connecting of the terms with "general" words that was the challenge.

But not everyone is satisfied with their English skills. A professor of education educated in an Anglophone country suggests that those educated in non-Anglophone countries are at a great disadvantage. A professor of humanities educated in an English center country says he does not get many comments on his writing from professional proofreaders, but when working with an English-speaking colleague, "he usually does a lot of editing of my work, see". He says he has no special issues having "an advantage as I lived for so long in [an English center country]". Yet later, he mentions feeling "handicapped" and not being the same personality when writing in English as in Icelandic.

One participant, a natural scientist, does not think writing ERPP is much of a challenge and says that in his field "English with character" is accepted as the journal editors are, more often than not, plurilingual speakers themselves and therefore more tolerant of non-native nuances in the text. Others in the natural sciences/medicine expressed this view. The language is not as important as the content in the natural sciences as in education or humanities.

Respondents mention copying other people's style, collaborating on texts with others, having others put the "native touch" on their text, and about losing themselves and their voice in the publication process. As one respondent from social sciences puts it: "There is this fright lurking. I know what I want to say, but not how to say it. My personal style is lost. I start copying instead of using my own voice." They also imply that even though proof-readers don't make many comments, colleagues with expertise in the field do, suggesting that their text may not have the characteristics of the genre of their discipline, even after the text has been "proofread".

The main finding of this study is that, despite reporting very good English skills, Icelandic scientists demonstrate a surprising lack of awareness of nature of the writing challenges they face. Their lack of genre awareness is revealed as many call for support in the form of compensation for costs incurred for purchasing translation and proofreading services. No one mentions the need for proofreaders to have content expertise. A second surprising finding is that scientists at the University of Iceland, although frustrated by the publication process, believe that any challenge in writing ERPP is specific to them personally, and do not question the legitimacy of the pressure placed on them to publish in English. They seem to uncritically accept the pressure to publish and how they each, individually, struggle with the process.

Discussion

The scholarly writing challenges faced by non-native writers of ERPP have been well documented (Flowerdew, 1999, 2001, 2015). Connor (1996) and Kaplan (1966), among others, have discussed the cross-cultural challenges plurilingual EAL writers face while composing text (Connor, Nagelhout, & Rozycki, 2008; Flöttum, et al., 2006), while others have focused on the burden (Hanauer & Englander, 2011) and barriers these writers face in the publication process (Bennett, 2015; Ingvarsdóttir & Arnbjörnsdóttir, 2013; Lillis & Curry, 2010). Issues pertaining to knowledge production and dissemination have been explored by Englander and Uzuner-Smith (2013) and Arnbjörnsdóttir and Ingvarsdóttir (2017a). These studies have focused on geographical areas with historically restricted English exposure or experiences by speakers of languages that are linguistically and culturally distant from English (Lillis & Curry, 2010). Subsequently, the assumption has been that speakers of Germanic languages with more proximity and access to English do not experience these challenges. This seems to be shared by university officials and even by the scholars themselves (Flöttum, et al., 2006; Hultgren, et al., 2014. This may explain the dearth of publications and academic discussion about plurilingual EAL scholars' challenges in the Nordic countries. This study has pointed out that academic writers in Iceland do face linguistic, cultural and institutional barriers while writing ERPP. Interviewees in this study collectively seem to agree that they have adequate English skills to fulfill their professional duties and that any difficulties in English they encounter are due to their own shortcomings rather than a consequence of policy that affects them as a professional group. They seem to have espoused the ideology that Nordic scholars have no issues when writing for ERPP, yet all the participants report being frustrated about the publication process and their role in global knowledge production (i.e. publishing research in English language journals). Interviewees only mention official support when asked whether they think there should be some. They call for support in the form of funding for proofreaders or translation services, as after all they believe that this is "only translation".

These research findings provide the foundation for a pedagogical intervention developed at the University of Iceland. The next section describes a short intensive writing ERPP workshop at the University of Iceland for seasoned researchers, many with a robust publication record in other languages and fluency in receptive, conversational English.

The Response: Programs to Support Writing ERPP

Partially due to dissemination of some of the findings described above (Ingvarsdóttir & Arnbjörnsdóttir, 2013, 2015), the English department at the University of Iceland was asked by individual participants whether the department could provide writing support to writers of ERPP. The department subsequently sought and received funding from the university's Instructional Development Fund to develop a series of intensive courses and workshops in writing for ERPP for novice and seasoned scientists. It should be emphasized that the department sought funding for this support from a university instructional development fund rather than the courses being viewed as a service to the entire University and thus paid for by the University directly. Offering ERPP courses has traditionally been beyond the scope of the English Department, which is an academic program in English language and linguistics.

In this section, the first in a series of interventions is described, an intensive workshop for seasoned plurilingual scientists in the humanities with publishing records in other languages. The content of the workshop is dually informed by the empirical findings reported above as well as successful courses reported in the literature (Englander, 2014; Cargill & O'Connor, 2006; Corcoran, 2017; Curry & Lillis, 2014; Swales, 2004). Given the lack of awareness of the issues pertaining to writing for publication revealed in the study above, a critical-pragmatic approach was adopted (Corcoran & Englander, 2016). Scholars' lack of agency, view of ERPP as a personal challenge rather than a collective one, and tendency to accept the status quo of being subordinate to native English speakers in the publication race indicated that a straightforward writing-based intervention would not suffice. A critical-pragmatic approach to ERPP according to Corcoran and Englander:

> . . . encourages [writers] to assess their options in particular situations rather than assuming they must fulfill expectations. After considering options, they may choose to carry out demands or challenge them" (in Benesch, 2001, p. 64). It encourages international scholars to have "a critical mind set" and at the same time, alert them "to the possible repercussions of some of the critical actions".
>
> *(Flowerdew, 2007, p. 23)*

Major themes addressed in the workshop include scholars' agency and national and institutional policies, participation in the international publication process, the role of networks and communities of practice, the development of ERPP skills, and the development of genre awareness and writing skills specific to participants' language background and discipline. The workshop described below is the first in a series of pedagogical interventions in the form of workshops for faculty and courses for graduate students in different disciplines. The workshops will be delivered by the University Language Center that provides development opportunities for faculty. Workshops focus on ERPP in the different disciplines within the humanities and social sciences. The first workshop in this series will be delivered to the faculty of the School of Humanities in the spring semester of 2018 and is described below. Instructors have been recruited from a pool of English writing experts in the Department of English, published scholars from the different disciplines who will provide individual coaching and mentoring support, and journal editors and research directors who will inform participants about the nature of the academic publishing process.

A Workshop in Writing ERPP in the Humanities

This is a 12 contact-hour workshop that targets plurilingual scientists with research degrees and publications records in the humanities who are at different stages of adopting more robust writing of ERPP. The goals and content are based on: (a) identified needs of Icelandic scientists; (b) adapted genre based/pragmatic instructional foci; and (c) a critical component. The latter two are heavily informed by Cargill and O'Connor (2006), Englander (2014), and Corcoran and Englander (2016), respectively, and, adjusted to the local context (see Table 5.1). The goals of the workshop are: (a) to increase awareness and agency in the publication process and understanding of how seasoned plurilingual writers who write in EAL are affected by local and international journals' impact factors, literacy brokers, the effect of policies on those who are required to publish in international journals; (b) to appreciate the role of research networks and communities of practice in developing and using relevant and current discourse; (c) to develop awareness of variation in cross-cultural rhetorical and discourse conventions and the skill to produce English texts representative of the genre expectations of their discipline; (d) to examine the development of their own voice in academic writing; and (e) to critically explore alternatives to traditional ENL standards in writing and the consequences of writing exclusively in English for world knowledge production.

The instructors will include two experts in ERPP and second language writing with a successful publishing record, the Research Director of the School of Humanities and two content experts. The writing experts will serve as primary teachers while the Research Director and content experts will mentor and coach individuals or groups working in the same or similar genres. The workshop will use a flipped classroom approach where lectures and writing assignments are required outside of class and class time devoted to critical

TABLE 5.1 A critical pragmatic approach to writing for ERPP for Icelandic scholars*

Perceptions of Icelandic scientists of ERPP	Genre based and pragmatic instruction	Critical approach
Limited awareness of ERPP. Exclusion of locals from research findings. Icelandic journals not valued.	The nature of plurilingual scientists' writing in ERPP. Communication within the disciplines. Genres.	Communication within dif. discourse communities. Politics of language choice and consequences for knowledge production.
Lack of awareness of the discourse characteristics of their discipline.	A genre-based approach to writing research articles in the humanities.	The characteristics of published papers.
Lack of awareness of L1, L2 rhetorical differences.	Rhetorical elements of research articles. Problematic features for Icelandic writers.	Accepted variability in rhetorical features. English with character/ELF.
Limited agency and voice in ERPP.	Stylistic elements and making a claim in English.	Style in relation to identity and voice, including variation.
Characteristics of Icelanders' English academic texts.	Academic and genre-based terminology.	The role of networks in the development of genre-based discourse.
Limited grasp of the editorial and publication process.	The submission and review process, editor and reviewer feedback.	Ideologies and global politics of publishing access, impact factors.
No official writing support. Limited awareness of the role of proofreaders and translators.	Institutional resources. The role of proofreaders, translators, editors, etc.).	Institutional ERRP support.
Unfamiliarity with collaborations and networks.	Collaboration with editors. Professional networks and research and publication agenda.	Editorial feedback. Strategies for developing academic networks.

*This table is adapted from Englander, 2014.

discussion and writing feedback (including peer review) and individual coaching. Participants prepare their own research findings for publication. Clearly, this work outside of class is not part of the 12 contact hours. Assessment is based on completed papers ready for submission to journals and surveys on self-efficacy. Texts will include articles from a journal in participants' discipline for analysis and various texts to raise awareness about the collective challenges of local and international plurilingual scholars writing in ERPP. Participants will use their own findings to draft an article, according to the conventions of their discipline. Table 5.1 provides a more detailed overview of the perceived needs of Icelandic scholars and the genre-based and critical features of the workshop that attend to their perceptions.

Conclusions

The goal of the efforts described here is to meet the "hidden challenges" revealed in a study of the experiences of Icelandic scientists writing ERPP. The study identified issues that reflect both language-specific and well-established broader challenges of (semi) peripheral scholars when writing for publication (Bennett, 2014; Lillis & Curry 2010; Flowerdew, 1991, 2015; Dimova et al., 2015). Because the study revealed concerns that surpass mere linguistic and compositional challenges—principally the lack of critical examination of their rights and their role in the publishing process—the course adopts a critical-pragmatic pedagogical approach (Corcoran & Englander, 2016; Englander, 2014). It covers the linguistic and structural issues associated with genre-based writing methodologies (Swales, 1990, 2007; Hyland, 2007), but also examines ways to empower writers to take a more critical stance in the publication process in relation to their needs for English writing support while participating in international knowledge production. Central to such an approach is explicit discussion of both scholars' and the University's obligation to disseminate research findings to the local community while at the same time participating in efforts to elevate their own and their University's international standing. The success of these empirically driven workshops has wide implications for individual scholars as well as for other universities. At the time of this writing, the interventions have been developed and advertised to faculty but not yet delivered.

The goals of this intervention are ambitious and participation will require substantial work outside class hours. Further, affecting change takes more than a handful of short workshops and only ongoing evaluation on behalf of all participants can speak to their eventual success. On the other hand, the University Instructional Development Fund has provided a grant for the creation of these interventions and there is a growing awareness among faculty that writing for publication in English calls for institutional support. As academic institutions such as the University of Iceland demand increased English language knowledge production, they must not only increase the resources available to their scholars (e.g. ERPP workshops or courses) in order to fulfill their professional obligations, but also reconsider policies that promote increasing homogeneity and hegemony in scholarly writing for publication.

References

Arnbjörnsdóttir, B., (2011). Exposure to English in Iceland: A quantitative and qualitative study. *Netla - Menntakvika 2011*. MenntavísindasviÐ HÍ. http://netla.hi.is/menntakvika201

Arnbjörnsdóttir, B., & Ingvarsdóttir, H. (Eds.) (2017b). *Language development across the lifespan: The impact of English on education in Iceland*. Berlin: Springer.

Arnbjörnsdóttir, B., & Ingvarsdóttir, H. (2017a). Issues of identity and voice: Writing English for research purposes in the semi periphery. In M. J. Curry, & T. Lillis, (Eds). *Global academic publishing Policies, perspectives, and pedagogies* (pp. 73–87). Clevedon, UK: Multilingual Matters.

Bennett, K. (2014). *The semi-periphery of academic writing: Discourses, communities and practices*. London: Palgrave MacMillan.

Cargill, M., & O'Connor, P. (2006). Getting research published in English: Towards a curriculum design model for developing skills and enhancing outcomes. *Revista Canaria de Estudios Ingleses*, 53, 79–94.

Connor, U. (1996). *Contrastive rhetoric: Cross-cultural aspects of second-language writing*. Cambridge: Cambridge University Press.

Connor, U., Nagelhout, E., & Rozycki, W. (2008). *Contrastive rhetoric: Reaching to intercultural rhetoric*. Amsterdam, the Netherlands: John Benjamins.

Corcoran, J. N., & Englander, K. (2016). A proposal for critical-pragmatic pedagogical approaches to English for research publication purposes. *Publications*, 4(1), 1–10. doi:10.3390/publications4010006

Corcoran, J. N. (2017). The potential and limitations of an intensive English for research publication purposes course for Mexican scholars. In M. J. Curry, & T. Lillis, (Eds). *Global academic publishing: Policies, perspectives, and pedagogies* (pp. 233–249). Clevedon, UK: Multilingual Matters.

Curry, M. J., & Lillis, T. M. (2014). Strategies and tactics in academic knowledge production by multilingual scholars. *Education Policy Analysis Archives*, 22(32), 1–28. http://dx.doi.org/10.14507/epaa.v22n32.2014

Deklaration om nordisk språkpolitik [Declaration on Nordic language policy]. [DNS] (2007). Copenhagen: Nordisk Ministerråd [Nordic Council of Ministers].

Dimova, S., Hultgren, A. K., & Jensen, C. (Eds.) (2015). *English-medium instruction in European higher education: English in Europe* (Vol. 3). Berlin: Mouton de Gruyter.

Englander, K. (2014). *Writing and publishing science research papers in English: A global perspective*. New York: Springer.

Englander, K., & Uzuner-Smith, S. (2013). The role of policy in constructing the peripheral scientist in the era of globalization. *Language Policy*, 12(3), 231–250. doi: 10.1007/s10993-012-9268-1

Flöttum, K., T. Dahl, & T. Kinn. (2006). *Academic voices – across languages and disciplines*. Amsterdam, the Netherlands: John Benjamins Publishers.

Flowerdew, J. (1999). Problems in writing for scholarly publication in English: The case of Hong Kong. *Journal of Second Language Writing*, 8(3), 243–264. doi:10.1016/S1060-3743(99)80116–7

Flowerdew, J. (2000). Discourse community, legitimate peripheral participation and the non-native English-speaking scholar. *TESOL Quarterly*, 34, 127–150. doi: 10.2307/3588099

Flowerdew, J. (2013). English for research publication purposes. In B. Paltridge and S. Starfield (Eds.). *The handbook of English for specific purposes* (pp. 301–322). Chichester, UK: John Wiley & Sons.

Flowerdew, J. (2015). Some thoughts on English for research publication purposes (ERPP) and related issues. *Language Teaching*, 48(2), 250–262. doi: 10.1017/S0261444812000523.

Flowerdew, J., & Wang, S. H. (2015). Identity in academic discourse. *Annual Review of Applied Linguistics*, 35, 81–99. doi:10.1017/S026719051400021X

Gregersen, F. (2014). *Hvor parallel: Om parallellspråkighet på Nordens universitetet*. Köbenhavn: Nordisk Ministerråd. [How parallel: Parallel language use at Nordic universities. Copenhagen: Nordic Council of Ministers].

Hultgren, A. K. (2016). Parallel language use. In A. Linn, (Ed.). *Investigating English in Europe: Contexts and agendas* (pp. 158–163). Berlin: Mouton de Gruyter.

Hultgren, A. K., Gregersen, F., and Thögersen J. (2014). *English in Nordic academia: Ideology and practice*. Amsterdam, the Netherlands: John Benjamins.

Hyland, K. (2007). Genre pedagogy: Language, literacy and L2 writing instruction. *Journal of Second Language Writing*, 16(3), 148–164. doi:10.1016/j.jslw.2007.07.005

Ingvarsdóttir, H., & Arnbjörnsdóttir, B. (2010). Coping with English at tertiary level: Instructors' views. *RáÐstefnurit Netlu–Menntakvika 2010*, 1–11. http://skemman.is/en/stream/get/1946/7800/20393/1/010.pdf

Ingvarsdóttir, H., & Arnbjörnsdóttir, B. (2013). ELF and academic writing: A perspective from the expanding circle. *Journal of English as a Lingua Franca*, 2(1), 123–145. doi: 10.1515/jelf-2013–0006

Ingvarsdóttir, H., & Arnbjörnsdóttir, B. (2015). English in a new linguistic context: Implications for higher education. In S. Dimova, A. K. Hultgren, & C. Jensen (Eds.). *English-medium instruction in European higher education* (pp.137–156). Berlin: Mouton De Gruyter. doi: 10.1515/9781614515272–008

Kaplan, R. (1966). Cultural thought patterns in intercultural education. *Language Learning*, 16(1), 1–20.

Lillis, T., & Curry, M. J. (2006). Professional academic writing by multilingual scholars: Interactions with literacy brokers in the production of English-medium texts. *Written Communication*, 23(1), 3–35. doi: 10.1177/0741088305283754.

Lillis, T., & Curry, M. J. (2010). *Academic writing in a global context: The politics and practices of publishing in English*. London: Routledge.

Lillis, T., & Curry, M. J. (2015). The politics of English, language and uptake: The case of international academic journal article reviews. *AILA Review*, 28(1), 127–150. doi: 10.1075/aila.28.06lil.

Lillis, T., Hewings, A., Vladimirou, D., & Curry, M. J. (2010). The geolinguistics of English as an academic lingua franca: Citation practices across English-medium national and English-medium international journals. *International Journal of Applied Linguistics* 20(1), 111–135. doi:10.1111/j.1473-4192.2009.00233.x

Patton, M. Q. (1990). *Qualitative evaluation and research methods* (2nd ed.). Thousand Oaks, CA: Sage.

Swales, J. (2004). *Research genres: Explorations and applications*. New York: Cambridge University Press.

Swales, J. (1990). *Genre analysis: English in academic and research settings*. Cambridge: Cambridge University Press.

6

THE UNREAL AND THE REAL

English for Research Purposes in Norway

Tom Muir

OSLOMET – OSLO METROPOLITAN UNIVERSITY, NORWAY

Kristin Solli

OSLOMET – OSLO METROPOLITAN UNIVERSITY, NORWAY

"Out With Norwegian!"

In an article entitled "Out With Norwegian!", *Morgenbladet*, a Norwegian weekly, published an interview with Curt Rice, the rector of Oslo Metropolitan University (OsloMet), one of the largest institutions of higher education in Norway. In the interview, Rice, who is American and a professor of linguistics, proposed a ban on publishing research articles in Norwegian. To ensure the quality of work, Rice argued, all research should be reviewed by an international community of scholars. He also insisted that research results should be available to as many people in the world as possible and highlighted that publishing in Norwegian does not serve this purpose well. Rice admitted that his position "is extreme, but possible to defend" (Time, 2017).

The article immediately spurred numerous responses. The majority disagreed with Rice and were deeply concerned that such a prominent figure in Norwegian academia (and a linguist at that!) could have such little regard for the well-being of Norwegian as an academic language and for the importance of national research communities (Graver, 2017; Gulbrandsen, 2017; Johansen, Jonsmoen, & Greek, 2017; Slaatta, 2017). One of the chief areas of disagreement—and one of our preoccupations in this chapter—was over the issue of whether research can be considered *first and foremost* an international domain.

As several chapters in this volume along with a substantial body of research illustrate, this kind of debate about the place of English is not unique to Norway (Ammon, 2001; Bennett, 2014; Lillis & Curry, 2010; Plo Alastrué & Pérez-Llantada, 2015). Indeed, the debate described above in many ways exemplifies what Hultgren, Gregersen, and Thøgersen (2014) call a tension between "internationalist" and "culturalist" discourses. Speaking specifically about a Nordic context, they argue that "internationalist" discourses are typical of policymakers and institutional leaders who strive to become "international" by attracting scholars and students from around the world and by increasing the global visibility of the institution's research activities. This move in effect positions English as a key instrument in becoming "international."

At the same time, there are voices that express a profound alarm about domain loss and argue for the preservation and nurturing of Nordic languages for teaching and research. Hultgren, Gregersen, and Thøgersen say the proponents of this kind of "culturalist" discourse can be found among a disparate mix of leftist cultural elites, academics, and right-leaning politicians and populists (2014, p.2). Although these "culturalist" groups might be anxious for different reasons, they share a sense of unease about the future of Norwegian language and culture and argue for the need to preserve and develop Norwegian as an academic language.

While often discussed as a simple dichotomy between English and local languages, the tensions between "internationalist" and "culturalist" discourses are also crosscut by disciplinary concerns. As noted by some of Rice's critics, professional fields such as law, nursing, social work, and teacher education are often deeply embedded in national regulatory policies and professional practices. Some scholars in these fields posit that for their research to effect change, the national arena is crucial. One researcher in the field of social work and law argued in response to Rice that "If I were to publish in English only, my research would be meaningless" (Gording Stang as cited in Lie, 2017). These kinds of claims, then, are not only about "culturalist" arguments to preserve Norwegian language for the sake of Norwegian culture. Rather, they are arguments about what research should do and whom it should be for.

Tensions over language-choice and disciplinary configurations are very much alive in our institutional context. We work in the English for Academic Purposes Unit at OsloMet. We work primarily with PhD candidates and academic staff to support them in writing for international publication. Many of the researchers at our institution are in professional fields, so we frequently meet scholars for whom writing in English involves not only linguistic challenges of working in an additional language. Rather, the choice of writing in English is wrapped up in larger epistemological, ideological, and political questions. This, in turn, means that our pedagogical practices must also address these questions.

In what follows, we situate our work within current research about language, discipline, and authority to argue for approaches that provide scholars with analytical tools that offer room to navigate in rhetorical spaces that sometimes seem constricted and constricting. In many ways, this chapter is an attempt to think through a paradox—academic writing is real and, at the same time, not real. To adapt some phrasing from Jacques Derrida, academic writing has no essence—that is to say, its properties are conventional and contingent, not permanent and *essential* (an idea we will treat in more detail below). At the same time, of course, it is very real, as policy and debate around research languages illustrates. So our chapter plays out this tension in its structure, as we move from a discussion of publication policies in Norway to some of our own pedagogical initiatives, and then, ultimately, to the historical and philosophical analyses of Karen Bennett and Derrida, whose work compels us to reflect on this essence-less quality of academic writing. We look, along the way, at some of the practical implications of this: Legitimation Code Theory (LCT), as pioneered by Karl Maton, is useful because it allows us to think of academic language, and academic disciplines, as changing rather than rigid. We begin, then, with some thoughts about publication practices in Norway, and the backdrop they form for our work and institution.

Language Policies and Publication Practices in Norwegian Higher Education

In Norway, as in the rest of the Nordic countries, "parallel language use" has become the most common position advocated by higher education leadership. This position recognizes English as necessary to reach international research communities, and yet, at the same time, encourages the use of local languages to reach local audiences (Nordisk ministerråd, 2007). In a report from 2017 written by a working group convened by the Nordic Council to make language policy recommendations for the HE sector, institutions are urged to ensure that research fields are both sufficiently international and sufficiently local. English is recognized as the dominant language for international research. Yet, the report argues,

> The universities in the Nordic countries can be said to have a national responsibility to ensure that the Nordic national languages continue to develop so they may be used as scientific languages at a national level; this is a question of democracy and knowledge-building.
>
> (More parallel, please!, *2017, p. 23*)

The working group's appeal to "responsibility" and "democracy" exemplifies a hierarchy of knowledge in which English-language work is considered to be what really counts in the world of research, whereas work in the national languages is valued for other reasons. Ragnhild Ljosland has noted that language debates in the HE sector tend to be characterized by an opposition between a "rhetoric of responsibility" to argue for the importance of using local languages and a "rhetoric of excellence and competition" to argue for the importance of writing in English (2016, p. 57).

This hierarchy in which English is associated with "excellence" and Norwegian with "responsibility" is one reason why the idea and ideal of "parallel language use" might be said to have had limited impact on scholars' actual language choices (McGrath, 2014). The most significant factor influencing publication patterns arguably has to do with disciplinary configurations and hierarchies. The natural sciences, for example, are already primarily international, and language policies are unlikely to change that configuration. In the social sciences and humanities (SSH), scholars often have a more meaningful choice in terms of publishing in English or in other languages, but language policies do not seem to be the primary driver in those choices.

Performance-based research funding policies, on the other hand, have had a significant impact on publication patterns. Introduced in 2004, these policies established a system whereby a portion of the government's funding for HE institutions is calculated by research output in terms of number of publications and external grants. As a part of this system, journals are ranked at two levels. The highest, level 2, is intended to represent the top 20% of the journals in a given research field. Publishing in journals at this level is deemed more prestigious, and yields more "points" than publishing in level 1 journals. Since very few of the level 2 journals are Norwegian-language journals, this policy rewards researchers and institutions who publish in international journals.

There has been considerable debate about the impact of this system (Hagen & Johansen, 2006). An evaluation of the policy shows that the most significant effect is that scholars at Norwegian HE institutions overall publish more frequently than they did before the policy was implemented (*Evaluering af den norske publiceringsindikator*, 2014, p. 6). The language choices vary considerably among fields and disciplines, but the overall patterns in the different fields have remained fairly stable (*Evaluering af den norske publiceringsindikator*, 2014, p. 6). In the natural sciences, the vast majority of the publications (recent figures indicate 95%) are in English (Kristoffersen, Kristiansen, & Røyneland, 2014, p. 213). In the SSH, about 50% of the publications are in international languages, while the other half are in Norwegian (Sivertsen, 2016, pp. 361–364). Based on a range of bibliometric studies, Gunnar Sivertsen concludes that "Researchers in the SSH are *normally bilingual* in their publication practice (if their native language is not English)" [italics in original] (2016, p. 362). In sum, although researchers in Norway are expected to publish in English, most scholars in the SSH also publish in Norwegian.

This situation resonates with studies of European multilingual scholars in the SSH (Lillis & Curry, 2010). Many of these scholars, then, have to make choices about what kind of studies or research questions would be interesting for an international audience and which ones are more appropriate for a local audience. Such deliberations also involve assessing the "cost" of publishing in Norwegian—which might count less towards promotion and status. The "costs" of publishing in English, on the other hand, involve writing in a second language, shifting the focus of research to more general, and often more theoretical discussions, and, in some fields, writing with less of a chance of having an impact on the "real world" in terms of policy, professional or pedagogical practices.

Disciplinarity, Language, and Pedagogy

In a Norwegian context, these kinds of debate about the purpose of research are particularly pronounced in relatively new academic fields, e.g. nursing, teacher education, and social work. As we move from the national scale of the previous section to an institutional focus in this one, then, we begin to see how national policies around publication shape the institutional culture of a discipline. This gives us an initial sense of academic writing and disciplinarity as things that are mutable, but not in a way that scholars always experience as positive or tension-free.

The term "academic drift" has been used to describe the way professional fields have been perceived to adopt the ideals and practices of older and established academic disciplines (Smeby, 2015). The concept of "drift" is intended to capture how these professions have moved from vocational fields outside the university structure into the academic sphere. As several scholars have shown (Smeby & Suthpen, 2015), this movement is contested and complex. It comes with concerns that a professional or vocational field's aspirations to become established as an academic field can make it become less relevant for professional practice (Agevall & Olofsson, 2015). As the term "drift" implies, the field seems to be moving away from a perceived ideal core. In these fields, publishing in English might also be seen as a part of this drift away from professional relevance and credibility towards an academia seen as sterile, non-credible and removed from crucial "real-world", practice-based issues. Ultimately, then, what is at stake in such debates are questions of authority, power, hierarchy, and different rationales for doing research in the first place.

These debates form an important backdrop for our work at OsloMet because our institution is the result of several mergers of specialized professional colleges, and many of the educational programs OsloMet offers are within professional occupations. Our remit includes work with scholars who have come to academia from professional fields. Some of these have completed a PhD, others have not. A growing body of scholarship refers to scholars who transition into higher education from professional fields as "second-career academics." A number of studies document the challenges facing this group (Moriarty, Manthorpe, Stevens, & Hussein, 2015; Smith & Boyd, 2012; Murray, 2008). This literature suggests that many second-career academics continue to feel a strong sense of loyalty and obligation to their field of practice, and sometimes experience considerable tension because of a contradiction between what is considered relevant for the profession and what is considered relevant for research (Boyd & Smith, 2016).

In short, among both PhD candidates and academic staff, we meet scholars who struggle not just with academic language but also with the academic identities and epistemological configurations of their fields. Questions of audience, focus, and research agendas are, thus, central issues in our writing support initiatives. Understanding the political economy of international academic publishing and negotiating the dilemmas that face both individual researchers and institutions are key academic literacies for the researchers we work with.

Our pedagogical initiatives are very much inspired by an academic literacies approach because this approach allows us to focus not only on specific textual or rhetorical features, but also on why particular forms of writing are privileged (Barton & Hamilton, 1998; Lea & Street, 1998, 2006). In a way, "academic drift" can be a useful, illustrative concept: it allows scholars to see that disciplines are not immutable. But at the same time, academics are often expected to behave as though disciplines, knowledge and the contexts of knowledge *are* immutable. As we have mentioned, this is the paradox that we wrestle with in this article, and it comes into focus for us and our course participants alike when we include a segment called "The Case of Norway." Since many of the scholars we work with use empirical data from Norway, international journals will often expect these writers to justify why Norway would be an interesting case for an international readership. Such are the realities—if that is the right word—of international publishing. But this segment is also a space to reflect on how "parochialism" (Lillis & Curry, 2010) is configured in international publishing, and to discuss the hierarchies that dictate who is asked to include such explanations and who is not. These discussions show how the textual work involved in academic writing depends on a whole set of extra-textual circumstances that are historically contingent, culturally determined and, at root, economic. Texts, textual conventions and the circumstances that produce them are both real, because powerful, and unreal, because they have always changed and will always change. So in some ways, "The Case of Norway" is a study in frustration—"Why must I behave as though my research context is less meaningful, and why must I use writing conventions that seem, precisely, to reify this perception?"

These are big questions, of course, and we will not solve them at a stroke. But because of the attention it pays to the constructedness of knowledge, we wonder if LCT might be a way of bringing these issues into a clearer light, and perhaps beginning to map some ways through them.

LCT in the Classroom and Beyond

"Academic drift," as we have seen, is an instance of disciplinary change that researchers and teachers may feel is forced on them, and may feel unnerving. LCT, we suggest in this section, may be a way of perceiving, working with and responding to disciplines as, precisely, modes of knowledge and expression that change (cf. Molinari, 2015).

Using LCT as an extension of academic literacies approaches gives researchers an opportunity to think through the constructedness of their disciplines and, indeed, of disciplinarity itself. It is versatile, metacognitive and transdisciplinary, being, as Maton says, a toolkit to be developed rather than a theory to be applied (Maton, 2014). Each instance of its use can develop the toolkit further. It can be used at a micro or meso way to think about the individual sections of a research article, but also at a macro level to chart the development of a discipline as Maton does with the field of cultural studies in the UK (Maton, 2014) and as McNamara does with the field of academic nursing in Ireland (McNamara, 2010).

Our starting point for using LCT for researchers was with a group of physical rehabilitation PhD students and postdocs. Many PhDs in Norway proceed by the article compilation method, so using LCT to think about the individual sections of an article was an appropriate way to work. In this case, the aim was to reveal the underlying shape and structure of the Discussion section of an article, using the concept of semantic waves (Maton, 2013; Kirk, 2017), with a view to developing models that could be applied in the candidates' own writing. The semantic wave employs the LCT tool of semantic gravity, often in conjunction with semantic density (which can be taken to mean "relationality": "the more relations with other meanings, the stronger the semantic density" (Maton, 2016, p. 15)). Semantic gravity can be stronger (SG+) or weaker (SG-), depending on how context-dependent the meaning of a text is at a given point in that text. The text's points of maximal SG (SG+) are where its meaning is most context-dependent. As the text moves towards abstraction, speculation, generalization, and theoretical positions, we can say that the semantic gravity lessens, and the meaning becomes less context-dependent (SG-). Kirk (2017), for example, working with reflective statements written by Masters-level anthropology students, uses the semantic wave to show how such statements move between the recollection of actual experience and conceptual discussions based on theoretical understanding. This is the approach we applied to the Discussion section of a paper on ultrasound in the diagnostic process (Nam, Hensor, Hunt, Conaghan, Wakefield, & Emery, 2016). Following Kirk, we opted to do this without a detailed explanation of LCT, but instead using a language of enactment (Kirk, 2017; Maton, 2014). Table 6.1 shows the text levels distributed across the Discussion section.

These levels allow a reader to think about the way a discipline constructs, or legitimizes, knowledge by threading together meanings that are context dependent with those that are not.

The aim for the candidates was to describe the text's movements between these levels, and to then represent that movement visually (see Figure 6.1).

TABLE 6.1 Text level distribution

Greater abstraction (SG-)	5	Speculation
	4	Established knowledge
	3	Patterns, generalizations
	2	Comparisons
Context-dependence (SG+)	1	"This study"

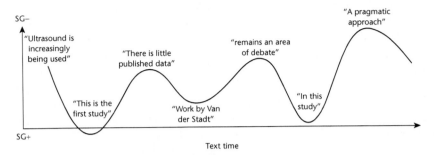

FIGURE 6.1 The semantic wave in a research article discussion section from *Annals of the Rheumatic Diseases*.

An important thing for the candidates to notice was not only the movement between the levels, but also the language used at the different levels. This would allow them to more effectively transfer the movement of the semantic wave into their own texts.

Using the semantic wave, then—with or without explicit mention of the LCT concepts of semantic density and semantic gravity that it draws on—is an approach congruent with the academic literacies approaches already in play in EAP at OsloMet. The researchers we worked with responded positively to it, and found the visual representation of the text a useful way of capturing the dynamic quality of an article. We have subsequently begun using the semantic wave with other groups of researchers, and we are currently working on ways of refining its use with multidisciplinary groups. As Maton, Hood, and Shay (2016) show, LCT can be a fertile resource in a range of educational situations.

LCT has an additional value, however, in its potential for researchers to reflect on and perhaps even change the trajectories of their disciplines, and conceivably to collapse the binary opposition between the "regional" and the "international." LCT sees disciplines as being constructed out of "languages of legitimation" (Maton, 2014; Maton, Hood, & Shay, 2016). Part of its advance from Basil Bernstein's notion of "codes" is the specificity and depth LCT brings to codes: the semantic codes we have been discussing are one instance of this. Maton argues that the semantic codes can be shown visually on a semantic plane, as shown in Figure 6.2.

This brings us back to the topic of academic drift discussed above. One way of thinking about academic drift in practices such as nursing and teacher education is to imagine it moving from the "prosaic" quarter of the plane—where semantic density is low, and semantic gravity is high—to the "rarefied" quarter of the plane, where semantic density and gravity are lowest. In other words, this shows a changing language of legitimation—rarefied, generalizable, abstract, theoretical work becoming more academically valuable than the more context-specific, experience-rooted work that is valued in disciplines that construct legitimacy using

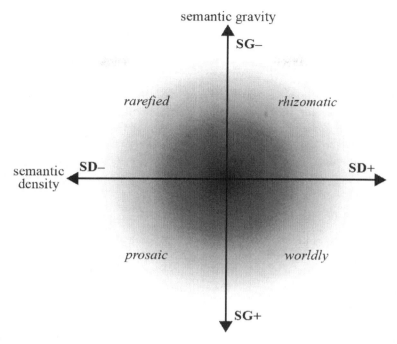

FIGURE 6.2 The semantic plane. (Image from Maton, 2016, p.16. Used with permission.)

greater semantic gravity (i.e., falling into the "worldly" or "prosaic" sections of the plane). Indeed, Maton specifically points out that the worldly codes that structure professional and vocational knowledge fields have been "rendered invisible by dominant visions of education" (Maton, 2016, p. 17). These visions have tended to posit a dichotomy between theoretical knowledge (rhizomatic codes) and practical knowledge (prosaic codes). LCT, thus, offers a different way of thinking about professional knowledge than through this rigid opposition.

It is not for nothing that Maton refers to LCT as a "sociology of possibility," therefore. One pedagogical value of LCT is to assist learners in mapping the underlying codes of their disciplines; but a step beyond this might be to change those codes (cf. Maton 2016, p.3). If a researcher is worried, for example, by academic drift, a tool such as the semantic plane provides an opportunity to think about reversing that drift. A writer can use the tool not just to reproduce the existing legitimation codes, but to begin pushing back at them. And because the writer is doing this with a knowledge of the codes, the process is not blind, or haphazard. It would be inadequate, doomed, even, for a writer to say, "I am going, in such and such an article, to step right back into the worldly or prosaic quarters," because the processes of legitimation have moved elsewhere; but the writer might think, "By using increments or instances of language more associated with the other quarters, I can begin a process of re-legitimation for more context-dependent work."

We have only just begun to explore the uses of LCT in our pedagogical work and in our own thinking about knowledge production, but we wonder if something similar might be possible with the regional/international binary. One of the benefits of equipping researchers with a deeper understanding of LCT—rather than just an appropriate language of enactment—might be to allow them to analyze the trajectories of legitimation in their own fields, including the legitimation codes that privilege the international over the regional. Might a discipline be positioned differently on the semantic plane depending on where in the world one is?

From Epistemicide to Onticide

Another way of thinking about these topics is via Karen Bennett's concept of epistemicide (Bennett, 2007). As mentioned in the first section, an attendance, such as Bennett's, to the historically-constructed and contingent features of "academic writing in English" leads to the unsettling question of "What object are we actually talking about?" In other words, if the object of study ("academic writing") is to a large extent the accretions of cultural processes—fall-out, the rubble of history—can it be said to have any properties that are *essential*, that are absolutely proper to it? We suggest here that a useful corollary to English Academic Discourse (EAD) as it appears in Bennett's work is the sense of literature as similarly "essence-less," a proposition advanced by Jacques Derrida.

One of the distinctive features of Bennett's work is its engagement with EAD as a cultural artefact, an artefact with a history. One of her concerns is that the dominance of EAD leads to epistemicide—that is, the extinction of other modes of thinking (Bennett, 2007, 2014). In this, she differs from other researchers, whose focus tends to be on English as a language. Bennett's interest is in the positivist, empiricist nature of the discourse itself, which she sees as a distinctive product of the English Reformations, and quite different to the rhetorical and analytical traditions of Southern Europe, where the Reformation didn't happen. "In the Catholic countries of southern Europe," she notes, "the scholastic tradition was maintained long after it had been overturned in the Protestant countries of the north," with the result that the plain style that would become EAD never took hold; instead, a worldview remained whereby "Verbal abundance and linguistic complexity were valued as signs of inner worth, and knowledgeable texts were expected to be beautiful artifacts, rather than transparent windows onto some outer reality" (Bennett, 2007, p.163).

Two observations may be made from this: one is that the positivist, empiricist dimensions of EAD may be said to inhere in research even when the language of research is not English; and two, that in the spread of EAD from the physical sciences to the SSH, EAD has in some sense colonized itself, by expelling or repelling alternative modes of thought. It is not simply that "English" is the Tyrannosaurus Rex (to borrow John Swales's (1997) metaphor); it is, rather, that English fell victim to itself, resulting in a monolithic "EAD" where there could have been a profusion, a forest, of "Englishes."

What this perhaps invites, though, is a kind of onticide—that is, the cancelling out of an ontology of academic writing, any idea that academic writing is a thing in the world, is a "thing" at all. A useful correspondence here is from one of Jacques Derrida's comments on the concept of literature. Derrida writes, in an essay called "Demeure":

> There is no essence or substance of literature: literature is not. It does not exist. . . . No exposition, no discursive form is intrinsically or essentially literary before and outside of the function it is assigned by a right, that is, a specific intentionality inscribed directly on the social body. The same exposition may be taken to be literary here, in one situation according to given conventions, and non-literary there. This is the sign that literarity is not an intrinsic property of this or that discursive event. Even where it seems to reside [*demeure*], literature remains an unstable function, and it depends on a precarious judicial status. Its passion consists in this—that it receives its determination from something other than itself
>
> (Derrida, 2000, pp. 28–29)

In all of this, Derrida could be talking about academic writing. It has no essence—it is a product of historical circumstances, and different things are called "academic" at different points in time and place. This is what he means when he says "it receives its determination from something other than itself"—there is no essential property of a text that guarantees that we call it academic, that guarantees it will always be thought of as academic.

Out With Conclusions!

As we have outlined above, the participants we introduced to LCT found the work useful. While we may pat ourselves on the back for the ways in which we think of our work as "useful," we would like to question what we perceive to be the value and purpose of writing pedagogy. What do we mean by "useful"? Should any academic discipline or practice be reduced to "use value"? And what is the *time* of use, or usefulness? A discussion of extreme positions may not generate "rules of the game," immediately transferable into "text"; but it may generate thinking, now or in the future. Writing pedagogy, we suggest, should be about thinking—perhaps, indeed, thinking without a prespecified end point—as much as any other discipline. This might be a way of doing justice to Nicholas Royle's

A Microscopic Digression

Microscopic, because we will not detain you long; and a digression, because this sits at a tangent to the issues discussed above. But having thought about the artificiality and contingency of "academic writing," are we not compelled to digress? Is it not more than a license, but a compulsion? It would be appropriate to Derrida's use of the word "passion": this is a word that doesn't appear very often in academic texts, and so we would like to linger over it here for a few seconds.

The idea that both literature and academic writing are essence-less—and that hence, neither exists—provokes us to think that there might be other correspondences between the two concepts. It implies that there is a "literariness" to academic writing, that might be linked to a "passion." We are not talking here of writing pretty sentences, or using figurative language; it would be a concern, as for Derrida, with the etymological relation between "passion" and "passivity." A passion is a passion because one does not choose it, one must undergo it—one is passive in its face or its approach. Such, perhaps, is the "passion" of literature: for Derrida, literature's "non-existence" means that texts are never finished, reading is never finished. Paradoxically, there is always something left over, something is always waiting to be read, thought, interpreted. Perhaps this is true of academic writing, also, or some kinds of academic writing; a new reader will always find new meanings, and reading can never be said to be complete or ended.

What we have been discussing, over the course of these remarks, is the relationship between agency and "the rules of the game." Most forms of writing pedagogy aim to make their participants well-versed in the "rules of the game," to make them confident about participating in various discourse communities. What we have been thinking about in this chapter—the paradox we began with, and have not been able to escape or resolve—is how teaching the rules reifies the rules, even, or especially, while revealing the rules to be constructs (and fragile ones, at that).

Consequently, when we look back now at Curt Rice's "Out with Norwegian!" provocation, we see a statement that is powerful and tissue-thin at the same time. It reasserts—albeit wryly, mischievously—a particular ideal of research and research languages, which assumes that research is always international in intent; but precisely through being a provocation, it demands an interrogation of the modes of power that produce "international" as something to be aspired to. It becomes a site of critique.

As we have seen, the thinking of Bennett and Derrida represents two steps beyond this, by historicizing the construct "academic writing in English" and by insisting on the essence-less, non-real quality of a form that "receives its determination from something other than itself". A meaningful question, then, concerns the extent to which these processes of interrogation and reflection can increase a writer's agency. We have begun exploring LCT because it offers an opportunity to join critique to a greater sense of agency. It creates an awareness of texts and disciplines as dynamic and in flux, and therefore offers ways of pushing back at disciplinary conventions. (Although, as we write these words, we reflect now that the version of this outlined above is perhaps rather cautious, and maybe even does some reifying work of its own. Can writing pedagogy throw caution to the wind? Can it aim at radical, blockbusting texts like Benjamin's "Theses on the Philosophy of History"?)

(extremely satirical) remark that English for Academic Purposes made as much sense to him as "English for dream purposes" (Royle, 2016).

At the same time, embedding an awareness of LCT and Bennett's historical analysis may create opportunities for a new kind of discourse, one that allows both regional and local elements. Added to this might be Canagarajah's notion of code-switching (2003). Ann Torday Gulden (2013) has discussed the experience of being a Norwegian speaker teaching academic English in the Sudan, and the implications this might have for academic English in Norway. Something that might be drawn out of this is the possibility of not translating certain words—the word *fag*, for example, cannot be translated context-free. It can mean "academic discipline" or "field" in some contexts, but also denotes professional knowledge. Code-switching like this—with the appropriate explanatory scaffolding—would be one way of allowing the regional into the international.

In the end, code-switching might still not be a solution that solves the issues of power and hierarchy that underpin the logics of international academic publishing. In a way, "code-switching" as of yet still functions as a "marked" category in contrast to the "unmarked" writing of the dominant center. Yet, it might be a step toward encouraging a tolerance for, or even developing an appreciation of, a diversity of approaches. Ultimately, such a diversity might open up possibilities for new ways of being scholars, new ways of doing scholarship, and new ways of thinking.

References

Agevall, O., & Olofsson, G. (2015). Tensions between vocational and academic demands. In J.C. Smeby & M. Suthpen (Eds.). *From vocational to professional education: Educating for social welfare* (pp. 26–49). London: Routledge.

Ammon, U. (2001). *The dominance of English as a language of science: Effects on other languages and language communities* (Vol. 84). Berlin: de Gruyter.

Barton, D., & Hamilton, M. (1998). *Local literacies*. London: Routledge.

Bennett, K. (2007). Epistemicide! The tale of a predatory discourse. *The Translator 13*(2), 151–169. doi: 10.1080/13556509.2007.10799236

Bennett, K. (2014). (Ed.) *The semiperiphery of academic writing: Discourses, communities and practices*. Basingstoke, UK: Palgrave Macmillan.

Boyd, P., & Smith, C. (2016). The contemporary academic: Orientation towards research work and researcher identity of higher education lecturers in the health professions. *Studies in Higher Education*, *41*(4), 678–695. doi: 10.1080/03075079.2014.943657

Canagarajah, A. S. (2003). *Resisting linguistic imperialism in English teaching*. Oxford: Oxford University Press.

Derrida, J. (2000). Demeure: Fiction and testimony. Trans. Rottenberg, E. Published with Blanchot, M. *The instant of my death*. Stanford, CA: Stanford University Press.

Evaluering af den norske publiceringsindikator [Evaluation of the Norwegian publication indicator]. (2014). Aarhus: Dansk center for forskningsanalyse [The Danish Centre for Studies in Research and Research Policy].

Gording Stang, E. (2017, April 4). *Får kritikk for å bannlyse norsk i forskningsartikler* [Criticized for banning Norwegian in research articles]. (T. Lie reporter). *Khrono*. Retrieved from http://www.khrono.no

Graver, H. P. (2017, April 1). *Juridisk forskning trenger norsken* [Legal research needs Norwegian]. *Morgenbladet*. Retrieved from http://www.morgenbladet.no
Gulbrandsen, E. (2017, March 31). *Språk og uspråk* [Language and unlanguage]. *Morgenbladet*. Retrieved from http://www.morgenbladet.no
Gulden, A. T. (2013). Writing across cultures: English as a common denominator after all that history. In H. B. Holmarsdottir, V. Nomolo, A. I. Farag, & Z. Desai (Eds.). *Gendered voices: Reflections on gender and education in South Africa and Sudan* (pp. 171–184). Rotterdam/Taipei: Sense Publishers.
Hagen, E. B., & Johansen, A. (Eds.). (2006). *Hva skal vi med vitenskap? 13 innlegg fra striden om tellekantene* [What do we want from science? 13 contributions to the debate on bibliometrics]. Oslo, Norway: Universitetsforlaget.
Hultgren, A, Gregersen, F., & Thøgersen, J. (2014). Introduction. English at Nordic universities: Ideologies and practices. In A. Hultgren, F. Gregersen, & J. Thøgersen (Eds.), *English in Nordic universities: Ideologies and practices* (pp.1–25). Amsterdam: John Benjamins Publishing Company.
Johansen, S. J., Jonsmoen K. M., & Greek, M. (2017, April 7). Ut med norsk og inn med engelsk? [Out with Norwegian and in with English?]. *Morgenbladet*. Retrieved from http://www.morgenbladet.no
Kirk, S. (2017). Waves of reflection: Seeing knowledges in academic writing. In J. Kemp (Ed.). *Proceedings of the 2015 BALEAP Conference – EAP in a rapidly changing landscape: Issues, challenges and solutions* (pp. 109–118). Reading, UK: Garnett.
Kristoffersen, G., Kristiansen M., & Røyneland, U. (2014). Landrapport Norge: Internasjonalisering og parallellspråklighet ved norske universitet og høyskoler [Country report Norway: Internationalization and parallel language use at Norwegian universities and colleges]. In F. Gregersen (Ed.). *Hvor parallelt? Om parallellspråklighet på Nordens universitet* [How parallel? On parallel language use at universities in the Nordic countries]. TemaNord 2014:535 (pp.197–259). Copenhagen, Denmark: Nordisk ministerråd. URL: http://www.norden.org/da/publikationer/publikationer/2014-535
Lea, M. R., & Street, B. V. (1998). Student writing in higher education: An academic literacies approach. *Studies in Higher Education 23*(2): 157–172.
Lea, M. R., & Street, B. V. (2006). The "academic literacies" model: Theory and applications. *Theory into Practice, 45*(4), 368–377.
Lie, T. (2017, April 4). *Får kritikk for å bannlyse norsk i forskningsartikler* [Criticized for banning Norwegian in research articles]. *Khrono*. Retrieved from http://www.khrono.no
Lillis, T. M., & Curry, M. J. (2010). *Academic writing in a global context: The politics and practices of publishing in English*. London: Routledge.
Ljosland, R. (2014). Language planning in practice in the Norwegian higher education sector. In A. Hultgren, F. Gregersen, & J. Thøgersen (Eds.). *English in Nordic universities: Ideologies and practices* (pp. 53–81). Amsterdam: John Benjamins Publishing Company.
Maton, K. (2013). Making semantic waves: A key to cumulative knowledge-building. *Linguistics and Education 24*(1), 8–22.
Maton, K. (2014). *Knowledge and knowers: Towards a realist sociology of education*. Abingdon, UK: Routledge.
Maton, K. (2016). Legitimation Code Theory: Building knowledge about knowledge building. In K. Maton, S. Hood, & S. Shay (Eds.), *Knowledge-building: Educational studies in Legitimation Code Theory* (pp. 1–23). Abingdon, UK: Routledge.
Maton, K., Hood, S., & Shay, S. (2016). *Knowledge-building: Educational studies in Legitimation Code Theory*. Abingdon, UK: Routledge.

McGrath, L. (2014). Parallel language use in academic and outreach publication: A case study of policy and practice. *Journal of English for Academic Purposes*, *13*, 5–16. doi:https://doi.org/10.1016/j.jeap.2013.10.008

McNamara, M. S. (2010). What lies beneath? The underlying principles structuring the field of academic nursing in Ireland. *Journal of Professional Nursing*, *26*(6), 377–384.

More parallel, please! Sprogbrug i internationaliseringsprocesser [More parallel, please! Language-use in internationalization processes]. (2017). Nordisk gruppe for parallelsproglighed [The Nordic Group for Parallel Language Use].

Molinari, J. (2015). An archaeology of academic writing(s): Using history to understand the present and future of academic writing. Paper presented at EATAW 2015. Tallinn, Estonia.

Moriarty, J., Manthorpe, J., Stevens, M., & Hussein, S. (2015). Educators or researchers? Barriers and facilitators to undertaking research among UK social work academics. *British Journal of Social Work*, *45*(6), 1659–1677. doi: 10.1093/bjsw/bcu077

Nam, J. L., Hensor, E. M., Hunt, L., Conaghan, P. G., Wakefield, R. J., & Emery, P. (2016). Ultrasound findings predict progression to inflammatory arthritis in anti-CCP antibody-positive patients without clinical synovitis. *Ann Rheum Dis*, *75*(12), 2060–2067. doi:10.1136/annrheumdis-2015-208235

Nordisk ministerråd. [Nordic Council of Ministers]. (2007). *Deklaration om nordisk språkpolitik* [Declaration on Nordic language policy]. Copenhagen, Denmark: Author.

Plo Alastrué, R. N., & Pérez-Llantada, C. (Eds.). (2015). *English as a scientific and research language: Debates and discourses: English in Europe* (Volume 2). Berlin/Boston: De Gruyter.

Royle, N. (2016). The sense of unending. Plenary paper presented at NFEAP 2016: EAP and Creativity. Oslo, Norway.

Sivertsen, G. (2016). Patterns of internationalization and criteria for research assessment in the social sciences and humanities. *Scientometrics*, *107*(2), 357–368. doi: 10.1007/s11192-016-1845-1

Slaatta, T. (2017, April 7). *Rektor Rice on the norsk issue* [Rector Rice on the Norwegian issue]. *Morgenbladet*. Retrieved from http://www.morgenbladet.no

Smeby, J. C. (2015). Academic drift in vocational education? In J.C. Smeby & M. Suthpen (Eds.). *From vocational to professional education: Educating for social welfare* (pp. 7–24). London: Routledge.

Smith, C., & Boyd, P. (2012). Becoming an academic: The reconstruction of identity by recently appointed lecturers in nursing, midwifery and the allied health professions. *Innovations in Education and Teaching International*, *49*(1), 63–72.

Swales, J. (1997). English as *Tyrannosaurus Rex*. *World Englishes*, *16*(3), 373–382.

Time, J. K. (2017, March 31). *Ut med norsken!* [Out with Norwegian!]. *Morgenbladet*. Retrieved from http://www.morgenbladet.no

REGION 3
Eastern and Southern Europe

7
RESEARCH WRITING IN ENGLISH IN A ROMANIAN ACADEMIC ECOSYSTEM

A Case Study of an Experienced Multiliterate Researcher

Laura-Mihaela Muresan
BUCHAREST UNIVERSITY OF ECONOMIC STUDIES, ROMANIA

Carmen Pérez-Llantada
UNIVERSITY OF ZARAGOZA, SPAIN

Introduction

Over the past decades numerous claims have been made regarding the challenges that English for Research Publication Purposes (ERPP hereafter) poses to non-Anglophone researchers worldwide. The scholarly debate has brought to the fore the linguistic marginalization of these researchers by conceptualizing it in terms of binary categorizations. Some categorizations specifically refer to the socio-historic context of research knowledge production of plurilingual academic communities (Canagarajah, 2002; Lillis & Curry, 2010). Others, such as 'publish in English or perish' (Englander, 2014; Englander & Uzuner-Smith, 2013), "core vs. semi-periphery writers" (Bennett, 2014; Liu, 2004), "stigmatized vs. non-stigmatized scholars" (Flowerdew, 2009), have been deployed to discuss the widespread perception of linguistic inequity felt by those communities whose first language (L1) is not English. Broadly, the literature reports that the current geopolitics of English continues to favour its spread for global knowledge production and dissemination purposes. This "asymmetrical market of knowledge production" (Corcoran, Englander, & Muresan, this volume) explicitly points at the effects of an English-dominant research publication context on multiliterate writing practices and evince the ways in which writing practices are shaped by global and regional policies for scientific knowledge production.

A further set of categorizations revolves around the linguistic factors in academic writing. Categorizations such as "good vs. awkward scholarly writing features" (Englander, 2010) or "canonical vs. non-canonical" grammar usage (Rozycki &

Johnson, 2013) serve to qualify distinctive features of L2 English academic texts that are not used in L1 English. Studies have shown that these features reflect processes of lexical and phraseological L1 transfer in L2 academic English texts (Mauranen, Pérez-Llantada, & Swales, 2010). Research concludes that these features ought to be attributed to different L1 academic styles and academic writing cultures (Duszak, 1994; Kourilova, 1998; Loi & Evans, 2010).

Particular attention has been paid to situational and cognitive factors related to learning to write academic texts. These are disciplinary enculturation, or learning in the community, and literacy development. Barton (2007) argues that literacy is acquired through processes of informal learning of social practices in a community. Research on multiliterate writing in communities of researchers whose L1 is not English has drawn on qualitative methods such as narratives, autobiographic accounts, interviews and case studies. For example, Swales (1998) and Prior (2009) examine processes of disciplinary enculturation. Johns (1997), Belcher and Connor (2001) and Lillis and Curry (2010) also report formative literacy experiences of single researchers based on autobiographical narratives.

Drawing on the perspective of bilingualism, Gentil and Séror (2014) define bi-/multiliteracy as the writing ability in two or more languages. These authors explain that biliteracy development is challenging and time-consuming, as it is constrained by an English-dominant research publication context and a disciplinary context. Using longitudinal case studies of scholars from an L1 French academic setting, Gentil (2011) concludes that bilingualism has a positive influence in L2 writing, as writers can draw on their knowledge of genre conventions in their L1 to draft texts in L2 English. As Gentil explains, because a multilingual writer can develop and use genre expertise in more than one language, a bilingual genre-based instructional approach can focus on "underdeveloped/transferable components in two academic languages" (p. 6).

Ethnographically-oriented research on academic writing prompts insiders' reflections on the context of academic text production, the relationship between research (disciplinary content and research interests) and writing for publication, by this means approaching both "text as process" and "text as product". Furthering this line of enquiry, in this study we focus on an individual subject's case study to explore different dimensions of academic literacy development, namely, the sociocultural/sociohistoric dimension, the socially-situated dimension, the cognitive dimension and the linguistic dimension. The research questions posed were the following:

- What was the researcher's perception of English as the main international language of science?
- How does her participation in a disciplinary culture enhance academic literacy skills development?
- What metacognitive strategies does the researcher draw upon to improve her writing skills?

- In what ways does the researcher's writing expertise (both in L1 and L2) assist her in the process of writing L2 English academic texts?

A secondary aim of this chapter is to illustrate the value of some key constructs in the broad field of SLA—biliteracy, L1/L2 writing development and writing expertise—for describing and better understanding L2 English academic writing processes.

Methodology

Building on the experience of training professional researchers within the framework of an academic development Master of Arts (MA) programme established at the Bucharest University of Economic Studies (Bardi & Muresan, 2014; Muresan & Nicolae, 2015), we first outline some of the key features of the academic ecosystem selected for the present study, as well as the developments introduced in this programme over the last few years in response to identified language learning needs.

Useful references for understanding the Romanian context can be found in previous studies on attitudes towards publishing research in English of cohorts of researchers participating in the English Language Education and Research Communication for Business and Economics (EDU-RES) master's programme. This programme, which was awarded the European Language Label 2011 by the EU Commission DG for Education and Culture (through the Romanian Agenția Națională pentru Programe Comunitare în Domeniul Educației și Formării Profesionale), is an interdisciplinary master's designed to support the development of integrated competencies in communication in international academic and professional contexts. It integrates language and culture in the curriculum, as well as research-oriented skills practice. Its main focus is on research/study design, methodological aspects and communication skills for presenting and publishing research internationally. It is within this context that we contacted an experienced researcher in the field of social sciences, with expertise in project management and management information systems. She is a full professor, highly-cited researcher with a strong publication record (according to bibliometric data) who is participating in the 2016–2018 EDU-RES programme. She had learnt English as a second foreign language in high school and was first exposed to academic English in 1985, after graduating from university, when she started working in research groups at university and read the first articles in English. Since then, the researcher has been publishing research, involved in projects and acted as an expert evaluator in research assessment throughout her academic career. Considering her background and expertise, we selected this particular scholar because we believed this was a case representing learning derived from extensive researching/writing experience and autonomous learning in L2 writing processes.

We specifically applied the methods proposed by Johns (1997, pp. 76–77) to English for academic purposes (EAP) instructors to investigate aspects of individuals' academic skills learning and literacy development. These methods have also been applied in ethnographic studies of cohorts of non-Anglophone academics in Europe and elsewhere (Belcher & Connor, 2001; Lillis & Curry, 2010; Phothongsunan, 2016). We selected case study research as we wanted the study to be "explanatory, exploratory and descriptive" (Creswell, 2013, p. 97). The data collection instruments were a self-reflective questionnaire and a semi-structured interview (included in Appendix 7.1). The former was designed for initial interaction with the individual subject as well as pedagogically oriented, as it sought to prompt self-reflection on past/current writing practices and written commentary on individual literacy skills learning and academic writing development.

The self-reflective questionnaire was administered prior to the final onsite session of the 2nd semester of the masters' course. Following previous studies (Hanauer & Englander, 2011; Johns, 1997; Lillis & Curry, 2010; Muresan & Pérez-Llantada, 2014), it aimed to elicit the insider's view of some of the key contextual aspects of research communication pointed out by the literature, particularly the impact of language and research policies, the geopolitics of ERPP and the dominant role of English in today's academia. We were also interested in knowing her past and present writing for publication experiences, her perceptions of text as both process and product, as well as her self-perceived writing skills, above all, her skills in linguistic and rhetorical aspects of genres and her text-composing strategies (how to go about it, linguistic resources at hand, reliance on prior genre knowledge, approach to self-assessment, techniques for text improvement, etc.).

The interview protocol, which turned out to be close to the think-aloud protocols and the narrative account format used in Belcher and Connor (2001) and Lillis and Curry (2010), was based on Phothongsunan's (2016) study on Thai academics, but was adapted to the particular academic setting investigated. The interview questions focused on aspects that the self-reflective questionnaire had prompted regarding the researcher's formative literacy experience and her own approaches to writing. We wanted to understand how an experienced researcher goes about doing research and about publishing research results, how research (disciplinary content and research interests) relates to writing; whether there was an intrinsic relationship between content, research objectives and writing, and how results are disseminated. We also sought to gain further insight into the preparation stages and her approach adopted prior to writing, her commitment to values and high standards and peer cooperation and values attached to it. The interview lasted 50 mins. A final follow-up face-to-face discussion with the scholar (approx. 20 minutes) was conducted for further clarification. Put together, the questionnaire, interview and follow-up responses, the data source amounted to an approximate total of 4,000 words.

Data were analyzed with a view to identifying some of the factors determining advanced L2 writing and literacy development through the participant's current perspectives and retrospective reflections on her biliterate experiences. Using *Atlas.ti* 8, we conducted thematic analysis (paying attention to the qualitative aspects)

[Word cloud figure]

FIGURE 7.1 Word cloud of the researcher's narrative (threshold = words occurring at least five times)

putting all the transcribed data together (questionnaire, interview, follow-up). Data coding corresponded with the following dimensions of writing mentioned previously: the sociocultural/sociohistoric dimension (RQ1), the socially-situated dimension (RQ2), the cognitive dimension (RQ3) and the linguistic dimension (RQ4). The word cloud generated with *Atlas.ti* shows the recurring concepts that surfaced in the researcher's narrative (Figure 7.1). These concepts were linked to the different dimensions of writing so as to systematize the Discussion section of this chapter.

Results

Focusing first of all on the theme of the geopolitics of ERPP, the data showed that the researcher's perception of English as the main international language of science was similar to that of other scholars in Europe and other world regions (Bardi & Muresan, 2014; Buckingham, 2014; Chiu, 2001; Englander, 2014; Englander & Uzuner-Smith, 2013; Ferguson, Pérez-Llantada, & Plo, 2011; Lillis & Curry, 2010). Her responses contained frequent references to aspects of English-medium text production and to journal article writing in English. Various interests were associated with writing for publication in English, namely, finding solutions to large-scale societal problems, carrying out research to cater for the particular needs and demands of private and public companies, sharing science with peer colleagues and reaching the international scientific community. Acknowledging that she was a senior researcher, she noted that publishing involved personal and social satisfaction:

[. . .] to demonstrate, mainly to myself that I am still able to do research, I am still active and productive. Secondly, I enjoy continuing working with my colleagues from the research group. Doing research is the opportunity to interact with them and this is a good thing for me.

She considered scientific knowledge dissemination at a local level as important as publishing globally because it responded to local/national-based needs. Publishing internationally was not ideologically-laden. In her narrative there were no references to the importance of rewards or regulations regarding ERPP or feelings of "English-dominance", "linguistic disadvantage" or "stigmatization" (Flowerdew, 2009). When asked specifically about her reasons for publication and her decisions regarding staying local vs. going global, the researcher underlined that "being local" offered opportunities for scientific knowledge exchange with peer colleagues and participation in a particular disciplinary culture.

Like other Romanian academics and academics with other non-Anglophone L1 backgrounds (Bardi & Muresan, 2014; Englander & Uzuner-Smith, 2013; Ferguson et al., 2011; Muresan & Pérez-Llantada, 2014), she highlighted the role of English as the world's international language of science (Canagarajah, 2002). She also stated that she read in English and wrote papers in her L1 early in her career, but eventually shifted to English-only: "In 1985, I started research by reading papers in English and writing papers in Romanian. After 2000, I have read and written papers almost exclusively in English."

The researcher viewed writing in the global context as a way of disseminating research and, in this respect, she acknowledged the functionality of English. Although she described writing for publication in high-profile journals as highly competitive, requiring her to highlight the value, contribution and implications of the research for persuasion purposes, in her view, the process of planning and designing new research was motivated by the preoccupation of having an innovative idea that could contribute to the pool of existing knowledge and be valuable for other researchers in the field. Such a view was supported by comments on the intrinsic research and writing relationship and perceptions of texts as processes. For example, when asked about the process of selecting a research topic, she underlined that researching extensively, finding an idea and, afterwards, identifying publication possibilities in her research areas were crucial steps towards producing a publishable piece of writing:

[. . .] a paper is only the end-result of a research process, which has already been started, and the selection of the topic depends on what I have already done, on what I have done before and on what I feel confident I'm capable of doing, or it may depend on the team I'm working with. The article comes only in the end, after I have done the research. If you don't have your research there's no article to write.

As the researcher reiterated, aspects such as knowledge of the journals in her field, the process of selecting the journal, investigating who is publishing, what topics and assessing the chances she and her research team have involved collaborative assessment of the situation, the journals and so on. She attached more value to the research process itself and viewed texts as "only the end-result of a research process", as she explicitly notes when she comments on how her research on management information solutions can support the educational field.

> Publication comes at the end [of the process], and to me it seems to be the easiest part, not in the sense that it is the easiest but because it is the final step; the most difficult part is to have an idea and to have something to work on, trying to obtain a better or more interesting eLearning solution, to improve functionalities, to extend the range of users, to make better financial analyses in projects, and only then to consider where it would be better to publish, what journal has a higher ranking; so this comes only at the end.

The main places the researcher engaged in activity and social interaction were both her own local environment (i.e. interacting with her group members) and the international context (i.e. through participation in numerous international conferences and European projects). She referred to learning from colleagues and working together with the texts (as part of co-authoring practices) and pointed out that collaboration and team complementarity resulted in careful decision-making regarding the method of analysis and the provision of data for developing case studies in her field of research expertise:

> One team member works on the text/draft, and then the draft is read by another co-author. The manuscript goes through two/three draft versions, especially for refining the language. I usually work in two/three teams, and we have a lot of experience of working with each other. We agree on the structure from the very beginning, and then everybody writes directly in English. [. . .] each of us takes on a role in the research process and the efforts are evenly distributed; this involves harmonisation of the work style, compatibility, years of team consolidation.

The researcher's high level of perceptiveness was crucial for learning "the content of disciplinarity", that is, learning "registers, textual genres, rhetorical features and semiotic forms" (Prior & Bilbro, 2012, p. 21) specific to her disciplinary community. She reported "considerable efforts, but not frustrating, to acquire research communication abilities", "in getting to know who is going to read the journal, not only as reviewer, but also those for whom the articles are written, those to whom they are addressed". Such perceptiveness may explain her "familiarization with the requirements of the different journals, the work put into getting to understand the style, the topics addressed and the readership of a particular journal". As shown below, she acknowledged the difficulty of getting research published in scientific journals as opposed to publishing in conference proceedings.

> As compared to [*Procedia*[1]], a journal is more difficult "to penetrate", the requirements are higher, you don't know the people on the editing board directly, or even if you know them, you don't know who will be doing the peer review, and I also don't think they [a journal] would publish work in progress. This is why you have to follow a lot of issues of that journal, to read several issues and articles in that journal and to feel you can fit with your research within the journal's thematic field and that your research style is compatible with that of the journal.

Several L2 reading and writing connections became evident in the researcher's academic (bi)literacy development:

> In order to read an article I needed several full days, working a lot with the English-Romanian dictionary. I had to go through the text several times, in order to understand the content. But, eventually, it became easier and easier, so that after some months I could read specialised literature with a certain ease. The progress was unexpectedly rapid, considering the initial difficulties.

Further, while she noted that writing in academic English came "naturally" out of extensive reading of English-medium texts, when she had to produce both an English and a Romanian version of the same article for *Revista Amfiteatru Economic* (an ISI-indexed journal that publishes full articles in both languages), she felt that work on the Romanian version involved greater effort, and reliance on her knowledge of the English rhetorical and linguistic conventions.

The theme of the L2 writing processes in English revealed some of the researcher's strategies to approach writing. "Visualising the readers", i.e., having a target audience in mind, helped the researcher to frame the literature review section of articles. This was eloquently expressed with a sense of responsibility when carrying out research:

> I must confess that [when writing] in most of my articles I see my colleagues or I see those who are my peer researchers, those who do research in the same field, who could be interested, and then I make sure. . . it is like an obligation, anyway, to do work which makes sense in the current research environment and you refer to this in the literature review.

The researcher drew on extensive revision "for improving the clarity of the formulations, e.g. rephrasing, restructuring of some sentences, synonyms" before submitting a manuscript to a journal. Other strategies for approaching the process of writing, setting herself very high standards also in the intermediate steps (e.g. preparatory work prior to the writing process), included reading texts from the target journal in preparation for writing, peer-reviewing for journals and analyzing and understanding the reports received from journal reviewers. The "main lessons learned" from being peer-reviewed were the importance of reading the reports closely and paying attention to the reviewers' relevant feedback:

> The reviews received often refer to language, although the feedback received from reviewers sometimes seems contradictory. Sometimes there are also content related aspects, for instance one reviewer recommends reducing the material, the text you have written, while another asks for more text. If you analyze the text and the feedback received better, you actually realise that both reviewers are right and that their feedback is not contradictory; in some parts you have probably written too much, indeed, and maybe not everything is relevant or necessary, and in other parts you have not been sufficiently explicit.

To her, the reviewers' feedback had an educational goal, as it enabled her to critically reflect on her own writing and improve her style. As she put it, "[o]ver time I have understood that it is important to express yourself as clearly as possible, in a simple, easy to follow manner." Use of online resources for writing, such as spell-checkers, online dictionaries and thesauri for checking vocabulary and finding appropriate synonyms, was associated with specific areas for improvement ("I have to pay more attention to vocabulary and the writing style").

Attention to the discourse pragmatics and the functions of linguistic resources for conveying pragmatic nuances were reported to be direct learning outcomes of the EDU-RES masters' programme instruction. In this respect, the researcher enumerated some of the typical features of the academic written register (formulation of ideas, reader-oriented metadiscourse resources, intertextuality and citation, rhetoric and argumentation, and authorial/disciplinary voice) and, having identified areas for improving language skills, she readily stated that she was determined to "deliberately and purposefully" pay greater attention to specific linguistic resources in academic discourse.

Lastly, reflection on the beginnings and the process of acquiring relevant skills for research writing, the researcher said that, in retrospect, receiving formal instruction could have helped her to discern the "difference between general English and academic English". Yet, she added that since such training was not available at the beginning of her career, she relied on extensive reading and learning how to write within her community of practice. In the follow-up interview, the scholar acknowledged and reiterated the importance of both "high-level instruction" and "experience" for achieving expertise in writing.

Discussion

In this section we discuss the main dimensions of writing explored through the case study, namely, the socio-historic, socially-situated, cognitive and linguistic dimensions (Berkenkotter & Huckin, 1995; Gentil, 2011). We introduced the term 'ecosystem' as a metaphor for the L1 context in which academic literacy is acquired while being shaped and influenced by these interrelated dimensions. All in all, reflection on the above dimensions does not simply enable us to understand a researcher's literacy journey and his/her experiences in composing research genres in an L2. As discussed below, it helps us create robust synergies between the key SLA conceptualizations such as "conscious attention", "awareness" and "noticing/noticing the gap" (Schmidt, 1993), those of the field of socioliteracies (Johns, 1997; Prior, 2008) and those of EAP and ethnographically-oriented research on commentary around texts (Berkenkotter & Hukin, 1995), textographies (Swales, 1998), observation of fieldwork disciplinary practices (Dressen-Hammouda, 2014), think-aloud protocols over text composing (Salö & Hanell, 2014) and/or manuscript drafting journeys (Guo, 2012; Paltridge, 2008).

Firstly, the case study showed that the emic perspective of the socio-historic context of scientific knowledge production brings to the fore issues of current scholarly concern, namely, the geopolitics of English and individuals' perceptions of interests, regulations (policies) and rewards ascribed to writing in English for an international (global) audience. English-only research publication practices was a "taken-for-granted" reality for the researcher interviewed in the present case study. Further, in this case study, the researcher's main motivation was based on participating in trans-national research efforts where English is the lingua franca and where results are deliberately intended for a multilingual audience. In sum, her motivation confirmed that there is a strong non-linguistic dimension underpinning international publication, as claimed previously in the literature (Uzuner, 2008; Lillis & Curry, 2010; Pérez-Llantada, Ferguson, & Plo, 2011; Englander & Uzuner-Smith, 2013).

This study also showed that the researcher did not shift to English for reasons of prestige, recognition and international visibility. Her choice of language was not motivated by ideological discourses or the existing system of supra-national and institutional research policies, but by her own "personal satisfaction" in producing research and sharing it with peers so as to move the disciplinary field ahead. Instead of siding for or against "staying local" (i.e. publishing in Romanian) or "going global" (i.e. publishing in English), the researcher appeared to feel satisfied with her plurilingual literacy practices because these allow her to participate in distinct ways with each of her intended readers. This somehow contradicts the extant literature, or rather, adds complexity to it, as her English-only writing practices are not influenced by the widespread ideologies of English associating this language with prestige and international recognition (Corcoran, 2015; Englander, 2010; Lillis & Curry, 2010).

Regarding the socio-situated dimension of writing, case studies such as the present one can be insightful from the point of view of understanding the context of research knowledge production and academic writing activity from an emic perspective. The process of writing and learning to write in an academic L2 is complex and thus needs to be analyzed from multiple perspectives. Qualitative insights such as those reported in this study reveal how a small community of practice enculturates its members into disciplinary practices and how its members acquire "the content of disciplinarity" (Prior, 2008). A focus on "discipline" enables us to identify relevant aspects such as the role of cooperation and the values attached to collaborative work in planning, designing, preparing and, finally, drafting and submitting a text for publication. The link between research and writing and the view of publication at the end of an enquiry-based collaborative process emerges as an additional factor in understanding writing practices and approaches to writing in ERPP. Further, it suggests that the challenges of publishing in an additional language are just part of such processes within the community of practice. As stressed in this study and in previous studies (Belcher & Connor, 2001; Berkenkotter & Hukin, 1995; Corcoran, 2015; Guo, 2012; Paltridge, 2008; Salö & Hanell, 2014; Swales, 1998), spaces of disciplinary enculturation become appropriate loci to investigate literacy development and writing practices—hence the metaphor of "ecosystem". Enquiry into ecosystems enables us to capture the particular ways in which each surrounding environment shapes both knowledge construction and influences the researchers' decisions that make knowledge beget text.

Closely interrelating with the socio-historic, socially-situated dimensions, the cognitive and linguistic dimensions of writing enable us to map out the stages of literacy development towards advanced literacy. The validity of an individual researcher's narrative might be critiqued and, in a way, contested if it is taken as a subjective and, therefore, non-generalizable view of literacy development. Notwithstanding the obvious limitations of any case study, we would argue here that personal narratives of what it takes to attain and master academic literacy skills, the efforts involved and the challenges faced in this process provide valuable information on strategies, resources and approaches to writing that help this researcher (and may likewise help other researchers) to overcome language-related challenges when writing for publication.

This case study also sought to enquire into the cognitive dimension of learning to write and raise critical discussion on key constructs of SLA research—"incidental learning", "consciousness and awareness", "noticing" and "conscious attention to input" in language learning (Schmidt, 1993)—to assess their impact on writing and literacy development. The researcher's narrative illustrates the crucial role played by these constructs. Her high level of perceptiveness has turned over time into a very systematic approach to the process of carrying out research and preparing for writing, always seeking to continuously improve.

Her strategies to prepare for writing and her approach to the writing process point at processes of incidental learning and foreground the connections between reading and writing (Belcher & Hirvela, 2001). She reported extensive exposure to linguistic input. She read texts (genres) from the target journal in preparation for writing and paid conscious attention to their recurring rhetorical and linguistic features. Rich input from English-medium texts over time and, on the other hand, lack of reading and writing in her academic L1 could explain why she reported that academic Romanian is challenging while academic English comes naturally.

Given that genres are "typified responses" to recurrent communicative situations within disciplinary communities (Miller, 1984; Swales, 2004), it seems feasible to deduce that the insiders of the community gradually become acquainted with the conventions of recurring genres. From the researcher's narrative, the journal article was the prevailing text-type for communicating research. Exposure to this genre through reading might have contributed to her increasing familiarity with the relatively stabilized linguistic and rhetorical features of this genre. Because major and minor academic genres (Swales, 2004) are highly typified, it can be surmised that the researcher gradually became confident in handling the contents of the discipline and familiarized with the social interaction practices of her community.

In addition to increased awareness of generic typification through extensive reading, self-reflection on the quality of her own writing (e.g. through the close analysis of reviewers' reports) can account for advanced literacy in English. According to the data, formal instruction on the pragmatic nuances of academic English has helped her become more aware of those features and improve the metacognitive skill of "noticing the gap" (Truscott, 1998). Through consciousness and attention to form, she became able to identify areas of improvement in her own writing such as discourse pragmatics and style. Her confident use of metalanguage in her responses (with references to "rhetorical moves", "literature review", "genre differences", "publishing requirements", "language nuances', "the academic register" managing information flow between and within paragraphs) suggests that formal instruction guided and made more comprehensive her own approach to writing. In the interview data, and re-iterated also in the follow-up discussion, she mentioned that the formal instruction received through the master's programme has contributed to her paying greater attention, deliberately and purposefully, to the functionality of the recurring linguistic resources in the academic written discourse.

Gentil (2011) convincingly argues that genre expertise, even if it is dependent on the knowledge of a language system, may be exploited in an L2 and thus serves as a scaffold in L2 text-composing processes. Although the researcher involved in the present study did not explicitly mention that genre knowledge in her L1 influenced her performance in composing L2 academic English texts, she tacitly acknowledged that what Gentil defines as "layered linguistic experiences of practice"—in the case of our Romanian researcher, her knowledge of genre in her academic L1 was transposable to her L2 academic English writing practices.

A critical area for further investigation would be to assess the subject's "ability to transfer, adapt, and innovate with genres cross-linguistically" (Gentil, 2011, p. 10). In the present case study the researcher explicitly noted that she relied on her knowledge of the English rhetorical and linguistic conventions. Examining "interdiscursive connectivity", a text-composing strategy deployed by bilingual writers that involves "draw[ing] on other linguistic experiences by patching together generics from similar texts in other languages" (Salö & Hanell, 2014, p. 13), thus emerges as an important area of enquiry in future L2 academic writing research.

Finally, some reflections on independent, non-formal academic literacy learning are also worth discussing. Through the questionnaire/interview data we were able to identify some of the hurdles encountered by the Romanian researcher and the strategies she developed to draft and refine her texts. The data showed that writing for publication in high-profile journals was a demanding task, as it required the expression of certain communicative functions that highlight the value, contribution and implications of the research. As reported in other stories of L2 academic writers, the Romanian researcher found it challenging to construct arguments successfully when writing for publication. Adhering to Gentil (2011), we assume that the researcher in our case study, as an expert writer, could draw on her "whole repertoire of genres and rhetorical strategies across languages strategically" (p. 19) to write texts both in her L1 and in English as an L2. Yet this is a tentative claim that needs further exploration.

It is likely that her success as an advanced writer results from developing her own perspective about what quality of research writing means and setting high standards for her writing as a result of systematic critical analysis of her own writing and that of others. As reported earlier, she exhibited a high level of perceptiveness and was inclined to reflect and learn from all possible situations and interactions with others (colleagues, reviewers, experts in other fields, etc.). Such proactive behaviour might have contributed to her advanced academic writing skills.

Conclusions and Pedagogical Implications

Ethnographic case studies on individual subjects' accounts of academic literacy experiences can be particularly effective for gaining insights into the closely interrelated dimensions that shape L2 writing processes. This case study has sought to move towards "deep theorizing" (Lillis, 2008) and contribute a better understanding of ERPP writing processes. Case studies can be an opportunity to inform pedagogically sound means of addressing and overcoming language challenges and supporting multilingual writing development. An additional value of case study research lies in its implications for EAP instruction. We therefore turn to several pedagogical implications below.

As previously proposed (Bardi, 2015; Cheng, 2008; Pérez-Llantada, & Swales, 2017), a pedagogy offering rich linguistic input and genre-based and rhetorical consciousness-raising tasks can raise awareness of the formal (structural), discourse and pragmatic functions of recurring academic genres. Data-driven learning and analysis of texts exemplars from specialized corpora also seem an appropriate pedagogical intervention. From the case study results, other tasks that seem pedagogically appropriate are peer review tasks and tasks involving self-assessment of drafts and close analysis of journal reviewers' reports.

The data gathered in this exploratory case study did not yield sufficient evidence to ascertain the exact nature of the researcher's language challenges and gatekeeping experiences with a view to deepening into linguistic and rhetorical aspects of the researcher's textual production. The SLA literature explains that learning cannot take place without noticing. Aligning with this claim, a close analysis of journal reviewers' reports can become a useful classroom material to enhance noticing and awareness processes.

Throughout this chapter, we have sought to stress the complexity of L2 academic writing processes in relation to processes of advanced academic literacy development. At the same time, it has also been our aim to underline the complexity of academic literacy development beyond the challenges that writing in an L2 poses. As illustrated in this case study, such complexity involves aspects such as an individual's institutional, pressure to publish, her challenges of doing so in an L2, her reliance on previous experience and the deployment of various cognitive processes (e.g. analysis, enquiry and self-assessment of her own written production and writing practices).

In acknowledging the value of multilingualism in support of research writing practices, it seems reasonable to advocate an instructional approach involving materials and tasks oriented towards bi-/multiliteracy skills development, as genre knowledge in the L1 is transferable to L2 writing (Gentil, 2011). Compilation of multilingual corpora of relevant genres in academia—e.g. articles and abstracts—can become a productive source for materials designers. As Cheng (2008) demonstrates, analyzing genre exemplars proves a useful pedagogical task to prepare for writing. These corpora can also serve as a starting point to teach how to draw on knowledge of one academic language to communicate effectively in another language.

Using ethnographic tools for self-reflection on individual writing practices in the EAP classroom such as those applied in this case study facilitate the compilation of repertoires of strategies used by different individual researchers to overcome the challenges of publishing in an additional language. Sharing these repertoires, and sharing individual accounts on how to use them when writing, both in the EAP classroom and outside of it (e.g. with the other members of the community of practice a researcher collaborates with), can offer useful guidance for self-directed, independent lifelong learning.

Like others (Swales, 2004; Belcher, 2007; Gentil, 2011), we wish to stress that many non-native speakers of English can eventually acquire high quality academic writing skills, learn how to write publishable texts and succeed in their publication endeavours. The study reported here provides the framework of an ecosystem for examining individual subjects' trajectories of plurilingual writing development. It is hoped that, looking forward, it will encourage scholarly dialogue on theoretically-grounded innovative pedagogic approaches to assist individual subjects' academic writing/literacy needs and train them for lifelong language learning.

Acknowledgements

We wish to thank the Spanish Ministry of Economy and Competitiveness for the financial support to conduct this research under the project "Ecologies of genres, ecologies of languages: an analysis of the dynamics of local, cross-border and international scientific communication" (FFI2015-68638-R MINECO/FEDER, EU). The chapter is also an outcome of the projects "Improving Standards of Quality in Adult Language Education" (LLP-2011–1-BG1-GRU06-04962) and "Quality Assessment Training" (LLP-2013–1-BG1-GRU06-00108), funded by the European Commission.

We would also like to express our gratitude to the researcher who participated in this study, for her generous time and consideration, as she truly helped us gain a better understanding of L2 academic writing.

Note

1 *Procedia* is Elsevier's "online collection of high quality conference proceedings" in different subject categories. "Peer-review is under responsibility of the scientific committee of the conference" (https://www.elsevier.com/books-and-journals/procedia).

References

Bardi, M. (2015). Learning the practice of scholarly publication in English—A Romanian perspective. *English for Specific Purposes, 37*, 98–111.

Bardi, M., & Muresan, L.-M. (2014). Changing research writing practices in Romania: Perceptions and attitudes. In K. Bennett (Ed.). *The semiperiphery of academic writing. Discourses, communities and practices* (pp. 121–147). Basingstoke, UK: Palgrave.

Barton, D. (2007). *Literacy. An introduction to the ecology of written language.* London: Blackwell.

Belcher, D. (2007). Seeking acceptance in an English-only research world. *Journal of Second Language Writing, 16*(1), 1–22.

Belcher, D., & Connor, U. (Eds.) (2001). *Reflections on multiliterate lives.* Clevedon, UK: Multilingual Matters.

Belcher, D., & Hirvela, A. (2001). *Linking literacies. L2 reading writing connections.* Ann Arbor, MI: Michigan University Press.

Bennett, K. (Ed.) (2014). *The semiperiphery of academic writing. Discourses, communities and practices.* Basingstoke, UK: Palgrave.

Berkenkotter, C., & Huckin, T. N. (1995). *Genre knowledge in disciplinary communication. Cognition/Culture/Power.* Hillsdale, NJ: Lawrence Erlbaum.

Buckingham, L. (2014). Building a career in English: Users of English as an additional language in academia in the Arabian Gulf. *TESOL Quarterly*, *48*, 6–33.
Canagarajah, S. (2002). *A geopolitics of academic writing*. Pittsburgh, PA: University of Pittsburgh Press.
Cheng, A. (2008). Analyzing genre exemplars in preparation for writing: The case of an L2 graduate student in the ESP genre-based instructional framework of academic literacy. *Applied Linguistics*, *29*(1), 50–71.
Chiu, Y. (2001). Exploring non-native science scholars' perspectives of writing for publication in English. *The Asia-Pacific Education Researcher*, *20*(3), 469–476.
Corcoran, J. (2015). English as the international language of science: A case study of Mexican scientists' writing for publication. Unpublished dissertation, University of Toronto. https://tspace.library.utoronto.ca/bitstream/1807/70842/1/Corcoran_James_201511_PhD_thesis.pdf (accessed 10/12/2017)
Creswell, J. W. (2013). *Qualitative inquiry and research design. Choosing among five approaches*. Los Angeles, London: Sage.
Dressen-Hammouda, D. (2014). Measuring the voice of disciplinarity in scientific writing: A longitudinal exploration of experienced writers in geology. *English for Specific Purposes*, *34*(2), 14–25.
Duszak, A. (1994). Academic discourse and intellectual styles. *Journal of Pragmatics*, *21*, 291–313.
Englander, K. (2010). But it would be good in Spanish: An analysis of awkward scholarly writing in English by L2 writers. In S. Santos (Ed.). *EFL writing in Mexican universities: Research and experience* (pp. 55–71). Nayarit, Mexico: Universidad Autónoma de Nayarit.
Englander, K. (2014). *Writing and publishing science research papers in English. A global perspective*. New York: Springer.
Englander, K., & Uzuner-Smith, S. (2013). The role of policy in constructing the peripheral scientist in the era of globalization. *Language Policy*, *12*, 231–250.
Ferguson, G. R., Pérez-Llantada, C., & Plo, R. (2011). English as an international language of scientific publication: A study of attitudes. *World Englishes*, *29*(3), 41–59.
Flowerdew, J. (2009). Goffman's stigma and EAL writers: The author responds to Casanave. *Journal of English for Academic Purposes*, *8*(1), 69–72.
Gentil, G. (2011). A biliteracy agenda for genre research. *Journal of Second Language Writing*, *20*(1), 6–23.
Gentil, G., & Séror, J. (2014). Canada has two official languages—Or does it? Case studies of Canadian scholars' language choices and practices in disseminating knowledge. *Journal of English for Academic Purposes*, *13*, 17–30.
Guo, Y. H. (2012). The manuscript drafting journey of a NNE scientific writer: An ethnographic case study. *Sino-US English Teaching*, *9*(10), 1580–1589.
Hanauer, D. I., & Englander, K. (2011). Quantifying the burden of writing research articles in a second language: Data from Mexican scientists. *Written Communication*, *28*(4), 403–416.
Johns, A. M. (1997). *Text, role and context. Developing academic literacies*. Cambridge: Cambridge University Press.
Kourilova, M. (1998). Communicative characteristics of reviews of scientific papers written by non-native users of English. *Endocrine Regulations*, *32*, 107–114.
Lillis, T. (2008). Ethnography as method, methodology, and "deep theorizing": Closing the gap between text and context in academic writing research. *Written Communication*, *25*(3), 353–388.

Lillis, T., & Curry, M. J. (2010). *Academic writing in a global context: The politics and practices of publishing in English*. New York: Routledge.

Liu, J. (2004). Co-constructing academic discourse from the periphery: Chinese applied linguists' centripetal participation in scholarly publication. *Asian Journal of English Language Teaching, 14*, 1–22.

Loi, C. K., & Evans, M. S. (2010). Cultural differences in the organization of research article introductions from the field of educational psychology: English and Chinese. *Journal of Pragmatics, 42*, 2814–2825.

Mauranen, A., Pérez-Llantada, C., & Swales, J. M. (2010). Academic Englishes: A standardised knowledge? In A. Kirkpatrick (Ed.). *The World Englishes handbook* (pp. 634–652). London, New York: Routledge.

Miller, C. R. (1984). Genre as social action. *Quarterly Journal of Speech, 70*, 151–167.

Muresan, L.-M., & Nicolae, M. (2015). Addressing the challenge of publishing internationally in a non-Anglophone academic context. Romania—a case in point. In R. Plo Alastrué & C. Pérez-Llantada (Eds.). *English as a scientific and research language. Debates and discourses. English in Europe* (pp. 281–310). Berlin: De Gruyter Mouton.

Muresan, L.-M., & Pérez-Llantada, C. (2014). English for research publication and dissemination in bi-/multiliterate environments: The case of Romanian academics. *Journal of English for Academic Purposes, 13*, 53–64.

Paltridge, B. (2008). Textographies and the researching and teaching of writing. *Ibérica. Journal of the European Association of Languages for Specific Purposes, 15*, 9–24.

Pérez-Llantada, C., & Swales, J. M. (2017). English for Academic Purposes. In E. Hinkel (Ed.). *Handbook of research in second language teaching and learning III* (pp. 42–55). New York, London: Routledge.

Phothongsunan, S. (2016). Thai university academics' challenges of writing for publication in English. *Theory and Practice in Language Studies, 6*(4), 681–685.

Prior, P. A. (2009). *Writing/Disciplinarity. A sociohistoric account of literate activity in the academy*. New York, London: Routledge.

Prior, P., & Bilbro, R. (2012). Academic enculturation: Developing literate practices and disciplinary identities. In M. Castelló & C. Donahue (Eds.). *University writing: Selves and texts in academic societies* (pp. 19–31). Bingley, UK: Emerald.

Rozycki, W., & Johnson, N. H. (2013). Non-canonical grammar in best paper award winners in engineering. *English for Specific Purposes, 32*(3), 157–169.

Salö, L., & Hanell, L. (2014). Performance of unprecedented genres. Interdiscursivity in the writing practices of a Swedish researcher. *Language and Communication, 37*, 12–28.

Schmidt, R. (1993). Awareness and second language acquisition. *Annual Review of Applied Linguistics, 13*, 206–226.

Swales, J. M. (1998). *Other floors, other voices. A textography of a small university building*. Mahway, NJ: Lawrence Erlbaum.

Swales, J. M. (2004). *Research genres. Explorations and applications*. Cambridge: Cambridge University Press.

Truscott, J. (1998). Noticing in second language acquisition: A critical review. *SLA Research, 14*, 103–135.

Uzuner, S. (2008). Multilingual scholars' participation in core/global academic communities: A literature review. *Journal of English Academic Purposes, 7*, 250–263.

Appendix 7.1

SELF-REFLECTIVE QUESTIONNAIRE

Dear colleague,

Here are some questions for self-reflection, in preparation/as inspiration for tomorrow's round-table (the 3rd suggested topic, related to your research writing). After a quick look at the questions, decide for yourself in which order you want to start reflecting on the various aspects.

- How does your experience of writing in your L1 (Romanian) compare with your experience of writing in L2 or L3 (English, French? another language?) What is your experience in L1 academic writing (how many years and what genres)?
- What is your experience in L2 academic writing? How many years and what types of texts (genres)?
- How do you select the topics for writing papers for publication?
- Is your research targeted at different projects?
- What text types (genres) do you have to produce?
- Who are the target audiences of your research?
- How has writing changed over time and what factors/reasons have contributed to that change?
- What are your reasons for publication: staying local, going global? (The importance of the local in scholars' writing lives.)
- How would you qualify 'good research writing'?
- Why do you like the texts selected? In what ways do they stand out from the other texts you have published?
- Do you use the following resources for text production? (e.g. academic research networks, local-transnational network activity in academic text production) Why?/Why not?

SEMI-STRUCTURED INTERVIEW PROTOCOL

- Do you publish regularly in journals or proceedings? What language do/will you use for publication?
- How do you perceive the pressure to publish? How does it influence the quality of your writing in terms of . . .
    - efforts put into writing?
    - resources used?
    - duration of the writing process?
- What do you think about publishing your work in English? Is it easy or hard to write in a second language?

- If any, what problems do you have when trying to publish your work in English? How do you approach them and how do you deal with them?
- Do you need any kind of support to publish your research successfully?
- Overall, what does it take for you to write for publication in English?
- What's your contribution in journal articles and your contribution to the writing/composing process?
- How do you distribute the writing task with your co-authors?
- If any, where do difficulties lie?
- What copying strategies did you use? And what strategies do you use now?
- Do you draw on your knowledge of different genres to write these generic text types in different academic languages?
- Can you explain in which ways this knowledge or other types/sources of knowledge help you in the writing process?
- How similar/different are each of these linguistic features to/from the realizations in English L1?
- Did you make use of technologies to cope with the difficulties? Do you make use of them now? Which ones?
- Finally, are there any other comments or observations that you may wish to add?

8

ENGLISH OR SPANISH FOR RESEARCH PUBLICATION PURPOSES?

Reflections on a Critical Pragmatic Pedagogy

Sally Burgess
UNIVERSIDAD DE LA LAGUNA

Pedro Martín
UNIVERSIDAD DE LA LAGUNA

Diana Balasanyan
YEREVAN HAYBUSAK UNIVERSITY

Introduction

It has long been essential for academics working in the natural and social sciences to publish in English for research recognition and professional promotion. More recently, English as a vehicle for research publication has begun to make inroads into arts and humanities disciplines (Flowerdew & Li, 2009). In Spain, scholars in these fields, like their colleagues elsewhere in the world (see Nederhoff, 2006 for a review), are now experiencing increasing pressure to publish in English (Burgess, 2014, 2017; Burgess, Gea-Valor, Moreno, & Rey-Rocha, 2014). In the light of the social and political inequalities that both arise as a result of and reproduce the dominance of English as a language of research publication, it is important to explore approaches to the teaching of research publications skills which move beyond a simple acceptance of this situation. Contexts where the process of encroachment of English is on-going and still incomplete, as is the case of research publication in the humanities, are important sites for such exploration. These "niche disciplines" (Ammon, 2006) where publication in languages other than English is still a viable option and, arguably, a principled choice, provide a potentially more appropriate arena for contestation than the hard or social sciences, where English as a language of research publication is more firmly established (Nederhoff, 2006). In a course intended to introduce arts and humanities PhD students to writing for research publication purposes—designed and implemented at the University of La Laguna—we asked participants to examine the viability of publishing in Spanish, thus contesting the increasing pressures to publish in English.

In this chapter, we reflect upon and discuss the two occasions on which we have taught this credit-bearing course to date. In our reflection and discussion, we explain how we sought to acknowledge and address issues surrounding the relative status of Spanish and English as languages of research publication and presentation, while seeking to develop multilingual publication skills through a critical-pragmatic approach (Corcoran & Englander, 2016; Harwood & Hadley, 2004). Drawing on our own observations and those of course participants, we discuss the efficacy and appropriateness of such an approach in the training of bilingual novice writers working in the arts and humanities.

In the first part of this chapter, we examine the ways in which Spanish and English are currently positioned as languages of research communication in Spain. We then briefly discuss the means by which Spanish scholars acquire research publication skills in the two languages. We also explain the context in which we designed and taught the course, particularly the recent reforms of doctoral education at Spanish universities and the specific ways in which these reforms have been implemented in our university, a large provincial university in the Canary Islands. The next section provides a descriptive account of the two instances of the course we offered. This is followed by a review of critical pragmatic approaches to the teaching of research publication skills and a discussion of how our course fits within the critical pragmatic pedagogy paradigm. We conclude by reflecting upon the appropriateness and efficacy of the methodology we adopted and consider how future courses might be adapted to graduate students' changing needs and desires in an era of increasing English language hegemony.

Spanish and English as Languages of Research Publication in Spain

The increasing pressure on Spanish academics to publish in English comes from various quarters, not least the Spanish research evaluation agencies which have, since the 1980s, adopted a policy of rewarding publication in ISI journals (Burgess, 2017). By choosing to measure research productivity and quality in terms of impact, the agencies have prompted many Spanish researchers to publish largely or exclusively in English. It is well known that papers published in English attract a wider readership and accrue more citations (see, for example, Ramos-Torre & Callejo-Gallego, 2013; Whitehand, 2005). Knowing that one's work is being read and potentially cited can, for some, be a powerful incentive for writing in English rather than Spanish (Lorés-Sanz, Mur-Dueñas, Rey-Rocha, & Moreno, 2014). As a result, Spanish is experiencing a decline as a language of research publication.

This decline has not occurred at the same rate across disciplines. The natural sciences were the first to experience the shift to a strong preference for publication in English, followed by the medical sciences, with the social sciences following suit not long after. Today, as González-Alcaide, Valderrama-Zurián, and Aleixandre-Benavent (2012) note, only the clinical medical sciences, the applied social sciences and the humanities remain "holdouts", where there is still robust publication in Spanish and where convincing arguments remain for continuing to publish in that language. Among these arguments are the special relevance of the research reported to local communities of practitioners who may not read English (López Navarro, Moreno, Quintanilla, & Rey-Rocha, 2015) and the difficulty of expressing complex argumentation elegantly in an additional language (Burgess, 2017; Hanauer & Englander, 2011; Pérez-Llantada, Plo, & Ferguson, 2011).

Attitudes to publication in English and Spanish vary across disciplines as well. Whereas among researchers in the natural and medical sciences there is generally an attitude of "qualified acceptance" (Pérez-Llantada, et al., 2011 p. 22) of what is regarded as a "fait accompli", in the humanities there is evidence of some resentment and resistance (Burgess, 2017; Burgess, et al., 2014). Even where there is such resentment, there is a reluctant recognition that acquiring proficiency in English for Research Publication Purposes (ERPP) and writing in English has many advantages (Bocanegra-Valle, 2014; Burgess, 2017; Muresan & Pérez-Llantada, 2014).

ERPP at the University of La Laguna: The Doctoral Programme

Currently, doctoral programmes throughout Spain follow the same basic format: students are required to attend a research seminar related to their thesis topic as well as research methodology courses. They are also generally required to produce a research publication over the course of the four years before submission of the thesis and, in some cases, present a paper at a conference. English is generally included as one of the languages in some or all of the components, though for the most part there is no specific instruction in English or in any other language of research communication, the assumption being that doctoral students already possess the necessary research communication and publication skills or will be able to acquire these skills through the other course components.

The University of La Laguna is somewhat unusual in that it has in the past—and does still—offer some training in ERPP and, more recently, Spanish for Research Publication Purposes (SRPP), through its doctoral programmes. After a series of workshops run by Margaret Cargill in our department in 2005 and 2006 drawing on her work with Patrick O'Connor (Cargill & O'Connor, 2006; Cargill & O'Connor, 2013), members of our research group offered similar workshops to staff and postgraduate students in the Psychology Faculty. Over several years, we also offered a doctoral course in ERPP in Medicine (see Burgess & Cargill, 2013 for an account of this course). The underlying assumption of the workshops and doctoral course was that the attitude of participants was likely to be one of "pragmatic resignation" (Pérez-Llantada, et al., 2011, p. 9) in the face of pressures to write in English. In fact, scholars often responded to post-course questionnaires by commenting that these workshops were among the most useful training experiences they had had in their university careers. Participants responded particularly positively to the genre-based methodology and the fact that the corpus used was made up of papers they themselves had selected as good examples of publications in their field.

When the opportunity arose to offer a similar course as part of the doctoral programme in the humanities, we began our planning for the course by reflecting on our experience as members of the ENEIDA (Spanish Team for Intercultural Studies on Academic Discourse) research group. The initial stage of the group's project involved an online survey aimed at identifying the scientific fields where the need for training in writing for research publication purposes was greatest. One of our findings was that humanities scholars, unlike their colleagues in other disciplines, did not always see publication in English as a desirable goal, preferring to publish in Spanish or in other languages relevant to their research (Burgess, et al., 2014). We also brought to bear on our preparation for the doctoral course our understanding of the geopolitics of English as a language of research publication and presentation and the work of Bennett (2007) on "epistemicide". This led us to the conclusion that if ERPP courses were to be run for humanities doctoral students, they should of necessity be couched in terms of a critical or a critical pragmatic approach in which the choice of language of publication would be discussed in the context of the pressures on scholars to publish in English.

The course we designed and taught was part of a new doctoral programme in the arts and humanities implemented at the University of La Laguna in the academic year 2014–15. The programme represented a considerable departure from earlier programmes and was intended to achieve greater uniformity in doctoral studies in Spain and to bring these into line with other universities in the European Higher Education Area (see Ramírez, 2016). The programme seeks to develop six basic competencies including the ability to design a research project, choose appropriate tools for analysis of results and the ability to critically appraise findings. The fifth competence is expressed as "the capacity to communicate with the academic and scientific community and with society in general about specific fields of knowledge in the manner and languages commonly used in the international scientific community" (Real Decreto 99/2011, art. 5.1). It was this competency our course sought to address through a critical-pragmatic approach.

Researching and Delivering a Humanities Doctoral Course in Research Writing for Publication

Action Research

An introductory email was sent out to doctoral students two weeks before we met for the first time explaining that during the course we would be analyzing the most salient textual features of various research genres, among them research articles from the arts and humanities. To this end, we asked students to send us one or two examples of articles in English from the references they had used when writing for their thesis proposals. These articles formed a corpus through which we collectively and individually analyzed the genre-specific structures presented in Swales (1990) and (2004), Weissberg and Buker (1990) and MacDonald (1994), one of relatively few studies of research writing in the humanities. Though such a corpus-based genre analysis can be considered a pragmatic pedagogical approach, we began the course with a debate on whether the focus should be on English only or partially or entirely on Spanish as a language of research publication, employing a critical stance. We provided students with information drawn from our own and others' studies of research genres and of Spanish scholars' motivations for writing in the two languages (e.g. Moreno, Burgess, Sachdev, López-Navarro, & Rey-Rocha, 2013; and López-Navarro, Moreno, Quintanilla, & Rey-Rocha, 2015). We made explicit to them the ways in which the geopolitics of academic publishing privileges English and offered reasons why they might choose to resist this privileging. We returned to these issues at various points throughout the course, asking students to critically consider the advantages and possible consequences of choosing to publish in one language or the other. We were wary of producing a design that might be labelled as an instance of "vulgar pragmatism" (Cherryholmes cited in Pennycook, 1997), an approach which sidesteps critical evaluation and appraisal of norms, beliefs and ideologies in order to meet practical requirements. We were also conscious of our privileged position as either first language users of English or highly competent multilingual users of English and fully aware of the fact that this potentially gave us far greater access to and prominence in the communities of practice we might seek to address than that of our monolingual Spanish-speaking colleagues. We did not want our course to run the risk of "reinforcing norms, beliefs and ideologies that maintain inequitable social and cultural relations" (Pennycook, 1997, p. 256). By making explicit to participants that the course itself was an instance of action research, we attempted to challenge an asymmetrical power relationship with participants which Barthomae (cited in Harwood & Hadley, 2004) characterises as expert informing neophyte. We came far closer to Cadman's (2017) position, which she terms, drawing on her own earlier work, "dialogic pedagogy" (see Cadman, 2005). There were, however, many elements in the course that cannot be regarded as instantiating a critical pedagogy in any of the ways Pennycook (1997 and 2001) or Benesch (1996 and 2001) have described. Taking up an extreme critical approach would have, in our estimation, been unduly disconcerting and unhelpful to our colleagues and their students. We needed to find an approach which fell somewhere between these extreme critical and vulgar pragmatic positions.

A Critical Pragmatic Approach

The middle ground we sought was provided by Harwood and Hadley's (2004) paper. They problematize the pragmatic approach taken in UK university pre-sessional and in-sessional EAP courses, where there is an attempt to equip students to meet the often unrealistic expectations of supervisors and lecturers. This they argue leads to a situation where the students learn to pretend they hold the privileged position of fully-fledged members of the discourse community without having had the experience of "discovery and invention" (Bartholomae cited in Harwood and Hadley 2004, p. 359). Harwood and Hadley argue, as we do, that a refusal to teach the discourse norms of Anglo-American English for academic purposes (EAP) runs the risk of further limiting these students' rights to participation in the conversations of their disciplines by means of publication in Anglophone journals. Ultimately, they define a critical pragmatic approach as one that combines "the restive questioning of Critical EAP" (p. 366) while still offering students access to the dominant discourse norms through a corpus-based pedagogy. They suggest that by means of such a pedagogy it is possible to arrive at a check list of conventions that are inviolable and those that might be more readily challenged or flouted.

Our approach was also informed by Corcoran and Englander (2016) who, working in a non-Anglophone context, suggest the efficacy of a programme that focuses on effectively navigating the manuscript submission and review process (Cargill & O'Connor, 2006, 2013). Importantly, their analysis of such a genre-based approach resulted in the espousal of a more critical approach that goes further than an avoidance of normativity to problematize and discuss questions of language choice, systems of evaluation, and inequity in a market of knowledge production that prejudices those using English as an additional language. Their critical pragmatic pedagogical approach suggests providing their course participants with not only the linguistic skills and genre awareness necessary for publishing success in such a market but also the critical awareness to negotiate their evolving voices as plurilingual scholars using English as an additional language in an asymmetrical market of scientific knowledge production.

By asking our students to reflect upon the geopolitics of global publishing in relation to their first language and English as an additional language and to decide whether to, as Benesch puts it, "carry out demands or challenge them" (2001, p. 64), we believe we are justified in regarding our course as an instance of a critical pragmatic approach. In common with Cadman (2017), we also sought to introduce students to elements of research methodology by explicitly stating that the course itself was an instance of action research through which we would be critically reflecting upon our approach, design and procedures with a view to developing future courses.

The course, taught by two members of staff and a research student, all actively involved in studies of research writing, was conducted through four three-hour seminars over a two-week period. Our stated objectives were the following:

TABLE 8.1 Classification of course activities and objectives

Course session and activity/task	Approach	Objective(s) addressed
Debate on language to be used in the course.	Critical	2, 3, 6
Presentation of our research backgrounds in cross-disciplinary studies of academic discourse and Spanish scholars' experiences of research publication.	Critical	2, 6
Presentation of theoretical underpinnings of research we had previously conducted on ERPP and SRPP.	Critical pragmatic	2, 6
Students decide which language they would use to write key research genres.	Critical pragmatic	1, 2, 4
Discussion of ENEIDA project findings on Spanish scholars' reasons for publishing in Spanish or English.	Critical pragmatic	2, 6
Discussion of how Spanish scholars acquire expertise in research writing based on the ENEIDA questionnaire.	Critical pragmatic	2, 6
Students use schemata for structure of research articles to analyse their chosen examples.	Pragmatic	1, 3, 4, 6
Students prepare a short statement on an area of controversy or debate in relation to their thesis topic.	Pragmatic	1, 3, 4
Discussion of students' statements and using online tools to check spelling and grammar.	Pragmatic	1, 2, 5
Students put key research genres in order of priority in terms of their short- and long-term goals.	Pragmatic	1, 3
Introduction to Manchester Academic Phrasebank (Morley, 2014). Discussion of its relevance to writing in the Humanities.	Pragmatic	1, 3, 4, 5
Introduction to posters as a mode of presentation.	Pragmatic	1, 3
Students analyze the generic structure of humanities posters.	Pragmatic	1, 3

Introduction to abstracts and their generic structure.	Pragmatic	1, 3, 4
Students analyze example abstracts, suggesting modifications and improvements.	Critical pragmatic	1, 3, 4, 6
Analysis of a typical conference "call for papers".	Pragmatic	1, 3, 4
Students locate conference calls for papers in their research area.	Pragmatic	1, 3, 4
Students prepare an abstract for one of the calls they have identified as of interest.	Pragmatic	1, 3, 4
Students display their draft abstracts and suggest modifications and improvements.	Pragmatic	1, 3, 4
Plenary presentation on manuscript preparation and submission.	Pragmatic	1, 3
Introduction to editing and translation resources: assessing the quality of services.	Critical pragmatic	1, 5
Students prepare final version of conference abstract to send for assessment.	Pragmatic	1, 5
Introduction to lexical bundles and concordancing (see Balasanyan, 2017).	Critical pragmatic	1, 3, 4, 5, 6

1. To familiarise students with the international conventions of writing for publication and presentation in the humanities.
2. To stimulate critical reflection on the origins and consequences of pressures to choose English over Spanish as a language of research publication.
3. To introduce students to the key research genres in the humanities.
4. To introduce students to genre analysis as a tool in the development of research writing skills.
5. To introduce students to language development resources for research writing.
6. To introduce students to aspects of our action research methodology by explicitly informing them of our ongoing reflections on the course design and implementation.

Table 8.1 provides an overview of the ways in which we sought to achieve these objectives through course activities and tasks. In the middle column of the table we identify whether we regard each of these activities and tasks as realizing a critical, critical pragmatic or pragmatic approach.

Reflections on the Appropriateness and Efficacy of Our Critical-Pragmatic Approach

A genre-based pedagogy and the use of a small but authentic corpus of research articles, posters and conference calls for papers were elements of the course that participants perceived to be useful and appropriate. Their response to the follow-up workshop on concordancing and lexical bundles based on Balasanyan (2017) was also very positive. None of these elements involves a critical pedagogy though they do go beyond the presentation of stylistic norms or non-discipline specific guidance on how to produce ERPP. By drawing on a corpus effectively selected by the students themselves and by providing them with tools to continue to examine instantiations of research process genres in their disciplines, we encouraged a critical rather than a normative stance in which genre is seen as dynamic and as social action (Miller, 2015). Further, we invited discussion of the tensions surrounding choice of language of publication and gave them access to our research methods and instruments and to our findings on professional researchers working in Spanish and English. In this way, we sought to present ourselves as both language and research professionals, challenging the notion that these two activities should be regarded as discrete (see Cadman, 2017).

What we did not do, and what we now consider might have produced a less unilateral presentation of our critical stance on the geo-politics of global publishing, was to draw on the students' backgrounds in post-structuralist, feminist and post-colonial studies. We might well have included among the papers in our corpus writing those that employ critical theoretical positions and critical ERPP, for example Pérez-Bustos (2017) as well as examples of transgressive academic writing that deliberately flouts normative or dominant conventions (see Swales, 2017 for some examples).

Unlike Corcoran and Englander (2016), and indeed Harwood and Hadley (2004), our course involved little or no "language work" at the sentence level in the actual sessions, though we did offer written feedback on the two short pieces of written work the students submitted. We provided information on authors' editing services, particularly the highly professional work carried out by colleagues in the Mediterranean Editors and Translators group (see Matarese, 2016 for an account of this work). Further, we did not seek to problematize the relationships between L1 English user editors or indeed to question the role of inner circle (Kachru, 1985) users of English as a norm-determining group. In the workshop on lexical bundles we uncritically compared L2 user frequencies of bundles with L1 user frequencies assuming rightly that the participants would share with us the view that solving the "puzzles of native-like selection and fluency" (Pawley & Syder, 1983) was a desirable goal. Finally, we did not introduce participants to the notion of English as an academic lingua franca (Mauranen, Hynninen, & Ranta, 2010), use of codemeshing in research writing (Canagarajah, 2011), or discuss ways in which English, even in high stakes publications, can be and is being "pluralized" (Heng Hartse & Kubota, 2014).

It would certainly be possible to bring all these critical considerations to bear on the design of future editions of the course. What remains an open question—for us and for others offering such courses outside Anglophone contexts—is whether students would in fact welcome a more explicitly critical stance. On the two occasions we have offered the course so far participants were interested in what we had to say about questions of equity and social justice in relation to languages of research publication and presentation; however of greater concern to them was their immediate need to learn as much as they could about the accepted or normative conventions of ERPP and to acquire the necessary skills to meet these conventions. Surprisingly, this pragmatic focus was shared even by those students working in fields such as Spanish literature. We contend, nevertheless, that it is our responsibility to raise students' awareness of the injustices of current research publishing practices in relation to the status of languages other than English, particularly major world languages like Spanish. By drawing attention to these issues of hegemony and resulting inequity we are positioning scholars to make educated decisions about whether or not it is viable to challenge particular conventions of language choice and use at various points in their academic careers. We believe that by informing our students and raising their critical awareness while still sharing our expertise on ERPP we are best serving their interests in a context in which they are expected to publish internationally before defending their theses and afterwards. It is essential, at the same time, to see these interests and concerns as subject to shifting tensions that are themselves responses to changes in the conditions of "intellectual workers" (Connell, 2006; Connell & Wood, 2002).

Ultimately, in each instance of a course such as ours the precise balance to be struck between the critical and the pragmatic should be a response to these tensions and should be negotiated with participants in the lead-up to and in the initial session of the course rather than established *a priori*. The needs and desires of a given cohort of students may be very different from those of their colleagues or predecessors. A willingness to include participants in the decision-making around course design is, in our view, a core component of a critical pragmatic approach.

References

Ammon, U. (2006). Language planning for international scientific communication: An overview of questions and potential solutions. *Current Issues in Language Planning, 7*(1), 1–30.

Balasanyan, D. (2017). *The acquisition of lexical bundles in English for Academic Purposes: A multidisciplinary study of novice authors*. Unpublished Doctoral thesis: Universidad de La Laguna.

Benesch, S. (1996). Needs analysis and curriculum development in EAP: An example of a critical approach. *TESOL Quarterly, 30*(4), 723–738.

Benesch, S. (2001). *Critical English for academic purposes: Theory, politics, and practice*. London: Lawrence Erlbaum Associates.

Bennett, K. (2007). Epistemicide! The tale of a predatory discourse. *The Translator, 13*(2), 151–169.

Bennett, K. (2011). *Academic writing in Portugal: Discourses in conflict*. Coimbra, Portugal: Imprensa da Universidade de Coimbra/Coimbra University Press.

Bocanegra-Valle, A. (2014). 'English is my default academic language': Voices from LSP scholars publishing in a multilingual journal. *Journal of English for Academic Purposes, 13*, 65–77.

Burgess, S. (2014). Centre-periphery relations in the Spanish context: Temporal and cross-disciplinary variation. In K. Bennett (Ed.). *The Semiperiphery of academic writing: Discourses, communities and practices*, (pp. 93–105). London: Palgrave MacMillan.

Burgess, S. (2017). Accept or contest: A life-history study of humanities scholars' responses to research evaluation policies in Spain. In M. Cargill and S. Burgess (Eds.). *Publishing research in English as an additional language: Practices, pathways and potentials* (pp.13–32). Adelaide, Australia: Adelaide University Press.

Burgess, S., & Cargill, M. (2013). Using genre analysis and corpus linguistics to teach research article writing. In V. Matarese (Ed.). *Supporting research writing: Roles and challenges in multilingual settings* (pp. 55–71). Oxford: Chandos Publishing.

Burgess, S., Gea-Valor, M. L., Moreno, A. I., & Rey-Rocha, J. (2014). Affordances and constraints on research publication: A comparative study of the language choices of Spanish historians and psychologists. *Journal of English for Academic Purposes, 14*, 72–83.

Cadman, K. (2005). Towards a 'pedagogy of connection' in critical research education: A REAL story. *Journal of English for Academic Purposes, 4*(4), 353–367.

Cadman, K. (2017). Introducing research rigour in the social sciences. In M. Cargill & S. Burgess (Eds.). *Publishing research in English as an Additional Language: Practices, pathways and potentials* (pp. 33–54). Adelaide, Australia: Adelaide University Press.

Canagarajah, S. (2011). Codemeshing in academic writing: Identifying teachable strategies of translanguaging. *The Modern Language Journal, 95*(3), 401–417.

Cargill, M., & O'Connor, P. (2006). Developing Chinese scientists' skills for publishing in English: Evaluating collaborating-colleague workshops based on genre analysis. *Journal of English for Academic Purposes, 5*, 207–221.

Cargill, M., & O'Connor, P. (2013). *Writing scientific research articles: Strategy and steps* (2nd Ed.). Oxford: Wiley-Blackwell.

Connell, R. W. (2006). Core activity: Reflexive intellectual workers and cultural crisis. *Journal of Sociology, 42*(1), 5–23.

Connell, R. W., & Wood, J. (2002). Globalization and scientific labour: Patterns in a life history study of intellectual workers in the periphery. *Journal of Sociology*, *38*(2), 167–190.

Corcoran, J., & Englander, K. (2016). A proposal for critical-pragmatic pedagogical approaches to English for Research Publication Purposes. *Publications*, *4*(1), 1–10.

Flowerdew, J., & Li, Y. (2009). English or Chinese? The trade-off between local and international publication among Chinese academics in the humanities and social sciences. *Journal of Second Language Writing*, *18*(1), 1–16.

González-Alcaide, G., Valderrama-Zurián, J. C., & Aleixandre-Benavent, R. (2012). The Impact Factor in non-English-speaking countries, *Scientometrics*, *92*, 297–311.

Hanauer, D. I., & Englander, K. (2011). Quantifying the burden of writing research articles in a second language: Data from Mexican scientists. *Written Communication*, *28*(4), 403–416.

Harwood N., & Hadley, G. (2004). Demystifying institutional practices: Critical pragmatism and the teaching of academic writing. *English for Specific Purposes*, *23*, 355–377.

Heng Hartse, J., & Kubota, R. (2014). Pluralizing English? Variation in high-stakes academic texts and challenges of copyediting. *Journal of Second Language Writing*, *24*, 71–82.

Kachru, B. B. (1985) Standards, codification and sociolinguistic realism: The English language in the outer circle. In Quirk, R., & Widdowson, H. G. (Eds.). *English in the world: Teaching and learning the language and literatures* (pp. 11–31). Cambridge: Cambridge University Press for the British Council.

López-Navarro, I., Moreno, A. I., Quintanilla, M.A., & Rey-Rocha, J. (2015). Why do I publish research articles in English instead of my own language? Differences in Spanish researchers' motivations across scientific domains. *Scientometrics*, *103*, 939–976. DOI: 10.1007/s11192-015-1570-1

Lorés-Sanz, R., Mur-Dueñas, P., Rey-Rocha, J., & Moreno, A. I. (2014). Motivations and attitudes of Spanish Chemistry and Economics researchers towards publication in English-medium scientific journals. *Revista Canaria de Estudios Ingleses*, *69*, 83–100.

MacDonald, S. (1994). *Professional academic writing in the humanities and social sciences*. Carbondale, IL: SIU Press.

Matarese, V. (2016). *Editing research: The author editing approach to providing effective support to writers of research papers*. Medford, NJ: Information Today, Incorporated.

Mauranen, A., Hynninen, N., & Ranta, E. (2010). English as an academic lingua franca: The ELFA project. *English for Specific Purposes*, *29*(3), 183–190.

Miller, C. R. (2015). Genre as social action (1984), revisited 30 years later (2014). *Letras & Letras*, *31*(3), 56–72.

Moreno, A. I. (2011). English for research publication purposes and cross-cultural academic discourse analysis. In J. Ruano, M. Fernández, M. Borham, M. Díaz, S. Bautista, P. Álvarez & B. García (Eds.). *Current trends in Anglophone studies: Cultural, linguistic and literary research* (pp. 53–69). Salamanca, Spain: Ediciones.

Moreno, A. I., Burgess, S., Sachdev, I., López-Navarro, I., & Rey-Rocha, J. (2013). The ENEIDA questionnaire: Publication experiences in scientific journals in English and Spanish. http://eneida.unileon.es/eneidaquestionnaire.php (Accessed 22 December 2016)

Morley, J. (2014). *Academic phrasebank*. The University of Manchester. Retrieved December, 9, 2014 from http://www.kfs.edu.eg/pdf/2082015294739.pdf

Muresan, L. M., & Pérez-Llantada, C. (2014). English for research publication and dissemination in bi-/multiliterate environments: The case of Romanian academics. *Journal of English for Academic Purposes*, *13*, 53–64.

Nederhoff, A. J. (2006). Bibliometric monitoring of research performance in the Social Sciences and the Humanities: A review. *Scientometrics*, *66*, 81–100.

Pawley, A., & Syder, F. H. (1983). Two puzzles for linguistic theory: Nativelike selection and nativelike fluency. In J. Richards. & R. Schmidt (Eds.). *Language and communication* (pp. 191–225). London: Longman.

Pennycook, A. (1997). Vulgar pragmatism, critical pragmatism, and EAP. *English for Specific Purposes*, *16*(4), 253–269.

Pennycook, A. (2001). *Critical applied linguistics: A critical introduction*. Mahwah, NJ: Lawrence Erlbaum.

Pérez-Bustos, T. (2017). "No es sólo una cuestión de lenguaje": Lo inaudible de los estudios feministas latino-americanos en el mundo académico anglosajón. *Scientiae Studia*, *15*(1), 59–72.

Pérez-Llantada, C., Plo, R., & Ferguson, G. R. (2011). "You don't say what you know, only what you can": The perceptions and practices of senior Spanish academics regarding research dissemination in English. *English for Specific Purposes*, *30*(1), 18–30.

Ramírez, M. J. (2016). Doctoral studies in Spain: Changes to converge with Europe in the internationalisation of the doctorate. *Educational Research and Reviews*, *11*(23), 2097–2107.

Ramos-Torre, R., & Callejo-Gallego, J. (2013). 'El español en las ciencias sociales'. In J.L. García-Delgado, J.A. Alonso & and J.C. Jiménez (Eds.). *El español, lengua de comunicación científica* (pp. 29–74). Madrid: Ariel and Fundación Telefónica.

Real Decreto 99/2011, de 28 de enero, por el que se regulan las enseñanzas oficiales de doctorado. Boletín Oficial del Estado. núm. 35, de 10 de febrero de 2011, páginas 13909 a 13926.pdf/2011/BOE-A-2011-2541-consolidado.pdf [Royal Decree 99/2011 of 28 January to regulate official doctoral teaching. Official State Gazette, no. 35, 10 February 2011, pages 13909 to 13926, pdf/2011/BOE-A-2011-2541-consolidado.pdf]

Swales, J. (1990). *Genre analysis: English in academic and research settings*. Cambridge: Cambridge University Press.

Swales, J. M. (2004). *Research genres: Explorations and applications*. Cambridge: Cambridge University Press.

Swales, J. M. (2017). Standardisation and its discontents. In M. Cargill & S. Burgess (Eds.). *Publishing research in English as an additional language: Practices, pathways and potentials* (pp. 239–253). Adelaide, Australia: University of Adelaide Press.

Weissberg, R., & Buker, S. (1990). *Writing up research*. Englewood Cliffs, NJ: Prentice Hall.

Whitehand, J. W. R. (2005). The problem of Anglophone squint. *Area*, *37*(2), 228–230. doi: 10.1111/j.1475-4762.2005.00625.x

REGION 4
East Asia

9

OBSERVING AND REFLECTING IN AN ERPP "MASTER CLASS"

Learning and Thinking About Application

Yongyan Li
UNIVERSITY OF HONG KONG, CHINA

Margaret Cargill
UNIVERSITY OF ADELAIDE, AUSTRALIA

Introduction

In this chapter, we characterize emerging Chinese English for Academic Purposes (EAP) teachers' collective activity of learning to teach international publication skills, a pedagogical domain that has become known as ERPP (English for Research Publication Purposes) (Cargill & Burgess, 2008), by enlisting the theoretical lens of cultural-historical activity theory (CHAT) (Engeström, 1987, 2001; Leont'ev, 1978; Vygotsky, 1930/1978). These emerging Chinese EAP teachers are English as a Foreign Language (EFL) teachers in mainland Chinese universities who have traditionally been teaching general English to undergraduate and (post)graduate students across disciplines. Yet a growing number of these teachers are endeavoring to re-orient themselves to become EAP teachers, in the wake of the wide recognition of the need to develop students' English competencies in their academic disciplines, and no less significantly for these teachers, in view of the accompanying pressure to retain and reinforce their (traditionally marginal) institutional positions in an increasingly competitive academic environment (Cheng, 2016; Li & Ma, 2018). The change has been characterized as a paradigm shift from the traditional general English education to EAP-oriented English education in Chinese universities (Cai, 2012), a trend which started around the early 2000s (Cargill, O'Connor, & Li, 2012), and which is witnessing the rise of EAP courses at a growing number of universities (e.g., Gao & Bartlett, 2014). Current EAP implementation at Chinese universities is commonly based on a general, as opposed to a specific, approach. Beyond the widespread adoption of an English for General Academic Purposes (EGAP) model (Flowerdew, 2016), however, for the emerging Chinese EAP teachers in general, how to provide ERPP instruction, or more specifically, how to teach English academic writing to facilitate students' English publication, is a question of intense interest. Students' level of attainment in English publication, as it were, has a direct impact on when they can graduate/whether they can graduate with a degree, and what kind of a career path they could follow in the future (Cargill, O'Connor, & Li, 2012; Li, 2016).

The widely perceived need at Chinese universities to teach English academic writing for research publication purposes to students across disciplines, in particular those studying at the post(graduate) level, bears a number of similarities to what is happening elsewhere in the world. Firstly, the Chinese scenario resembles initiatives to install 'graduate writing support' on US campuses (see Simpson, Caplan, Cox, & Phillips, 2016). Secondly, the issue of training and professional development for emerging Chinese EAP teachers finds many echoes in discussions of EAP practitioners' education in British and broader European contexts, such as in terms of the knowledge base that EAP practitioners need to develop (Ding & Bruce, 2017), and the learning curves they are expected to experience when moving from general English teaching to the field of EAP (Martin, 2014). Thirdly, within the Asian context, while apparently lagging behind the EAP enterprise in locales such as Hong Kong (Hyland, 2014), the rise of EAP in mainland China is part of the broader picture of EAP provision becoming a growing necessity in Asian higher education. In this scenario EAP practitioners are found to "face various contextual struggles and difficulties" in negotiating "the implementation of locally situated academic practices in the provision of EAP" (Liyanage & Walker, 2014, p. ix).

In light of the literature as well as our long-term engagement with the Chinese context, we anticipate that the "various contextual struggles and difficulties" (Liyanage & Walker, 2014, p. ix) faced by emerging Chinese EAP practitioners will manifest at multiple levels: challenges from their lack of content knowledge in their students' disciplines (Flowerdew, 2016; Hyland, 2016; Spack, 1988), potential difficulty in engaging the participation of content specialists (Chanock, 2017; Hyland, 2014; Simpson et al., 2016), and lack of institutional structures that could facilitate systematic institution-wide planning for pedagogical support of EAP or, more specifically, academic writing (Shapiro, 2015; Sundstrom, 2016).

Alongside these challenges and difficulties, EAP teachers' training and professional development (PD) are prominent issues in China. It has been suggested that EAP professionals, with relevant training and experience in providing academic English support, are well-positioned to provide instructional support aimed at developing competencies in academic writing and international publication (Burgess & Pallant, 2013; Simpson, et al., 2016). However, a survey of recent reports (published in Chinese journals) on the teaching of English academic writing has concluded that there is an urgent need for the emerging Chinese EAP teachers to receive training to develop their expertise in the teaching and researching of English academic writing (Li & Ma, 2018).

A crucial channel of PD for the emerging Chinese EAP teachers is potentially offered by conducting classroom observation to facilitate learning from experienced peers, a time-honored practice of teacher education that can help to contextualize self-evaluation and promote reflection (Richards & Nunan, 1990). In the Chinese context where local, experienced ERPP practitioners are perhaps still in the process of being cultivated, inviting an experienced professional from the outside can be a valuable strategy to undertake. It is against this backdrop that MC, the second author of the paper, an experienced ERPP practitioner based in Australia, has, on invitation, run workshops and short courses at research institutes and universities in China regularly since 2001 (see Li, 2017, for details of MC's commitment to teaching in China). The study to be reported in this chapter concerned a set-up where a group of fledgling EAP teachers, coming from a range of universities in different parts of the country, voluntarily participated in a week-long PD program and observed MC's teaching. In a teacher development program such as this one, an issue of significance for institutions and individual teachers alike is the learning that takes place during such training, and its likely outcomes for trainees in their working contexts. Thus our investigation to be reported in this paper was guided by this research question: From the teacher participants' perspectives, what have they learned from observing MC's teaching, and what challenges do they anticipate in applying their learning to their own teaching context? Given the dearth of literature on ESP/EAP teacher education in general (Basturkmen, 2014) and on ERPP teacher education in particular, our study will provide an example of researched practice, and hopefully will inspire future researchers to tackle this under-studied area.

Theoretical Perspective

We propose that the emerging Chinese EAP teachers are engaged in a collective learning activity which can be examined in the light of cultural-historical activity theory (CHAT) (Engeström, 1987, 2001; Leont'ev, 1978; Vygotsky, 1930/1978). CHAT, or activity theory as it is commonly known, has its origin in the developments of Russian psychology in the late 1920s, when Vygotsky (1930/1978) proposed that human action is mediated by cultural artifacts. This theory of mediation was carried forward by Vygotsky's student, Leont'ev (1978), who introduced a historical perspective on activity by analyzing activity at the three levels of motive-directed activity, goal-oriented actions, and routine operations. This early iteration of activity theory was later developed by Engeström (1987, 2001), a Finnish activity theorist, as eminently represented in his triangular model of activity system analysis. In Figure 9.1, we adopt this model to characterize emerging Chinese EAP teachers' collective activity of learning to teach English academic writing to students across disciplines in the triangular structure of an activity system.

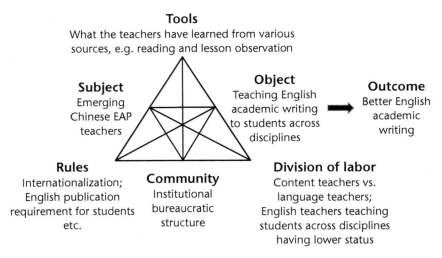

FIGURE 9.1 Emerging Chinese EAP teachers' collective learning activity of teaching English academic writing to students across disciplines

A tool-mediated and object-oriented activity system is a unit of analysis of individual or collective human behavior; it is dynamic, historically conditioned, and constantly recreated through the interactions between the nodes of the triangular structure (Engeström, 1987). In Figure 9.1, emerging Chinese EAP teachers' point of view is chosen and therefore they take the Subject position. To the new activity shown in Figure 9.1, they bring a shared motive of teaching English academic writing to students across disciplines, which is embedded in the Object. The Object points to the Outcome of students' better English academic writing. A crucial part of the Tools that mediate the activity is what the teachers have previously learned from various sources, such as from reading and lesson observation, for the Outcome of such previous learning activities would 'flow' (Engeström, 2009) and become the Tools mediating their activity of teaching English academic writing to students across disciplines.

At the bottom of the triangular structure in Figure 9.1, the Rules or the explicit or implicit norms that govern the activity in question include internationalization, an institutional mandate prevalent in Chinese universities (Yang, 2016), the English publication requirement for students (Li, 2016), and other norms. The Community or the sociocultural environment of the activity is the institutional bureaucratic structure. The traditional compartmentalization between disciplines at Chinese universities has led to a separation between content teachers and language teachers (Cargill et al., 2012), which is shown in the node of Division of Labor. Another important element in the node is that, at Chinese universities, English teachers teaching students across disciplines tend to have a lower status than their colleagues who teach English majors (Cheng, 2016).

According to CHAT, in the context of an activity system, problems or challenges can be understood in terms of contradictions and tensions within and between its nodes. Such tensions are the source of dynamism in an activity system; resolutions of the tensions would ultimately lead to qualitative changes of the system. The activity represented in Figure 9.1 is thus dynamic and changeable, characterized by systemic tensions and their resolutions over time and space.

Methodology

Research Setting

The present study capitalizes on a PD activity hosted by a university in a major coastal city in mainland China. In January 2017, MC taught an 18-hour international publication skills course to a mixed-disciplines class of 20 graduate students (mostly Master's students) over six days. The six three-hour sessions were observed by 34 English teachers, who occupied the seats behind the students in the classroom. After observing these sessions in the mornings, the teachers also had four 2.5-hour afternoon seminar meetings with the instructor. The teachers came from 22 universities in 12 cities and had voluntarily registered for the PD program in response to an announcement sent out by the host university.

The course was entitled "Preparing to Write an International Science Article (PWISA)" and was a version of the course whose genesis and content are described in detail in Cargill, Gao, Wang, and O'Connor (2018). The overall approach was descriptive, not prescriptive—students learned about their own discipline writing by applying analysis tools to texts they had selected. A common refrain was, "Check your target journal!"

Research Question

Our study was guided by this question: As a result of observing the teaching of the external ERPP specialist (MC), how did the class of emerging Chinese EAP teachers envision the application of the learning to their own teaching context? The question evokes three interconnected activities in the CHAT sense (Engeström, 2001). The Object of MC's teaching demonstration activity can be designated as teaching international publication skills, while that of the teacher participants' lesson observation activity is making sense of MC's teaching of international publication skills. These two Objects have an overlapping area (Engeström, 2001), which in our conceptualization represents the teacher participants' learning from the lesson observation, and this will become a source of the Tools to be drawn upon in their envisioned activity of application to their own institutional context.

Data Collection and Analysis

The study reported here had access to the following types of data: a) video-recordings of the four seminar sessions (made by the host university for archival purposes and accessed by us with informed consent); b) YL's fieldnotes as a participant observer of the seminars; c) the teacher participants' anonymous written responses in English to a one-page questionnaire in the final seminar session; and d) their follow-up group discussions (in Chinese, lasting about 20 minutes) based on their responses in the questionnaire. Types c) and d) provided the most relevant data for this analysis.

The questionnaire responses were typed up, relevant segments of the seminar recordings were transcribed, and the group discussion recordings (in Chinese) were translated and transcribed in English by YL herself (but see Li, 2014, for a critique of this strategy adopted with group discussion recordings in order to save time), with group numbers (Group 1, Group 2, etc.) randomly assigned. The English scripts were then coded in turn in NVivo. The early stage of coding used both "descriptive codes" and levels of "categorization codes" (Bazeley, 2013). Three broad categories of meaning were identified in our data that collectively addressed our research question: what is learned from observing MC's teaching (a source of Tools potentially to be applied); perceived challenges; and partial resolutions to the challenges.

Building on Figure 9.1, we then represented the teachers' envisioned activity of applying their learning to their own teaching context in Figure 9.2.

Compared with Figure 9.1, which is based on the literature, Figure 9.2 addresses our study. Thus the Object is more specifically designated as teaching international publication skills to students across disciplines, the Tools node is more concrete, and to the node of Rules "language teachers working as a team" is added, in light of the data.

Finally, as a step of analytical coding (Bazeley, 2013), we interpreted the seven types of perceived challenges we had identified in the data as manifestations of systemic tensions in the teachers' envisioned activity. Accordingly, we added in Figure 9.2 dotted lightning-shaped arrows, which signal tensions within this activity system, to represent these challenges.

Findings

What Can Be Learned From Observing MC's Teaching

As described above, this learning would become a source of the Tools to mediate the teachers' envisioned activity of teaching in their own context. Three types of learning stood out.

Understanding of how such a course can be taught. In responding to the questionnaire item "What has been your most important learning from Margaret's course and seminars?", the teacher participants provided general statements such

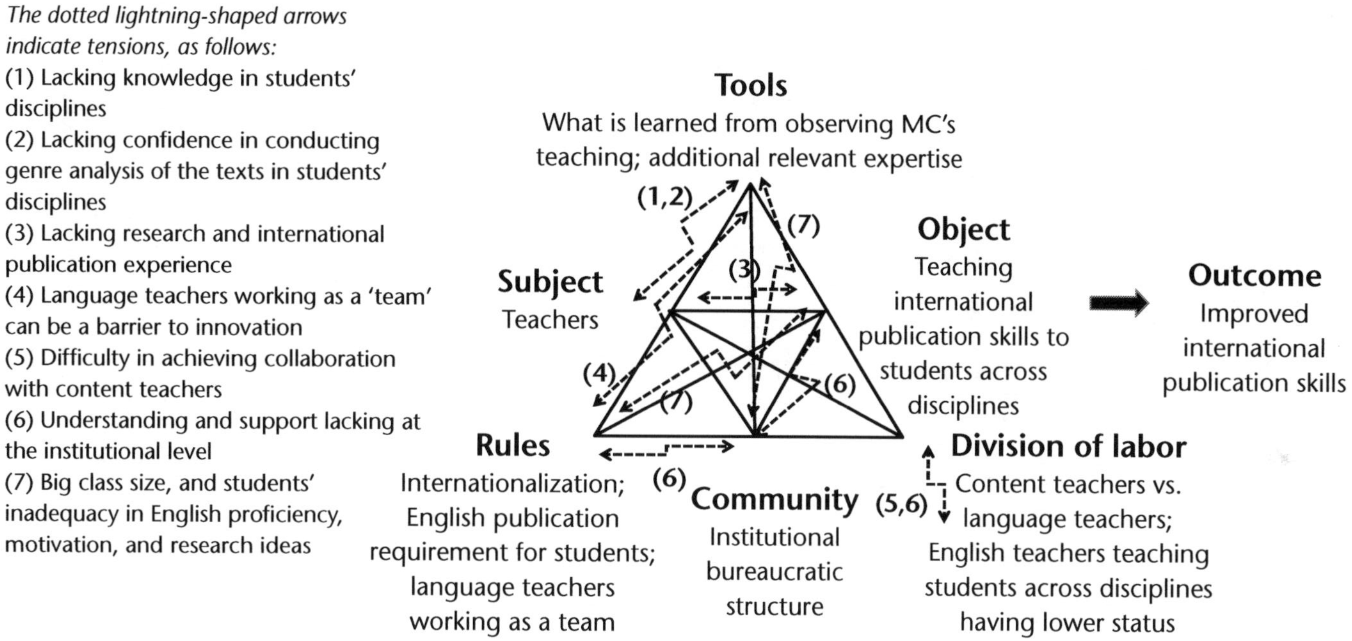

The dotted lightning-shaped arrows indicate tensions, as follows:

(1) Lacking knowledge in students' disciplines

(2) Lacking confidence in conducting genre analysis of the texts in students' disciplines

(3) Lacking research and international publication experience

(4) Language teachers working as a 'team' can be a barrier to innovation

(5) Difficulty in achieving collaboration with content teachers

(6) Understanding and support lacking at the institutional level

(7) Big class size, and students' inadequacy in English proficiency, motivation, and research ideas

Tools
What is learned from observing MC's teaching; additional relevant expertise

Subject
Teachers

Object
Teaching international publication skills to students across disciplines

Outcome
Improved international publication skills

Rules
Internationalization; English publication requirement for students; language teachers working as a team

Community
Institutional bureaucratic structure

Division of labor
Content teachers vs. language teachers; English teachers teaching students across disciplines having lower status

FIGURE 9.2 The activity system of teacher participants' envisioned application of their learning to teaching in their own context

as "got clearer ideas about teaching EAP" and "better understanding of how to implement an English academic writing course". Teachers also mentioned their gains in terms of the course design, process and organization, teaching strategies, and activity and assignment design. During group discussion, a teacher in Group 7, who had not taught academic writing before, commented:

> For me it is about systematically getting to understand the course. I think we can achieve a certain theoretical height, to see this whole course; how to teach such a course, and what is the research support behind all this.

Another teacher in Group 7, who reported that he had been adapting some of MC's PowerPoint slides (accessed on the Internet) for teaching writing to undergraduate students, said: "My purpose of coming to attend this class is to see how this course is taught." He had "gained a lot" from the course: "It's been hard for me to go deeper. She shows us how to go deeper. She talked about the use of language, tense, sentence templates, vocabulary, and use of corpus. I think these are all worth studying by us."

Knowledge of scientific research article writing. Quite a few teachers also referred to learning about the "structure" and "language conventions" of scientific research articles as their most important learning. A teacher in Group 6 commented:

> I feel in the past, our teaching focused too much on details. Thus the students were confused. My biggest gain from attending this course is that I developed an understanding of the structure of a research article. There are several types of structure.

In terms of learning about scientific language, there was mention of "strength of the wording" (questionnaire response), "distinguishing between the words from weak to strong" (Group 8), and "the use of tenses" (Groups 1 and 6). On learning about the use of tenses, a teacher in Group 1 commented:

> I have been aware of certain things, for example, the use of tenses. But previously I was not able to confirm that it's a phenomenon. I thought it's only something accidental, but now I realized there is regularity, and it can also be regarded as something that has more universal presence.

Adopting a "descriptive" approach based on "checking the target journal" and using corpus methods. The teachers often referred to adopting a "descriptive" as opposed to a "prescriptive" approach as a very important message they got from MC's teaching: "Be descriptive. Offer patterns. Let students decide which style or what features to use based on their observation of the papers in their discipline." (questionnaire response). The comments demonstrate the teachers' understanding that the "descriptive" approach demonstrated by MC relates to advising students to "check the target journal". This advice is in turn closely associated with MC's demonstration of using corpus methods, including encouraging the students to check a self-compiled corpus of their own discipline articles (ODAs). The teachers also got the point: "Check your target journal. Make their own corpus. Motivate students to investigate on their own" (questionnaire response).

The teachers agreed that such a "descriptive" approach builds the students' learning autonomy as well as confidence in writing for publication, which in fact should be an important aim of teaching: "The most important is to let students acquire the ability of self-teaching based on their target journals and build their confidence." (questionnaire response)

As a result of observing the use of a 'descriptive' approach, the teachers themselves also developed confidence: "I recognize the importance of students' autonomy. The teachers are playing a role of scaffolding. I feel more confident about my teaching even though I do not have discipline-specific expertise."(questionnaire response)

Teachers' Perception of Challenges and Partial Resolutions to the Challenges

The seven types of perceived challenges identified in the data are specified below, together with their partial resolutions as noted by the teachers. Our representations of the challenges in Figure 9.2 are explained in turn.

(1) **Lacking knowledge in students' disciplines.** Although our teacher participants believed that adopting a "descriptive" approach based on "checking the target journal" and using corpus methods would be the way out for them in teaching students of different disciplines, as illustrated earlier, they still considered lacking knowledge in students' disciplines a major challenge in their envisioned writing instruction. Relevant questionnaire responses included these:

> get myself familiarized with the content of the discipline I am going to teach;
>
> to read the articles in the target discipline;
>
> to make myself deal with some difficulties in discipline and read a professional paper.

The teachers' listing "lacking knowledge in students' disciplines" as a challenge seems bound to their concern over providing "language support" to students. Thus "to embed language teaching in the framework [demonstrated by MC]" and "the explanation of language features in specific disciplines" were also noted as challenges in the teachers' questionnaire responses.

In Figure 9.2, the challenge of "lacking knowledge in students' disciplines" is represented as manifesting a tension between the Subject and the Tools, for content knowledge in a target discipline is a tool (a type of "additional relevant expertise") which could mediate the teachers' activity in question. One resolution proposed by Group 1 was to read a few articles in the target discipline closely to understand well: "Maybe you can select just one paper in one discipline each semester, understand everything—otherwise your workload is too big."

(2) **Lacking confidence in conducting genre analysis of the texts in students' disciplines.** Conducting genre analysis in students' disciplines was listed as a challenge in questionnaire responses: "the application of genre analysis"; "increase my awareness of genre analysis of academic journals". In Figure 9.2, this challenge is also represented as manifesting a tension between the Subject and the Tools.

A teacher in Group 1, who admitted that she had "started to touch upon genre analysis long time ago", commented: "Knowing the moves and steps is one thing, but when I try to analyze a text, there will be many difficulties". To this teacher, to address the problem, "Apart from doing genre analysis, you should also read about experts' research on genre."

(3) **Lacking research and international publication experience.** To our teacher participants, their own lack of research and international publication experience undercut their confidence in teaching a course on the topic to students across disciplines, as shown in Exhibit 9.1. This challenge is interpreted as indicating a tension between the Subject and the Object in Figure 9.2.

Exhibit 9.1

[The first seminar session. The class of teachers were responding to MC, in English, for her to take notes on the blackboard, regarding what they would hope to hear from her during the seminars.]

Teacher 1:	Provide information on recent research on ERPP.
Teacher 2:	[. . .] To help our own paper to be published in the English journals. [Laughing from the class]
MC:	So strategies for writing for publication. [Writing on the blackboard]
Teacher 3:	As English teachers, we also need to improve our language competence and research skills. So if we can publish internationally sometimes, we'll have more competence to teach students to publish internationally. [. . .]
MC:	[. . .] You're also talking about YOU publishing, English language teacher publishing. You want to get parallel experience, so that students are more likely to listen to you.
Teachers:	Yes! [Laughing from the class]

YL's fieldnotes also recorded her being approached after class by a number of teachers for consultation on their research plans. Thus for these teachers a resolution to address the challenge of their lack of publication experience is learning about and engaging in ERPP research and publication themselves.

(4) **Language teachers working as a "team" can be a barrier to innovation.** This challenge was coded based on just one piece of data, found in Group 4's discussion, as shown in Exhibit 9.2.

Exhibit 9.2

Teacher 1:	In our case, the higher level asked us to work in a team rather than on our own. A big problem is—to be frank, [Turning to Teacher 2, who was her colleague] you know whom I'm talking about—I don't support that teacher's way of teaching reading, which I don't think has any good for my teaching of writing, but I can't topple hers.
Teacher 2:	We also have a problem of communication between courses.

In this extract, Teacher 1 implied that having to follow the institutional rule that language teachers should work in a team rather than on their own had created a barrier to initiating the kind of innovation she would have desired. Teacher 2 chose to interpret the situation in a more hedged way, as an issue of "communication between courses", which at the same time also indicated in effect what she saw as a resolution to the challenge, namely, teachers of different language courses should communicate with each other. In Figure 9.2, we characterize the challenge described here as manifesting a tension between the Tools (which can be used for pedagogical innovation) and the (institutional) Rules.

(5) **Difficulty in achieving collaboration with content teachers.** The teachers expressed a strong wish to collaborate with content teachers, as shown in the following questionnaire response:

> I strongly hope that some content teachers will collaborate with me in teaching writing to undergraduates because I'm not so confident in explaining some concrete content in writing.

At the same time, however, they tended to feel that such collaboration would be hard to achieve, as attested to by these questionnaire comments:

> I do not expect to collaborate with the content teachers or scientists because they are too busy to focus on teaching.

> In our university it is not likely to invite content teachers to the writing course because they would not be paid.

Although team-teaching was considered unlikely by the teachers, a few indicated the following form of cooperation may be possible: "In the preparation stage to have some personal contacts with content teachers to clear up some discipline problems and collect information about what problems they think the students have when writing RAs [research articles]." (questionnaire response)

In Figure 9.2, we represent this challenge as signaling a tension within the node of Division of Labor.

Four lines of resolution to the challenge were proposed by the teachers. The first is relying on personal contacts: "If you want to have a break-through, you have to use your own resources. Or you don't do it." (Group 3)

The second is institutional intervention: "I wonder if there should be some top-level design, not we ourselves trying to liaise with them, 'make friends' [English in the original], asking for a favor." (Group 3)

The third is to facilitate collaboration between students and their supervisors: "If we cannot let the collaboration happen between teachers, we can let it happen between students and supervisors. We can remind the students, ask your supervisor on this language point." (Group 4)

The fourth is to collaborate with students instead: "Even if the teachers are too busy to come, can I invite their students, to come and become TAs? I think establishing this connection is possible." (Group 3) Another teacher in Group 3 supported her groupmate's proposal by recounting that a doctoral student in her writing class, after receiving help from her on a paper, actually said to her: "We can do something together."

(6) Understanding and support lacking at the institutional level. Questionnaire responses indicated some support from universities, Graduate Schools, Deans of Foreign Language Studies, or Heads of English Departments. Nevertheless, various challenges led to a lack of support for EAP teachers at different levels of the institution. At the level of the department/School of Foreign Studies, language teachers teaching students across disciplines are accorded a lower status than their colleagues teaching English majors:

> Our Dean said: "Ah, we should be teaching our own English majors [in our own department]! What is 'major'? Teaching college English [to students across disciplines or in other departments] is to serve others! Our own stuff [focusing on teaching the English majors in our own department] is called 'major'!"
>
> *(Group 4)*

This problem is represented as a tension also within the node of Division of Labor, in Figure 9.2. At the university level, these English teachers may likewise be undervalued. A teacher in Group 3 said:

> They [the university authorities] are indeed doing something. But to me, what they are doing is quite empty and general: following the path of internationalization, aiming for the first-class, etc.. At the concrete level, they did not associate that with this, and consider what foreign language teachers can do.
>
> *(Group 3)*

In our interpretation, the comment above implies a tension between an institutional Rule (internationalization) and the Community (Figure 9.2), in which these language teachers are not valued or supported in a way that allows them to contribute to the commitment to internationalization.

Another two teachers in Group 3 observed:

> EAP is a new phenomenon in China, and hasn't yet taken a firm foothold. Our universities do not have good understanding of it.
>
> Utilitarianism is strong. After we've finished teaching the course, there'll be questions thrown at us: we have not seen students publish more papers, we can't see effect, quantifiable result.

The teachers' perception of a lack of understanding on the part of university authorities of EAP and the nature of EAP work is shown as a tension between the Community and the Object in Figure 9.2.

For this challenge of "Understanding and support lacking at the institutional level", which involves multiple nodes in the teachers' envisioned activity, just one resolution was proposed:

> Maybe we should pick some excellent students, out of 100 students, to aim to help them publish 1–2 papers in international journals in one or two years. Publish one paper first. Don't aim too high, not *Nature*. Then when we defend ourselves, we may have some evidence.
>
> *(Group 3)*

This idea is both accommodationist, aimed to cater for the university-level "utilitarianism" referred to above, and defensive, aimed to demonstrate to the university authorities that language teachers are capable.

(7) **Big class size, and students' inadequacy in English proficiency, motivation, and research ideas.** The teacher participants also identified a number of problems surrounding students. In Figure 9.2, we have represented this group of problems as reflecting a tension between the Tools (which might have been able to work effectively) and the Community. A teacher expressed concern over class size:

> If my class is small, I can circulate, and let students raise questions. But if it's a big class, it'll be very hard for me to take this form [that of MC's teaching] and finish the task. I can only leave it after class. But if leave it after class, the effect will be reduced by a large measure.
>
> *(Group 7)*

For this teacher, a related question is "what to include in class and what to put outside class". In discussing the same question, a teacher in Group 6, one of the few who had been teaching academic writing to graduate students, pointed out that she had been partially "flipping" her classroom (Berrett, 2012), as a resolution to address the tension posed by class size and to achieve efficient use of class time.

Students' inadequate English proficiency would also make it difficult to implement MC's approach, according to some. A teacher in Group 4 said: "You can teach them about the structure, but what they write is not readable." Another teacher who had been teaching doctoral students in medicine claimed: "I don't need to tell them about the IMRD structure. [. . .] There's also no need to go into detail; they all know it. My experience told me that their greater problem is in language, in expressing themselves." (Group 2)

To address students' need for greater help in language, this teacher incorporated much "practice", in the form of joint writing of an individual section of a research article in groups in class, revision after class, and group-based feedback from the instructor in class.

Students' motivation is also an issue. An experienced teacher in Group 5 described how she motivated students through material selection (e.g., students reading a text on the topic of 3D printing) and task design (e.g., asking students to translate short sentences from Chinese to English, so that they would realize the wide difference between the two languages in syntax).

Finally, as a teacher in Group 3 pointed out: "If students can't publish, we can't take the full responsibility." Another teacher in the same group echoed and suggested that a main cause of the failure is that students "have no ideas", which is "to a large extent attributable to their education in their disciplines". She wondered: "If they do have ideas, that is, the so-called 'innovative views', I wonder if the rest might be easier to deal with?" For the "ifs" to become true, it is not just a matter of content teachers needing to take responsibility, according to this teacher, it is also about collaboration: "We need even more collaboration from content teachers."

Discussion and Implications

Drawing upon the theoretical lens of cultural-historical activity theory (CHAT) (e.g., Engeström, 1987, 2001), in the study reported in this chapter we conceptualized emerging Chinese EAP teachers' teaching English academic writing to students across disciplines as a collective tool-mediated learning activity characterized by systemic contradictions and tensions. We focused on obtaining our teacher participants' perspectives on what they had learned from the teaching observation and the challenges they anticipated in their teaching context. We found that as a result of the teaching observation, the teacher participants' confidence grew, through developing an understanding of how such a course can be taught as well as knowledge of scientific research article writing, and through gaining insights into a "descriptive" approach based on "checking the target journal" and using corpus methods. None of these came as a surprise, perhaps. However, as one comment went: "The experience leaves us transformed." This highlights the significance of such a PD experience for emerging EAP teachers in a country like China, where EAP is burgeoning at universities and the need to develop EAP pedagogy and research is urgent.

The teachers' reported learning can be characterized as knowledge of and confidence in the use of genre pedagogy and corpus-informed approaches. While these may have become commonplace in the EAP instruction delivered in Anglophone countries and English-dominant universities in some parts of Asia and Europe, understandings of these pedagogical practices may only be starting to grow in other places of the world. From this perspective, the role that experienced ERPP specialists (like MC) can play, through cross-cultural teaching, can be significant.

The participants identified seven types of challenges which represented a wide range of systemic tensions within the activity of envisioned application of their learning to teaching in their own context. Echoes can be recognized in the relevant discussions in the literature (e.g., Chanock, 2017; Flowerdew, 2016; Hyland, 2014; Simpson et al., 2016). We would further suggest that, taken as a whole, the challenges and proposed partial resolutions highlight the issue of discipline specificity in EAP and its implications for EAP instructors' professionalization, as elaborated below.

The teacher participants in our study embraced the "descriptive" approach based on "checking the target journal" and corpus methods, that is, they were enthusiastic about a specific approach to EAP; meanwhile, they expressed grave concerns over their lack of knowledge in their students' disciplines, which in turn was bound to their concern about how to provide "language support" to the students. Although they proposed a few partial resolutions (e.g., reading a small number of articles in a target discipline closely to understand them well), from our perspective, it seems they were yet to develop an in-depth understanding of their need to engage in "analyzing academic subject texts and related discourse knowledge" and of how they could do so (Bruce, 2011, p. 73).

Both Flowerdew (2016) and Hyland (2016) argued that EAP teachers developing expertise in the specific discourse of their students' disciplines is an issue of professionalism. The concept of professionalization of EAP provides counter evidence to the traditional perception of EAP teachers and the language centers/departments they work in as merely playing a remedial, service role (e.g., Flowerdew, 2016; Hyland, 2016). The same argument would hold true in China. In the process of professionalizing their commitment, the emerging Chinese EAP teachers could consider experience from other contexts in teaching specificity-based EAP (e.g., Cargill, Cadman, & McGowan, 2001; Hyland, 2014). Through engaging with specificity, and meeting the many related challenges surrounding their work, the Chinese teachers will be creating new channels for their own research and their aspirations for international publication. Their current inadequacy in research training and lack of experience in international publication was indeed poignantly acknowledged by the teacher participants in our study as a barrier that undercut their credibility as aspiring ERPP teachers. Research training thus needs to be part of the PD programmes targeting Chinese EAP teachers. Overseas-trained EAP researchers in China as well as overseas-based EAP researchers can play a valuable role in this context (Lei & Li, 2018).

In our study, the teacher participants' perspectives upon their envisioned activity of applying what they had learned from the teaching observation were richly informed by their experience in their respective institutional settings, rather than decontextualized and only imaginary. The theoretical lens of CHAT helped us bring to light a holistic and contextualized picture. In this vein, illuminating collective perspectives upon an envisioned activity, as we aimed to do in this chapter, can provide a useful foundation or baseline for future investigation of teachers' actual practices. Future research could also incorporate a longitudinal dimension and capture qualitative changes in EAP practitioners' learning activities in their distinctive institutional and national settings.

Finally, we should highlight the innovative nature of the PD design that provided the research venue for our study reported here.[1] In the PD program, MC was teaching a class of science students and at the same time she was observed by a large group of 34 language teachers. This resembles the setting of a "master class", "rather like they have in classical music, where a famous musician instructs one or more students and an audience is able to observe it" (Email communication, John Flowerdew, September 8, 2017).[2] As mentioned earlier in the chapter, the teachers came from 22 universities in 12 cities of the country. The innovative PD approach thus has the potential to train large numbers of EAP teachers—a matter of significance in the contemporary scene of higher education (Email communication, Karen Englander, October 15, 2017)—and may, excitingly, be replicable or adaptable elsewhere.

Notes

1 We would like to thank Karen Englander for reminding us that this is worth highlighting.
2 We must acknowledge that this innovative PD approach, in the case of our research setting, was the design of a Chinese colleague, who initiated and hosted the event and who remains anonymous in the present chapter.

References

Basturkmen, H. (2014). LSP teacher education: Review of literature and suggestions for the research agenda. *Ibérica, 28*, 17–34.

Bazeley, P. (2013). *Qualitative data analysis: Practical strategies.* London: Sage.

Berrett, D. (February 19, 2012). How 'flipping' the classroom can improve the traditional lecture. *The Chronicle of Higher Education.* Retrieved June 7, 2017 from http://www.chronicle.com/article/How-Flipping-the-Classroom/130857

Bruce, I. (2011). *Theory and concepts of English for academic purposes.* New York: Palgrave Macmillan.

Burgess, S., & Pallant, A. (2013). Teaching academic writing in Europe: Multilingual and multicultural contexts. In V. A. Matarese (Ed.). *Supporting research writing: Roles and challenges in multilingual settings* (pp. 19–38). Cambridge: Chandos.

Cai, J. (2012). *Zhongguo daxue yingyu jiaoxue: Lu zai hefang* [A way out for EFL at tertiary level education in mainland China]. Shanghai: Shanghai Jiao Tong University Press.

Cargill, M., & Burgess, S. (2008). Introduction to the Special Issue: English for Research Publication Purposes. *Journal of English for Academic Purposes, 7*, 75–76.

Cargill, M., Cadman, K., & McGowan, U. (2001). Postgraduate writing: Using intersecting genres in a collaborative content-based program. In I. Leki (Ed.). *Case studies in TESOL: Academic writing programs* (pp. 85–96). Alexandria, VA: Teaching English to Speakers of Other Languages (TESOL).

Cargill, M., Gao, X., Wang, X., & O'Connor, P. (2018). Preparing Chinese graduate students of science facing an international publication requirement for graduation: Trialling an early-candidature course. *English for Specific Purposes, 52*, 13–26.

Cargill, M., O'Connor, P., & Li, Y. (2012). Educating Chinese scientists to write for international journals: Addressing the divide between science and technology education and English language teaching. *English for Specific Purposes, 31*, 60–69.

Chanock, K. (2017). Learning specialists working with faculty to embed development of academic literacies in disciplinary subjects. In S. Plane, C. Bazerman, F. Rondelli, C. Donahue, A. N. Applebee, C. Boré, P. Carlino, M. M. Larruy, P. Rogers, & D. Russell (Eds.). *Research on writing: Multiple perspectives* (pp. 243–262). Fort Collins, CO: The WAC Clearinghouse and Centre de Recherche sur les Médiations (CREM).

Cheng, A. (2016). EAP at the tertiary level in China: Challenges and possibilities. In K. Hyland & P. Shaw (Eds.). *The Routledge handbook of English for academic purposes* (pp. 97–108). London, New York: Routledge.

Ding, A., & Bruce, I. (2017). *The English for Academic Purposes practitioner: Operating on the edge of academia.* Cham, Switzerland: Palgrave Macmillan.

Engeström, Y. (1987). *Learning by expanding: An activity theoretical approach to developmental research.* Helsinki: Orienta-Konsultit.

Engeström, Y. (2001). Expansive learning at work: Toward an activity theoretical reconceptualization. *Journal of Education and Work, 14*(1), 133–156.

Engeström, Y. (2009). The future of activity theory: A rough draft. In A. Sannino, H. Daniels, & K.D. Gutiérrez (Eds.). *Learning and expanding with activity theory* (pp. 303–328). Cambridge: Cambridge University Press.

Flowerdew, J. (2016). English for Specific Academic Purposes (ESAP) writing: Making the case. *Writing & Pedagogy, 8*(1), 5–32.

Gao, Y., & Bartlett, B. (2014). Opportunities and challenges for negotiating appropriate EAP Practice in China. In I. Liyanage & T. Walker (Eds.). *English for Academic Purposes*

(EAP) in Asia: Negotiating appropriate practices in a global context (pp. 13–31). Rotterdam, The Netherlands: Sense Publishers.

Hyland, K. (2014). Re-imagining literacy: English in Hong Kong's new university curriculum. In D. Coniam (Ed.). *English language education and assessment: Recent developments in Hong Kong and the Chinese mainland* (pp. 139–151). Singapore: Springer.

Hyland, K. (2016). General and specific EAP. In K. Hyland & P. Shaw (Eds.). *The Routledge handbook of English for Academic Purposes* (pp. 17–29). London, New York: Routledge.

Lei, J., & Li, Y. (2018). Empowering emerging Chinese EAP teachers through research training. Paper presented at the 2018 International Conference on Teaching and Researching EFL Writing, October 12–15, 2018, Nanjing, China.

Leont'ev, A. N. (1978). *Activity, consciousness, and personality.* Englewood Cliffs, NJ: Prentice-Hall.

Liyanage, I., & Walker, T. (Eds.). (2014). *English for Academic Purposes (EAP) in Asia: Negotiating appropriate practices in a global context.* Rotterdam, The Netherlands: Sense Publishers.

Li, Y. (2014). Seeking entry to the North American market: Chinese management academics publishing internationally. *Journal of English for Academic Purposes, 13,* 41–52.

Li, Y. (2016). "Publish SCI papers or no degree": Practices of Chinese doctoral supervisors in response to the publication pressure on science students. *Asia Pacific Journal of Education, 36*(4), 545–558.

Li, Y. (2017). Teaching Chinese graduate students of science to write for publication: An interview with Margaret Cargill. Retrieved from http://www.ceapa.cn/d.asp?id=261

Li, Y., & Ma, X. (2018). Teaching English academic writing to non-English major graduate students in Chinese universities: A review and a transnational vision. In X. You (Ed.). *Transnational writing education: Theory, history, and practice* (pp. 222–243). New York, London: Routledge

Martin, P. (2014). Teachers in transition: The road to EAP. In P. Breen (Ed.). *Cases on teacher identity, diversity, and cognition in higher education* (pp. 287–315). Hershey, PA: Information Science Reference.

Richards, J. C., & Nunan, D. (Eds.) (1990). *Second language teacher education.* Cambridge: Cambridge University Press.

Shapiro, E. (2015). Towards an integrated graduate student (training program). *Across the Disciplines, 12*(3). Retrieved from http://wac.colostate.edu/atd/graduate_wac/shapiro2015.cfm

Simpson, S., Caplan, N. A., Cox, M., & Phillips, T. (Eds.). (2016). *Supporting graduate student writers: Research, curriculum, and program design.* Ann Arbor, MI: University of Michigan Press.

Spack, R. (1988). Initiating ESL students into the academic discourse community: How far should we go? *TESOL Quarterly, 22*(1), 29–52.

Sundstrom, C. J. (2016). Graduate writing instruction: A cautionary tale. In S. Simpson, N. A. Caplan, M. Cox, & T. Phillips (Eds.). *Supporting graduate student writers: Research, curriculum, and program design* (pp. 192–205). Ann Arbor, MI: University of Michigan Press.

Vygotsky, L. S. (1930/1978). *Mind in society: The development of higher psychological processes.* Cambridge, MA: Harvard University Press.

Yang, R. (2016). Internationalization of higher education in China: A national scenario. In H. de Wit, J. Gacel-Avila, E. Jones & N. Jooste (Eds.). *The globalization of internationalization: Emerging voices and perspectives* (pp. 142–152). London: Routledge.

10
PUBLISHING RESEARCH IN ENGLISH FOR CHINESE MULTILINGUAL SCHOLARS IN LANGUAGE-RELATED DISCIPLINES

Towards a Biliteracy Approach

Yongyan Zheng

FUDAN UNIVERSITY, SHANGHAI, CHINA

Yuan Cao

SHANGHAI INTERNATIONAL STUDIES UNIVERSITY, SHANGHAI, CHINA

Introduction

The scale of international scholarly publishing has been expanding rapidly on a global level. Some seven to nine million researchers participate in this worldwide activity with a growth rate at 3% per year, and the most rapid growth has taken place in South Korea and China (Hyland, 2016). Individual researchers see publishing research in prestigious international, usually English-medium, journals as the key to career development, to receiving wide acknowledgement, and to their successful integration into the global research community (e.g. Bocanegra-Valle, 2014; Flowerdew, 2015). At a more macro level, international scholarly publishing is increasingly related to a nation's innovative vitality and wealth creation potential (Englander & Uzuner-Smith, 2013) and determines its standing in the international academia (King, 2004).

Although heatedly debated, English has become the dominant academic language (e.g. Hyland, 2015; Lillis & Curry, 2010). English for research publication purposes (ERPP) has emerged as a recent focus (see Flowerdew, 2015, for a review), and publication-related writing practices of international scholars whose native language is not English and who use English as an additional language (EAL) have drawn much attention (Kuteeva & Mauranen, 2014). Research has shown that EAL scholars face discursive difficulties including nonstandard uses of academic English, stylistic and rhetorical differences (Duszak & Lewkowicz, 2008; Uzuner, 2008), and many feel that they are linguistically disadvantaged relative to native-speaking English scholars (e.g. Ferguson, Pérez-Llantada, & Plo, 2011; but see Hyland 2016 for counter argument). EAL scholars also face non-discursive difficulties, including a lack of network resources or material/financial access to the mainstream research community (e.g. Belcher, 2007; Canagarajah, 2002), so they are sometimes labelled as "off-networked" scholars in the "periphery".

Despite the challenges, EAL scholars around the world are ever more committed to practicing ERPP. They believe that by publishing in English, they can reach a wider audience and participate in the international community (Bocanegra-Valle, 2014; Flowerdew & Li, 2009; Lillis & Curry, 2010). But their language practices also vary across disciplines (Duszak & Lewkowicz, 2008; Kuteeva & Airey, 2014; Phillipson & Skutnabb-Kangas, 1999). While researchers in the hard sciences generally accept English as the uncontested academic lingua franca, researchers in the humanities and social sciences (HSS) are more ambivalent. More important, EAL scholars' language practices are affected by national and institutional research policies that prioritize research published in internationally indexed and English-language journals, which enacts a de facto policy (Shohamy, 2006) of publishing in English. EAL scholars from various contexts indicate that their choice to publish in English is out of the performative pressure and departmental assessment criteria as well as the incentive to receive financial rewards (Englander & Uzuner-Smith, 2013; Feng, Beckett, & Huang, 2013; Flowerdew & Li, 2009; Lee & Lee, 2013).

It needs to be noted that the language policy that primes English-language publications in non-Anglophone contexts virtually creates a competition between English and the local language in the space of research communication, sometimes wrapped in the discourse of "the threat of English" (Bocanegra-Valle, 2014; Olsson & Sheridan, 2012; Uzuner, 2008). The dominance of English may generate a potential risk of global diglossia and national language domain loss (e.g. Ferguson, et al., 2011; Olsson & Sheridan, 2012). Many EAL scholars by committing themselves to English writing rarely write in any language other than English, such as in the case of Chinese scholars in Hong Kong (Flowerdew & Li, 2009). But language choice in research communication is a complicated issue. Duzak and Lewkowicz (2008) argued that social sciences naturally invite localization and, thus, communication in English is an ideological choice, whereas McGrath (2014) examined the rhetoric and reality of the "parallel language policy" in the Nordic context and concluded that language practices are more determined by pragmatic forces, such as the intended audience, than by ideological or language-political reasons, such as safeguarding the national language. Gentil (2011) pointed out that current research on multilingual scholars' writing mostly emphasizes the EAL dimension, while neglecting that of native-language writing, and to redress the balance he advanced a biliteracy approach to genre studies.

The above review has highlighted several issues that merit further exploration. First, it seems that the current line of ERPP research mainly concentrates on European contexts where the national languages are spoken by relatively small populations. Sandelin and Sarafoglou's (2004) statistical analysis demonstrates a robust relationship between the use of English and the size of the population using a non-English domestic language: the larger the number of speakers of a domestic language, the higher the propensity to publish in the domestic language. Thus, it becomes important to re-examine the relationship of English and local languages in research communication in a different context, such as China, where there is the world's largest population of native speakers of a national language. Second, disciplinary variations have propelled us to further look at scholars engaged in English-language teaching and research. As language specialists, they may be more aware of language choice for research communication (Bocanegra-Valle, 2014; Flowerdew, 2015). How Chinese scholars in English-language studies deal with both languages in research communication is an underexamined area. Thirdly, the role of national/institutional language policy in individual scholars' ERPP practices needs further examination, particularly in a sociopolitical context different from the European ones. This chapter intends to explore Chinese EAL scholars' practices and beliefs in ERPP, and findings are believed to be conducive to a deepened understanding of the complex language dynamics in research communication. It needs to be noted that "EAL scholars" in this chapter particularly refer to Chinese scholars engaged in English-language teaching and research.

Chinese Context and Purpose of the Study

On the China mainland (henceforth China), there are 56 officially recognized ethnic groups. The national language, Chinese, is also known as *Hanyu* (Han language). The Chinese government attached great importance to foreign language education since 1949, with an initial focus on Russian and then a shift to English (Lam, 2005). Since the end of the "Cultural Revolution" in 1977 and the "Reform and Opening-up" policy in 1978, English gradually became the dominant foreign language in China's education system (Bolton & Graddol, 2012). The most recent national survey puts the number of English learners on the China mainland at around 390 million, and there are over one million English-language teachers all over the country at different levels of education (Wei & Su, 2012).

The Chinese government has placed high priority on Chinese research development. Along with China's growing economic and geopolitical influence, the research policy is oriented to "going-out", namely, promoting the Chinese language, culture, and research to the world. The Central Committee of the Communist Party of China (CCCPC) issued the "Views to further promote the development of philosophy and social sciences" in 2004[1], and the "Decision to further reform the cultural system and promote cultural prosperity" in 2011[2]. These two policies explicitly state that "Chinese culture goes out, Chinese research goes out", and implicitly encourage internationally-indexed English-language publications. A shift has been observed in the most recent document issued in 2017, "Decision on Accelerating the Construction of Philosophy and

Social Sciences with Chinese Characteristics"[3], which accentuates the imperative to construct a China-centered discourse system in international research communication. In various other channels, government officials have stressed that Chinese-language publications are as important as, if not more important than, English-language publications.

China's HSS research output increased dramatically during the past decades. As of 2015, Chinese science researchers published 8,176 articles in the SSCI database (ISTIC, 2016) in just one year, ranking 6th in the world. But there is a conspicuous imbalance in the language choice, as 95.3% of Chinese scholars published in English-medium journals, whereas Chinese-language publishing concentrates on the three Chinese-medium journals indexed in the SSCI (Zheng & Gao, 2016). However, little information is available up to today on their beliefs and practices in ERPP. To this end, the present paper intends to explore the following questions:

1) What beliefs do Chinese EAL scholars hold towards Chinese and English as the language for research communication?
2) What challenges do Chinese EAL scholars meet in ERPP practices?

The Study

The study reported in this chapter stems from a larger project that aimed to investigate the research capabilities of multilingual scholars in China. We used a survey questionnaire to elicit information on Chinese EAL scholars' ERPP beliefs and practices.

Instrument

The survey questionnaire included a mix of open-ended and closed multiple-choice questions. We consulted the question items used in three earlier studies conducted in the European contexts (Bocanegra-Valle, 2014; Muresan & Pérez-Llantada, 2014; Olsson & Sheridan, 2012) to address the research questions. We also intended to examine the Chinese EAL scholars' attitudes towards the competition between global English and Chinese in research communication, so we added several questions in this regard.

The survey questionnaire was divided into three sections. Section A sought to obtain information on the respondents' biographic and academic backgrounds, including age, gender, major of study, the number of foreign languages learned and the degree of mastery, education history, and overseas experience (Q1–Q15). Section B intended to elicit the respondents' beliefs and attitudes towards English-language and Chinese-language publication (Q16–Q21). Section C aimed to address the respondents' actual language practices for research publication purposes and the challenges in ERPP as well as the support they could receive (Q22–Q32). The questionnaire items drew on a combination of multiple choice and open-ended questions, so that we could obtain some qualitative insights into the situated details of the respondents' ERPP experience. For example, in Q19 "Which is more important to you, publishing in English or publishing in Chinese?", the respondents were required to choose from three items: publishing in English is more important, publishing in Chinese is more important, and both are important. Then they were required to elaborate on their reasons in the space given below.

Data Collection

As the current study aims at EAL scholars in language studies, we decided to target six national foreign studies universities, namely, Beijing Foreign Studies University, Shanghai International Studies University, Guangdong University of Foreign Studies (located in Guangzhou), Sichuan International Studies University (located in Chengdu), Tianjin Foreign Studies University, and Xi'an International Studies University. These universities are among the first batch of institutions established by the Chinese government since 1949 specifically to cultivate foreign-language specialists, and they are geographically spread across the east (Beijing, Tianjin, Shanghai, and Guangzhou) and the west (Xi'an and Chengdu) of China. It is estimated that there are around 4,800 full-time faculty members in the six universities, 50% of which are in English literature and linguistic research. As such, the total population of EAL specialized in English-language studies is estimated to be around 2,400 in these universities.

The survey questionnaire was written in Chinese, and was distributed to around twenty social media groups of English-language professionals on Wechat (the most widely used Chinese mobile messaging app) via an Internet link during January and March 2016. Efforts were made to reach the teaching staff in the six universities. A total of 463 questionnaires were collected, and we excluded respondents whose first foreign language was not English and those who did not work in subjects of literature or linguistics. The filtering process resulted in 210 questionnaires, representing approximately 9% of English literature and linguistic researchers in the target universities. Descriptive statistical analysis was applied to the quantitative data, and content analysis was applied to the open-ended comments. These comments complemented the quantitative findings, as they revealed more detailed personal experiences and opinions in relation to the question items and enhanced our interpretation of the quantitative data.

Findings

Language and Academic Backgrounds of the Respondents

Data collected from Section A of the questionnaire sketch out the backgrounds of the respondents. Among the 210 respondents, 41 were male (19.52%) and 169 were female (80.48%), reflecting a disproportional distribution of gender among English-language professionals in Chinese universities. 142 respondents were under 45 years old (67.62%) and 137 were either Assistant Professors or Associate Professors (65.24%). It seems that the respondents were mostly at a stage when the pressures of career development and promotion were at their peak. All of them learned English as the first foreign language and considered their language mastery ranging from "proficient" (30.95%) to "highly proficient" (45.24%), which suggests that the majority of the respondents were confident of their English-language abilities.

70.95% reported at least six months of overseas experience in the US, UK, Canada, the Netherlands, Singapore and Hong Kong SAR, and 31 of them gained post-graduate degrees in these areas. 59.52% reported having received some degree of training in English academic writing at different stages of their academic studies. Their widely reported overseas experience is related to the Chinese "going-out" policy. The Chinese government actively supports, especially financially, Chinese scholars for overseas exchange, so they are increasingly more connected with the international academic community. However, it needs to be noted that only 20.95% of the respondents successfully published internationally in English, suggesting a still low rate of international scholarly publishing for the language specialists.

Language Beliefs in English and Chinese for Research Publication Purposes

Section B of the questionnaire offers some insights into the Chinese EAL scholars' beliefs in using English and Chinese for research communication. In Q16 respondents were asked: "Do you tend to publish in international or domestic journals?" 57.14% chose to publish in domestic journals, 25.24% chose to publish in international journals, and 17.62% believed that it did not matter. The reasons to prioritize domestic journals included unfamiliarity with international publishing practices (29.33%), lack of academic training (23.92%), and not feeling encouraged by the policy (19.92%). All these discouraged the respondents from submitting manuscripts to international journals. But 11.91% of the respondents also indicated that to publish in Chinese was to increase domestic research quality.

Content analysis revealed more details. Some respondents pointed out that the international journals' publication cycle is much longer than that of domestic journals, and they would rather start from more familiar publishing practices with domestic journals. One respondent discussed the research assessment practice as follows: "It was difficult for the research review panel in our institution to judge the quality of a certain international journal, so papers published in it sometimes cannot be appropriately recognized as good research."

The reasons for favoring international publication are presented as follows. Their principal motivation to publish in international journals was related to the belief in the more advanced research level of the English-medium international journals, as 25.42% believed that English-medium publication signals better research quality and 29.66% believed in self-improvement through international publishing. On the other hand, the respondents were also aware of the national research policy of "Chinese research going out", as 27.12% regarded international publications as the channel to disseminate Chinese research and to raise the visibility of Chinese scholars; and 15.25% of the respondents indicated that institutional policy encourages international publication.

Content analysis of the open-ended comments highlighted the respondents' concerns over the complicated domestic publication culture, which steered them away from domestic publishing. One respondent commented that: "Domestic publication is more difficult as it requires more connections with the journals. The reviewing process is not transparent enough compared to international journals, so it may be easier to publish internationally."

Q19 tapped the issue of language choice by asking: "Which is more important to you, publishing in English or publishing in Chinese?" 12.38% chose Chinese, 10.48% chose English, and 77.14% believed that both were important. Content analysis of the open-ended comments suggested that reasons to stress Chinese over English in research publication were mostly out of an ideological drive, including: 1) "We are obliged to contribute to the development of local research community", 2) "Publishing in Chinese can safeguard the local culture against the global English tendency", and 3) "Using Chinese is to speak with scholars in the local research community." By contrast, the reasons to prioritize English over Chinese in research publication were related to the Chinese EAL scholars' professional needs to participate in the international community, to gain international recognition and facilitate international exchange through the use of English. Some others also believed that the international community needs to know more about China, and English-language publication serves as a channel to publicize Chinese scholars' research and increase Chinese scholars' visibility in the international academia.

Our data showed that 77.14% of the respondents believed in using both languages for research publication purposes. They recognized the pros and cons of publishing in English and Chinese, and realized the two-fold need to simultaneously engage in the global and local communities. For example, one respondent commented: "English-language publication helps us connect with the international community, and Chinese-language publication helps increase the domestic research quality."

Some respondents drew on their professional identity as English teachers to justify the biliteracy approach. For example, one respondent believed that "language specialists should be able to use two languages proficiently". They also expressed a sense of obligation as bilingual researchers:

> As an English-language teacher, it is important to write in English habitually. But as a Chinese, we can't abandon Chinese writing either.

> We need to make our research output known to Chinese readers, but at the same time, we should make our voices heard in the international community.

We also explored the respondents' perception of "the threat of English" (e.g. Bocanegra-Valle, 2014; Olsson & Sheridan, 2012; Uzuner, 2008) to Chinese research academia. Responding to Q20, "Do you agree with the opinion that publishing in English would result in English hegemony and pose a threat to language security of Chinese?", 72.86% disagreed, while 17.14% agreed and 10.00% were unsure. Content analysis of the open-ended comments revealed more details. Some respondents tended to assume a neutral position towards the role of language in research communication:

> Academic research is academic research, and the medium of language is the medium of language. They should be treated separately.
>
> Communication in academic research is a free and equal process, and the use of language for research communication is a free choice.

Respondents of this view also leaned towards an apolitical stance, as one respondent commented "there is no need to bring in political elements into the discussion of academic issues." Furthermore, the respondents expressed confidence in their native language by arguing that "mother tongue will always remain mother tongue, and will never be replaced."

Interestingly, their opposition to "the threat of English" is closely related to their bilingual identity and biliteracy approach to research communication. For example,

> So long as we attend to both sides of English- and Chinese-publishing, the use of English for research communication will not result in English hegemony.
>
> A good foreign-language user should be able to use both the foreign language and native language proficiently, so neither will be undermined.

Only 17.14% of the respondents agreed with "the threat of English" and were more aware of the "textual ideology" involved in English-medium publishing activities (Lillis & Curry, 2010), as illustrated by the following comment: "An overemphasis on English-language publications would result in hegemony of the English language over Chinese in the ideological aspect. In fact, there are already some voices looking down upon Chinese culture and Chinese research around us."

Challenges in ERPP Practices

Section C of the questionnaire intended to address the Chinese EAL scholars' actual language practices in terms of the challenges encountered during ERPP. Q21 asked them about the biggest challenge associated with ERPP. Formulation of research questions (28.00%) and research design/methodology (28.00%) amounted to the greatest difficulties, which corresponds to the previously listed factor of "lack of academic training" as a reason to steer away from international publishing practices. "Not having channels of publishing" was also chosen (24.00%), suggesting the respondents' unfamiliarity with the international academia. Language and rhetoric (17.09%) and other difficulties (2.91%) were also indicated by the respondents.

Q24 further specified the types of language-related difficulties (Figure 10.1). It can be seen that only a small proportion of the choices focused on pure linguistic elements, such as vocabulary (19.12%) and grammar (3.59%). The mastery of appropriate rhetorical styles and academic norms were seen as the greatest language-related difficulties for the respondents to engage in ERPP activities.

However, although they reported different types of difficulties, only 36.67% of the respondents have used or intended to resort to language editing services, whereas 63.33% never have or do not intend to do so. This is probably due to the absence of such help available to the respondents at the institutional level. Figure 10.2 shows that most of the respondents' institutions did not provide any research paper editing service or regular ERPP training such as activities organized by a writing center. Some serial lectures or workshops were conducted to help improve the ERPP practices, but these measures are rather temporary.

Discussion

Following Flowerdew (2015) and Bocanegra-Valle (2014), this study focuses on a sub-group of Chinese EAL scholars who were intensively engaged with English-language linguistic and literature studies. Findings demonstrated their awareness

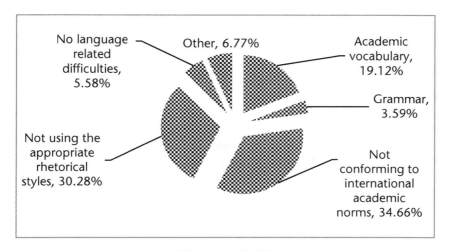

FIGURE 10.1 Language-related difficulties in ERPP

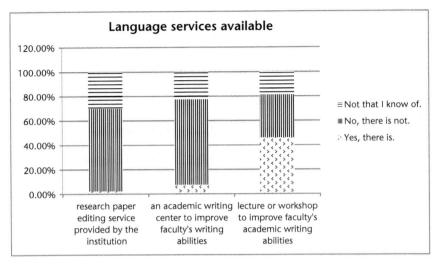

FIGURE 10.2 Language services available at the institutional level

of language choice for research communication purposes, and showed that they share most of the concerns about ERPP in other fields of research and other geographical contexts. However, they are also unique due to the specific disciplinary, ethnolinguistic, and national policy contexts.

The findings of the respondents' academic background and overseas experience probably defy the stereotype of EAL scholars as linguistically disadvantaged or off-networked. As language specialists, they were confident in their English abilities and thus did not seem to be bothered by their non-native status, as also found with the Swedish scholars (Kuteeva & McGrath, 2014) and Romanian scholars (Muresan & Pérez-Llantada, 2014). It is probably inappropriate to portray the Chinese EAL scholars merely in the terms of "non-native", "periphery" or "off-networked" scholars (Belcher, 2007; Canagarajah, 2002) in past literature. However, the rate of successful international publication remains quite low, probably because of the unfamiliarity with international publishing practices and lack of academic training as shown in the findings. Specifically, the finding that the formulation of research questions and research design/methodology, rather than language-specific difficulties, were listed as the biggest challenges for Chinese EAL scholars' ERPP practices supports the claim that the level of professional expertise plays a key role in successful international publishing (Hyland, 2016).

In addition, Chinese EAL scholars' challenges encountered in ERPP, as reported in the present study, also implicate insufficient communication between the international and Chinese research circles in language studies. Despite the respondents' self-reported satisfactory language proficiency and abundant overseas exchange experience, they seemed to be unfamiliar with the common practices of international publishing and incognizant of possible channels to disseminate their research internationally. This lack of knowledge may also engender the difficulty for the review panels to judge the quality of some international journals in the local institutional context, which diverted the scholars away from international publishing. Indeed, unfamiliarity may result in a lack of trust between international and local researchers (Li, 2014), which may further perpetuate the gap between international and domestic academia. From this perspective, one initiative to support local scholars in international publishing can be to help them enact the network practices in the disciplinary context (Curry & Lillis, 2010; Lillis & Curry, 2010).

The beliefs in ERPP held by the Chinese EAL scholars surveyed in this study are not much different from scholars in other contexts (e.g. Bocanegra-Valle, 2014; Duzak & Lewkowicz, 2008), as they also aspire to participate in international academia through the use of English. However, our findings seem to suggest some top-down influence of the macro-level research policy upon individual scholars' ERPP practices and beliefs (Feng, et al., 2013; Lee & Lee, 2013; Muresan & Pérez-Llantada, 2014). In particular, the nationalist rhetoric of "Chinese research going out" seems to have been internalized by the respondents as they regarded ERPP as a means to help achieve the nationalistic objective of promoting Chinese culture and research. Furthermore, we found that the nationalistic rhetoric was intertwined with their professional and ethnolinguistic identity as Chinese scholars in language studies. They believed in the professional need to publish in their research language English, and considered it their own obligation to promote Chinese culture and research through ERPP. This finding implies an ideological impetus behind their ERPP attempts, which aligns with China's national research policy emphasis. From this perspective, individual language practices and beliefs seem to be merged into the macro-level policy narrative.

A unique finding of our study is Chinese EAL scholars' articulated preference for a biliteracy approach to research communication. In Bocanegra-Valle's (2014) survey with language specialists (mostly from European backgrounds), only 15.2% of the respondents considered publishing in English and in their national language equally valued, and the justification largely depended on the research topic and the primary target groups. Quite differently, our study showed that a predominant majority (77.14%) considered that both languages are important, mostly because they identify themselves as bridging the global and local academia by using two languages proficiently for research communication. Thus, the biliteracy approach (Gentil, 2011) seems to fit the mentality of the Chinese EAL scholars in our study. It needs to be noted that, different from the "parallel language policy" enacted by the Nordic countries in a top-down manner (McGrath, 2014), there is no explicit language policy to direct Chinese scholars' language practices for research publication purposes. However, the recent emphasis on promoting Chinese research and on constructing a China-centered discourse system in the national research policies implies the government's strong will to (re)instate the position of Chinese to counterbalance the global spread of English. In this sense, the scholars' preference for a biliteracy approach can be seen as their attempt to negotiate a space between the professional need to participate in the international academia through English-language publishing and the nation's ideological rhetoric to promote Chinese culture and research. McGrath's (2014) study in the Swedish context suggested that publishing in Swedish was less determined by ideological or language-political factors. But our findings seem to suggest that in the Chinese context, where national policies have strong influences on social life, scholars' language choice can also be determined by ideological or sociopolitical forces.

With regard to the competition between English and the local language in the academic domain, the European scholars (Bocanegra-Valle, 2014; Bolton & Kuteeva, 2012; Olsson & Sheridan, 2012) tend to perceive that the use of English poses a threat to the local language, whereas the Chinese EAL scholars in our study mostly considered English not to be a threat to Chinese academia. The reasons for this finding are complicated, and one possible explanation might be linked to the characteristics of the Chinese ethnolinguistic context. Chinese is a language with the largest population of native speakers in the world, and the local language is connected with a lively local research community. It nurtures a large domestic publication culture, where the Chinese scholars can find a local audience to speak to. According to Sandelin and Sarafoglou (2004), the larger the number of native speakers of the domestic language, the greater the propensity for the people to publish in that language, and the less the propensity to publish in English. Therefore, the existence of a local audience and local publication culture seems to influence individual scholars' language practices and beliefs.

Alternatively, the Chinese EAL scholars' neutral perception of ERPP is probably related to how English has been promoted in China in general. In China's national policy and public imagination, the political or ideological connotations of English as a language of capitalism or imperialism is avoided as much as possible, and English is promoted as a foreign language mainly for the instrumental purposes of economic development, modernization and internationalization (Pan, 2011). By the same token, ERPP in the domain of research communication is mostly conceived of as a way to increase Chinese scholars' visibility in the international academia and to facilitate "Chinese culture going out, Chinese research going out". It is thus imbued with a patriotic purpose, whereas the discourse on English as a threat is downplayed. In other words, the macro-level policy discourse focusing on the pragmatic aspect of ERPP instead of the critical aspect encapsulated by the "textual ideology of ERPP" (Lillis & Curry, 2010) may have affected Chinese scholars' perception of the use of English in research communication. It is thus not difficult to understand that the respondents maintained an apolitical stance for ERPP. However, it needs to be clarified that the Chinese scholars' perception of ERPP as not being a threat to Chinese does not mean that ERPP is value-free. Nor does it mean that language choice for research communication is a completely neutral or free choice. Rather, we interpret this finding as implying that the macro-level narrative profoundly permeates Chinese scholars' language beliefs and practices.

Conclusion

As ERPP has been extensively researched in the European contexts and discussed by Anglophone scholars, this chapter aims to bring in the perspective of Chinese EAL scholars by highlighting the distinctive ethnolinguistic and disciplinary context they are situated in as well as the mediating role of national research policy involved in individuals' language beliefs and practices in research communication. Although this study mainly employed descriptive statistical analysis of the quantitative data, the complemented qualitative data help to present a more nuanced picture of the Chinese local scholarship in language studies.

With regard to Chinese EAL scholars' language beliefs in research communication, we found that they overtly preferred a biliteracy approach and did not perceive English as a threat to the Chinese language. We interpreted this finding as signaling their efforts to negotiate their professional identity as English-language teachers/researchers with the nation's policy initiative to promote "Chinese culture and research going out". It is argued that macro-level sociopolitical factors, such as national research policy and historical contingencies of foreign language education, may exert top-down influences upon individual scholars' language beliefs and practices.

Despite the willingness to publish in English, however, the Chinese EAL scholars' ERPP attempts were somewhat thwarted mainly by the unfamiliarity with the international publishing practices and a perceived lack of academic training, which calls for more discipline-embedded training including research design and methods. It also needs to be noted that their articulated preference for a balanced biliteracy approach was not translated to actual biliterate practices in academic publishing. In view of the discrepancy between language beliefs and language practices, it is desirable to advance the ERPP research by in-depth examinations of the bi/multiliterate academic environments like the Chinese context and by critical inquiries into the bilingual scholar identity involved in academic publishing practices. Lastly, future research may also foreground the role of national/institutional research policy and examine ERPP in its own right as a language policy in higher education.

Acknowledgements

We would like to thank the editors for their constructive feedback. This study was partially supported by Shanghai Philosophy and Social Sciences Fund (2017BYY008).

Notes

1 The Chinese version of the 2004 "Views" can be found in http://www.gov.cn/test/2005-07/06/content_12421.htm.
2 The Chinese version of the 2011 "Decision" can be found at http://www.gov.cn/jrzg/2011-10/25/content_1978202.htm.
3 The Chinese version of the 2017 "Decision" is available at http://www.gov.cn/xinwen/2017-05/16/content_5194467.htm.

References

Belcher, D. (2007). Seeking acceptance in an English-only research world. *Journal of Second Language Writing, 16*(1), 1–22.
Bocanegra-Valle, A. (2014). "English is my default academic language": Voices from LSP scholars publishing in a multilingual journal. *Journal of English for Academic Purposes, 13*(1), 65–77.
Bolton, K., & Graddol, D. (2012). English in China today. *English Today, 28*(3), 3–9.
Bolton, K., & Kuteeva, M. (2012). English as an academic language at a Swedish university: Parallel language use and the "threat" of English. *Journal of Multilingual and Multicultural Development, 33*(5), 429–447.
Canagarajah, S. (2002). *The geopolitics of academic writing*. Pittsburgh, PA: University of Pittsburg.
Curry, M. J., & Lillis, T. (2010). Academic research networks: Assessing resources for English-medium publishing. *English for Specific Purposes, 29*, 281–295.
Duszak, A., & Lewkowicz, J. (2008). Publishing academic texts in English: A Polish perspective. *Journal of English for Academic Purposes, 7*, 108–120.
Englander, K., & Uzuner-Smith, S. (2013). The role of policy in constructing the peripheral scientist in the era of globalization. *Language Policy, 12*(3), 231–250.
Feng, H., Beckett, G. H., & Huang, D. (2013). From "import" to "import-export" oriented internalization: The impact of national policy on scholarly publication in China. *Language Policy, 12*(3), 251–272.
Ferguson, G. R., Pérez-Llantada, C., & Plo, R. (2011). English as an international language of scientific publication: A study of attitude. *World Englishes, 29*(3), 41–59.
Flowerdew, J. (2015). Some thoughts on English for Research Publication Purposes (ERPP) and related issues. *Language Teaching, 48*(2), 250–262.
Flowerdew, J., & Li, Y. (2009). English or Chinese? The trade-off between local and international publication among Chinese academics in the humanities and social sciences. *Journal of Second Language Writing, 18*(1), 1–16.
Gentil, G. (2011). A biliteracy agenda for genre research. *Journal of Second Language Writing, 20*, 6–23.
Hyland, K. (2015). *Academic publishing: Issues and challenges in the production of knowledge*. Oxford: Oxford University Press.
Hyland, K. (2016). Academic publishing and the myth of linguistic injustice. *Journal of Second Language Writing, 31*, 58–69.
ISTIC (2016). Statistical data of Chinese S&T papers. Retrieved 01 Feb, 2017, from http://conference.istic.ac.cn/cstpcd/newsrelease.html
King, D. A. (2004). The scientific impact of nations. *Nature, 430*, 311–316.
Kuteeva, M., & Airey, J. (2014). Disciplinary differences in the use of English in higher education: Reflections on recent language policy. *Higher Education, 67*(5), 533–549.

Kuteeva, M., & Mauranen, A. (2014). Writing for publication in multilingual contexts: An introduction to the special issue. *Journal of English for Academic Purposes*, *13*(1), 1–4.

Kuteeva, M., & McGrath, L. (2014). Taming *Tyrannosaurus rex*: English use in the research and publication practices of humanities scholars in Sweden. *Multilingua*, *33*(3/4), 365–387.

Lam, A. S. L. (2005). *Language education in China*. Hong Kong: Hong Kong University Press.

Lee, H., & Lee, K. (2013). Publish (in international indexed journals) or perish: Neoliberal ideology in a Korean university. *Language Policy*, *12*(3), 209–213.

Li, Y. (2014). Seeking entry to the North American market: Chinese management academics publishing internationally. *Journal of English for Academic Purposes*, *13*(1), 41–52.

Lillis, T., & Curry, M. J. (2010). *Academic writing in a global context: The politics and practices of publishing in English*. London: Routledge.

McGrath, L. (2014). Parallel language use in academic and outreach publication: A case study of policy and practice. *Journal of English for Academic Purposes*, *13*(1), 5–16.

Muresan, L.-M., & Pérez-Llantada, C. (2014). English for research publication and dissemination in bi-/multiliterate environments: The case of Romanian academics. *Journal of English for Academic Purposes*, *13*, 53–64.

Olsson, A., & Sheridan, V. (2012). A case study of Swedish scholars' experiences with and perceptions of the use of English in academic publishing. *Written Communication*, *29*(1), 33–54.

Pan, L. (2011). English language ideologies in the Chinese foreign language education policies: A world-system perspective. *Language Policy*, *10*, 245–263.

Phillipson, R., & Skutnabb-Kangas, T. (1999). Englishization: One dimension of globalization. In D. Graddol & U. H. Meinhof (Eds.). *English in a changing world. AILA Review* (pp. 19–36). Oxford: The English Book Center.

Sandelin, B., & Sarafoglou, N. (2004). Language and scientific publication statistics. *Language Problems and Language Planning*, *28*(1), 1–10.

Shohamy, E. (2006). *Language policy: Hidden agendas and new approaches*. London: Routledge.

Uzuner, S. (2008). Multilingual scholars' participation in core/global academic communities: A literature review. *Journal of English for Academic Purposes*, *7*(4), 250–263.

Wei, R., & Su, J. (2012). The statistics of English in China. *English Today*, *28*(3), 10–14.

Zheng, Y., & Gao, X. (2016). Chinese humanities and social sciences scholars' language practice in international scholarly publishing. *Journal of Scholarly Publishing*, *48*(1), 1–16.

REGION 5

South Asia

11
THE IMPACT OF ENGLISH LANGUAGE TEACHING REFORMS ON PAKISTANI SCHOLARS' LANGUAGE AND RESEARCH SKILLS

Sarwat Nauman

INSTITUTE OF BUSINESS MANAGEMENT, PAKISTAN

Introduction

Higher Education Commission (HEC) Pakistan is an independent, autonomous, and constitutionally-established institution responsible for overseeing, regulating, and accrediting higher education in Pakistan (HEC, n.d). This responsibility puts HEC Pakistan in a position where it draws rules and regulations for Pakistan's higher education institutions in order to maintain and improve their quality. One of the benchmarks of improved quality by HEC focuses upon the number of research papers published by the faculty of a Higher Education Institute (HEI). Not only is the number of research publications highly valued in recruitment and retention of faculty, as expressed in HEC's Minimum Criteria for the Appointment of Faculty Members (2015), but publication is also a prerequisite for an MPhil or a PhD degree. The issue, of course, is that 80% of the research work published in international journals is in English and out of many criteria set by HEC for a journal to be recognized, one is that a Pakistani journal must either publish all of its content, or at least its abstracts, in English (Mahboob, 2017; Standard Operating Procedure (SOP) for Recognition, Upgradation & Funding of Journals and Equivalency of Book with Research Article, n.d). It thus becomes incumbent for Pakistani scholars to be well versed in not only conducting research but also in writing research in the English language. To support its faculty with the English language and in various research procedures, HEC has initiated capacity building programs, workshops and training under the aegis of English Language Teaching Reforms (ELTR).

This chapter investigates the need for, the deliverance and the fruitfulness of these English Language Teaching Reforms. Drawing on the extant literature on Pakistani higher education policy, I evaluate the current state of reforms and give recommendations to be acted upon in order for Pakistani scholars to be able to actively and effectively participate in global knowledge production. This chapter is divided into five sections: an explication of Pakistan's language dilemma; my own experiences as an English language teacher and an Associate Editor of a Pakistani journal; the functions and policies of HEC Pakistan; a description of the English Language Teaching Reforms (ELTR) initiated by HEC; an analysis of the efficacy of these reforms; and some resulting recommendations for Pakistani policymakers.

Pakistan and English Language Learning

Pakistan comfortably fits in Kachru's Outer Circle, which is comprised of countries that were formerly British colonies and use English as their second language (Xu, 2017). Pakistan achieved its independence from the British Raj in 1947 and one of the legacies that the British left behind was the prestige, power and privilege that came with the English language (Rahman, 1996; Shamim, 2008). Even though Urdu is officially Pakistan's national language, to this day English remains the language of government, military and higher education.

The 1973 constitution ensured that steps would be taken to make Urdu the official language of Pakistan. However, Pakistani governments over the past 70 years have been delaying the implementation of this constitutional clause. As Gulzar and Farooq (2009) suggest, "sociopolitical realities of Pakistan brought English into the limelight and most importantly uncertain/indecisive language policy about the role/status of regional languages and Urdu has come to support English" (p. 10). Lack of interest or initiative from Pakistani governments to promote the vernacular language, Urdu, has created a niche in the domain of language for pragmatic purposes which English has helped to fill. Instead of promoting the Urdu language as per the 1973 constitution, the 2009 National Education Policy (NEP) explicitly announces that the Ministry of Education "shall develop a comprehensive plan of action for implementing the English language policy in the shortest possible time" (National Education Policy, 2009, p. 27). The NEP further states that the English language needs to be reinforced in schools from grade one and that it should be the medium of instruction in science and mathematics from grade four onwards, thus ascribing a special status to the English language. Critics argue that such a policy could be counterproductive as children should first be proficient in their first language before moving on to the second one, that the first language is natural, and that using it has a positive impact on the mental and emotional health of a child, facilitating increased learning capacity (Gulzar & Farooq, 2009; Khan, 2016).

Prior to analyzing the efficacy of current reforms, it is important to understand the place of English and Urdu in Pakistan's education system(s). Since there was no clear cut government stance on language policy in the previous education policies, the Pakistani education system was divided into two types of schooling systems, with public schools only offering English as a subject as of Grade 6 and private schools using English as the medium of instruction from pre-school until Grade 12. Despite the majority of Pakistanis studying in Urdu until Grade 5, there has historically been no provision of Urdu curriculum in higher education. The language of instruction at the higher education level throughout Pakistan has been English. This policy has created a great divide between public and private school students. As Rahman (2011a) suggests, students are often unable to fully achieve their intellectual potential due to their limited English language skills. He elaborates, "They are not prepared to constructively engage with texts (both oral and written) in their courses" (Rahman, 2011a, p. 5).

Experiences with English language teaching and journal editorship. My experiences as an educator support Rahman's (2011a) claims that Pakistani scholars are unprepared to meaningfully engage with advanced English language textual analysis and production. During my 15 years of teaching English writing and comprehension to students at the secondary, undergraduate and post-graduate levels, at various HEIs, there were numerous incidents where the students asked me to teach English in Urdu. Curious about their schooling background, I often asked them about their prior schooling. Students often revealed that it had been either from public schools or low standard private schools. Many private schools hire untrained teachers who have been part of the Urdu medium public school system and teach English in Urdu. English in such schools across Pakistan is taught by reading aloud the English text and then translating it into Urdu, whereas the answers to the comprehension questions and grammar exercises are dictated by the teachers which students learn and later produce in exams (Nawab, 2012). Over time, I discovered that a lack of what I perceive to be necessary perquisite English skills was not restricted to undergraduate students alone, but was persistent through scholars' educational trajectories, with graduate students as well as HEI faculty demonstrating a lack of necessary English language proficiency.

I was appointed to the role of Assistant Editor of a Pakistani research journal in 2015. During the tenure of my editorial post, I came to realize that a vast majority of Pakistani scholars were unable to compose a clear, coherent and cohesive text in English. Even if their research was robust, their writing skills often proved to be insufficient for the task. My experience with the Pakistani journal tells me that there are several main challenges for Pakistani scholars attempting to write research in English: the clear formulation of a research question; the ability to erect a coherent and cohesive text; logical reasoning; lexicogrammatical errors such as subject verb agreement and effective use of clauses and modifiers; and stylistic issues such as the lack of parallel writing structure. As a result, more than 90% of the time, we returned the papers to the authors and asked them to re-submit the papers after revising and eliminating all English language errors. However, very often they would re-submit the paper after making amendments to it themselves, without seeking professional help, which resulted in total rejection of their hard work. Given the potential mismatch between the expectations for publication facing Pakistani scholars and their English (research writing) proficiency, the question remains: Can this problem be tackled at such an advanced level of education? The following sections include an analysis of current reforms being enacted in Pakistani higher education.

Higher Education Commission (HEC) Pakistan: Background and Analysis

According to the NEP, Pakistan (2009), in order to keep abreast with today's fast-paced and ever-changing world of research, science and technology, the people of Pakistan must be competent in the English language. However, low levels of English proficiency at Pakistani HEIs suggests that HEC needs to step up its efforts on this front. HEC Pakistan has multiple roles to play: it is responsible for drafting and implementing the policy for higher education, it assures quality in higher education; and it must develop and upgrade university offerings (Dar, Jabeen, Jadoon, & Dar, 2016; HEC, n.d). The HEC thus provides a guideline for HEIs to keep up with the international standards. Following the lead of developed countries, HEC introduced vision 2025 which aims to develop Pakistani HEI's into TIER 1 research universities that should be the highest bastions of learning and discovering creative solutions to real life challenges facing Pakistan (Dar, et al., 2016). Hence, HEC Pakistan has emphasized research production, making it a fundamental criterion in university ranking and the Tenure Track System (TTS).

Through the TTS system, universities across Pakistan pay competitive salaries to faculty of Pakistani origin who are working in more "advanced" countries to assist local scholars and help create a research culture in the universities where they are appointed. In the TTS a faculty member is appointed for a period of three years following the submission of letters of reference from his/her PhD supervisor and review of all his/her publications in internationally recognized abstracted journals. These credentials are first reviewed by the Technical Review Panel (TRP), which consists of eminent international academics and researchers in the relevant area. The panel then gives its recommendation to the university's selection board where the final decision to induct the faculty member is taken (Model tenure track process statutes, 2008). The TTS is similar to the scheme implemented by the Chinese Education Ministry to upgrade its international universities' ranking where post-docs and foreign qualified Chinese PhDs are hired for short-term contracts that are renewable only upon the fulfilment of their "high-impact" journal publication requirement.

For Pakistani universities to become centers of knowledge development, the HEC has made it mandatory for students at the post-graduate level to be involved in research courses/projects. Further, production of quality research is also expected from the higher education faculty and is monitored through the number of their publications in Pakistani, HEC-recognized journals included in the ISI Web of Knowledge, e.g. Science Citation Index, SCI-Expanded, Social Science Citation Index (SSCI), and Arts & Humanities Citation Index (A&HCI) databases (Mahboob, 2017; Standard Operating Procedure (SOP) for Recognition, Upgradation & Funding of Journals and Equivalency of Book with Research Article, n.d.). In order to increase the visibility of Pakistani research, HEC demands publication in ISI journals and books; however, the ISI database reveals that only 11 out of 14,000 ISI journals are from Pakistan. Adding to this challenging situation is the fact that even though the highest numbers of PhD students come from the social sciences, there is not a single social sciences journal from Pakistan on the ISI list. The vast majority of the research work published in these international journals is in English and for a Pakistani journal to be included in HEC's journal database, it must publish, if not full articles, then at least article abstracts in English (Mahboob, 2017; Standard Operating Procedure (SOP) for Recognition, Upgradation & Funding of Journals and Equivalency of Book with Research Article, n.d). It seems unfair that the criterion set by HEC for research to be recognized as being worthy is so high and not in line with the actual research skills of the HEI faculty.

To fulfill the HEC research publication criteria, it is important that faculty be trained from their very early careers in the fundamentals of research, such as research ethics and academic writing skills (Dar, et al., 2016). Nasreen and Mirza (2012) explain that in order for this training to be fruitful, it should have the following qualities: i) be needs based; ii) be continuous; and iii) results must be monitored after the training/programs have been conducted. From my perspective, trainer effectiveness and transparency in trainee selection, which will be discussed in length later in this chapter, should also be included as necessary features of such sustainable research support.

Even though HEC Pakistan has developed policies and initiatives to upgrade the research skills of PhD scholars and university faculty via various courses and training, scholars' lack of English language proficiency at this advanced level of academe may be responsible for their insufficient disciplinary knowledge and/or critical thinking skills as their knowledge base was built using curriculum in a language (English) in which they were not fully proficient (Atta-ur-Rahman, 2001; Mahboob, 2017; Nauman, 2017). To expect a high level of research work from Pakistani scholars given their poor language skills seems like a far-fetched idea. Admittedly, language issues may not be the only reason why Pakistani papers have been rejected by international journals; scholars may fail to achieve publication of their work due to the choice of uninteresting topics, lack of access to resource materials, and physical, scholarly or financial isolation (Canagarajah, 2002; Hyland, 2016).

HEC Pakistan is well aware that English is the lingua franca of the scientific community (Ammon, 2006; Mahboob, 2017). Thus, enhancing English language proficiency is a precondition for advancement in research work

(Mahboob, 2017; Parvez, Anjum, & Khawaja, 2014; Sajid & Siddiqui, 2015); but producing research writing in English is not always easy for those using English as an additional language (Ammon, 2006; Durand, 2006; Hanauer & Englander, 2011). The "language proficiency problem" is once again highlighted in the 2016 report, Review of Research Performance in Higher Education Sector in the Last Decade, where it was suggested that scholars did not possess the skills to write a formal proposal as they had never received any explicit training or guidelines for doing so (Kumari, Babur, & Siddiqui, 2016). In this report, faculty further complained about their lack of ability to gain scholarships and research grants due to low levels of English language proficiency (Kumari, et al., 2016; Rind & Kadiwal, 2016; Shamim, 2008). Ultimately, all discussion boils down to the fact that there is a mismatch between the English proficiency levels and the unrealistic publishing requirements for Pakistani scholars, which has led to the current dilemma. HEC hopes to address this problem by improving English language and research skills of Pakistani scholars and faculty and has thus introduced a set of English Language Teaching Reforms (ELTR).

English Language Teaching Reforms (ELTR)

English Language Teaching Reforms (ELTR) were introduced by the Higher Education Commission in 2004, with the aim of building capacity and proficiency of English language teachers in higher education. Ostensibly, this is to stimulate effective and sustainable development in English language teaching and in research through short- and long-term courses (HEC, n.d; Rind & Kadiwal, 2016). HEC Pakistan has recognized that traditional English language courses at the post-graduate level could not prepare students for the academic English writing necessary for research activities (Mahboob, 2017; Parvez, et al., 2014; Sajid & Siddiqui, 2015). Others have noted that PhD scholars and faculty lack the ability to critically evaluate and analyze a text written in English, which is a necessary axiological skill in post-graduate studies (Sajid & Siddiqui, 2015). In response to this need, the Pakistani HEC enacted the six-part English language teaching reforms (ELTR) project, including faculty development program, curriculum material development, testing and evaluation, reorganization of ELT departments, computer aide language learning and research and publication (see figure 1).

According to the HEC Pakistan website, this project is divided into two phases: the first phase was completed in 2010 and the second phase will be completed in 2020. HEC claims that the first phase has been completed successfully, where out of 1400 targeted teachers, 1398 college and university teachers have been trained (HEC, n.d). Under phase II of the ELTR program, HEC has introduced the International Resource Person (IRP) training (in collaboration with the US and UK) where it recruits experts from abroad to work with college and university English language faculty and scholars. During this training, they

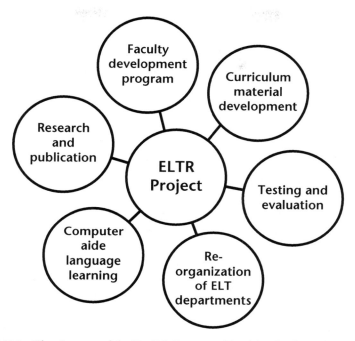

FIGURE 11.1 The six parts of the English Language Teaching Reforms (ELTR)

are provided with support from well-reputed and distinguished foreign experts not only in TEFL/Applied Linguistics/TESOL but also in basic and advanced research techniques. These experts are invited to Pakistan to conduct 100 hours of specified professional development and capacity building workshops in the following areas through the ELTR (HEC, Pakistan, n.d):

- Computer Assisted Language Learning (CALL)
- Testing and Evaluation
- Research Methodology and Skills
- Open and Customized Programs in ELT related areas (EAP, ESP, ESL, ELT)
- Andragogical and Pedagogical Skills.

The HEC website also touts the long-term ELTR courses, which include a two-year Master's degree in Applied Linguistics/TESL/TEFL/ELT. The ELTR also includes the Virtual Education Program Pakistan (VEPP), where students pursuing post-graduate degrees develop their language and literacy with support from a global network of scholars contributing through video conferencing lectures. It is suggested that this training allows Pakistani scholars to more fully engage with and contribute to their international disciplinary communities (HEC, n.d). Next, HEC has developed faculty training programs under the aegis of the ELTR, such as the

Continuous Professional Development (CPD) courses, where faculty capacity is built through two-week seminars, workshops and courses based on the university proposals. The IRP program and the organization of seminars/conferences aims to enhance the research capacity of faculty and provide a forum for them to upgrade their research skills as per the global standards. This naturally leads us to the pressing question: How effective has the ELTR program been at improving Pakistani scholars' (English) language and research skills?

Assessing the Impact of the ELTR Program

The ELTR program was initiated after realizing two fundamental problems that postgraduate university students were facing: the first one being their inability to use their "higher order" thinking skills; the second one being their inadequate command over the English language (Khan, Majoka, & Fazal, 2016; Nauman, 2017). Malik (2013) concludes that much effort was made in designing the ELTR training modules where help and assistance was taken from experts from both within and outside the country. She calls the first phase of ELTR a success, noting a recognizable impact of the ELTR training on faculty work both in and outside the classroom, leading policymakers to move on to phase II of the project. She further explains that it is the responsibility of the program planners and the policymakers to do away with the weaknesses in phase II of the program that were visible in phase I: gaps between the training objectives and their realization in real classroom settings; formulation of transparent selection criterion of trainees; and the development of a mechanism to follow up on trainee outcomes (Khattak, Abbasi, & Ahmad, 2011). Since HEC has linked research projects and publications with monetary and promotional incentives, both faculty and graduate students have shown acute interest in upgrading their research skills; therefore, ELTR courses that dealt with research development were often exceedingly competitive, where for 30 seats there were often 180 applicants who were then shortlisted according to regional distribution (Azam, 2009).

Have the HEC initiatives impacted Pakistani scholars' ability to produce "visible", "high impact" research? Thomson Reuters' recent report "Pakistan, Another BRIC in the Wall" (2016) paints a very positive image of progress in Pakistani research, highlighting that there has been a dramatic increase in the number of publications coming out of Pakistan in the last ten years from 2000 articles per year in 2006 to 9000 articles in 2015. It further acknowledges that the number of highly cited papers from Pakistan has also increased tremendously, from nine articles in 2006 to 98 in 2015. The report makes a comparison between Pakistan and the BRIC (Brazil, Russia, India and China) countries and concludes that the most cited articles in Pakistan during the period of 2006 to 2015 was 62.27% of the total published work, which is more than the citations made from published work of all the BRIC countries combined, which was 59.73%

(Herciu, 2016). Thus, HEC's efforts may have positively impacted the number of publications coming out of Pakistan, with some being published in ISI journals; nevertheless this number remains very low (Mahboob, 2017).

On the surface, the Thomson Reuters report would seem to challenge the claims made by the critics of HEC, who claim that very little impactful research is coming out of Pakistan (Hoodbhoy, 2009; Mahmood, 2017; Shamim, 2008); that Pakistani scholars lack the requisite English language skills to achieve publication (Kumari, et al., 2016; Rind & Kadiwal, 2016; Shamim, 2008) as well as claims of lack of requisite critical thinking skills among Pakistani researchers (Khan, et al., 2016; Nauman, 2017). Upon deeper reflection, this positive contribution may be partly due to HEC initiatives taken to send PhD candidates in more advanced countries for the completion of their degrees in various fields where 3000 PhD scholarships were granted during 2003–2009, which was about the same as in the previous 55 years (Rahman, 2011b). These scholars have often been trained by their supervisors to publish in highly cited research journals, therefore, as a result the number of research publications in respectable international journals shot up from about 500 per year in 2000 to 4,600 per year by 2009 (Rahman, 2011b). Ultimately, it seems highly unlikely that increase in visible knowledge production highlighted in the Thomson Reuters report is the direct result of the ELTR program, but there does appear to be some evidence of the program's impact.

Saleem, Masrur, and Afzal (2014) also suggest the effectiveness of the ELTR program. Their results stem from an investigation of ELTR training that was conducted over a period of 12 weeks, where the training focus was on the development of faculty research skills. Their research methodology was a simple one; a pre-test was conducted prior to the training and a post-test was conducted after the training to gauge the difference in the knowledge of the attendees. Their data revealed a positive impact of the training on the trainees as their knowledge increased significantly. The problem with such studies is that knowledge is the lowest of the cognitive domains in Bloom's taxonomy and at the post-graduate level, higher cognitive skills such as critically analyzing, evaluating and creating are essential ones which can only be measured if those involved in learning are made to use the knowledge obtained to create something new. In this case, having the knowledge of study design or research methodology does not guarantee their fruitful usage. As suggested by Shamim (2010) in an article published in the *Guardian*:

> There has been a focus on numbers—so many teachers trained, so many courses held. The reports produced haven't indicated how these courses and seminars have made a difference to the teaching and learning of English in universities. I worry about the focus on numbers in the second phase as well.
>
> *(para 11)*

How can we call a program a success when there has been little well-defined assessment criteria? In my view, a more pragmatic approach is needed where the trainees must use this learned knowledge and create something new from it, especially given that these Pakistani researchers have studied in an education system that does not always robustly promote critical thinking skills (Shamim, 2008 Nauman, 2017). The study by Saleem, et al., (2014) does not convincingly elucidate whether or not the ELTR really made a difference in the higher order cognitive skills of the participants. Also, Raabi and Mamoon (2017) and Nauman (2017) explain that research cannot be impactful until and unless it gives solutions to the problems that exist in a society. Hence, although there is some evidence of increased research production from Pakistani scholars (Herciu, 2016; Rahman, 2011b), I contend that if they are not making any difference in the society then they can hardly be called impactful. Ultimately, even though there has been a significant increase in research, there is still a lot more that needs to be done; particularly keeping in view that the report points out that research publication from Pakistan is still relatively very small when compared with other BRIC nations' research output.

Further critique of the ELTR comes from Malik (2013), who is of the view that one major problem in conducting this program successfully was the combined lack of interest from universities along with resistance to change by the teaching fraternity. For example, courses offered in the ELTR program that cater to teaching, curriculum management and assessment needs are of less interest to scholars because they have to work extra without getting a study leave from their respective institutions (Azam, 2009). Further, most of the faculty in these programs were nominated by the universities rather than scholars self-selecting, which is problematic in that programs are not necessarily responsive to the needs of scholars (Azam, 2009; Malik, 2013).

Conclusions

The Pakistani situation with reference to English language and research production is a complex one. Some reports suggest a substantial increase in Pakistani research published in indexed English language journals. Conversely, critics, scholars, and faculty have suggested the weakness of Pakistani researchers' English language proficiency and overall research skills, pointing to the divide between reality and expectations for scholars' research production. My final analysis, outlined in this section, draws upon the limited research on the topic as well as my own experience as an English language educator and Pakistani scholar.

In considering directions forward, we must bear in mind that Pakistani society is a mixture of those who have been through private, highly effective school systems where the whole curriculum is in the English language and based upon British or American schooling models; and those who have come from public school systems where all subjects are taught in Urdu and rote learning is often the teaching methodology. This contrast in students from two starkly different education systems leads to varied skill sets in individuals later in life. Another contributing factor to the quality of research and publication outcomes in Pakistan is the return of Pakistani scholars to Pakistan after completing their higher education in more "advanced" countries. In 2016 alone, 65% of those availing of the HEC scholarship have returned to Pakistan (Haq, 2017; The Nation, 2017). Hence, I would suggest that many of these scholars are contributing positively and have had the requisite training in order to successfully publish research in international research journals. However, the question remains of how to increase the publication outcomes of Pakistani scholars, many of whom have not been educated abroad and have less robust traditions of research and writing?

It is important to mention that Pakistani universities should not solely rely on efforts made by the HEC; they need to be active in promoting a research culture in their respective institutions. It seems that universities are lacking when it comes to facilitation of their faculty research writing, which creates a gap between their reality and the HEC vision. This gap can be bridged through a more dynamic university role. The NEP Pakistan, HEC Pakistan, and Pakistani universities should all be on the same page in order to produce more positive and sustainable research production results. No policy can be wholly effective unless all stakeholders hold the same vision and make substantial contributions accordingly.

Programs like the ELTR have contributed significantly to stimulating the research activities in Pakistan and have tried to shape the rough edges around English language proficiency and research writing expertise. However, like any program, it has its weaknesses. One apparent weakness is the lack of follow-up with scholars after English language research and writing support has been provided. There has been no systematic measure of the impact and effectiveness of ELTR programs and their trickle down effects. Not only is there a need for more research in this area, but HEC needs to devise a methodology to measure the effectiveness of these programs on a regular and ongoing basis. Currently, there is only one report available (Kumari, et al., 2016) and it does not exclusively focus on any one program, but rather provides an overall picture of HEC initiatives.

Another clear shortcoming of the ELTR is the lack of transparency or systematicity used to select either the language and research trainers or the participants. This is evidenced by the fact that there are no guidelines available on the HEC website or elsewhere that demonstrate the selection criterion for the trainers or the trainees. There is also no way to find out how HEC decides which training programs to offer. There seems to be a gray area in the selection of trainers, trainees and the topics chosen for training programs which can be easily manipulated, and is being manipulated to some extent, as highlighted by Kumari, et al. (2016) in their report. It seems that the faculty chosen for various HEC-led training programs is selected in accordance with the will of their respective department heads or the university administrators (Kumari, et al., 2016; Malik, 2013), which is problematic on many fronts. Further, there is neither a needs analysis conducted to see which faculty is in want or need of particular training, nor does merit appear to be considered. The HEC should ask universities to develop consistent faculty selection criteria for various training programs and workshops. This would have a positive effect on the training through substantiated learning while reducing the stigma of biased selection based upon favoritism (Kumari, et al., 2016). Further, training programs such as the CPD and IRP need to be more frequent and should attempt to reach the maximum number of scholars. In addition, another potentially useful tweak to the ELTR initiatives could include making available temporary study/training leave for faculty. HEC needs to make sure that universities implement such policies whereby faculty members are given short study leaves to attend various training programs and workshops organized by HEC. Such a move may increase faculty receptiveness to these courses and workshops, resulting in increased capacity for Pakistani knowledge production.

Finally, to presume that after studying in an inefficient schooling system that stresses low level thinking skills (Shamim, 2009; Nauman, 2017), PhD students (and faculty) will suddenly acquire higher order thinking skills at the university level is, in my estimation, unrealistic. HEC can introduce as many ELTR programs as possible, but with a weak base in English language and higher order thinking skills, there will likely only be limited progress. Although revamping the whole Pakistani education system from pre-primary to the higher education needs is perhaps unrealistic, attention needs to be paid to creating a system that is more pragmatic in nature and helps students function in global contexts. Ultimately, when considering the mismatch between Pakistani scholars' capacities and expectations for their research production, I am skeptical about the initiatives taken by the HEC and NEP to adequately address the situation. Only if great care is taken to adopt concurrent reforms introducing English from grade one at the school level (NEP, 2009) alongside capacity building reforms such as the HEC's ELTR, can there be hope for lasting and fruitful results in the arena of Pakistani research production.

References

Ammon, U. (2006). Language planning for international scientific communication: An overview of questions and potential solutions. *Current issues in language planning*, 7(1), 1–30.

Azam, M. K. (2009). Professional development of English language teachers in higher education in Pakistan. In N. Hussain, A. Ahmed, & M. Zafar (Eds.). *English and Empowerment in the Developing World* (pp. 77–83). Newcastle upon Tyne, UK: Cambridge Scholars Publishing.

Canagarajah, A. S. (2001). *A geopolitics of academic writing*. Pittsburgh: University of Pittsburgh Press.

Dar, S., Jabeen, N., Jadoon, Z. I., & Dar, I. S. (2016). Faculty development programs and their effect on individual and organizational performance in Pakistan. *Pakistan Vision*, 17(2).

Durand, C. X. (2006). "If it's not in English, it's not worth reading!" *Current Issues in Language Planning*, 7(1), 44–60.

Gulzar, M. A., & Farooq, U. (2009). Linguistic controversy: Promotion of English. *Journal of Social Sciences and Humanities, 17*(1), 1–12.

Haq, R. (2017, August 07). *65% of those availing HEC scholarship returned after studies*. Retrieved from Tribune Express: https://tribune.com.pk/story/1475147/65-availing-hec-scholarship-returned-studies/

Higher Education Commision (n.d.). Retrieved from http://hec.gov.pk/english/services/faculty/ELTR/Pages/Introduction.aspx

HEC minimum criteria for the appointment of faculty members at HEIs/DAIs (18 July 2015). Retrieved from http://hec.gov.pk/english/services/universities/QA/Documents/H.pdf

Hanauer, D. I., & Englander, K. (2011). Quantifying the burden of writing research articles in a second language: Data from Mexican scientists. *Written Communication, 28*(4), 403–416.

Herciu, I. (2016). *Pakistan, another BRIC in the wall*. Cape Town: Thomson Reuters.

Hoodbhoy, P. (2009). Pakistan's higher education system—What went wrong and how to fix it? *The Pakistan Development Review, 48*(4), 581–594.

Hyland, K. (2016). Academic publishing and the myth of linguistic injustice. *Journal of Second Language Writing, 31*, 58–69.

Khan, M. I., Majoka, M. I., & Fazal, S. (2016). Post/graduate academic writing problems: A Pakistani case. In C. Badenhorst, & C. Guerin (Eds.). *Research literacies and writing pedagogies for masters and doctoral writers* (pp. 389–406). Boston, MA: Brill.

Khan, M. T. (2016). Mother tongue an effective medium of education—(education which is a factor of human capital development). *International Journal of Information, Business and Management, 8*(3), 207–225.

Khattak, Z. I., Abbasi, G., & Ahmad, A. (2011). Impact analysis of the in-service teacher training programmes of the testing and evaluation sub-committee of the ELTR project in Pakistan. *Procedia Social and Behavioral Sciences, 15*, 1479–1483.

Khattaka, Z. I., & Abbasib, M. G. (2010). Evaluation of the effectiveness of in-service teacher training courses of the CALL sub-committee of the ELTR project in Pakistan. *Procedia Social and Behavioral Sciences, 2*, 4911–4917.

Kumari, R., Babur, M., & Siddiqui, N. (2016). *Research and development: Review of research performance in higher education sector in the last decade*. Islamabad: Higher Education Commission.

Lotbinière, M. D. (2010). *Pakistan struggles to reverse falling university language skills*. Retrieved from the *Guardian*: https://www.theguardian.com/education/2010/jun/15/pakistan-struggles-to-reverse-falling-university-language-skills

Mahmood, K. (2016). *Overall assessment of the higher education sector*. Islamabad: Higher Education Commision.

Mahboob, A. (2017). English medium instruction in higher education in Pakistan: Policies, perceptions, problems, and possibilities. In I. Walkinsah, B. Fenton-Smith and P. Humphreys (Eds.). *English as a medium of instruction in higher education in Asia-Pacific: Issues and challenges* (pp. 71–92). London: Springer.

Malik, N. A. (2013). Advances in teacher education and innovative professional development initiatives to address emerging challenges. In A. Ahmed, M. Hanzala, F. Saleem, & G. Cane (Eds.). *ELT in a changing world: Innovative approaches to new challenges* (pp. 203–214). Newcastle upon Tyne: Cambridge Scholars Publishing.

Model tenure track process statutes. (2008, January 1). Retrieved from HEC Pakistan: http://www.hec.gov.pk/english/services/universities/tts/Documents/Model%20TTS%20Ver%202%200%20%2805-07-12%29.pdf

Nasreen, A., & Mirza, M. S. (2012). Faculty training and development in the public sector universities of Punjab. *International Journal of Business and Social Science, 3*(3), 229–240.

Nauman, S. (2017). Lack of critical thinking skills leading to research crisis in developing countries: A case of Pakistan. *Learned Publishing, 30*(3), 233–236. DOI: 10.1002/leap.1091

Nawab, A. (2012). Is it the way to teach language the way we teach language? English language teaching in rural Pakistan. *Academic Research International, 2*(2), 696–705.

National Education Policy (2009). Islamabad: Ministry of Education.

The *Nation* (2017, August 06). *Over 3,000 scholars returned after completion of studies.* Retrieved from http://nation.com.pk/islamabad/06-Aug-2017/over-3-000-scholars-returned-after-completion-of-studies

The *Guardian*. (2010, June 15). *Pakistan struggles to reverse falling university language skills.* Retrieved from https://www.theguardian.com/education/2010/jun/15/pakistan-struggles-to-reverse-falling-university-language-skills

Parvez, A., Anjum, M. A., & Khawaja, I.-U.-D. (2014). Quality assurance: The standards for teaching and learning in higher education institutions of Pakistan. *Journal of Applied and Emerging Sciences, 5*(2), 105–118.

Raabbi, A., & Mamoon, D. (2017). Short term versus long term economic planning in Pakistan: The dilemma. *Journal of Economics Library, 4*(1), 1–20.

Rahman. A. (2011a). *The higher education network and virtual education project Pakistan: A model for educational change for the developing world.* Islamabad: Higher Education Commission.

Rahman, A. (2011b, June 7). *Faculty development in higher education.* Retrieved from The Express Tribune: https://tribune.com.pk/story/190946/faculty-development-in-higher-education/

Rahman, T. (2008). *Language, ideology and power: Language-learning among the Muslims of Pakistan and North India.* Hyderabad: Orient Longman Private Limited.

Rind, I. A., & Kadiwal, L. (2016). Analysing institutional influences on teaching-learning practices of English as second language programme in a Pakistani university. *Cogent Education, 3*(1), 1–13.

Sajid, M., & Siddiqui, J. A. (2015). Lack of academic writing skills in English language at higher education level in Pakistan: Causes, effects and remedies. *International Journal of Language and Linguistics, 2*(4), 174–186.

Saleem, A., Masrur, R., & Afzal, M. T. (2014). Effect of professional development on enhancing the knowledge level of university teachers in Pakistan. *Journal of Research and Reflections in Education, 8*(2), 162–168.

Shamim, F. (2008). Trends, issues and challenges in English language education in Pakistan. *Asia Pacific Journal of Education, 28*(3), 235–249.

Standard Operating Procedure (SOP) for Recognition, Upgradation & Funding of Journals and Equivalency of Book with Research Article. (n.d.). Retrieved from HEC, Pakistan. http://hec.gov.pk/english/services/faculty/SSAH/Documents/JCR/Social%20Sciences%20Policy%20Booklet-Final.pdf

Xu, X. (2017). Study on the English varieties of "One Belt, One Road" countries. *Theory and Practice in Language Studies, 7*(3), 201–208.

REGION 6
Africa

12

TEACHING THE CRAFT

From Thesis Writing to Writing Research for Publication

Hayat Messekher
ECOLE NORMALE SUPÉRIEURE DE BOUZARÉAH, ALGERIA

Mohamed Miliani
UNIVERSITY OF ORAN 1, ALGERIA

Algerian Higher Education and Research Writing for Publication

Until quite recently, higher education (HE) institutions in Algeria did not encourage their graduate students to produce quality papers during their studies, let alone to publish them. However, in June 2016, the Algerian Ministry of Higher Education and Scientific Research issued a policy document (arrêté[1]) whereby publishing became an official requirement for the viva examinations to take place. The only drawback is that no formal training in writing for publication is offered at university level. Hence, much focus is put on publishing as it became a condition to earn a doctorate under both the classical[2] HE system and the new HE reform known as the LMD[3] (License – Master – Doctorate) system. Therefore, graduate students need to develop the ability to write and present papers as partial fulfilment of their doctoral degrees. Likewise, academic promotion requires publishing in national and international refereed journals cited in the established Scopus, ISI Thomson Reuters, etc. Although the 2016 policy document did not specify in which language doctoral candidates should publish, the point system allocated to different ranks of publications meant that publishing in English will secure the highest points compared to the other languages used, i.e. Modern Standard Arabic, Tamazight, French, or any other additional language. Hence, given that international publications in English will secure not just greater visibility but also the highest points, this might explain why English was made a compulsory course at the doctoral level with a focus on the two skills of speaking and writing. Yet, there was no indication in the policy document as to how this requirement of research writing (in English) will be supported or explicitly taught.

Publishing is becoming a pressing concern for most graduate students and faculty members. This puts a burden on doctoral candidates and faculty seeking tenure and promotion as they compete with other scholars who may also be non-native or native speakers of English despite issues of inequality (Ammon, 2007; Corcoran & Englander, 2016; Hanauer & Englander, 2013; Muresan & Pérez-Llantada, 2014). As noted above, the reward points given to a publication vary depending on whether it is published in a high-impact factor international/national journal, which increases the pressure to publish internationally; a trend that has been noted globally (Hanauer & Englander, 2011; Hyland, 2016; Pérez-Llantada, 2014; Uzuner-Smith & Englander, 2015). According to the policy document, the scale specifying the earned points for scientific productions (publishing, conference presentations, and patents) allocates at least 50 points to be eligible to defend a dissertation. This means that graduate students need to publish at least two articles. Furthermore, the journals need to be listed in the SCI. If the article is published in a journal indexed in the ISI Web of Science, the author gains the maximum, 50 points. However, if students publish nationally, they only earn half the points for each publication, i.e. 25. Hence, writing for publication in English is a skill that graduate students need to be prepared for when starting their MA program, especially as most MA students aspire to pursue a doctoral degree (Messekher & Miliani, 2017).

Previous Writing Experiences of MA Students

In post-colonial Algeria, publishing in English is problematic in that English is often learned as a third or fourth language after the acquisition of the mother tongue and the learning of French. In recent years, there has been an increase in the demand for English in private language schools linked to migration and employability (Cherfaoui & Khennour, 2016), but the level of mastery of English is far below that of Arabic and French. English is introduced as a subject in middle school and taught through high school. In tertiary education, English is taught as a subject, and not a medium of instruction, except at the Algerian Petroleum Institute and the Institute of Electric and Electronic Engineering at the University of Boumerdes. English is the language of instruction for English majors. If Ferris and Hedgcock (2014, p. 34) state that FL students "may have had limited opportunities to read and write extensively in the L2", we can safely posit from our personal experience that students have more limited exposure to English than to Arabic or French. Academic writing is taught for English majors at undergraduate and graduate degree programs. However, the students' writing practices are more likely to be affected by their level of proficiency in English, and the language(s) they speak. Students are also affected by the writing instruction they received in middle and high schools. In fact, the authors' personal experiences indicate that little writing instruction in English is provided in schools. As such, when English majors enter university, they have little experience with writing instruction and practice relevant to the development of the skill. Most of the writing they produced previously was in-class writing that was either *expository* or *argumentative*. Such writing is in the form of group-work, allowing students to contribute collectively. It can also be individual writing pieces produced by highly performing students and used by teachers as samples to display for the rest of the class. However, writing assignments are rarely free in-class activities, but tasks given during exams. The usual triptych, purpose-audience-content, is given to students as a way to determine the necessary rhetorical patterns.

Overall, when these majors write in English, similarly to what Manchon (2011) describes, they write to demonstrate mastery of content across the various courses they take especially for end of term sit-in exams. Furthermore, class sizes are large at the undergraduate and graduate levels. This means that there is less one-to-one teacher-student interaction when revising writing, less class-time for multi-drafting, and peer-review from personal experience can be resisted. Moreover, when students need help, there is no support or tutoring service available for them. In light of these constraints, academic publication in English becomes more of a burden in academia as academics would have had little to no training in academic writing to begin with. Therefore, writing for publication in English is a skill that graduate students need to be prepared for during their MA programs.

At the graduate level, the main focus of MA programs is to conduct degree-oriented research and then write up the results according to set academic standards. The essay examination is the most used writing assignment while other writing tasks such as summaries and book reports are only occasionally given if the teacher feels it necessary. If thesis writing is part of the MA programs, writing for publication is nearly ignored or it takes the form of seminars mostly for teachers with a scientific background. Given the focus on eventual publishing, and with English increasingly becoming a gatekeeper, it is clear that today's graduates will face the requirement of academic publication as a stipulation for career advancement. With insights gained from this exploratory research, we propose implications for the design of a writing-for-publication MA course.

The Present Study

Writing for publication is required from graduate students to further their studies, develop their own research agendas, and advance their academic career. In the long run, they might even help their institutions gain more visibility through publications in English in indexed journals. As such, we attempt to give an opportunity to 44 Algerian MA students to voice their concerns and experiences of writing or aspiring to publish in English in the future. The study builds on the theories of Communities of Practice (CoP) (Wenger, 1998), and Imagined Communities (ICs) (Anderson, 1991). CoPs focus on learning that occurs through practice and participation while ICs are imagined in language and require one to get socialized in activities adopting identities in order to be recognized by other members of the imagined community as a legitimate member. The notions of CoP and ICs are used to provide an analysis of the practice of writing and the communities imagined by the MA students in relation to future publication in English.

Methodology

The present study aims at examining: a) the perceptions of these multilingual MA students regarding their writing ability in the different languages they use and their previous experiences with both aspects of writing instruction and writing experience, and b) their future intentions of publishing in English in order to gauge the students' imagined conceptions of publishing in English.

Data was collected by means of two questionnaires developed to examine students' perceptions of writing and of future imagined writing for publication. The first questionnaire (cf. Appendix 12.1) consisted of three large components: (a) information background—the participants' age, gender, specialization, mother tongue and additional languages used; (b) their experience in composing in the different main languages they speak and the obstacles they face; and (c) their perceptions of the process-product, writing literary or ESP texts, and their writing process. The second questionnaire (cf. Appendix 12.2) was composed of five questions to gauge students' intentions for future co/publication in English, in national or international journals and any existing publishing experience. Open-ended questions to gather data on the participants' beliefs, attitudes and concerns in relation to writing were used. The participants were 36 students in an MA program at a Western university in Algeria and 8 students at a Teacher Training College (henceforth TTC) in Algiers. The students were majoring in Didactics of English and ESP, as well as Didactics of English and Applied Linguistics respectively. This makes them interesting to survey because they are immersed in writing in an English-rich field, are required to write an MA thesis in English, and may further their studies in English. The study also investigated these students' intentions and attitudes towards publishing in English.

The primary research questions are as follows:

1. What are MA students' perceptions and previous experiences of writing in English?
2. How do these students imagine their future publication endeavors in English?

The participating students were asked to fill out questionnaires. Responses were analyzed using descriptive statistics for the demographics and language mastery sections with content analysis used to reveal trends and common themes (Corbin & Straus, 2007) in terms of the most significant problems and processes that these students highlighted in their responses.

Findings

There were 44 participants in this study. Table 12.1 sums up the exogenous factors of gender, age group, mother tongue, and specialty. The majority of the participants were female, a trend quite common in HE demographics in the humanities, and were aged between 20 and 25. Algerian Arabic was the mother tongue of the majority and Tamazight of the minority; again, a very representative sample of the linguistic landscape in Algeria. Self-evaluation of the language proficiency of the languages they spoke showed an equal distribution between intermediate and advanced levels in English and French, and an overwhelming majority with an advanced level in Modern Standard Arabic.

The answers to question seven, related to students' experience in composition/essay writing in English, showed a limited experience in this respect. Most essay writing was exam-based with a daunting focus on grammatical accuracy and vocabulary. Much emphasis was put on paragraph writing used as a scaffolding to develop essay writing with a felt need for guidance. Some of the students were able to answer question eight related to the differences between writing a composition and an essay. For question nine, the majority of university students were positive and preferred to write in English, while students from TTC were equally divided, some showing preference to writing in English and some feeling comfortable while writing creatively in Arabic.

Talking about obstacles, the questions were intended to help students identify their difficulties in the use of Arabic (Q.10), French (Q.11) or English (Q.12) in writing assignments. Two linguistic items were transversal and recurrent in the three experiences: punctuation problems and vocabulary for the university students, while TTC students found no difficulties in writing in Arabic. Besides, these students seem to have the same obstacles when writing in English and French because of punctuation, lack of vocabulary, and interference from Arabic. Other peculiarities related to French were the difficulties of conjugation, and tenses and tense concord in English. The surprise came from students'

TABLE 12.1 Exogenous factors of participants

Exogenous factors	Options	Western university	Algiers Teacher Training College
Gender	Male	15	2
	Female	21	6
Age group	20–25	24	6
	> 25 year	12	2
Mother tongue	Algerian Arabic	33	–
	Tamazight	3	8
Specialty	Linguistics	11	–
	Language sciences & didactics	16	8
	ESP	9	–

shared views about French and English concerning their limited motivation. But it is French that has a more negative image in the eyes of a number of students: almost a quarter of the respondents highlighted its vocabulary not being rich enough, its grammar being boring, complicated, and having confusing tenses. This has developed in the students a passive attitude that pushes them to admit to understanding it without being able to write in it. The question may legitimately be asked whether this is not the same in English. However, some justify this feeling by pointing to their teachers' lack of expertise. Two students went as far as saying that they had difficulties with the Latin script, hence their negative attitude towards the language. At the other extreme, Arabic seemed to enjoy a high percentage of positive feedback (21): wide vocabulary, rich language, with very few students admitting having problems with its syntax and vocabulary. The majority of the students reported that their writing was limited to class assignments, homework, or exams.

As for the writing skills, the majority of students (33) confessed that they were not familiar with the product-process dichotomy (Q.14). When asked about their focus in writing (Q.13), many (32) declared that they aimed at the product, which is a token of the traditional method of teaching writing. The remaining (10) pointed towards process and product as being their target. Only two students from TTC favored a process approach to writing, while no one from the university stated that they favored process-writing: a contradiction with what was suggested in the answers to question 18, which asked them to describe the process they go through when they write. It was logical that to question 15, they disclosed their difficulties in process-writing though 14 students from the university and 6 from TTC acknowledged that they had problems in none, while only 2 from TTC found difficulties with the approach. A paradox that is apparent with their answer about their lack of familiarity with the process-product approach. This pushes us to question the consensus (44) about their knowledge of the differences between writing literary and ESP texts, a fundamental characteristic of writing for publication. Some students went as far as associating emotions and organization of ideas (25) with literary texts. ESP texts were said (18) to convey and/or transmit information, which could be seen as a good start to writing for publication.

Asked to describe the process they went through in order to write (Q.18), students revealed a lot about their skill practices. The question aimed at understanding if students had a particular organized way of planning and systematizing their writing practice, whether this meant following their teachers' lessons or at least their own understanding of what writing consisted of. More often than not, it was the traditional, introduction, body and conclusion pattern (27 students) that was suggested. At least, that showed a concern for a safe route to successful writing. A more sophisticated way was put forward when several students (14 from the university and 8 from TTC) sequenced their writing as follows: jot down ideas, evaluate your stretch of discourse, rearrange according to meaning building, expand, finally, check if it fulfils the intended goal. Some (13 from the university and one from TTC) displayed an interestingly creative way that is described as "write with the flow of ideas". A word of caution has been given by Rose as to when (1984, p. 91) ". . . the student generates a mass of ideas that can lead to more disorder". Others were more concerned with the "norms" of writing (17) that were felt to be a hindrance, stating that they bored them to death (2). Punctuation remained a real obstacle. Very few students did mention the editing aspect of writing tasks, giving a sense of linearity in composition or essay writing, unlike the students from TTC, who emphasized editing.

When invited to define what could be considered as a successful writing product (Q.19), the students seemed not to have understood the question. A number of them still talked about their own experience, while others simply pointed to process writing as a way to succeed in writing. The majority of students (19 from the university and seven from TTC) pointed towards the ultimate aim of communication in writing: i.e., transmission of intended message, while several indicated a more practical issue: answering a given exam question, which is after all what teachers are very frequently looking for. It was somehow a relief to read some mentions of the concepts of cohesion and coherence, even if the explanations were not totally in agreement with the admitted definitions of both terms. One student from TTC considers a successful writing product to be the one written voluntarily, without instructions from a teacher, not being part of an assignment, homework nor exam.

Finally, the ultimate question (Q. 20) asked students what they would consider a successful writing process. The majority of them chose safely: to follow the norms, even if one feels they would be at a loss if they were asked to name them. Only one student from TTC suggested writing without planning. A more common definition from most of them was the sequence pre-writing-drafting-editing-proofreading as a way to convention-oriented writing tasks. At the other end of the spectrum, there were few students who insisted on working with ideas before organizing them into coherent wholes. The last perceptions were a good omen as to how a course in writing for publication could benefit from these sophisticated views.

Results of the second questionnaire which aimed at uncovering the participants' envisioned intentions of writing for publication showed that the majority of the students plan to publish in English. Very few did not know nor had an intention to publish. The majority envisioned publishing in English locally; believing it will be difficult and competitive. Some students indicated they would start publishing locally, then in the Middle East and North Africa (MENA) region, and then worldwide. Reasons put forward by those who did not plan to publish internationally were again competitiveness, and local concerns and research agendas not being relevant to international audiences. In terms of authorship, a quarter of the respondents were inclined to single authorship as this was the only thing they had been doing and were instructed to do mainly because of exams and thesis writing. The majority had no idea what co-authorship meant while only two chose co-authorship, thinking that collaboration might render the process easier. Almost all students did not have any publishing experience, with the exception of two who published on a restricted-access blog and a closed social media group. They both found the process difficult and lengthy, and were not prepared to handle the criticism they received. This links into the last question related to previous writing experience or future publishing whereby the majority of the students expressed the need to learn more about writing for publication and to be initiated into it. Further, the majority felt at a loss in relation to the idea of writing for publication as they already found writing challenging and frustrating. However, a quarter felt the need to improve their writing skills in order to increase their chances of publication and only one student expressed her eagerness to develop writing for publication as they felt they could contribute to the field with their lived pedagogical experiences.

Discussion

Overall, exogenous factors like gender, age group, mother tongue, specialty, and students' proficiency in the three languages have not shown any particular difference between the students' answers. Despite the formal inclusion of writing in the curricula, it seems that the writing practices were a bit uncertain as far as some students' understanding of the differences between writing a composition or an essay and their own experiences in realizing these products were concerned. These students were able to express theoretical precepts but failed to reflect this when they shared their writing practice. Furthermore, students' attitudes towards their writing productions regardless of the fact of being positive or challenging is due to the fact that students are cognizant of the importance of the writing skill, which is required at MA level, and enables them to succeed in their studies. If students perform poorly in writing, chances are they will fail not only the writing course but others as well. In short, they will be penalized twice.

Further, students' sketchy descriptions are revealing enough of the absence of a "comprehensible input" (Krashen, 1981) from their previous learning years. When the answers were more elaborate, students did not go beyond the terms of norms they knew. Additionally, students from TTC voiced their frustration when writing in English because they automatically become stressed when they are asked to write. This, according to them, is mainly due to the fact that they started writing at university and not during their secondary education. Very often, the students singled out their limited vocabulary as being the cause of their misunderstanding of the ins and outs of the writing skills. Furthermore, the only difference they saw between composition and essay boiled down to the number of paragraphs each one is made up of. Strangely enough, concerning the feelings on writing in English, a good majority admitted they had no problem and even felt comfortable with the writing assignments given to them. A little surprising was the fact that some students, though a minority, preferred writing in Arabic or French as they felt comfortable using either language, and were able to take risks and write creatively. Our understanding is that there is little availability for risk-taking associated with autonomous use of a language any learner should experience to develop their competence. Unfortunately, teachers' obsession with error-making is the main obstacle posed to students who do not take enough risks when writing and thus develop instead a strategy of avoidance or simplification (for example, the frequent use of SVO sentence patterns). Furthermore, a plausible explanation to the ease of writing in Arabic for some of the English majors at TTC is the fact that the overwhelming majority of students come from a literary background prior to entering tertiary education, in which Arabic is important as reflected in the number of study-hours and the coefficient of the subject. Students, thus, tend to have a good command of Arabic.

Persistent Traditional Teaching Approaches to Writing

From the findings and discussions of the survey, it seems that teachers' vision of writing has not been transformed despite decades of new approaches to teaching the skill. Students have shown how the teaching of English is still looking backwards: most students referred to the formal teaching/learning of grammar and the learning of vocabulary lists out of context, along the lines of the Grammar-Translation Method. The present research has just underscored the huge gap witnessed by students between present-day theories and old practices that are still being pursued out of routine. In other words, the MA students' responses demonstrated that the reform is far from being implemented according to the rationale elaborated to teach foreign languages. The main objective of the reform was to teach "differently". However, students reported the persistent focus on the teaching of grammar and the prevalence of accuracy over fluency in writing.

Many differences exist between writing in English as an L2 or an FL, yet much of the pedagogy used in the latter context is inspired by L2 writing pedagogy. A simple overview of the state of the art of the teaching of writing presents a "swing of the pedagogical pendulum" because of the diverse methodologies that have invaded classroom practice. Despite that, the skill is still considered at a discrete-item level (grammar, vocabulary, spelling and even the mechanics of writing). In the Algerian context, splitting the skill into piecemeal levels is still the name of the game, which makes it all the more difficult to acquire than if a more integrative approach were used. The various approaches to writing: from register and genre analysis, to product-process dichotomy, to essay/composition writing, have not really impacted the classroom, or did so to a very small extent. Only cosmetic changes have been brought to a system that has been kept out of the paradigm-shifts operated worldwide. Many of the students' answers show a deep ignorance of present-day didactic debates: a sign of their teachers' lack of training or awareness of the pedagogical innovations in the field.

A Reflexive Evaluation of Teaching and Learning

An interesting aspect about the MA students' answers was the genuine evaluation of their own level, their learning context, and their teachers' pedagogies. Several questions were information-seeking devices to help the authors understand their environment from a different perspective. The aim of the questionnaire was to gauge the students' own awareness of the writing skill as much as their particular vision of the didactic practices they were subjected to. In fact, it is their representations of the writing skill that indicated nuances and even oppositions of viewpoints felt to be self-made rather than taught or acquired. For instance, students' descriptions of the differences between literary and ESP texts indicated a very limited understanding of each register. They differentiated between them by equating literary texts with academic, narrative and use of literary devices (particularly metaphors), while speaking about the practical and scientific aspects of ESP texts or genre. Likewise, confusion and unfamiliarity with the product-process dichotomy is more than an indictment. It is an admission of a pedagogical failure. Thus, building on the students' reflexive evaluation we infer that reflexive evaluation of and for learning should be encouraged in order to uncover aspects that need re/consideration while teaching writing. Reflection on recurrent, often not revisited, pedagogical practices is likely to help adapt existing didactic interventions and design tailored ones with a bottom-up approach.

Seeking Membership in an Imagined Community

Despite difficult and challenging previous experiences in writing in English, the majority of the surveyed students in this study sought membership in an imagined community to which they could contribute. Publishing locally seems to be the safest road prior to embarking upon an adventurous international publication for which they have not yet been prepared. To gain entry to the global publishing market, local, regional, and then worldwide international publication would smoothly prepare students to face the challenges of contributing to knowledge production based on local legitimate concerns. Having been initiated into writing in solo, it seems logical for students not to imagine themselves co-authoring. For all the writing they previously did, students were assessed individually. They still need much practice in writing in English and a sound preparation for writing for publication.

It is a well-known fact that publishing in English is not easy not only for ESL but also for native English speakers (Casanave & Li, 2008; Casanave & Vandrick, 2003). Again, if most graduate students in North America and Europe are trained and mentored to publish and present at conferences, graduate students in Algeria suffer from a lack of such training opportunities both locally and regionally. Moreover, the degree of mastery of English is decisive for such active scientific participation although graduate students majoring in English might seem to be at an advantage compared to other graduate students in other disciplines.

Our final remark about writing practices at university level is that it depends more on the teacher's individual initiatives than on well-established curricula that can spell out the many ways to go about writing. Additionally, one should never forget the deeply-ingrained way of writing in Arabic that has a definite impact on the students' vision of the things to do (grammatically-oriented practices), namely at word order level, use of articles, paragraph writing, etc. Our feeling is that teachers need to do away with the belief in a magic trick to bring about idealistic techniques to help students produce an accepted piece of discourse that answers the teachers' demands. Practice more than lecturing is the key to bringing more awareness of the mechanics of writing in a foreign language. This is why developing a real CoP inside the classroom might help students "share their experiences and knowledge in free-flowing, creative ways that foster new approaches to problems" (Wenger & Snyder, 2000, p. 140), which means transmitting best writing practices between them. To this end, in the following section we attempt to propose a "writing for publication" MA course.

Imagining a 'Writing-for-Publication' MA Course

This paper contends that Writing for Publication should be integrated within MA and doctoral curricula despite the fact that fundamental research is the prerogative of professional researchers, not university teachers. Yet, to this end, and building on students' inherent remarks related to the persistent traditional teaching approaches, criticisms of lack of practice and expectations to publish in English internationally, we attempt to draw up a course that should be conceived as a series of workshops that could help would-be research writers to not only improve their writing (for publication) but also, in doing so, respond more effectively to editors' and reviewers' feedback. Though many of the processes are similar, writing for publication and writing a thesis are two very different endeavors. The expectations of the targeted scientific communities are not the same. In fact, a career in academia makes it compulsory today for teacher-researchers to publish in order to gain visibility and promotion. We suggest a three-tiered approach that can help students prepare themselves for the upcoming challenges:

1. Planning the writing project
2. Writing under constraints
3. Reviewing

Table 12.2 displays the phases that consist of the following objectives, tasks and assignments.

It goes without saying that writing for publication entails a series of decisions that are not always taken into consideration by students or by teachers. One should always consider first the student/researcher's writing ability. The latter is

TABLE 12.2 Three-tiered approach to a Writing-for-Publication MA Course

Planning the writing project	Writing under constraints	Reviewing
Target audience	Writing conventions	Self-editing
Established editors	Writing standards	Self-reviewing
External reviewers/evaluators	Paper organization	Peer-reviewing
Type of research	Length and writing style	Blind reviewing
Research design	Genre	Self-discipline
Titling	Outlining	Publication process
	Citations and ethics (addressing plagiarism)	

a difficult skill to develop, and a real issue worth dealing with at pedagogical and cognitive levels. Hence, a proper assessment of the writing skill is needed prior to embarking on writing for publication.

As to the learning/teaching techniques, one thinks it is more relevant to use a combination of approaches, namely scaffolding (i.e., overall scientific claim-evidence-reasoning/CER framework), think-aloud protocol (describing one's own way of solving writing process-product assignments) or even staging (breaking stretches of discourse/text into smaller units of meaning then synthesizing into a whole).

Planning the Writing Project

Students apprehended the fact that the research community will not be interested in learning about their local concerns. Such considerations should be part of the complex planning phase that is reflected in the three phases of an introduction identified by Swales (1993) as *establishing a territory*, *establishing a niche*, and then *occupying the niche*; something a great number of researchers would not know unless taught explicitly. We need to raise students' awareness that reading widely is the only safe route to becoming more knowledgeable and finding a niche for a significant topic worth researching. This will enable students to avoid the constant headache of ensuring the originality of the thoughts to be included in the research paper. Many supervisors systematically attack students' research work if they feel it is not demonstrating originality. The class should be conceived of as a CoP whereby members give support and feedback to each other regarding topics. Next is audience analysis, to be considered at earlier stages. Any author is not always capable of knowing who will read them. At this stage, the researcher should develop a reader-centered approach in order to meet the readership expectations (is it to inform practice, to influence policymakers, or to advance science?). Next comes working with established editors, a component unknown to students. One aspect to consider is who the editors are; what their task is, and what to expect from them; reviewers/evaluators that might have a say in their work. These can be determined depending on who the audience is. Another aspect to consider is the type of research: is it an empirical, a case study, a methodology or a theory paper? This will have an impact on the research design (context, target population, research method, etc.). Having a working title that is short, informative, self-explanatory and catchy right from the beginning is important even if it might be revised.

Writing Under Constraints

Writing in English following writing conventions (grammar, punctuation, spelling, capitalization, etc.) is a requirement. If students' level of English is poor, we suggest they take a remedial EAP class especially in a context where writing centers and external support are not available. This will ensure they meet writing standards. Additionally, workshopping with a focus on paper organization and structure, length in terms of number of pages and word limits, writing style, genre, citation, etc. will be used. Ethics and preventing plagiarism should be included, especially in an era when the copy-paste function is so easy to use, and so difficult to control.

Reviewing

The easiest tool to use for self-editing is spell-check for grammar and punctuation. However, not all spell-check edits are correct. When self-editing, students should be made aware that rewriting is envisioned. After editing the paper, it is useful to take a break and then self-review it by looking at the picture before moving into the next stage of peer-reviewing. Encouraging students to peer-review their manuscript is important and can be done at milestones (planning followed by writing phase).

Before students experience blind reviewing from established editors, it is useful to initiate them into blind peer-review to get objective feedback. From experience, students tend to focus on positive feedback when reviewing their peers' papers. Initiating students to self-and peer-reviewing contributes to self-discipline of working under a strict timeline, of receiving feedback and on addressing it. Last, students will be introduced to the publication process of choosing a journal, submission, acceptance with revisions, or rejection of paper and re-submission to another journal.

The assessment of this course will be done at milestones of the paper production, reviewing the process and the outputs. This course should be designed and built around individual and peer-to-peer learning, and should be results-driven with the aim of improving writing for publication.

This chapter, then, has covered a post-colonial context, a former French colony, where English is used as an additional language, and where writing for publication in English is becoming a pressing need. However, it is taken for granted that students will move on from writing to demonstrate mastery of content during sit-in exams, to writing up a thesis after conducting research which is part of MA programs, to writing for publication in English, that is nearly ignored.

As we have noted in this chapter, one can but acknowledge the fact that graduate students are somewhat caught between the devil and the deep blue sea, between their shaky initiation steps for thesis writing that is not systematically found in university curricula and the requirements of publishing internationally in English; the latter calls for a sophisticated process of writing for publication that is more demanding and that requires preparation through *planning the writing project, writing under constraints,* and *reviewing.*

In fact, the constraints and exigencies are to some extent different on the writing continuum, which should link up the two major stages of thesis writing and writing for publication. If thesis writing is still the concern of individual students and is done in isolation, in this chapter, we conceive of writing for publication as a skills development course through a community of practice model to help students gain membership in the imagined community of scholars. To this end, we strongly believe in the harmonizing of this first phase (thesis writing) that will pave the way for the second one (writing for publication) that is norm-oriented, taking on board not only the mechanics of writing/style, the conventions of scientific writing (Cargill & O'Connor, 2009), but also other exigencies including the impact factor of scientific journals, editors' exigencies, reviewers' evaluative scientific demands (Englander & Lopez-Bonilla, 2011) and the expectations of the scientific community. But there seems to be a distance to travel before the desired outcome is reached, even if Einstein makes it sound easy by stating that "The whole of science is nothing more than a refinement of everyday thinking"; hence, our suggestion to produce a curriculum that systematizes what is yet in the domain of interest of a happy few individual university researchers.

Notes

1 Arrêté 547 dated June 2, 2016. Retrieved from the Ministry of Higher Education and Scientific Research website: https://www.mesrs.dz/afficher//asset_publisher/nFmcv2f FsM1O/content/chapitr-2;jsessionid=218395B0A45EBD47D125E2A9BF805FED
2 Classical system of higher education in Algeria was based on the French model. It comprised a first cycle of five years of study in professional technical and scientific fields, and four years for the humanities and social sciences. The LMD system was introduced in 2004 in line with the Bologna Process.
3 The LMD system (License, Master, Doctorate) is an HE reform that was progressively implemented throughout most higher education institutions since 2004 following the Bologna process with the exception of the medical and veterinary schools and the Teacher Training Colleges that continued to implement the classical HE system. For more information cf. Messekher & Miliani, 2017.

References

Anderson, B. (1991). *Imagined communities: Reflections on the origin and spread of nationalism* (2nd Edition). New York: Verso.

Ammon, U. (2007). Global Scientific Communication: Open questions and policy suggestions. In U. Ammon & A. Carli (eds.). *Linguistics inequality in scientific communication today* (pp.123–133). *AILA Review 20*. Amsterdam, The Netherlands: John Benjamins.

Cargill, M., & O'Connor, P. (2009). *Writing scientific research articles: Strategy and steps*. Chichester, UK: John Wiley & Sons Ltd.

Casanave, C. P., & Li, X. (Eds.) (2008). *Learning the literacy practices of graduate school: Insiders' reflections on academic enculturation*. Ann Arbor, MI: University of Michigan Press.

Casanave, C. P., & Vandrick, S. (Eds.) (2003). *Writing for scholarly publication: Behind the scenes in language education*. Mahzah, NJ: Lawrence Erlbaum Associates.

Cherfaoui, F. Z., & Khennour, S. (2016). Langues et marché du travail en Algérie: Cas de la Sonatrach et de la Sonelgaz [Languages and Labor Market in Algeria: The case of Sonatrach and Sonelgaz]. *Synergies Algérie, 23*, 111–119.

Corbin, J., & Strauss, A. (2007). Basics of qualitative research: Techniques and procedures for developing grounded theory (3rd ed.). Thousand Oaks, CA: Sage.

Corcoran, J. N., & Englander, K. (2016). A proposal for critical pragmatic approaches to English for publication purposes. *Publications, 4* (6), 1–10.

Englander, K., & Lopez-Bonilla, G. (2011). Acknowledging or denying membership: Reviewers' responses to non-anglophone scientists' manuscripts. *Discourse Studies, 13* (4), 395–416.

Ferris, D. R., & Hedgcock, J. S. (2014). *Teaching L2 Composition: Purpose, process, and practice*. New York: Routledge.

Hanauer, D. I., & Englander, K. (2011). Quantifying the burden of writing research articles in a second language: Data from Mexican scientists. *Written Communication, 28*, 403–416.

Hanauer, D. I., & Englander, K. (2013). *Writing science in a second language*. West Lafayette, IN: Parlor Press.

Hyland, K. (2016). Academic publishing and the myth of linguistic injustice. *Journal of Second Language Writing. 31*, 58–69.

Krashen, S. (1981). *Second language acquisition and second language learning*. New York: Prentice-Hall.

Manchon, R. M. (Ed.) (2011). *Learning-to-write and writing-to-learn in an additional language*. Amsterdam, The Netherlands: John Benjamins.

Messekher, H., & Miliani, M. (2017). Algeria: Challenges and perspectives. In S. Kirdar (Ed.). *Education in the Arab world* (pp. 263–284). London: Bloomsbury.

Muresan, L. M., & Pérez-Llantada, C. (2014). English for research publication and dissemination in bi-/multiliterate environments: The case of Romanian academics. *Journal of English for Academic Purposes. 13*, 53–64.

Pérez-Llantada, C. (2014). *Scientific discourse and the rhetoric of globalization: The impact of culture and language*. London: Bloomsbury.

Rose, M. (1984). *Writer's block: The cognitive dimension*. Carbondale, IL: Southern Illinois University Press.

Swales, J. (1993). Genre and engagement. *Revue Belge de Philologie et Histoire, 71*(3): 689–598.

Uzuner-Smith, S. & Englander, K. (2015). Exposing ideology with university policies: A critical discourse analysis of faculty hiring, promotion and remuneration practices. *Journal of Education Policy*, *30*(1), 62–85.

Wenger, E. (1998). *Communities of Practice: Learning, meaning and identity*. Cambridge: Cambridge University Press.

Wenger, E. C., & Snyder, W. M. (2000). Communities of Practice: The organizational frontier. *Harvard Business Review*, Jan-Feb. Reprint R00110.

Appendix 12.1

Questionnaire on Your Experience in Academic Writing

1. Age: below 20 ____, between 20 and 25 years ___, over 25 _____
2. Gender: male ___, female ____
3. Specialization: _____
4. Mother tongue: Algerian Arabic ____, Tamazight _____, French _____

   Other, please specify: ....

5. Which language(s) do you use in writing?_____
6. Describe your proficiency in the following languages, circle one:

   Modern Standard Arabic

   Basic   intermediate   advanced

   French

   Basic   intermediate   advanced

   English

   Basic   intermediate   advanced

   Other language, please specify: _____

   Basic   intermediate   advanced

7. Please describe your experience in composition/essay writing in English.
   _____
   _____
   _____
   _____

8. What are the differences between writing a composition and an essay?
   _____
   _____
   _____
   _____

9. How do you feel about academic writing in English compared to the language you usually use?
   _____
   _____
   _____
   _____

10. What are the main obstacles you face when writing in Arabic?

11. What are the main obstacles you face when writing in French?

12. What are the main obstacles you face when writing in English?

13. When writing, are you more focused on the product or the process?

14. Are you familiar with the process and product approaches?

    Yes   No

15. Which one do you have difficulties with?

16. Are there differences between writing literary and scientific (ESP) texts?

    Yes   No

17. What are they?

    Product:

Process:
_____
_____
_____
_____

18. Could you describe the process you go through when you write?
_____
_____
_____
_____

19. What do you consider to be a successful writing product?
_____
_____
_____
_____

20. What is according to you a successful writing process?
_____
_____
_____
_____

Thank you for your cooperation!

Appendix 12.2

Questionnaire on Future Publication Intentions

1. Do you plan to publish articles in English?

    Yes_____ No_____ Don't Know_____

    Why?
    _____
    _____
    _____
    _____

2. If yes, do you plan to publish in local _____, regional _____, or international journals _____ ?

Why?

_____
_____
_____
_____

3. Do you plan / would you like your publications to be:

   single authored _____ or co-authored _____ ? No idea _____

   Why?

   _____
   _____
   _____
   _____

4. Do you have any experience publishing research in English so far?

   Yes_____ No_____

   If yes, can you describe your experience composing the research in English?

   _____
   _____
   _____
   _____

5. Is there anything else you wish to add regarding a previous writing experience or a future publishing experience in English?

   _____
   _____
   _____
   _____

Thank you for your cooperation!

13

SCHOLARLY PUBLISHING IN NIGERIA

The Enduring Effects of Colonization

Ayokunle Olumuyiwa Omobowale

UNIVERSITY OF IBADAN, NIGERIA

Olayinka Akanle

UNIVERSITY OF IBADAN, NIGERIA

Charles Akinsete

UNIVERSITY OF IBADAN, NIGERIA

Introduction

English has gained a dominant competitive edge globally. It is arguably the global lingua franca and, more than ever before, has assumed the status of the global language of scholarship. Failing to publish in English can result in a scholar's academic invisibility often referred to as "perishing" (Kilonzo & Magak, 2013; Bajerski, 2011; Beigel, 2009; Thompson, 2009; Harris, 2001). Scholarly publication media, which solely or partly publish in English, have greater visibility, circulation and impact than others with comparable standards (Englander, 2011; Vanderstraeten, 2011, 2010; Curry & Lillis, 2004). In the academia, the intellectual reality of "preference" for English makes it the "queen" of all languages, in which most scholars wish to publish as a statement of academic excellence and global competitiveness (Englander, 2011; Curry & Lillis, 2004; Ryan, et al., 2002).

The place of English in international publishing and global inequality in scholarly dissemination is well documented (Collyer, 2018; Englander, 2011; Vanderstraeten 2011, 2010; Salager-Meyer, 2008; Duszak & Lewkowicz, 2008; Meriläinen, Tienari, Thomas & Davies, 2008; Paasi, 2005; Curry & Lillis, 2004; Harris, 2001; van Dalen & Henkens, 1999). In fact, available evidence reveals that Nigerian scholars and graduate students who specialise in local languages such as Hausa, Igbo, Ijaw, Efik and Yoruba and European languages such as French, German and Russian disseminate their research in English (see for example Ayeleru, 2011; Ayeleru & Ajah, 2011; Ogúndèjì, 1998, 1997). Of course, when colleagues raise queries about why such research is not disseminated in the language of specialisation, the usual response is: "If we wrote it in a language other than English, you would not be able to read it." Simply put, scholars of non-English language disciplines are also caught in the web to publish in English to ensure wider dissemination of research and remain relevant. To address these issues more thoroughly, this chapter discusses the colonizing effect of the English language in scholarly publishing in Nigeria.

The essentiality of the English language reverberates in the post-colonial discourse. English is a transferred language in colonies and many writers and speakers are unable to grasp standard principles in oral and written forms of the language. Arguments to move away from "standard English" discourse are presented by Rose and Galloway (2017), and Shi (2013) who demonstrate that the move is needed to appreciate and recognise the glocalization and context of global Englishes that have evolved due to diffusion of the language. Similarly, in a discussion of the domestication of ideas and language, Onwuzuruigbo (2018), dwelling on the thoughts of Alatas (2000, 1974, 1972), advocates the freedom of the "captive mind" through scholarly indigenisation. It is our view that irrespective of the calls for recognition of global Englishes and scholarly indigenization, it is important to note that English is still the language of communication of these indigenization and relativity calls; English remains the dominant language of research and scholarship, outside of which research communication becomes limited. Indigenized Englishes would remain largely understandable only to the local audience; if the research is intended for the global audience it is our view that it should abide by standard structures of the English language.

This chapter discusses the colonizing effect of English in Africa, language challenges and extra-pedagogical strategies used to circumvent difficulties in writing in English for international publishing. In the first section we examine the effects of colonialism in Nigeria on the English language and more specifically on academic publishing. In the second section we look more closely at some specific instances of divergence from the norms of prestigious standard varieties such as British and US English. Finally, we provide some reflections on the sociology of English as a language of research publication in the Nigerian context, the strategies that scholars adopt to meet the challenges of satisfying the linguistic and rhetorical requirements of international journals.

Colonialism, English Language and Academic Publishing

Colonialism is a historical fact in Nigeria's existence, and its effects on the country continue to impact contemporary post-colonial social reality. Nigeria was under British colonial rule from 1893 (Lagos was earlier declared a British Colony in 1861) and until it gained independence in 1960. In Nigeria and across Anglophone Africa, English became an instrument of colonial perpetration, perpetuation and acceleration. Beginning with the so-called "Age of Discovery" by the European explorers as from the fifteenth century (and afterwards), eventual colonisation of Africa was very resolute and systematic. Africa's colonialism was accentuated in the 19th and 20th Centuries with scramble and partitioning of the continent (Akanle, 2012). At the point of partitioning, little or no attention was paid to existing culture and language peculiarities, thereby creating language and cultural complications in Africa (Muchiri, et al., 1995). Colonisation of Africa and domination of African languages were not without resistance, but the resistances were largely unsuccessful.

Elevation of English as the preferred colonial language thus meant that everyone aspiring to modernity must of necessity learn and speak English. Implicitly, the capacity to speak English became elitist. Natives incapable of speaking English became the low class and restricted in colonial operations. English speaking colonial court clerks, colonial domestic servants and errand personnel somewhat became the elites. Traditional class structures and systems became reconfigured because of the English language to the extent that traditional rulers and chiefs had to rely on interpreters to communicate with the colonialists. English became Nigeria's official language, as well as the main language of pedagogic instruction. Ayo Banjo (2012, p. 3) notes that "the spread of primary education in the country from the 1950s onwards greatly boosted the ranks of mesolectal and basilectal speakers of the (English) language." Today, there is a good percentage of speakers of the language at every level; it is also noteworthy that thousands of graduates of the English language are churned out by Nigerian tertiary institutions annually.

The elitism of the English language degraded local languages to vernacular status, unacceptable in official circles and formal education (Bgoya & Jay, 2013; Pavlenko & Norton, 2007; Rymes & Pash, 2001; Muchiri, et al., 1995). Vernacular, local languages attracted (and still attract) punitive sanctions, especially in private schools and other formal climes where such languages must not be spoken even in informal relations. In fact, in many homes, English is the language of communication, such that children learn English earlier than they do local languages, if they ever gain proficiency in them at all. Throughout the Nigerian social structure, the English language has the elitist status of privileged communication, which most people strive to attain, even though imperfectly most times. English preference is meant to aid wide-reaching communication, but not without more fundamental political economy and cultural outcomes. This is because, according to Ngugi wa Thiong'o (1986, p. 108):

> Languages as communication and as culture are often products of each other. Communication creates culture: culture is a means of communication, language carries culture, and culture carries, particularly through orature and literature, the entire body of values by which we come to perceive ourselves and our place in the world. How people perceive themselves affects how they look at their culture, at their places, politics and at the social production of wealth, at their entire relationship to nature and to other beings. Language is thus inseparable from ourselves as a community of human beings with a specific form and character, a specific history, a specific relationship to the world.

Language is central to personal and social constructions of existence and reality. Language is not just a means of communication but a strategy of self and group identities (Lovesey, 2000). Language is important and germane for identity, communication, relevance, culture and survival. It is about identity because language demonstrates the identity of a people. This is why there are the Yoruba language (for Yoruba people), Ashanti language (for the Ashanti people), French language (for French people), English language (for English people), Zulu Language (for Zulu people) and Hausa Language (for Hausa people), among others. It is the embodiment of culture and vehicle of socialisation (Rymes & Pash, 2001). Language is about people and their existence.

Language is also a powerful cultural tool. Expertise in a dominant standard language puts the speakers in an advantageous position. The culture of the dominant language is propagated, while its speakers are esteemed, irrespective of their nationality or ethnicity. Confirming this position, Currey (2013, p. 9) notes that European editors acknowledge the expertise and unique "sophistication" of early post-independence African writers in English. In Nigeria, Wole Soyinka, Chinua Achebe and Christopher Okigbo, among other early authors, were the cream of Nigeria's literary and scholarly writers, with an expertise and sophistication in English that awed the international audience (Currey, 2013).

Language is also a vehicle of communication driving social relations; it shows the relevance of a people in local and external engagements. Use and misuse of language symbolise groups' dominance. When different groups interact, there are bound to be power relations and cultural and linguistic exchanges (Pavlenko & Norton, 2007). These exchanges could be mutually rewarding and peaceful and can be forceful and exploitative, depending on the power structures and motivations emergent in the relationships. In the case of African countries, the latter options were the case. Language is also about the survival of a people. For instance, expertise or (in)competence in a language can determine if an individual will gain employment, earn income and survive, especially if competence in the language is required in the job. In other words, once a language is dominant, the careers and existential survival of an individual or a group then depend on expertise in the dominant language.

Once a language is adopted as a major medium of communication, it simply shows the degree of dominance of the group that owns that language. In the case of English, this started with colonialism and is accentuated in post-colonial scholarship. Interestingly, English was systematically entrenched during colonialism, in post-colonial times, and English remains the dominant language of the academy and scholarship. It remains a national language and the country's lingua franca.

The compulsion to learn and use English language is not only political but also economic. Academic and scholarly careers are dependent on competence in English, thus forcing scholars who use languages other than English to either learn English or employ author-editors or translators; especially native speakers of English. Unfortunately, the second option is far more expensive and means that most scholars see gaining a mastery of English or using author-editors as their only options if they are to experience career advancement.

Despite the argument that Nigeria should have surpassed its colonial challenges, the colonial heritage remains nationally ingrained (White, 2000). This is particularly so when accounts of colonial occurrences and events continue to be relevant in understanding current realities in Nigeria. A case in point that would benefit from a post-colonial critique is the interface of English language and academic publishing (Omobowale, Akanle, Adeniran, & Adegboyega, 2014; Olukoju, 2004; Osundare, 2000). Even in Francophone Africa, it is important to note that English is increasingly gaining popular use, based on the recognition that it is the dominant language in scholarship capable of giving research wide reading coverage (Kamwangamalu, 2016; Omobowale, Sawadogo, Sawadodo/Compaoré, & Ugbem, 2013). For example, many frontline scholars in the Benin Republic, Senegal and Cameroon are competent in the use of English even though the official language of instruction and lingua franca is French.

While this situation ingrains a neocolonial language mentality, African scholars appear unable to escape the ascendancy and dominance of English because of pressures to publish. It, therefore, becomes an issue of choosing between career survival and ideological/epistemic debates. Thus, for many African academics, irrespective of colonial heritage, "publishing in English is the beginning of wisdom", in fact, it is the pragmatic approach to having a successful academic career. This is because competence in English language would enhance the possibility of publishing in the dominant English journals, which promotion committees increasingly identify as the ones competitively indexed, with impact factor and so the standard journals. Publishing in such journals enhances promotion opportunities, expands the spread of the reading audience and the possibility of wide citation as well as the likelihood of international scholarly collaborations, consultancies and other opportunities.

As English continues to ascend as the language of scholarship and the academia in the post-colonial era, it is difficult to resist the systemic language dominance beyond mere stereotypical and ideological conjectures, intellectual rhetoric and political exemplifications. This is because English represents and reflects multi-layered interests in the global academia, scholarship and beyond. Hence, political, ideological and career motivations of academics, scholars and language learners and users are multifaceted and traverse schools, offices, communities and relationships. According to Canagarajah (1999), against the background, scholars face publication realities that advance scholarly dissemination through the English language as the panacea. Canagarajah further notes that the dominance of English in post-colonial scholarship reveals profound consequences of colonial territorial power relations in knowledge production, development and scholarship commodification. Simply put, the domination of the English Language in postcolonial scholarship somewhat gives something of a scholarly advantage to those who publish in English, especially in terms of wider dissemination of findings and consequent ranking advantage to such scholars and their institutions. Also, the publishing economy thus favours

English dissemination outlets, as they attract high patronage, readership and of course, profit viz-a-viz the non-English journals and publishers.

English is thus the language of the "center" propagating the "center's interest" while Africa (and Nigeria) is part of the "periphery", which must learn the language of the centre to be relevant in the global schemes of knowledge production and certification. Hence, publishing in English is largely an effective strategy that accentuates the dominance of English in global scholarship. Publishing as a legitimation strategy of English language is very dynamic and assertive. The tide has shifted from just publishing in reputable journals to largely English indexed journals with impact factor. For example, in Nigeria, as from about the year 2000, university management have supposedly tried to redress poor-quality scholarship and predatory publishing, and enhance global ranking of universities by adopting the "internationalization policy". The internationalization project primarily prioritises "international publishing" in foreign English journals. More often than not, the responsibility to "internationalize" research findings is that of the individual researcher (with little or no funding support) at the pain of career stagnation, psychological trauma at loss of prestige, honour, seniority and of course, subtle or total obscurity (Omobowale, et al., 2014; Omobowale, et al., 2013).

Publishing in English is also about ideologies extension, structures' legitimization and practices that legitimize and reproduce unequal power systems between Anglo-Saxon West and the South on the basis of English as the language for scholarship (Cook, 1992; Bourdieu, 1991; Canagarajah, 1999). Irrespective of ideological stances on the colonizing effect of English language, it is a fact that Nigerian scholars must write (and speak) standard English to have their manuscripts reviewed and possibly published. The next section discusses the Nigerian English in context, focusing on some of its characteristics, discrepancies from standard English and editorial remedies.

Nigerian English in Context: Characteristics, Discrepancies and Editorial Remedies

As argued above, in Nigeria, English remains a requisite as a result of a range of complex factors such as the significant social relevance that use of the language proffers, as well as its publishing advantage. Kachru (1995) foregrounds the world canonization of the English and Awonusi (2016) equally states that "English assumes a hegemonic status as the most widely studied foreign language". Consequently, the language is an essential constituent for learning across all tiers of education in Nigeria. The potential advantage that Nigeria's long-standing contact with the language represents is, on the one hand, threatened by declining expertise in the standard varieties (Amakaeze & Abana, 2017; Akande, 2016). Further, linguistic influences from local languages and declining expertise in the language result in common errors and use of non-standard English. In this section we describe characteristics of Nigerian English and how it differs from the standard form.

Fakoya (2015, p. 46) observes that although the English language is thriving in Nigeria, there is an assemblage of lexical and phraseological differences that separate the Nigerian variety of English from the international standard. This scenario is often described as a reflection of the fallen standard of education in Nigeria (Amakaeze & Abana, 2017; Akande, 2016; Schneider, 2010; Osundare, 2000; Akere, 1978). However, it also reflects examples of glocalized English, locally popular and understood, but with little or no international communication and publishing advantage.

Writing for the British Broadcasting Corporation (BBC), Adaobi Tricia Nwaubani affirms that it is not uncommon to encounter official documents and research writing exhibiting verbose and flowery English (see BBC, 2017). The BBC (2017) report cited an example of a press release by the military High Command that reads as follows:

> The Nigerian Army in synergy with other security agencies under its constitutional mandates. . . acted responsively in order to de-escalate the deteriorating security scenario in-situ.
>
> Instructively, the military and other security agencies exercised maximum restraints against the odds of provocative and inexplicable violence that were employed against them. . .
>
> It is rather inconceivable for any individual or group to have decided to inundate the general public with an anecdote of unverified narratives in order to discredit the Nigerian Army in the course of carrying out its constitutional duties despite the inexplicable premeditated and unprovoked attacks. . ..

The quote above is an example of the verbose style often found in Nigeria's official and academic circles. Though a communication from the military, the extract is a good representation of everyday use of the English language in both spoken and written forms. The communiqué simply states that

> the military, in cooperation with other security agencies is doing its best to improve security in Nigeria. . . Despite attacks against its forces, the military utilised minimal force to maintain order. . . False claims of acts of brutality against the Nigerian Army by individuals and groups (civil society) are unfortunate. . . .

Quite a number of Nigerian writers employ an army of ostentatious expressions to needlessly embroider a particular idea. This tendency is particularly common in the nation's geopolitical space. One prominent example is that of a member of the Nigerian National Assembly in recent times, whose verbose style of speaking has attracted wide interest among Nigerians. Honourable Patrick Obiahiagbon's contribution to national development was largely viewed from a comic perspective, rather than a meaningful critique of the depraved state of the nation. Here is a compilation of some of his vocabulary:

1	Crinkum-crankum	—	elaborate or detailed
2	Mephistophelean	—	wicked
3	Kakistocracy	—	government under the control of a nation's worst citizens
4	Braggadocio	—	arrogant attitude
5	Jiggery-pokery	—	misrepresentation, tricky

When asked why he chose to confuse his audience, the politician simply apologized, stating that his "intention is not to deliberately befuddle or obfuscate them (the audience). I do not set out to deposit my audience in a portmanteau of indecipherability (Obiahiagbon, 2008, *Vanguard Newspaper*)". The point is that whenever Honourable Obiahiagbon speaks, his Nigerian audience must make a quick dash for the dictionary. When he was asked to speak on the death of former president of the Academic Staff Union of Universities (ASUU) in 2016, he had this to say:

> The grand initiation of Professor Festus Iyayi is a lancinating loss of another stentorian voice, against retrograde and prebendel forces of primitive mercantilism. That he passed through transition on matters pro bono public, bears eloquent testimony to our state of dystopia. Such is the evanescence of life. It's all vanitasvanitatum.
>
> *(Ugobude, 2016)*

The summary of the above quote is that Mr Patrick mourns the loss of the deceased and therefore sees life as transient. And when he thought that the Nigerian footballer, Mikel Obi, deserved the Player of the Year Award in 2014, Obiahiagbon did ironically express his feelings in clear-cut terms:

> I am maniacally bewildered, overgassted and flabberwhelmed (sic) at the paraplegic crinkum-crankum that characterized the GLO-CAF awards culminating in an odoriferous saga cum gargantuan gaga. The jiggery-pokery of CAF in crowning YayaToure instead of our own prodigy John Mikel Obi is a veritable bugaboo that must be pooh-poohed by all compos mentis homo sapiens. The perfidy and mendacity of all the apparatchik of sports suzerainty are not only repugnant but also insalubrious.
>
> *(Ugobude, 2016)*

We should note the introduction of new expressions in the first sentence. The words "overgassted" and "flabberwhelmed" did go through the process of lexical mutilations. It is apparent that a mental state of chaos is created in the mindset of the listener, which runs parallel to the distressed situation of the speaker. Hence, there is a deliberate switch to further bewilder the audience, who are most assuredly used to the correct expressions "overwhelmed" and "flabbergast". Nevertheless, what remains pertinent is that communication is hindered by this outlandish linguistic noise; the result is an unavoidable distraction from the essence of the message.

As a prominent leader and national figure, Obiahiagbon's lucid expressions are quite inspirational to many young writers. There is a strong temptation to follow in his footsteps, especially with the huge fame that he has attracted to himself. However, the effect of his idiosyncratic use of language has far reaching consequences, particularly in a formal setting. Be it a manuscript, essay, research proposal, grant proposal, thesis or any formal documentation, the presence of verbose expression is always counter-productive.

Furthermore, the use of incomplete expressions is another common problem which features regularly in publications written in English. There is a striking connection between verbosity and incomplete expression. The underlining factor is the desire to be seen as an elite proficient speaker of English. Unfortunately meaning is distorted when sentences are not well constructed. The value-chain of cohesion and coherence in any given language, in this case English, is immediately lost in the sea of incomprehension. Here are a few excerpts from essays written by undergraduate students.

Example 1. It was on a Tuesday evening 14th of March 2017 at the faculty of art the class was supposed to hold in Room 40 precisely why we were at the premises waiting for our tutor, and that faithful day was our first class.

Example 2. And I see him as a very hardworking man, because he did not just only rely on the lecturing job but has extra three jobs, all because of the welfare of his family members.

The two examples are derived from two descriptive essays with the same title, "My English Lecturer". The first example is meant to be an introductory paragraph, while the second is culled from a transitory paragraph of the second essay. The common problem associated with both excerpts is incomplete expressions.

In everyday spoken interaction, it is not uncommon to hear phrases such as "I came to your office, but met your absence" (I called at your office, but you were not in), "you are welldone" (you have done well), "I had go-slow" (I was held up in traffic) or "I flashed your number yesterday" (that is, I called (or telephoned) you yesterday, but terminated the call before you answered).[1],[2] Nigeria thus has usages that diverge from the standard, but which are locally regarded as "standard", due to fallen standards and as a result of a conscious desire to celebrate the local varieties. Whereas this has negative implications for global competitiveness in English and publishing, there is little deliberate pedagogical effort put into enhancing written English among scholarly and literary writers. Needless to say, the challenge of divergent use of the English Language is generally noted in Nigeria, though it is assumed that scholarly and literary writers are in fact expert users of the English language. It is this assumption that results in an almost complete lack of formal training for professional writers.

Common errors and non-standard usage affect different units of the English Language such as phonology, morphology, syntax, and so on. In this chapter we present data focused on divergence within the Nigerian context that is commonly seen in political views, edited manuscripts, theses, dissertations and essays. The objective here is to foreground archetypal non-standard grammatical constructions and/or unclear structural presentation of the English language, possibly influenced by linguistic elements of Nigeria's local languages. These grammatical, lexical and orthographic infelicities are well represented in public speeches as well as in quite a number of publications by Nigerian authors. Among these infelicities we would include verbosity, inappropriate expressions, wrong usage of punctuation marks and morphological errors among other linguistic infractions.

It should be emphasized that it is not our intention to undermine the creative enterprise of Nigerian publications. In terms of global recognition, Nigerian writers are among the best in the world. As was noted earlier the likes of Wole Soyinka, Chinua Achebe and Elechi Amadi are pioneers in the arts of creative writing and many have, over the years, followed in their footsteps. Contemporary Nigerian writers such as Ben Okri, Chimamanda Adichie, among others, have successfully navigated linguistic pitfalls that many other writers have fallen into, with respect to combining the English language effectively with indigenous idiosyncrasies. More often than not, quite a number of writers suffer the ill-effects of a general belief that language use must go beyond communication. In other words, authors are inclined to think that by using the English language in an exaggerated fashion, they generate respect and admiration from the reader. In actual fact, the reverse is the case.

In addition to turns of phrase, bad punctuation is the nemesis of any good publication. Although punctuation marks may appear to be of no consequence due to the way writers usually flout punctuation rules, it is arguably one of the most important guidelines that aids acceptance of manuscripts for publication. The import of the full-stop, comma, semicolon, colon, question mark, among others, cannot be overestimated. Wrong use or the lack of these punctuation marks in publications causes unintended alteration. Without appropriate use of punctuation, the readers are easily misinformed. Babajide (1996, p. 71) affirms that if there is a proper usage of punctuation, "it facilitates correct interpretation of the message encoded. If, on the other hand, it is not used properly, it either leads to utter meaninglessness or gives an unintended meaning." Here are some examples culled from written essays, in which the use of the comma is omitted.

Excerpt 1: During my free periods I love watching football including gymnastics athletics judo and wrestling.   (wrong use)

Excerpt 2: Before they knew he had escaped.   (wrong use)

Excerpt 1: During my free periods, I love watching football, including gymnastics, athletics, judo and wrestling.   (correct)

Excerpt 2: Before they knew, he had escaped.   (correct)

First, it is difficult to have an orthographic reading in the first example. Also, the second example is complex and quite tricky in terms of absolute comprehension. But reading the two sentences in Excerpt 2 ultimately saves the day.

There are other morphological concerns that also affect the quality of publication. These include a varied number of errors such as spelling mistakes, homophone errors, slang, colloquialisms, to mention a few. Focus would however be on certain morphological misrepresentations, which are quite common in publications. In fact, this problem cuts across all levels of the education sector, right from primary schools to tertiary institutions. For instance, the use of "its vs it's"; "their vs there"; "lose vs loose"; "whose vs who's", "I vs me" are usually misrepresented in terms of usage. Listed below are common examples:

Its raining	(wrong)	
It's raining	(correct)	
Their is a need to change status quo.	(wrong)	
There is a need to change status quo.	(correct)	
Chelsea will not loose the next match.	(wrong)	
Chelsea will not lose the next match.	(correct)	
Who's car is outside?	(wrong)	
Whose car is outside?	(correct)	
Dad will take Gbemi and I	(wrong)	
Dad will take Gbemi and me	(correct)	
interprete	(wrong)	interpret
arguement	(wrong)	argument
early fourties	(wrong)	early forties
faithful	(wrong)	fateful
being	(wrong)	been

Grammatical and fundamental errors are prime linguistic setbacks that affect the quality of publications in general. There are nonetheless other challenges that should also be mentioned, especially in relation to journal articles, including other forms of academic writing. Reviewers of publications are often challenged by some other forms of errors, namely, poor abstract, bad reference style, poor titles and in-text citations (Omobowale, et al., 2014; Papaioannou, Machaira, & Theano, 2013). A poor abstract is often as a result of verbosity and lack of focus on the gap in knowledge. Using the appropriate reference style for any article or publication is not negotiable. Attention is usually not paid to appropriate reference style by some scholars. All these contribute to poorly written publications. The art and act of writing significantly determines the success of any given publication.

Author-Editing and Other Interventions

The challenges of producing a manuscript that meets the demands of journal editors are most often remedied through peer and professional authors' editing of manuscripts. Willing colleagues are often requested to assist in reading through manuscripts to assess the intellectual worth of such works, but very importantly, to also address grammatical issues that may be identified. This option is common among close colleagues. Peer editing does not necessarily confer such a transient editor with the role of an author. It is often a job done gratis, based on collegial values. Readiness to continue to offer such free services is not commonplace. Whereas a peer editor continually consulted may not decline, again due to collegial value, the enthusiasm, speed and frequency of assistance declines over time. As colleagues provide less of these free editing services, the author is stymied and consults professional editors. Hence, professional author-editing is the preferred option. In short, the need for international publishing portends the need to redress English language deficiency in scholarly manuscripts through author-editing. Peer-editing works, but professional author-editing is a relative panacea.

The art of author-editing is increasingly gaining ascendancy in Nigeria's intellectual and literary circles. Author-editing in the twenty-first century Nigeria has indeed reached a remarkable equilibrium, despite the fact that there are quite a number of linguistic and non-linguistic challenges. Author-editors do not only cross Ts, and dot Is, they practically ensure manuscripts are linguistically presented in Standard English. Hence, the English language has transcended its communication purpose alone. It is also a source of economic value.

There is an explosion of job opportunities across the nation as far as author-editing is concerned. Author-editors charge between N200 and N400, which is between 60 US cents and 1.3 dollars, per page. This avenue is now a steady source of livelihood for both exceptionally brilliant postgraduate students and professional author-editors in Nigeria. Unfortunately, quacks have also joined the teeming population of author-editors, claiming expertise in English language author-editing, which they obviously lack. Also, customers do not usually take the time to learn from the mistakes made. Since copy-editors are always available, quite a number of scholars have been lackadaisical with the necessity to learn how to use the English language appropriately. Nonetheless, with the use of the English language, author-editing in Nigeria has become a socio-economic and intellectual remedy in terms of both economic and intellectual values.

To meet the demand to publish, scholars are also known to take advantage of the opportunity to publish in less recognized outlets. We have seen that "there are journals, and there are journals" is a sordid reality among Nigerian scholars. Not only have journals sprung up in Nigeria that are characterized as "predatory", but some scholars actively seek them out, since for a fee they can quickly add a publication to their vitae even though it may have little credibility in the larger academic world (Omobowale, et al., 2014). While this does not serve the goal of disseminating Nigerian scholars' research on the international stage, it does respond to the need driven by universities and others to publish frequently and in English.

Author-Ethnographic Reflections and the Sociology of English and Publishing

Our experience and success have been guided by the need to as much as possible present research reports in Standard English. It is important to note that Nigerian universities do allow scholars to publish in other international languages such as French, Russian and Spanish among others, provided English interpretations are included for internal review. However, Nigeria's intellectual establishment sees the English language as the epitome of research (and publication). Works published in other languages are rarely assessed for appointment and promotion review. Though an unwritten code, it is expected that most scholars' works (up to 99%) is presented in the English language.

Despite Nigeria's Anglophone heritage, it is difficult to claim a global optimal expertise in the English language among scholars and students. It is not sufficient to have wonderful research ideas, super and cutting edge methodology, funds and generate empirical findings without dissemination outlets. From personal and shared experiences from colleagues, it is not uncommon to have reviewers complain about the written English of authors, typographical errors, misplaced punctuation and wrong use of words among other issues that, ordinarily, should not be challenges to individuals whose training and practice are carried out in the English language. Manuscripts may have sound empirical data, but due to language deficiency, they may fail quality tests depending on the editorial magnanimity of journal or volume editors (Papaioannou, Machaira, & Theano, 2013). Lapses in spoken and written English are evident in research reports, making such manuscripts barely readable and understandable for native speakers of English. It is our view that writing for international publication should abide by the standard structures of the English language. Thus, as scholars ourselves, we continually seek to replicate the rhetoric and accuracy of standard English with our students and in our papers.

Conclusion

The English language is not just the linguistic form in Nigeria; it is a social reality which captures Nigeria's colonial and post-colonial linguistic experience. Nigeria's English heritage notwithstanding, verbose expressions, coarse grammatical constructions, spelling errors, unclear presentation and homophone errors are some common challenges in oral and written English among Nigerians, thus necessitating a growing industry of author-editors, who many at times do poor jobs. Aside from personal reading, reflection and re-reading to detect often overlooked errors, scholars employ the services of author-editors and colleagues, and lately editing software such as Grammarly has been helpful. Poor English disadvantages the publication opportunities of Nigerian scholars in the global scholarly community.

As long as the "Nigerian English" remains internationally unrecognized, scholars whose works are rendered in such English will remain disadvantaged. The research theories and methods adopted may be sound, and of course, findings may be groundbreaking. Writing research reports in non-standard English, and thus finding it difficult to publish in internationally acclaimed dissemination outlets, also denies the international community access to scholarly-worthy research from Nigeria. This detracts from the possible contribution of Nigeria to the global repository of knowledge. The growing industry of language editors is a home-grown fix for improving manuscripts, but it does not represent a long-term strategy for supporting Nigerian scholars in publishing their research. Hence, there is a need to design pedagogic strategies for English scholarly writing to advance the writing skills and competitiveness of Nigerian scholars and graduate students.

Notes

1 "Welldone" evolved in the Nigerian English about the 1990s as a form of gratification for a job done satisfactorily or mutual salutation
2 "Flashing" became a strategic telephony method right from the early days of mobile phones entry into Nigeria between 2000 and 2001. Calling was expensive, hence, "flashing" was a symbolic code for greeting while repeated "flashing" was (is still) a strategic means of saying that there is an important message to be relayed, call me urgently. In the West, "flashing" rather refers to illicit momentary nudity in the public space (see Curnutt, 2012; Lynch, 2007; Barcan, 2004).

References

Akande, A. T. (2016). Non-standard syntactic features in Nigerian university graduates' English. *Awka Journal of English Language and Literary Studies*, 4(1), 16–30.
Akanle, O. (2012). Childhood construction, child rights and development in Nigeria: Trajectories from the Yoruba of the south-western Nigeria. *African Journal for the Psychological Studies of Social Issues*, 15(2), 359–379.

Akere, F. (1978). Socio-cultural constraints and the emergence of a standard Nigerian English. *Anthropological Linguistics, 20*(9), 407–421.
Alatas, S. (1972). The captive mind in development studies. *International Social Science Journal, 24*(1), 9–25.
Alatas, S. (1974). The captive mind and creative development. *International Social Science Journal, 26*(4), 691–700.
Alatas, S. (2000). Intellectual imperialism: Definition, traits and problems. *Southeast Asian Journal of Social Science, 28*(1), 23–45.
Amakaeze, G., & Abana, B. (2017). English as a criterion for political exclusion in Nigeria. *Madonna Journal of English and Literary Studies, 2*(8), 119–130.
Awonusi, S. (2016). Codification, standardisation and communication: Linguistic and literary perspectives of English and indigenous language in Anglophone West Africa. In A. Odebunmi, A. Osisanwo, H. Bodunde, & S. Ekpe (Eds.). *Grammar applied linguistics and society* (pp.15–42). Ile-Ife, Nigeria: Obafemi Awolowo University Press.
Ayeleru, B. (2011). African cultural rebirth: A literary approach. *Journal of African Cultural Studies, 23*(2), 165–175.
Ayeleru, B., & Ajah, R. O. (2011). Transgressing borders or bodies, deconstructing geographies in Tahar Ben Jelloun's "Partir". *Áfrìca: Revista do Centro de Estudos Africanos, 29*(30), 187–202.
Babajide, A. (1996). *Introductory English grammar and writing skills.* Ibadan, Nigeria: Enicrownfit Publishers.
Bajerski, A. (2011). The role of French, German and Spanish journals in scientific communication in international geography. *Area 43*(3), 305–313.
Banjo, A. (2012). The deteriorating use of English in Nigeria. A. Akinjobi (Ed.). *English language clinic lecture series* 1–5 (pp. 2–29). Ibadan, Nigeria: University of Ibadan.
Barber, C. (1993). *The English language: A historical introduction.* Cambridge: Cambridge University Press.
Barcan, R. (2004). *Nudity: A cultural anatomy.* Oxford: Berg Publishers.
BBC (2017, 5 February). *Letters from Africa: Nigeria's art of flowery language.* Retrieved from http://www.bbc.com/news/world-africa-38827888
Beigel, F. (2009). *Sur les tabous* intellectuals: Bourdieu and academic dependence. *Sociologica 2*(3), 1–26.
Bgoya, W., & Jay, M. (2013). Publishing in Africa from independence to the present day. *Research in African Literatures, 44*(2), 17–34.
Bourdieu, P. (1991). *Language and symbolic power.* Cambridge: Polity Press.
Canagarajah, A. S. (1999). *Resisting linguistic imperialism in English teaching.* Oxford: Oxford University Press.
Collyer, F. M. (2018). Global patterns in the publishing of academic knowledge: Global north, global south. *Current Sociology, 66*(1), 56–73. DOI: https://doi.org/10.1177/0011392116680020
Cook, V. (1992). Evidence for multicompetence. *Language Learning, 42,* 557–591.
Curnutt, H. (2012). Flashing your phone: Sexting and the remediation of teen sexuality. *Communication Quarterly, 60*(3), 353–369.
Currey, J. (2013). Literary publishing after Nigerian independence: Mbari as celebration. *Research in African Literatures, 44*(2), 8–16.
Curry, M. J., & Lillis, T. (2004). Multilingual scholars and the imperative to publish in English: Negotiating interests, demands, and rewards. *TESOL Quarterly 38*(4), 663–688.
Duszak, A., & Lewkowicz, J. (2008). Publishing academic texts in English: A Polish perspective. *Journal of English for Academic Purposes,* 7(2),108–120.

Englander, K. (2011). The globalized world of English scientific publishing: An analytical proposal that situates a multilingual scholar. *Counterpoints, 387*, 209–228.

Fakoya, A. (2015). Sources and courses of errors in Nigerian English. In A. Akinjobi (Ed.). *English language clinic lecture series* 1–5. Vol *2* (pp. 45–67). Ibadan, Nigeria: University of Ibadan.

Harris C. D. (2001). English as international language in geography: Development and limitations. *Geographical Review, 91*(4), 675–689.

Kachru, B. B. (1995). *The other tongue: English across cultures.* Oxford: Oxford University Press.

Kamwangamalu, N. M. (2016). *Language policy and economics: The language question in Africa* (pp. 83–104). London: Palgrave Macmillan.

Kilonzo, S. M., & Magak, K. (2013). Publish or perish: Challenges and prospects of social science research and publishing in institutions of higher learning in Kenya. *International Journal of Sociology, 43*(1), 27–42.

Lovesey, O. (2000). *Ngugiwa Thiong'o.* New York: Twayne Publishers.

Lynch, A. (2007). Expanding the definition of provocative dress: An examination of female flashing behavior on a college campus. *Clothing and Textiles Research Journal, 25*(2), 184–201.

Meriläinen, S., Tienari, J., Thomas, R., & Davies, A (2008). Hegemonic academic practices: Experiences of publishing from the periphery. *Organization, 15*(4), 584–597.

Muchiri, M. N., Mulamba, G. N., Myers, G., & Ndoloi, D. B. (1995). Importing composition: Teaching and researching academic writing beyond North America. *College Composition and Communication, 46*(2), 175–198.

Ngugi wa Thiong'o (1986). *Decolonising the mind: The politics of language in African literature.* London: J. Currey; Portsmouth, NH: Heinemann.

Ogúndèjí, P. (1997). The communicative and semiotic contexts of àrokò among the Yoruba symbol-communication systems. *African Languages and Cultures, 10*(2), 145–156.

Ogúndèjì, P. (1998). The Image of Ṣàngó in Duro Ladipọ's Plays. *Research in African Literatures, 29*(2), 57–75.

Olukoju, A. (2004). The crisis of research and academic publishing in Nigerian universities. In P. T. Zeleza and A. Olukoshi (Eds.). *African universities in the twenty-first century* Vol. *2*: Knowledge and Society (pp. 363–375). Dakar, Senegal: CODESRIA.

Omobowale, A. O., Akanle, O., Adeniran, I. A., & Adegboyega, K. (2014). Peripheral scholarship and the context of foreign paid scholarship in Nigeria. *Current Sociology, 62*(5), 666–684.

Omobowale, A. O., Sawadogo, N., Sawadodo/Compaoré, E., & Ugbem, C. (2013). Globalisation and scholarly publishing in West Africa: A comparative study of Burkina Faso and Nigeria. *International Journal of Sociology, 43*(1),8–26.

Onwuzuruigbo, I. (2018). Indigenising Eurocentric sociology: The "captive mind" and five decades of sociology in Nigeria. *Current Sociology, 66*(6), 831–848. DOI: 10.1177/0011392117704242

Osundare, N. (2000). Yoruba thought, English words: A poet's journey through the tunnel of two tongues. In S. Brown (Ed.). *Kiss & quarrel: Yoruba/English strategis of mediation* (pp. 15–31). University of Birmingham, UK: Centre of West African Studies,.

Paasi, A. (2005). Globalisation, academic capitalism, and the uneven geographies of international journal publishing spaces. *Environment and Planning A, 37*(5), 769–789.

Papaioannou, A. G., Machaira, E., & Theano, V. (2013). Fifteen years of publishing in English language journals of sport and exercise psychology: Authors' proficiency in

English and editorial boards make a difference. *International Journal of Sport and Exercise Psychology*, *11*(1) doi.org/10.1080/1612197X.2013.753726

Pavlenko, A., & Norton, B. (2007). Imagined communities, identity and English language learning. *International Handbook of English Language Teaching*, *15*, 669–680.

Rose, H., & Galloway, N. (2017). Debating standard language ideology in the classroom: Using the "speak good English movement" to raise awareness of global Englishes. *RELC Journal*, *48*(3), 294–301. DOI:10.1177/0033688216684281

Ryan, J., Avelar, I, Fleissner, J., Lashmet, D. E, Miller, J. H., Pike, K. H., Sitter, J., & Tatlock, L. (2002). The future of scholarly publishing: MLA ad hoc committee on the future of scholarly publishing. *Profession*, 172–186. Retrieved from https://www.mla.org/content/download/3014/80410/schlrlypblshng.pdf

Rymes, B., & Pash, D. (2001). Questioning identity: The case of one second-language learner. *Anthropology and Education Quarterly*, *32*(3), 276–300.

Salager-Meyer, F. (2008). Scientific publishing in developing countries: Challenges for the future. *Journal of English for Academic Purposes*, *7*(2), 121–132.

Schneider, E. W. (2010). Developmental patterns of English: Similar or different? A. Kirkpatrick (Ed.). *The Routledge handbook of world Englishes* (pp. 372–384). New York: Routledge.

Shi, X. (2013). The glocalization of English: A Chinese case study. *Journal of Developing Societies*, *29*(2), 89–122.

Thompson, R. H. (2009). Publish and prosper: Scholarly publishing in anthropology at the University of Arizona. *Journal of the Southwest*, *51*(3), 423–444.

Ugobude, F. (2016). *4 times hon Patrick Obahiagbon confused us with grammar*. Retrieved 10 from http://omgvoice.com/news/hon-patrick-obahiagbon-grammar/

van Dalen, H., & Henkens, K. (1999). How influential are demography journals? *Population and Development Review*, *25*(2), 229–251.

Vanderstraeten, R. (2010). Scientific communication: Sociology journals and publication practices. *Sociology*, *44*(3), 559–576.

Vanderstraeten, R. (2011). Scholarly communication in education journals. *Social Science History*, *35*(1), 109–130.

White, L. (2000). *Speaking with vampires: Rumor and history in colonial Africa*. Berkeley, CA: University of California Press.

REGION 7
Persian Gulf

14
EXAMINING THE STATUS QUO OF PUBLICATION IN IRANIAN HIGHER EDUCATION

Perceptions and Strategies

Hesamoddin Shahriari

FERDOWSI UNIVERSITY OF MASHHAD

Behzad Ghonsooly

FERDOWSI UNIVERSITY OF MASHHAD

Introduction

In terms of scientific output, Iran is one of the fastest-growing countries in the world. Over a period of 12 years, ranging from 1996 to 2008, Iran's scientific publications in international journals rose from 736 to 13, 238 (Coghlan, 2011). This is even more surprising considering the low percentage of gross domestic product (GDP) allocated to research and development relative to industrialized countries in the world. The Expediency Discernment Council, an administrative assembly appointed to advise and shape national policy, has decreed that Iran's scientific growth rate should exceed that of all countries in the region by the year 2025 (Iranidoost, 2018. As of this writing, Iran ranks 22nd on the SCImago Journal and Country Rank (SJR), above most other countries in the region.

For any nation or scientific institution to achieve growth in scientific output, there is a need for advancements in the "production, circulation and diffusion of science" (Hamel, 2007, p. 67), and this is largely achieved through publishing scientific findings in international journals, most of which use English as their primary language of publication. One of the major obstacles on the path of Iranian scientists seeking to publish their research in international journals is meeting the English language expectations. This means effective use of the English language (i.e., the international language of global communication), including lexico-grammatical features and stylistic elements expected by journal editors and their readership (Hyland, 2007; Strauss, 2017). This problem is by no means unique to the Iranian context. In fact, this is a distinct challenge faced by many non-Anglophone academics (Flowerdew, 1999; Hanauer & Englander, 2011; Li, 2002;

Lillis & Curry, 2014) who, in addition to the content and methodology concerns that are shared by all authors, may struggle with language issues compared to their Anglophone peers who are said to enjoy a "free ride" based on their Anglophone privilege (Van Parijs, 2007, p. 72). To enable researchers to publish internationally, any education system must tend towards developing the language skills of scientists in addition to cultivating the scientific and technological foundations required for generating and disseminating scientific findings.

This chapter presents an investigation of Iranian scholars' perceptions of increasing expectations to publish their research papers in indexed, international English-language journals. First, we examine the policies set by Iran's Ministry of Science, Research and Technology and the type of support provided to Iranian researchers by this ministry in order to achieve publication. Second, we outline the perceptions of emerging and established Iranian researchers as to what constitutes a "good" research paper, what their main challenges are with achieving publication, and the strategies they employ in order to improve their chances of having their work published in international journals.

The Status of English in Iran's Education System

English is among the foreign languages taught in the Iranian education system. Until recently, it was one of the two mandatory languages taught in high schools; however, as of 2015, students are no longer obligated to study English and can choose from among other languages such as German, French, Spanish and Chinese. Arabic, as the language of the Quran, is the other language that must be learned by all high school students. Despite the choices provided to students, English remains in greater demand compared to the other languages, and many students attend private language schools to receive further practice and achieve greater proficiency in English.

The education system in Iran offers 12 years of schooling. Foreign language education begins from the seventh grade and continues all the way to the twelfth. Prior to entering university, students will have received six years of English as a Foreign Language instruction. Students are admitted to university through taking part in a nation-wide entrance examination which includes English among its tested subjects. University programs in Iran follow a core syllabus mandated by the Ministry of Science, Research and Technology. Persian is the language of instruction in all but a few university majors (English Literature, English Language Teaching and Translation Studies are the exceptions). However, almost all undergraduate students must take an English course during the first two years of their studies. This course mainly focuses on students' academic reading and vocabulary knowledge. Many programs also require students to take a course on technical English, which familiarizes students with discipline-specific vocabulary and terminology of their field.

English plays a much more important role in Master's and PhD programs, where students are required to conduct research and subsequently write a thesis or dissertation based on their findings. Although in most cases the thesis is written in the students' mother tongue (i.e., Persian), they are also encouraged to publish an article based on the findings of their studies in either a locally- or internationally-indexed journal. While this is not obligatory for Master's students who are only awarded an additional grade for doing so, doctoral students are barred from graduating until they manage to publish a paper extracted from their dissertation. Like many other academic contexts, publication is also a gateway to success in continuing to higher levels and obtaining better job opportunities after graduation (Flowerdew, 2015; Tian, Su, & Ru, 2016).

Students can choose to either publish their research in national outlets, most of which use Persian as their language of choice, or international journals, for which they are obliged to write in English. Little training is provided on how to write academic articles in English (including both language use and procedural content training) beyond what students learn in research methodology courses during their degree programs.

Challenges Faced by Iranian Researchers

There are numerous challenges facing Iranian graduate students and faculty who seek to publish their work in international journals. Kachru (1992) draws a distinction between inner-circle, expanding circle and outer-circle countries. The first category refers to countries that are home to Anglophone speakers. Most scholars from these inner-circle countries have the advantage of speaking English as their mother tongue and thus have a head start over their counterparts who have learned English as a second/foreign language. Expanding circle countries, such as Pakistan, Hong-Kong and India are those where English has been established throughout their history of colonial rule. Researchers from these countries are more likely to find it easier to use English for communicating their research findings than those from outer-circle countries. Finally, in outer-circle countries, including Iran, English is learned as a foreign language and is rarely encountered outside certain academic or educational settings. This combination of geographical and language features can cause additional difficulty for researchers from these countries and may lead to an unfair playing field (Buckingham, 2008; Canagarajah, 2014; Duzsak & Lewkowicz, 2008).

Another problem faced by Iranian researchers—one inextricably linked to the outer-circle locale of this knowledge production—is the difficulty with which researchers can access the latest books and publications in their field. Flowerdew (2013) refers to this as well as limited research funding and facilities as some of the other problems facing "off-network" academics (Belcher, 2007; Ferguson, 2007; Swales, 2004). This problem is magnified by the sanctions imposed on Iran, which severely limit the transaction of money abroad for the purpose of purchasing books, journal subscriptions, research/lab facilities, etc. Problems like this persist to this day despite the Joint Comprehensive Plan of Action signed by the six world powers and Iran in 2014 with the aim of offering sanctions relief.

Yet another issue that serves as common obstacle to publication of English language research articles for Iranian researchers is the lack of a solid academic research network. Lillis and Curry (2010) note that publishing is not an individual endeavor, but rather a networked activity, where, ideally, a group of individuals work together both locally and transnationally to prepare a manuscript, review it and submit it for publication. Once again, socio-political problems have made it very difficult both for internationally-renowned scholars and researchers to visit Iran and for Iranian academics to attend international events. It is through such exchanges that constructive dialogue often takes place and the necessary networks that underlie scientific production and academic publication may be established.

The present study seeks to better understand the current response of Iranian scholars to increased expectations surrounding English language research publication by answering three research questions:

1. What are the official policies for scientific publication laid out by the Ministry of Science, Research and Technology?
2. What are Iranian researchers' perceptions of what constitutes a "good" research article and academic journal?
3. What are some strategies employed by Iranian researchers for improving their chances of achieving publication in international journals?

Methodology

As faculty members of Ferdowsi University of Mashhad, a state-funded university in northeastern Iran, and with years of experience teaching EAP and academic writing courses, we were given privileged access to documents and data from the Ministry of Science, Research and Technology, which is in charge of governing educational and research policies for all universities in Iran. All official documents on publication and academic promotion issued by the Ministry as of 2017 were made available and reviewed in this study. With access to faculty members and graduate students in over 10 different faculties ranging from the Humanities to Engineering, we were able to interview scholars from a variety of backgrounds and levels of experience in research and publication. In this section, we will describe our participants, data collection and data analysis procedures.

Document Analysis

The first phase of this study involved reviewing the policies laid down by the Ministry of Science, Research and Technology as to what constitutes a "valid" research article. These guidelines and policies are used by university recruitment/promotion councils for the purpose of deciding on recruitment, promotions and the overall evaluation of academic staff. For this purpose, we reviewed documents that have been issued by the Ministry and have examined the criteria outlined for evaluating the quality or standards of a research article. As mentioned previously, universities in Iran are governed according to Ministry guidelines, which are in turn subject to change depending on the administration in charge. We decided to examine these documents during a ten-year period ranging from 2005 to 2015. This period of time is significant in that a surge in academic publication in Iran occurred during this time frame (Coghlan, 2011).

Participants

The second phase of the study was aimed at investigating the perception of academics (both university faculty members and graduate students) regarding what constitutes a "good" research article compared to those mandated by the Ministry. We also sought to identify some of the strategies employed by Iranian academics to increase their chances of publishing their research in international, top-tier journals. To this end, we interviewed 17 faculty members and 20 graduate students (12 Master's and 8 PhD students) at Iranian universities. Emails were sent out to a list of faculty members and graduate students calling for their participation. Those who responded to our invitation (response rate was 14%), were asked to either take part in a face-to-face or Skype interview depending on their location. Our sampling procedure yielded a list of both emerging and established academics. Participant details are provided in Table 14.1.

Individual, semi-structured interviews were conducted both face-to-face and via Skype. The interviewees were working/studying at a number of state universities across the country, including Ferdowsi University of Mashhad, Tehran University, Shiraz University, Guilan University, Hakim Sabzevari University, and Iran University of Science and Technology. The faculty members all held tenure positions at their universities and their years of experience ranged from 2–26 years. Eight of the interviewed faculty members held the academic rank of "Assistant Professor", five were "Associate Professors" and four held the highest academic title of "Full Professor". Their majors varied and included both the "soft" (management, sociology, applied linguistics and psychology) and "hard" sciences (mathematics, chemistry, biology, physics and electrical engineering).

TABLE 14.1 Interview participants and their respective academic disciplines

	Faculty members	Graduate students	
		Master's students	PhD students
Social Sciences	4	3	2
Arts and Humanities	3	2	1
Engineering	4	4	2
Science	6	3	3

The graduate students were studying in either a Master's (12) or a PhD (8) program. The Master's students who participated in this study were in the last semester of their studies, and, for the most part, trying to publish an article based on their thesis research. The PhD students, on the other hand, were studying at different points in their respective programs. Some of the PhD students were still involved with course work, while others had taken their comprehensive exams and were working on their dissertation. All PhD students in this study, however, had had the experience of writing at least one research article with the intent of publishing it in an English-language journal.

Interviews

The interviews followed a semi-structured format, where the interviewees began by answering a series of pre-defined questions (see Appendix 14.1) but were then asked follow-up questions depending on their response to previous items. On average, the interviews lasted 75 minutes, and respondents were assured that their answers would remain anonymous. Participants were assured that their responses would not be shared with any third party and that pseudonyms would be used in any report in order to protect their identity. All interviews were held in the participants' mother tongue (i.e., Persian) and were recorded with their permission. Notes were taken during the course of the interviews, complementing transcribed data which was later translated into English for subsequent analysis. Responses were translated by one of the researchers and were later checked for reliability. Responses were subsequently coded and categorized using NVivo 11, a software for qualitative data management and analysis. With the help of this software, emergent themes were identified and labelled.

Results and Discussion

Ministry of Science, Research and Technology, and "Validity"

A review of the policy documents issued by the Ministry of Science, Research and Technology indicates that there have been three recent stages of policy making in the Iranian academic promotion system. These stages correspond to the documents issued in the years 2008, 2010 and 2016. The documents are issued by the Ministry of Science, Research and Technology under the title of "Academic Faculty Promotion Regulations" and can be accessed through the archive of the said ministry. Each of these stages outlines the type of activities that qualify as the legitimate production of science. Research-related activities that count towards the promotion of an academic faculty member include, but are not limited to, authoring a book, compiling an edited volume, conducting and administering research projects (mainly at the national level), carrying out "innovative projects", and publishing research in foreign language journals. Foreign language journals do not necessarily refer to those that publish articles in English and could refer to any foreign language, including Spanish and Arabic.

The 2008 version classifies journals into three groups: local, national and international, with the highest credit given to the international journals which are those publishing articles in a foreign language. Considering that most international journals publish articles in English and that it is very rare for Iranian researchers to be able to write articles in any other language, this category is for all intents and purposes referring to English language journals. The 2008 version also assigns value to the publication of articles in journals that are registered in the Islamic World Science Citation Database (ISC). The ISC, which only indexes journals in the Islamic world, was established by Iran's Ministry of Science, Research and Technology in an attempt to combat what was believed to be the hegemony of certain Anglophone countries over the publication process.

The 2010 version differs only slightly from its predecessor in that it places more value on the grants that a researcher obtains in his/her academic record. This is an attempt at encouraging Iranian academics to involve themselves in projects, especially those on an international scale, where foreign investment and grants are involved. While publishing research in international journals is still mentioned as an important criterion for promotion, the document promotes publication in English-language journals by downplaying the value of non-English-language and ISC-indexed journals compared to the 2008 document.

Finally, the 2016 version, which is the latest document issued by the Ministry of Science, Research and Technology (as of this writing) explicitly mentions English as the primary language of publication when referring to international journals. This document places more value on publishing research in international journals compared to other research activities that were mentioned in previous versions. The 2016 version is also different in that it explicitly mentions both h-index and impact factor, metrics that assess author- and journal-level impact of published research. Specifically, there is use of the Journal Citation Index (JCR), which ranks academic journals based on impact factor, when evaluating journals.

These findings indicate that through time, the policies implemented by the Ministry have gradually shifted toward encouraging Iranian researchers to publish their work in English-language journals that enjoy greater visibility and are more likely to be read by an international readership, thus receiving more citations. In other words, through these policies, the Ministry seeks to draw researchers' attention to the importance of system rankings and metrics that are used to improve an institution and/or a country's standing among other competing nations and universities (Corcoran & Englander, 2016; Salager-Meyer, 2014). As discussed later in this chapter, such policies appear to have had an impact on perceptions and practices of both emerging and established Iranian scholars. Of note, such a policy assumes a level of scholarly research and writing expertise that likely requires substantial investment in the improvement of research facilities, information access, networking and, importantly, English for research publication purposes instruction. Without such provisions, many Iranian researchers are likely to feel discouraged by repeated rejection and may possibly experience low self-efficacy and/or burnout (Tian, et al, 2016).

Perceptions of a "Good" Research Article

In response to the first research question (i.e., the features of a "good" or high quality research article), Iranian researchers noted the importance of a rigorous methodology, thorough literature review, effective/accurate English language usage, application of the findings, and up-to-date citations. Methodology was referred to as an important feature of a good research article and many of the respondents claimed that among their rejected articles, most were turned down because of methodological issues. This aspect was more often referred to by faculty members from hard science disciplines, and fewer respondents from the soft sciences stressed its importance. The literature review, on the other hand, was a feature that was of relatively greater importance to faculty members from the soft sciences, especially those from the fields of sociology and applied linguistics. Many of the respondents stated that an awareness of other studies into the same area of research is vital and that, in the words of Amir, a faculty member from the field of Food Science, one must "link the findings to what has been established in the literature".

Language was another important feature identified by participation in a quality research article. Leila, one of the interviewed graduate students, who was completing her PhD studies in Economics, said that "grammar and vocabulary are the essential features of a good article. You may have done wonderful research, but if your language is poor, you might as well forget about having it published in a high-ranking journal." This is important as Evans and Green (2007) have emphasized the crucial role of grammar instruction in EAP for the purpose of conveying ideas of a complex nature, and other studies have also reported on the normative expectations of journal editors with regard to adherence to native-speaker standards of language use (Lillis & Curry, 2015; Heng-Hartse & Kubota, 2014).

While rhetorical strategies and style were mostly emphasized by respondents specializing in applied linguistics, participants from other backgrounds also showed some awareness of these features, and a few indirectly referred to the importance of organizing content through planning and preparing an outline for the different parts of their article. Another feature that was referred to by scholars from the fields of mechanical engineering and chemistry was the application of the findings. According to one faculty member, "a good research article should address a genuine problem and come up with findings that can somehow either improve our understanding of the problem or offer a solution for it." Finally, citation was referred to by most faculty interviewees as a significant characteristic of a high-quality research article. One of the respondents (Javid, a faculty member at the department of biotechnology) even stated that when deciding on an area to conduct research, he "often weighs the chances of being cited by other authors". Similar findings have also been reported by Tenopir, Dalton, Fish, Christian, Jones, and Smith (2016), who found that US-based researchers tend to consider impact factor and number of citations for the journal as indicators of a journal's quality. Other studies have also shown that citations can be an important factor in determining the quality of a journal (Rupp, Thornton, Rogelberg, Olien, & Berka, 2014).

Graduate students interviewed in this study mentioned methodology, literature review, language and "trendiness" as the most important features of a research article. The first three were also mentioned by the interviewed faculty members; however, trendiness was only pointed out by three of the PhD students. These students said that certain topics/agendas within sub-disciplines of their field of study tend to come into vogue. Research articles written based on these topics, they claimed, were more likely to be published and were generally of greater interest to readers because they had become "trendy". Graduate students generally held the same views regarding the importance of having a sound methodology, a comprehensive literature review and accurate use of language. In terms of language, most of the graduate students referred to the proper use of grammar and formal, academic vocabulary. Only three of the PhD students mentioned the importance of content organization and Babak, a PhD student from the field of Chemistry, said, "I think it's important to present a convincing argument in support of your findings." Limited experience in writing for publication might be the reason why structural organization was somewhat undervalued by graduate students (Cheng, 2006).

Criteria for Choosing a Journal

The second interview question asked respondents about their criteria for choosing a journal. The most common answer among both the interviewed faculty members and graduate students was indexing. Almost all respondents referred to this factor as the most important criteria. To those who mentioned this factor in their response, being indexed in a valid database was the most important factor for an academic journal. The *ISI Web of Science* and *Scopus* were the most commonly-mentioned databases. When asked why they thought this was an important feature of a good journal, most respondents, especially the graduate students, said that they were introduced to these databases through workshops and their professors/supervisors. That is, the priority given to research articles available on these databases could be the outcome of the university policies. A few of the university faculty members, however, believed that indexing alone cannot guarantee the quality of a journal. They argued that there are countless journals that are indexed in these databases, but do not follow a rigorous peer review system for the selection of articles. These respondents instead stressed the value of visibility and recognition within the research community as more important factors. One of the respondents, who had earned his PhD from a university in Australia, said that he had not been familiar with the mentioned databases prior to becoming a faculty member.

He said that when choosing a journal, he often opted for those which had formerly published the research of other notable academic figures from the same area. In addition to indexing, a number of the PhD students and most of the faculty members also mentioned the journal's H-index as an important factor in determining the level and prestige of a journal. Interestingly, when asked whether the respondents knew what an H-index was, many of them could not provide a definition or gave a narrow definition at best. For example, in the words of Raheleh, a graduate student of Sociology, "it's the number of citations the articles in a journal receive". This suggests that many of the researchers interviewed in this study were directly influenced by the policies that were handed down by the Ministry of Science, Research and Technology and were for the most part unquestioningly following the ministry's definition of what constitutes a valid journal for publication.

In response to the same question, many of the Master's students said that they did not have much say in which journal their articles were submitted to. They stated that this was a decision that was made by their thesis supervisors. New regulations require a faculty member (in most cases the supervisor in charge of the student thesis) to be the corresponding author of any research article written based on a thesis. As a result of this, most Master's students in Iran are not involved in the process of submission. Those Master's students who did mention other factors, such as indexing, as being important, had learned about these factors through academic writing/publishing workshops. This trend also exists in other non-periphery contexts, where more experienced researchers have been found to pass on their preferences for journals and outlets to younger generations (Tenopir et al., 2016).

Perceived Challenges and Strategies

The third interview question asked participants about the difficulties they face when preparing a research article for publication and the strategies they employ for overcoming these difficulties.

A range of difficulties were expressed by the participants, some of which were shared by both groups (i.e., faculty members and graduate students) and others were unique to one of the two. The most common problem was the perception of a bias against submissions received from Iran, an issue that has also been reported for other non-Anglophone contexts (e.g., Corcoran & Englander, 2016; Salager-Meyer, 2014). There seemed to be an idea shared by many of the faculty members and graduate students that their manuscripts were considered unfairly by gatekeepers (journal editors or reviewers). One faculty member from the social sciences explained that her articles were rejected during initial screening by the journal editor, without giving her the chance to have her work reviewed. Another faculty member from social sciences said that he often removed any indication of where the study was conducted from his manuscripts because he believed the reviewers formed negative opinions of his work upon discovering its place of origin. When asked if there was any evidence for this systematic bias against manuscripts submitted from Iran, a number of responses were provided. One of the graduate students mentioned that one of her peers who had experienced difficulty publishing during graduate studies had reported a shift in attitude upon moving to an English-speaking university and submitting manuscripts with that university's affiliation.

One of the faculty members suggested that perhaps one of the reasons why Iranian researchers from the natural sciences are more successful in publishing their work is because their studies tend to be more decontextualized and hence less likely to be discriminated against due to their background and/or place of origin. Another graduate student mentioned that he had once conducted a replication study based on research that had been published in an accredited journal, but his paper had been rejected for methodological shortcomings. He therefore argued that "the reviewers were more strict when evaluating my work because the same methodological problems could have applied to the original study". Ebrahim, one of the more established faculty members from the hard sciences (i.e., physics), who had graduated from a university in Australia, said that his submissions were rejected by the editors of many high-ranking journals without any clear explanation. He stated that most of these reviewers mentioned reasons that were unconvincing to him. For instance, he provided some examples of responses from the editor as evidence for his claim. He showed us an email from the editor, which read "We think that your study has generated quite interesting findings with regard to your [topic of study] but we are not sure whether they constitute significant knowledge contributions to the field. We suggest that you may consider sending your work to some regional or national journals."

Despite the widespread view that submissions by Iranian researchers are discriminated against, a number of respondents, specifically three of the faculty members, denied the existence of such bias. They referred to factors such as the vast quantity of submissions, low quality of research and language problems. They said that journals are overwhelmed with a great number of submissions and often have high rejection rates. Secondly, they said that because of wrong policies, Iranian graduate students aim for high-ranking journals. As a result, many of these journals began receiving poor-quality submissions by novice researchers from Iran, which in turn led to a bad reputation for all researchers from the country. They emphasized, however, that this does not mean there is systematic discrimination against all submissions from Iran. Finally, they referred to common language problems as another reason for the high rejection rate among Iranian researchers. They believed that lack of proper training and not having competent "shapers" (Burrough-Boenisch, 2003) also contributed to the high rejection rate.

When asked about how these researchers dealt with this problem, some of the respondents said that they tried to remove any indication that the study had been sent from Iran. They deliberately deleted the name of the country, origin of the participants and name of universities and institutions. One of the graduate students, who was doing his PhD in biotechnology, said, "I try to partner up with researchers from other countries". He claimed that international studies carried out jointly by two or more researchers, especially those from English-speaking countries, had a much better chance of getting published. Another one of the respondents, a PhD student of psychology, said, "I try to choose topics that are not local; instead, I go with topics that don't involve Iranian participants or organizations." These perceptions seem to echo claims of other researchers and scholars regarding a potential bias against authors from the outer circle (Clavero, 2011; Flowerdew & Li, 2007; Umakantha, 1997).

Language Proficiency

Language was another challenge mentioned by many of the respondents. They specifically referred to the limited support they received from their universities and institutions with regards to editing and proofreading services. A number of studies have emphasized the importance of proofreading in improving the quality of academic/research writing by scholars using English as an additional language (e.g, Salager-Meyer, 2014; Uzunder-Smith & Englander, 2014; Willey & Tanimoto, 2012). One of the faculty members from the field of chemistry with a good track record of publishing mentioned that for him, the most common cause for rejection was language-related issues. He noted that in one specific case, due to the lack of professional language support from his institution, the journal editor had asked a native speaker to revise his submission and later added his name as a co-author. This faculty member argued that in many cases, he or his colleagues and students had conducted valuable research that could significantly contribute to the knowledge of the field but were subsequently deprived of sharing their findings with the community simply because their manuscript had been rejected on the grounds that it did not meet the language standards of the journal. The graduate students interviewed in this study also mentioned language-related issues as a barrier to publishing. One of the PhD students of this study said that he was an English teacher and had even achieved an excellent IELTS band score of 8.0 but still encountered problems when writing academic articles in English. He believed that his problem was with achieving an academic style and presenting his claims in a "weighed tone".

In response to the question of how the participants dealt with the "problem" of language, a number of strategies and solutions were provided. Many of the respondents said that they often ask peers with a good command of academic English or language experts to review their manuscripts prior to publication, a practice that is widely reported in the literature (see Willey & Tanimoto, 2013). One respondent, a PhD student from the field of sociology, noted that he would like to use professional editing/proofreading services suggested by journal editors, but found it unfeasible, because "they are very expensive and the university doesn't devote a budget for these services". Another graduate student said that he often asked students majoring in English to help revise his articles but admitted that "they only deal with language-related problems and lack content knowledge to address all aspects of the article". One of the faculty members mentioned that he often sought help from professional language editing services inside Iran but warned that not all businesses in this area could be trusted as many of them merely corrected surface-level grammatical and lexical mistakes without attending to elements such as style and other discipline-bound features of language.

A number of respondents also mentioned attending workshops focusing on improving academic English as a way of improving their writing skills. One of the respondents (Babak) referred to this as the best possible strategy, because he claimed that it would allow him to be independent in the long run and be able to publish his research without the need to seek help from others. In line with this expressed need, Corcoran and Englander (2016) maintain that "ERPP support in courses and workshops in order to attend more fully to the concerns of multilingual scholars tasked... with the challenge of publishing their research in English as an additional language." (p. 7) This type of ERPP support appears lacking for many of the study participants, something that has been reported by plurilingual scholars in other periphery locales (Bardi & Muresan, 2014; Canagarajah, 2013).

Social Writing Practices and (Legitimate) Participation

A final challenge mentioned by the interviewees of this study was their difficulty in accessing and discussing their work with other members of the international research community. This problem was mainly mentioned by the faculty members. According to Amir, a faculty member who had visited an American university on sabbatical:

> US-based researchers can easily discuss their research with colleagues, many of whom are experts in their field. They can even send out their manuscripts to each other and get feedback before submitting their work to journals, so they can predict some of the problems and revise their work and increase their chances of publication in good journals.

Graduate students, on the other hand, lamented the fact that their supervisors often did not provide detailed comments on their work and that they were left with very few options when it came to seeking comments and advice on their research articles. To overcome this problem, some of the respondents said they use reviewer comments as a source for improving [their] articles. That is, they often used reviewer comments as the only source of input for preparing their work for future submissions. A number of the respondents also stated that they attended foreign conferences and events with the sole purpose of sharing their research ideas and preliminary data with other researchers from the international community and receiving their comments and suggestions on how to improve their work. These findings stress the importance of social practices of writing for publication, where establishing networks and giving/providing feedback become sustainable methods of research writing (Badenhorst & Guerin, 2016; Casanave, 2014; Lillis & Curry, 2010).

Conclusion

This chapter is an attempt to provide readers with a view of the status of research publication in Iran through reviewing the policies, examining the perceived challenges faced by Iranian researchers and looking at the strategies and solutions they employ in order to overcome these challenges. The present study involves a number of limitations and readers should therefore bear in mind the scope of the data and the participants' background. Future studies should attempt to collect more generalizable data by including a broader range of participants from this under-researched context. Our findings suggest that writing for publication decisions made by Iranian academics (including their choice of journals) may be linked to the recent policies laid out by the Ministry of Science, Research and Technology. These policies have raised expectations for publishing of research in highly-ranked, indexed journals. Yet Iranian researchers—both faculty members and graduate students—have not received much support to help them overcome the challenges of publishing in such journals.

Our findings also suggest that Iranian researchers could benefit from a number of changes to the current situation. First of all, effective literacy brokers (Lillis & Curry, 2010) and rigorous ERPP courses (Corcoran & Englander, 2016) could help remove some of the language barriers experienced by many Iranian academics. Furthermore, since academic literacies are inherently socially- and politically-situated (Casanave, 2014), improvement of ties with inner-circle countries could greatly improve Iranian researchers' chances of publication. This could be achieved through policies that allow for development of scholars' networks, including the easing/lifting of international sanctions. It is incumbent upon the policymakers (especially those within the Ministry of Science, Research and Technology) to address these concerns by devoting more credits within the higher education curriculum to improving both the general English and academic English (including scholarly writing proficiency) of university students. Another measure that could improve Iranian scholars' ability to meet knowledge production expectations would be the re-integration of Iranian scholars into the international community of scientists by increasing travel funds for attending international conferences and workshops as well as easing restrictions on visits by foreign scientists. Finally, although the removal of sanctions by Western countries promised a better future for Iranian academics, there are still severe limitations on purchasing materials and resources, thereby disadvantaging Iranian scholars. Ultimately, access to greater language (for scholarly publication) support, materials, resources, and international networks are necessary in order to bridge the gap between expectations and reality.

References

Badenhorst, C. M., & Guerin, C. (2016). Introduction: Post/graduate writing pedagogies and research literacies. In C. M. Badenhorst, & C. Guerin (Eds.). *Post/graduate writing pedagogies and research literacies* (pp. 3–28). Amsterdam, The Netherlands: Brill/Emerald Publishing.

Bardi, M., & Muresan, L. (2014). Changing research writing practices in Romania: Perceptions and attitudes. In K. Bennet (Ed.). *The semiperiphery of academic writing: Discourses, communities and practices* (pp. 121–147). Berlin: Mouton De Gruyter.

Belcher, D. (2007). Seeking acceptance in an English only research world. *Journal of Second Language Writing, 16,* 1–22.

Buckingham, L. (2008). Development of academic writing competence by Turkish scholars. *International Journal of Doctoral Studies, 3,* 1–18.

Burrough-Boenisch, J. (2003). Shapers of published non-native speaker research articles. *Journal of Second Language Writing, 12,* 223–243.

Canagarajah, A. (2013). *Translingual practice: Global Englishes and cosmopolitan relations.* London: Routledge.

Canagarajah, S. A. (2014). Local knowledge when ranking journals: Reproductive effects and resistant possibilities. *Education Policy Analysis Archives, 22*(28), 1–23.

Casanave, C. P. (2002). *Writing games: Multicultural case studies of academic literacy practices in higher education.* Mahwah, NJ: Lawrence Erlbaum.

Casanave, C. P. (2014). *Before the dissertation.* Ann Arbor, MI: University of Michigan Press.

Cheng, A. (2006) Understanding learners and learning in ESP genre-based writing instruction. *English for Specific Purposes, 25,* 76–89.

Clavero, M. (2011). Unfortunately, linguistic injustice matters. *Trends in Ecology and Evolution, 26*(4), 156–157.

Coghlan, A. (2011). Iran is top of the world in science growth. *New Scientist.* Retrieved from https://www.newscientist.com/article/dn20291-iran-is-top-of-the-world-in-science-growth/

Corcoran, J., & Englander, K. (2016). A proposal for critical-pragmatic pedagogical approaches to English for Research Publication Purposes. *Publications, 4,* 1–10.

Duzsak, A., & Lewkowicz, J. (2008). Publishing academic texts in English: A Polish perspective. *Journal of English for Academic Purposes, 7,* 108–120.

Evans, S., & Green, C. (2007). Why EAP is necessary: A survey of Hong Kong tertiary students. *Journal of English for Academic Purposes, 6,* 3–17.

Ferguson, G. (2007). The global spread of English, scientific communication and ESP: Questions of equity, access and domain loss. *Iberica, 13,* 7–38.

Flowerdew, J. (1999). Problems in writing for scholarly publication in English: The case of Hong Kong. *Journal of Second Language Writing, 8,* 243–264.

Flowerdew, J. (2013). Some thoughts on English for Research Publication Purposes (ERPP) and related issues. *Language Teaching, 48*(2), 250–262. doi: 10.1017/s0261444812000523

Flowerdew, J. (2015). Some thoughts on English for Research Publication Purposes (ERPP) and related issues. *Language Teaching, 48*(2), 250–263.

Flowerdew, J., & Li, Y. (2007). Language re-use among Chinese apprentice scientists writing for publication. *Applied Linguistics, 28*(3), 440–465.

Hamel, R. E. (2007). The dominance of English in the international scientific periodical literature and the future of language use in science. *AILA Review 20,* 53–71

Heng-Hartse, J., & Kubota, R. (2014). Pluralizing English? Variation in high-stakes academic texts and challenges of copyediting. *Journal of Second Language Writing, 24,* 71–82.

Hyland, K. (2007). English for professional academic purposes: Writing for scholarly publication. In D. Belcher (Ed.). *Teaching purposefully: English for specific purposes in theory and practice*. New York: Cambridge University Press.

Iranidoost, K. (2018, July 2018). *Iran science production shows fastest growth*, p.1. Retrieved from https://en.mehrnews.com/news/136116/Iran-science-production-shows-world-s-fastest-growth

Kachru, B. (1992). World Englishes: approaches, issues and resources. *Language Teaching*, 25(1), 1–14. doi: 10.1017/s0261444800006583

Lave, J., & Wenger, E. (1991). *Situated learning: Legitimate peripheral participation*. Cambridge: Cambridge University Press.

Li, Y. (2002). Writing for international publication: The perceptions of Chinese doctoral researchers. *Asian Journal of English Language Teaching*, 12, 179–194.

Lillis, T. M., & Curry, M. J. (2006). Professional academic writing by multilingual scholars: Interactions with literacy brokers in the production of English-medium texts. *Written Communication*, 23, 3–35.

Lillis, T. M., & Curry, M. J. (2010). *Academic writing in a global context: The politics and practices of publishing in English*. London: Routledge.

Curry, M., & Lillis, T. (2014). Strategies and tactics in academic knowledge production by multilingual scholars. *Education Policy Analysis Archives*. doi: 10.14507/epaa.v22n32.2014

Lillis, T. M., & Curry, M. J. (2015). The politics of English, language and uptake: The case of international journal article reviews. *AILA Review*, 28(1), 127–150.

Rupp, D., Thornton, M., Rogelberg, S., Olien, J., & Berka, G. (2014). The Characteristics of Quality Scholarly Submissions. *Journal of Management*, 40(6), 1501–1510.

SCImago Journal and Country Rank (2017, June 1). Retrieved from www.scimagojr.com/countryrank.php

Salager-Meyer, F. (2014). Writing and publishing in peripheral scholarly journals: How to enhance the global influence of multilingual scholars. *Journal of English for Academic Purposes*, 13, 78–82.

Strauss, P. (2017). "It's not the way we use English"—Can we resist the native speaker stranglehold on academic publications? *Publications*, 5(4), 27.

Swales, J. M. (1987). Utilizing the literatures in teaching the research paper. *TESOL Quarterly*, 21, 41–68.

Swales, J. M. (1990). *Genre analysis: English in academic and research settings*. Cambridge: Cambridge University Press.

Swales, J. M. (2004). *Research genres: Explorations and applications*. Cambridge: Cambridge University Press.

Tenopir, C., Dalton, E., Fish, A., Christian, L., Jones, M., & Smith, M. (2016). What motivates authors of scholarly articles? The importance of journal attributes and potential audience on publication choice. *Publications*, 4, 1–22.

Tian, M., Su, Y., & Ru, X. (2016). Perish or publish in China: Pressures on young Chinese scholars to publish in internationally-indexed journals. *Publications*, 4, 1–16.

Umakantha, N. (1997). Beyond the language barrier [Letter to the editor]. *Nature*, 385, 764.

Uzuner-Smith, S., & Englander, K. (2015). Exposing ideology within university policies: A critical discourse analysis of faculty hiring, promotion and remuneration practices. *Journal of Education Policy*, 30(1), 62–85.

Van Parijs, P. (2007). Tackling the Anglophone's free ride: Fair linguistic cooperation with a global lingua franca. *AILA Review*, 20, 72–87.

Willey, I., & Tanimoto, K. (2013). "Convenience editors" as legitimate participants in the practice of scientific editing: An interview study. *Journal of English for Academic Purposes*, 12(1), 23–32.

Appendix 14.1

Interview Questions

1. What are the main features of a quality research article?
2. How do you go about choosing a journal to submit your articles to?
3. What are some of the challenges you face when seeking to publish your research in valid, international journals?
4. What are some measures you take to increase your chances of getting published in valid, international journals?

15

WRITING LOUDER?

Coping With the Push to Publish in English at an Iranian University

Seyyed-Abdolhamid Mirhosseini

ALZAHRA UNIVERSITY, TEHRAN, IRAN

Zahra Shafiee

ALZAHRA UNIVERSITY, TEHRAN, IRAN

Introduction

The flow of science, research, and technology today is known to take place mainly through the medium of the English language worldwide (Flowerdew & Li, 2009; Hyland, 2016), and Iran is no exception in this regard. During the past decade the two Iranian ministries in charge of science, research, and healthcare, namely, the Ministry of Science, Research, and Technology, and the Ministry of Health and Medical Education, have increased their national-level focus on the significance of academic publication as an indicator of advancement in these areas, especially at the international level and in the English language. This policy direction is in line with the long-held national academic and educational orientation of encouraging the expansion of science, technology, and healthcare. To complicate the situation, however, there is also a tendency to give primacy to the national and Islamic identity, attempting to elevate the status of the national official language of Farsi (Persian) and even promoting it to the level of a language of modern science.

This challenging scene is shaped against the backdrop of the escalating competition created by global university ranking systems, as academic institutions around the world increasingly expect their faculty members to publish research papers. Regardless of the home language of universities, writing in English tends to be a taken-for-granted priority of this demand and is justified by the wider reach and the *louder* voice of English that can collect more ranking scores (Rezaeian, 2015). In this chapter we explore such an academic climate, characterized by a combination of global-local features, at an Iranian university of medical sciences. Our aim is to explore how its faculty members are encouraged to write and publish in the English language and, at the same time, how they are concerned with local needs and the Iranian language and culture. Based on an outline of the administrative policies of the university to promote the publish-in-English trend, we draw on questionnaire data, as well as interviews with faculty members, to understand aspects of how they deal with such policies and to explore some implications of the function of these diverging forces in the Iranian academic and social context.

Background

In discussing the historical trends that turned English into the dominant language worldwide and the contemporary realizations of those trends, an important current force that has been considered is international publishing (e.g., Curry & Lillis, 2017a; Flowerdew, 1999; Flowerdew & Li, 2009; Huttner-Koros, 2015; Politzer-Ahlesa, Holliday, Girolamod, Spychalskae, & Berkson, 2016; Salager-Meyer, 2008, 2009). This trend of publishing in English is also increasingly inter-related with the way global university ranking systems persuade universities around the world to publish academic research. Based on the notion of "impact" and the significance of the number of scholars reached by academic publications, English has become a top priority in academic writing for pursuing individual interests, professional gains, and especially within the competition for better positions in ranking systems (Flowerdew, 1999; Meneghini & Packer, 2007). However, a concern about the role of gatekeeping in indexing systems and the use of English as the language of research communication is how English can encounter local languages in this regard, and the bias in favor of native English speakers (Curry & Lillis, 2017b; Maniati, 2014; Muresan & Pérez-Llantada, 2014; Salö, 2017).

An increasing body of literature indicates the records of scholarly endeavors addressing this trend across the globe and the related concerns of linguistic hegemony and injustice (e.g., Huang, 2010; Muresan & Pérez-Llantada, 2014; Politzer-Ahlesa, et al., 2016; Salager-Meyer, 2008, 2009). As an example, Flowerdew and Li (2009) examined the trend of domination and hegemony of English as the so-called academic lingua franca in the fields of humanities and social sciences in China. The attitudes of Chinese academics turned out to be in favor of increasing international publication in English, although the participants also valued retaining Chinese as the language of sciences and research publication. Similarly, Bocanegra-Valle (2014) tackled "the hegemony of English for scholarly publishing in multilingual Europe" (p. 66). She investigated the attitudes of European academics about publishing in English in spite of the efforts of the Council of Europe (1997) for encouraging linguistic diversity across European academia. As reasons for submitting their manuscripts in English to a multilingual journal, the participants mentioned academic and professional promotion, "a wider authorship. . . wider recognition and acceptance by peer academics. . . [and being] cited extensively and by foreign authors" (p. 69). A minority, however, considered English as a threat to their own languages.

Even in regions and countries where the cultural climate may be at odds with the cultural norms accompanying the English language, university ranking criteria including high impact publishing in English tend to be widely embraced (Riazi, 2012). Such orientations, which are no less active in Islamic countries including Iran, tend to foster the mainstream global academic culture through the ascription of higher value to articles published in English that can benefit authors for academic and professional recruitment, promotion, and funds (Doostdar & Mirhosseini, 2009). Therefore, academic publication in Iran mainly follows the "global trend of the anglicization of academic publishing" (Flowerdew & Li, 2009, p. 2) that contributes to the dilemma of "publish in English or perish in academia" (Bocanegra-Valle, 2014, p. 65). In this respect, Thomson Reuters (2012) reports on the eight-fold increase of Iranian submissions to English language journals from 2005 to 2010, and a perfunctory examination of Iranian university policies that drive research and education through regulations like academic promotion mechanisms indicates an increasing enforcement of publishing in internationally indexed publications (Doostdar & Mirhosseini, 2008).

The trend of publishing in English is increasingly prevalent in Iran across all disciplines due to the policies and regulations that encourage English publication as a prerequisite of recruitment, academic and professional promotion, and research funding (see the section on "Policies of publishing in English" below). Whereas upstream documents based on national policies assert the necessity of publishing research articles in Farsi, regulations authorized by the same policy sources consider English publications as a major yardstick for academic and professional evaluation. Such a yardstick may act as a de facto reinforcement of the hegemony of English (Bocanegra-Valle, 2014), linguistic imperialism for academic publication (Muresan & Pérez-Llantada, 2014), and linguistic injustice and bias for the non-Anglophone researchers (Curry & Lillis, 2017b; Politzer-Ahles, et al., 2016). The official language policy in Iran, including the language-in-education policy, is overtly set to support and elevate the status of Farsi along with the preservation of local languages (Ghamari & Hassanzadeh, 2010; Mirhosseini & Khodakarami, 2016), and this is reflected in decades of activities of the Iranian Academy of Persian Language and Literature (Davari-Ardakani & Ahmadipour, 2009; Riazi, 2005). However, the covert language-of-publishing mentalities, policies, and practices in Iran seem to have been well influenced by the ranking systems in the *glocal* push to publish in English (Dootdar & Mirhosseini, 2009).

In addition to such general concerns about the dominance of English in academic publishing and the related challenges for academic writers with non-English background, the specific issue of English language writing and publishing in medical sciences and related fields has been discussed as a concern on its own (e.g., Man, et al., 2004; Monge-Najera & Nielsen, 2005). Among the rare cases of similar attempts conducted in Iran, Rezaeian (2015) has discussed the disadvantages of English language publishing by non-Anglophones in the specific area of biomedical research. Accordingly, overlooking local health issues can be a crucial disadvantage of a publishing trend that overly writes for publication in English and naturally follows a subtle line of research drawn by international publishers.

Although from a different angle, the study reported in the rest of this chapter addresses an issue related to Rezaeian's (2015) concern based on the perspectives of faculty members at an Iranian university of medical sciences.

Policies of Publishing in English

This section provides an overview of policies that set the ground for the trend of publishing research articles in English in Iranian academia. National policies in areas of science and research are chiefly set as The Comprehensive Science Roadmap. The Roadmap is devised by The Supreme Council for Cultural Revolution headed by the president of the Islamic Republic of Iran. In this council, Iranian top-level policymakers decide on national policies and goals for cultural, educational, and scientific affairs to be implemented by different government bodies, including the Ministry of Science, Research and Technology, and the Ministry of Health and Medical Education. Regarding academic publishing, these documents clearly delineate a path of intensive research, as well as dissemination of findings. The rise in the number of international research submissions and publications by Iranian academics during the last decade (Hyland, 2016; Thomson Reuters, 2012) may be an indication of the reinforcing role played by these policies.

The Comprehensive Science Roadmap sets two major policy lines in the Iranian academic arena. On the one hand, aimed at improving and disseminating science, it emphasizes the importance of enhancing Farsi, Iranian culture, and Islamic identity and "elevating the status of Farsi among the international languages of science" (p. 6). As one of the guidelines for achieving this goal, the Roadmap advises increasing "the number of research articles in Farsi, published in journals indexed in credible international indexing systems" (p. 10). More specifically, national goals are devised so as to reinforce the publication of research articles in the national language "to elevate Farsi to the status of one of the international languages of science" (p. 46); "the admission of foreign university students, so that Iran becomes a scientific pole among neighboring and Islamic countries" (p. 46); and "the facilitation of introducing Farsi equivalents for foreign scientific terminologies" (p. 47). On the other hand, the Roadmap emphasizes the education and application of the English language for facilitating communication with international scholarly communities. It highlights the importance of "organizing English language education based on the needs of Iran for international communication for scientific and technological purposes" (p. 50).

The Roadmap and other upstream documents are translated into formal regulations to provide administrable guidelines for operationalizing the policies. The most recent versions of the Regulations for Academic Promotion of Faculty Members provide detailed evaluative guidelines and specific measures for assessing and quantifying academic activities. This document puts special emphasis on research publication as perhaps the most important criterion for academic promotion. Moreover, the devised quantification procedures in these regulations clearly allocate higher scores for publishing in internationally indexed publications and specifically consider added points for publishing in "foreign languages" (which is almost equivalent to English in this context). In these documents, the preference for publishing in English can be observed in the form of three major directions. First, the Promotion document specifies higher scores for English language publications (the scores assigned to every publication based on which the faculty members' promotion profile is evaluated). Specifically, the score for books published by credible international publishers (which, again, practically means those in English) is 1.5 times higher than that for Farsi publications, and the score for "articles published in Science and Nature [published in English] is twofold" (p. 5).

Second, a major prerequisite for promotion in medical sciences is publishing articles indexed by Thomson Reuters, PubMed, or Scopus. Although the language of publication is not asserted, an absolute majority of journals published by these systems are in English. As specified by the document, to gain promotion from an assistant professor to an associate professor, faculty members in the field of medical sciences, similar to other fields, need to have at least "one original research article in English, as the major author, published in journals indexed in international indexing systems" (p. 42). This figure is three for promotion to a full professor rank. In addition, the four-year interval required for promotion is reduced to three years for those who publish "at least one original article, as the first author in *New England Journal, JAMA, Lancet, Science,* and *Nature* [published in English]" (p. 7). Third, regarding the funds allocated to the faculty members' research activities based on their publications, the most recent version of the promotion regulations for medical sciences no longer considers funds for Farsi publications, as only articles published and indexed in the systems mentioned above are granted funds. Although the same regulations highlight the importance of Farsi as the language of publication, and in spite of the fact that faculty members need to have at least one Farsi publication for their promotion, they no longer receive funds for their publications in Farsi, while they still receive them for their English publications. This omission of funds practically discourages writing in Farsi.

The actual embracement of the language of research publication is not the same in all disciplines. For instance, in the hard sciences, beside their local and contextual benefits of disseminating knowledge for national gain, the international cooperative and communicative nature of the disciplines encourages choosing English as the language of research publication. The social sciences and humanity disciplines tend to be rather local and contextualized, thus, in these fields Farsi is relatively more frequently used for publication. Medical sciences—as the particular disciplines considered here—incorporate both direct local application and international reach for scholarly communication. The regulations, however, exert the same pressure on faculty members across disciplines with different disciplinary necessities, different levels of English language proficiency and academic literacy, and different levels of awareness of ideological and political functioning (Maniati, 2014). In the rest of this chapter, we explore the position of faculty members at a university of medical sciences about these policies and regulations, their own language priorities in academic writing and publishing, and the assumptions and justifications underlying these priorities.

Dealing With the Policies

To provide a more contextualized view of language preferences in academic research publication in Iran, we explore issues related to English language publishing, taking a bottom up approach. The existing policies apply to all universities of medical sciences and all research fields across the Ministry of Science, Research and Technology and the Ministry of Health and Medical Education. Thus, the focus here is on a single university of medical sciences as a representative research site. We examine the views of medical science faculty members on the language of research publication and investigate their beliefs regarding the value of publishing in English as an indication of academic status and professional achievement in contrast with writing in the national language of Farsi. The site of the study is a nationally leading university of medical sciences with 12 faculties and about 1200 faculty members. Apart from its specific features, the university can represent the 42 other Iranian state-run medical science universities in terms of policies and general orientations as university policies are set at the national level for all state universities.

The discussion in this chapter is based on two procedures of gathering in-depth, emergent data: a questionnaire-based survey and semi-structured interviews. A questionnaire was designed building on our initial study of the above mentioned documents, as well as on our anecdotal knowledge of faculty members' views regarding the language of their publications. The questionnaire consisted of three sections addressing the respondents' agreement with the regulations regarding the language of publication; their own language of preference for publication; and their reasons for their preferences. After each item, an open-ended question asked the respondents to further elaborate on their answers in case they found it necessary. The questionnaire was administered through online survey websites, making sure the respondents were informed about the anonymity procedures. A group of 125 faculty members from various faculties of this university participated in the survey. Subsequently, the major themes of the questionnaire were determined, with a view to addressing them in semi-structured interviews. The interviews tapped some more in-depth accounts of questionnaire themes and probed the reasons behind the responses. To further explicate questionnaire findings, a group of 18 questionnaire respondents, selected on the basis of the variations in their responses, took part in individual interviews that lasted 15 to 30 minutes (a total of 6 hours and 20 minutes). Interviews were audiotaped and later transcribed for the purpose of data analysis. A coding scheme based on grounded theory perspectives (open coding, axial coding, and selected coding) (Charmaz, 2006; Strauss & Corbin, 1998) was applied to the remarks and statements expressed by the interviewees (transcripts), and the emergent themes were categorized based on questionnaire prompts.

To Write or Not to Write in English?

The first questionnaire section probed the respondents' positions regarding the policy emphasis on the higher value of English language publications. Of the 125 faculty members who responded to the questionnaire, 97 participants (more than 77%) agreed with the official orientations that prioritize publishing in English language publications for the purpose of recruitment, promotion, funding, etc. Among the participants who added their views in response to the open-ended questions, some highlighted the justification for such a position to be "exchanging scientific content in the world". A minor group of 11 respondents (less than 9%) reported that they neither agreed nor disagreed with these regulations. As a third position, 17 respondents (about 13.5%) disagreed with the directions set by the policies that prioritize the English language. In the section dedicated to explanations, one respondent mentioned: "We should pay attention to the publication of high quality Farsi journals so that we do not forget the scientific Farsi."

The prevalence of agreement with the policies that allot higher value to English language publications may be an indication of the grassroots embracement of the English language in the Iranian academic arena. Although the national language is Farsi and the higher order policy documents explicitly emphasize the elevation of its status as a language of science, the influence of English in the academic context may imply that the concern over the dominance of English and its possible consequence of linguistic injustice in academic research publication is more than a "myth" (Hanauer & Englander, 2011; Meneghini & Packer, 2007; Muresan & Pérez-Llantada, 2014; Politzer-Ahles, et al., 2016). In the context of the global push to use English as the language of academic publication, the official Iranian policies in this regard align with such a push, and faculty members seem to generally endorse such a trend (Curry & Lillis, 2017a). This might raise the concern that the academic efforts that are expected to originate from local needs, might instead be directed by externally defined policy paths that dictate the production of research reports in English (Doostdar & Mirhosseini, 2009).

The second section of the questionnaire asked about the respondents' language priority for their own academic research publication. English was explicitly stated to be the preferred language for publishing research articles by 95 respondents (76%). The preference was based on the assumption that "every faculty member should know English" in order to "become familiar with scientific findings in the world and to use them". A group of 16 respondents (about 13%) reported no preferences for a particular language of publication. Instead, they expressed different concerns involved in the promotion and academic status of Iranian faculty members including "the quality and authenticity of the articles" and "the probability of plagiarism and dishonesty in gathering and analyzing the data". Only 13 respondents (around 10%) preferred Farsi and believed that "forcing authors to publish in English sometimes becomes problematic" as the obsession with publishing in English could hurt academic integrity and the quality of publications. They primarily preferred a "logical acceptable extent" of publishing in English.

The respondents' preferences indicate that in spite of the challenges faced by the Iranian academics, such as limited English language proficiency (Maniati, 2014), English language publication is taken for granted as the preferred choice by the majority of faculty members. This may indicate that certain academic recruitment and promotion mechanisms have encouraged academics to comply with the regulations that value English. This has probably resulted in publication bias against these researchers (Meneghini & Packer, 2007; Politzer-Ahlesa, et al., 2016; Salager-Meyer, 2008, 2009) and further prevalence of English as a privileged language (Hyland, 2016). With respect to the interviews, most of the interviewees confirmed that English was their primary choice in writing for publication, although some of them expressed hesitation and dissatisfaction with this very trend. These attitudes ranged from strong statements like "definitely in English" and "I do not think I have ever had any Farsi article" to milder statements like "I prefer to write in English" and "it is 50–50, half of my articles are in English". The interviewees also mentioned that they "try to write important works in English" since "it has become a norm" due to "the importance of citation", and that it helps "authors be better seen across the world".

However, in accordance with questionnaire data, the interviews indicated that there are also a few cases of hesitation about the all-out embracement of English in this regard. One participant noted that: "It is because of the ministry's evaluation system. . . but if you asked me, I would prefer to write in our own language." Accordingly, some stated that "the yardsticks for the improvement of science and technology should go beyond publication and its language" and "academics should be evaluated and promoted based on their efforts in solving local problems". Although the interviews revealed the participants' concerns about the language of publication and their awareness of its outcomes, juxtaposing the results of interviews and questionnaires indicates that they have taken for granted the higher value of English and have surrendered to the dominant trend of publishing in English. These results align with the findings of previous studies about the linguistic hegemony and publication bias that is prevalent among the majority of non-Anglophone researchers (e.g., Bocanegra-Valle, 2014; Hanauer & Englander, 2011; Meneghini & Packer, 2007; Muresan & Pérez-Llantada, 2014; Politzer-Ahles, et al., 2016). As such, one may argue that the dominance of English as an academic lingua franca has probably influenced rules and regulations that direct the language preferences of academics and faculty members.

Why We Need to Write in English

The questionnaire section addressing the reasons for preferring English as the language of research publication included the following items as options that can justify this preference: prestige of English, personal promotion, increasing university ranking, international scientific cooperation, and presenting national advancements. The respondents were asked to add other reasons they would find influential in their preference for writing in English. Some of the respondents who did not select English as their preferences also responded to the questions in this section probably because they found some justifications for writing in English as well. Therefore, the number of the respondents to this question exceeds the number of those who selected English as their preference in the previous section. Moreover, as the respondents could select more than one item, the total number of responses exceeds the number of respondents. A majority of the participants stated two reasons for the publication of their research articles in English: 101 respondents (more than 80%) selected international scientific cooperation and communication of opinions with scholars of other countries, and closely related, 92 (more than 73%) respondents specified their reason to be presenting national advancements of Iranian scientists across the world.

In this regard, answers to the open-ended questions that were appended to the main questionnaire highlighted instances of beliefs about international visibility such as "being known across the globe", "increasing citation", and "connecting to other scholars at the international level". One of the respondents emphasized that "the local presentation of the studies through a global scientific language plays a vital role in introducing Iran to the world". More emphatically, another respondent attributed the purpose of research dissemination to the goal of international scholars' interaction. The third most reported reason, which was selected by 41 respondents (about 33%), was personal academic promotion and enhancing one's professional status. This can show a direct trace of policy lines on preferences of academics. Relatedly, a group of 36 respondents (about 29%) mentioned increasing university ranking as a reason for their priority to publish in English. The least frequently reported reason was prestige, selected by 11 (about 9%) respondents.

Analysis of the interviews revealed further aspects of the use of English for research article publication. Regarding the reasons for publishing in English, they held that "English is a universal currency" that has the "power of transferring information across the world". As a result, they would see "no reason to write in Farsi", as global communication is important for them. In fact, the interviewees considered using language for international interaction as "the investment and business", thus, they would need to use "a known currency". In other words, they seek global access to their publications, hence a wide range of audience for scientific communication (in the questionnaire, this point constituted one of the most frequently selected reasons for using English). In addition, global reach would provide their articles with a wide range of "citation at an international level". The interviewees also referred to "language as the medium for transferring Iranians' research findings to the world" and the optimum medium was specified as English.

The role of official policies in shaping the preference for English language writing is fairly visible in the interviews. The majority of the interviewees asserted that the evaluation of faculty members is "influenced by the language of the articles and the number of English articles", and faculty members "should comply with the Ministry's regulations" for academic promotion. Above all, "according to the new regulations, Farsi articles no longer receive funds". In this regard, one interviewee stated: "It is because they want us to publish English articles. We do according to the rules and regulations. Regarding the scores, they say Farsi has no value for us." Moreover, "publishing in journals indexed in prestigious indexing systems", which is a policy requirement, constitutes another reason for publishing in English. The interviewees mentioned that "Farsi journals are not indexed by Scopus" and "there are no Farsi ISI journals". Considering the "low grade assigned to Farsi articles", having at least "a certain number of English publications" indexed in "the indexing systems mentioned in regulations" is the prerequisite for academic promotion and funds. As put by one of the interviewees: "If there were no force from anywhere, then we would write in Farsi as well. But with this pressure from faculty, university, ministry, with the international condition, you have to publish in English."

Why We Like to Write in Farsi

The reasons indicated in the questionnaire for preferring Farsi as the language of academic publication included national identity, promoting Farsi as the language of science, increasing university ranking, presenting scientific and technological advancements to Iranian academics, and presenting findings to all Iranians. The respondents were also asked to add other reasons they would find influential in their preference. (As in the case of the previous questionnaire section, some of the respondents who did not select Farsi as their preference also responded to the questions in this section probably because they found some justifications for writing in Farsi as well.) The most frequently reported reason for preferring Farsi, selected by 21 respondents (about 17%), was presenting the latest scientific and technological developments to Iranian academics. The second most frequent reason, selected by 18 respondents (about 15%), was presenting findings to all Iranians. Next, 14 respondents (about 11%) considered using Farsi as the language of publication as an attempt to promote Farsi as the language of science. National identity was selected by 13 respondents (about 10%) and 9 respondents (about 7%) preferred Farsi for increasing university ranking

Shedding further light on questionnaire findings, interviews showcased some deeper concerns regarding publishing in Farsi. These mainly encompassed publication for a specified target audience; the need to improve Farsi academic writing style; the concept of the language of science and establishing national identity to the world through publication in Farsi; and complaining about the regulations that influence Farsi publications by spotlighting English as the language of value. The interviewees mostly mentioned that depending on the goal of writing and the audience, Farsi or English can serve their needs. Farsi was preferred for instructional purposes, local publication for "nurses or other undergraduate audience", "presentations in local conferences", and for ease of writing when authors are not proficient enough to deal with some specific aspects of their research articles in English. One of the interviewees said: "Although I have no problem with technical terms of my own major in English, when it comes to statistical procedures, I prefer to write in Farsi. Explanation and discussion on statistical analyses in English is not easy to me."

Some of the interviewees highlighted the importance of improving Farsi academic writing style, and explained that, as supervisors, sometimes they need to teach it to their students in MA and PhD programs. Some complained about "the shaky language of Farsi articles published by some Iranian scholars". Emphasizing the necessity of "fortifying Farsi infrastructures" of academic publication, one interviewee commented: "This push to academic publication in English is a threat as the identity of a nation depends on its language, and language is what preserves nations. National language is transferred generation to generation; its growth should be visible somewhere." Moreover, aligned with the upstream policy documents, the concept of elevating Farsi as a language of science constituted another concern, although a peripheral one. Whereas a few interviewees expressed that pursuing this goal necessitates "assigning more value and credit to publishing articles in Farsi" among other things, all of the interviewees mentioned English as the language of science, and one interviewee observed that "the owners of this language are trying to maintain their power by imposing their language".

Further clarifying some aspects of the questionnaire findings, the interviewees saw it as unlikely that Farsi would be elevated to one of the languages of science to establish Iran's national identity in the world. The majority of the interviewees said they would prefer "to establish Iran's national identity by publishing localized findings (specified to Iranian contexts) in English and being cited by scholars all over the world", rather than "writing in Farsi and being limited to the Iranian audience". However, some suggested that there should be a law "to permit publishing one article in both languages" and to assign at least equal grades to Farsi publication. They noted that "Farsi publication has been oppressed" by Iranian academic rules and regulations because a high quality Farsi article receives low grades and no funds whereas an English one, even a low quality article, receives higher grades and some funds. This said, since Farsi articles receive lower grades,— "grades given by the system not by academics"—academics prefer English and encourage their students to write and publish in English.

Conclusion

This chapter inquired into some aspects of the global trend of academic publication in the English language (Flowerdew & Li, 2009) by examining the Iranian medical science academics' positions and preferences for the language of research publication. The majority of the participants revealed a deep-seated belief in the importance of English as the language of publication, although they seemed to be aware of the importance of publishing in Farsi for raising the status of their national language and the advancement of science and technology in the field of medical sciences in the local context. The weight given to the indexing systems, which is reinforced by official policies and seems to be partly rooted in the global agendas to dominate through English as the language of science, appears to keep our faculty members satisfied with their promotion and academic status, as well as with the higher ranking of our universities. However, these superficial achievements (Politzer-Ahles, et al., 2016) might further entangle global academic communities by the linguistic bias and injustice that they create.

The perspectives of the participants as a representative group of this particular national context portray an inclination towards international research visibility and academic achievement fueled by official policies through publishing in English, apparently even at the expense of marginalizing the national language in this regard. Although there are traces of loyalty to the status of the national language as observed in other contexts (Bocanegra-Valle, 2014; Flowerdew & Li, 2009), the interviewees' preferences seem to have all but surrendered to the official policies that encourage publishing in English. In turn, the policies may appear to be undetermined between elevating the status of the official language of Farsi and the enthusiasm for gaining scores and stepping up the predefined university ranking ladders. The wider reach of articles written in English and their increased visibility and citation can be rather conveniently accepted as a justification in this regard only after embracing the global regimes of academic knowledge dissemination and an underlying concept of the dominance of English as the taken-for-granted global language of publication.

The question that may be raised here is about the power of policies truly rooted in local positions and perspectives that are likely to be overshadowed by orientations that remain ambivalent in promoting the local language and culture through academic writing on the one hand, and the enthusiasm for catching up with the global trend on the other (Muresan & Pérez-Llantada, 2014). One final point to consider is that the issue at stake here is beyond the problem of the ease of writing (Riazi, 2012) and inequality between native and non-native speaker writers. Inequality and injustice in this regard is an important issue, as those who write in local languages have the ability to conceptually maneuver within the realm of their own language. However, beyond the "increased burden of writing science articles in English as a second language" (Hanauer & Englander, 2011, p. 404), a more serious concern that invites attention is a possible fostering of the historical trend that has led to the dominance of the English language worldwide through new mechanisms such as academic publication.

References

Bocanegra-Valle, A. (2014). English is my default academic language: Voices from LSP scholars publishing in a multilingual journal. *Journal of English for Academic Purposes, 13*, 65–77.

Charmaz, K. (2006). *Constructing grounded theory: A practical guide through qualitative analysis.* London: Sage.

Council of Europe. (1997). *Language Learning for European Citizenship. Final Report (1989–96)*. Strasbourg, Austria: Council of Europe.

Curry, M., & Lillis, T. (2017a). *Global academic publishing policies, perspectives and pedagogies*. Cleavedon, UK: Multilingual Matters.

Curry, M. J., & Lillis, T. (2017b). Problematising English as the privileged language of global academic publishing. In M. J. Curry & T. Lillis, T. (Eds.). *Global academic publishing policies, perspectives and pedagogies* (pp. 1–22). Cleavedon, UK: Multilingual Matters.

Davari-Ardakani, N., & Ahmadipour, T. (2009). An introduction to language policy implementation in Iran: The case of the Third Academy. In G. M. Socarras, (Ed.). *Philological explorations* (pp. 339–352). Athens: ATINER.

Doostdar, H. M., & Mirhosseini, S. A. (2008). بررسی تطبیقی معیارهای ارتقای اعضای هیأت علمی در آموزش عالی [A comparative investigation of academic promotion criteria in higher education]. *Journal of Science and Technology Policy, 1*(3), 91–106.

Doostdar, H. M., & Mirhosseini, S. A. (2009). The core and cover of quality in higher education. *International Journal of Information Science and Management, 7*(2), 45–55.

Flowerdew, J. (1999). Problems in writing for scholarly publication in English: The case of Hong Kong. *Journal of Second Language Writing, 8*(3), 243–264.

Flowerdew, J., & Li, Y. (2009). English or Chinese? The trade-off between local and international publication among Chinese academics in the humanities and social sciences. *Journal of Second Language Writing, 18*, 1–16.

Ghamari, M. R., & Hassanzadeh, M (2010). نقش زبان در هویت ملی [The role of language in national identity]. *Zaban Pazhuhi (Language Research) 2*(3), 153–172.

Hanauer, D. I., & Englander, K. (2011). Quantifying the burden of writing research articles in a second language: Data from Mexican scientists. *Written Communication, 28*(4) 403–416.

Huang, J. C. (2010). Publishing and learning writing for publication in English: Perspectives of NNES PhD students in science. *Journal of English for Academic Purposes, 9*(1), 33–44.

Huttner-Koros, A. (2015). The hidden bias of science's universal language. *The Atlantic Daily*. Retrieved from: www.theatlantic.com/science/archive/2015/08/english-universal-language-science-research/400919

Hyland, K. (2016). Academic publishing and the myth of linguistic injustice. *Journal of Second Language Writing, 31*, 58–69.

Man, J. P., Weinkauf, J. G., Tsang, M., & Sin, D. D. (2004). Why do some countries publish more than others? An international comparison of research funding, English proficiency and publication output in highly ranked general medical journals. *European Journal of Epidemiology, 19*(8), 811–817.

Maniati, M. (2014). *Investigating linguistic problems of Iranian researchers in publishing articles in English language*. Unpublished Doctoral Dissertation, Shahid Chamran University, Ahvaz, Iran.

Meneghini, R., & Packer, A. L. (2007). Is there science beyond English? Initiatives to increase the quality and visibility of non-English publications might help to break down language barriers in scientific communication. *EMBO Reports, 8*(2), 112–116.

Mirhosseini, S. A., & Khodakarami, S. (2016). From "our own beliefs" to "out of who you are": Aspects of "English language education" policies in Iran. *Journal of Multicultural Discourses, 11*(3), 283–299.

Monge-Najera, J., & Nielsen, V. (2005). The countries and languages that dominate biological research at the beginning of the 21st century. *Revista de Biología Tropical, 53*(1–2), 283–294.

Muresan, L. M., & Pérez-Llantada, C. (2014). English for research publication and dissemination in bi-/multiliterate environments: The case of Romanian academics. *Journal of English for Academic Purposes, 13,* 53–64.

Politzer-Ahlesa, S., Holliday, J. J., Girolamod, T., Spychalskae, M., & Berkson, K. H. (2016). Is linguistic injustice a myth? A response to Hyland (2016). *Journal of Second Language Writing, 34,* 3–8.

Rezaeian, M. (2015). Disadvantages of publishing biomedical research articles in English for non-native speakers of English. *Epidemiology and Health, 37,* Article ID: e2015021. Retrieved from http://dx.doi.org/10.4178/epih/e2015021

Riazi, A. M. (2005). The four language stages in the history of Iran. In A. M. Y. Lin & P. W. Martin (Eds.). *Decolonisation, globalisation: Language-in-education policy and practice* (pp. 100–116). Clevedon, UK: Multilingual Matters.

Riazi, A. M. (2012). Producing scholarly texts: Writing in English in a politically stigmatized country. In C. Bazerman, C. Dean, J. Early, K. Lunsford, S. Null, P. Rogers, & A. Stansell (Eds.). *International advances in writing research: Cultures, places, measures* (pp. 449–466). Fort Collins, Colorado: The WAC Clearinghouse and Parlor Press.

Salager-Meyer, F. (2008). Scientific publishing in developing countries: Challenges for the future. *Journal of English for Academic Purposes, 7*(2), 121–132.

Salager-Meyer, F. (2009). Academic equality and cooperative justice. *TESOL Quarterly, 43*(4), 703–709.

Salö, L. (2017). *The sociolinguistics of academic publishing: Language and the practices of homo academicus.* London: Palgrave Macmillan.

Strauss, A. L., & Corbin, J. M. (1998). *Basics of qualitative research: Techniques and procedures for developing grounded theory.* London: Sage.

Thomson-Reuters (2012). Global publishing: Changes in submission trends and the impact on scholarly publishers. Retrieved from scholarone.com/media/pdf/GlobalPublishing_WP.pdf

16

"HOLISTIC ARGUMENTATION CREATION"

Integrated Principles for Helping Graduate Students Create a Journal Paper

Roger Nunn
THE AMERICAN UNIVERSITY OF SHARJAH, SHARJAH, UAE

Tanju Deveci
KHALIFA UNIVERSITY OF SCIENCE AND TECHNOLOGY, ABU DHABI, UAE

Introduction

This chapter presents a holistic support system designed for multilingual scholars in a graduate program taught in English in a science and engineering university in the Middle East. By "holistic" we refer to an approach that combines a number of principles and activities in combination as a coherent whole. Students at our university are strongly encouraged to publish in international journals during their studies or soon after graduating, thus a holistic approach is warranted. In this chapter, we principally focus on the rationale and description of the writing for publication course that is obligatory during one semester at the graduate level.

Our approach serves to counter an over-simplification that we see in many manuscripts concerning writing for publication that are submitted to the *Asian ESP Journal*, where we are both long-time editors. Many manuscript authors seem to see value in providing only sequentially organized move-structure templates for so-called "non-native" apprentice authors. We challenge this characterization in two ways: first, such a template approach is insufficient for academic argumentation; and secondly, we forgo the classification of our students in terms of native or non-native ability, which we believe represents a hegemony of the idealized native speaker. We only consider their competence in academic drafting based on the principles we teach and refer to in this chapter.

Our efforts focus on helping students draft journal papers, in addition to the thesis that all MSc students must produce. We propose a pedagogical approach we call "holistic argumentation creation", which, while drawing on genre knowledge, is enhanced by simple and accessible linguistic principles of competent academic communication in writing that are adaptable to context. The term holistic argumentation creation needs some explanation. When drafting a whole paper, we consider this an act of creation. We see the underlying rhetorical structure of an academic paper as argumentation, in that the author is persuading the reader to ultimately accept the scholarly contribution of the paper, based on the scientific method, results and conclusion presented. Finally, we characterize argumentation as holistic in that elemental arguments are expected to combine in a principled way through the different stages of the paper into a coherent whole. We emphasize here the strategic and adaptable use of language choices is based on sound principles of academic writing in building the whole argumentation of a research narrative. We also believe that this approach supports the creation of the students' own persuasive academic voice.

The basic structure of the course is simple.

1. We firstly engage in an analysis of a journal paper. This analysis is illustrated in class in 4 stages using teacher-led examples: holistic generic structure, referencing, transitivity and modality. It is intended to be a critical analysis. This analysis is the framework used for defining and illustrating principles of academic literacy.
2. Students then in small teams select a journal paper in their own specialization and conduct a similar analysis. Where possible, they choose one that has made a seminal contribution to their field.
3. In the last stage of the course, students then individually do a short 500-word introduction of a self-authored journal paper that puts the principles learnt through the analysis into practice in their own writing.

In this chapter, we first explain the underlying linguistic principles that are incorporated in the course. We then demonstrate their application through our own sample text analysis. Next, we discuss students' reactions to the novel, non-traditional writing approach found in papers published in *Nature*, and illustrate the way students go on to adapt rather than blindly adopt this approach in their own drafting.

Underlying Principles

We see "moves" (Swales, 1990) as important generic features of competent academic creation because they name individual acts of argumentation. However, one important component of our holistic approach in understanding the generic structure of academic papers is Grice's cooperative principle and its maxims of conversation (Grice, 1989) which we adapt to academic writing and literacy (White, 2001; Mackenzie, 2002) (see Table 16.1).

TABLE 16.1 Maxims

Quantity	Make your contribution as informative as is required (for the current purposes of the exchange). Do not make your contribution more informative than is required.	Relates to the balance and quantity of information among sections of a paper (stage 1 of the analysis below)
Quality	Do not say what you believe to be false. Do not say that for which you lack adequate evidence.	Relevant to choices of epistemic modality use which depend on the strength of evidence (stage 4 of the analysis below)
Relation	Be relevant.	Helps make decisions about the quantity of information needed in each section (stage 1)
Manner	Be perspicuous. Avoid obscurity of expression. Avoid ambiguity. Be brief. (Avoid unnecessary prolixity.) Be orderly.	Relates to language choices such as active/passive (stage 3 of the analysis below)

* Adapted from Grice (1989, pp. 26–27)

The cooperative principle and its maxims of conversation are based on the premise that interlocutors desire to make communication flow easily, and this is accomplished by four characteristics of speech by the speaker: quantity (be informative, yet brief), quality (be true, do not lie), relation (be relevant to the prior comment), and manner (be clear, not ambiguous). It is important to emphasize that we have adapted Grice's approach to conversational interaction and applied it to academic writing, as shown in Table 16.1. As in Grice's original model, the maxims are intentionally subordinated to a Cooperative Principle and a theory of implicature that requires us to decide what is required in context as the (written) communication develops stage by stage. Note that we do not present even the more categorical sub-maxims to the maxim of manner, "be brief", "avoid ambiguity" as absolute rules of writing etiquette. In fact, Grice's principle to which the maxims are subordinated is very flexibly worded: "Make your [conversational] contribution such as is required, at the stage at which it occurs, by the accepted purpose or direction of the [talk] exchange in which you are engaged" (1989, pp. 26–27). In terms of written argumentation, what is "required" in terms of "quantity", "quality", "relation" and "manner" is context dependent and therefore requires the reader and writer to determine what is appropriate at any particular stage of the written argumentation.

Another linguistic concept that we adapt for our writing for publication course comes from systemic functional linguistics (Halliday & Matthiessen, 2004) namely, the principle that authors have choices, which are neither totally free nor overly restricted, at each stage of their argumentation. In this sense we see a research paper as a whole developing narrative that aims a persuading an academic audience that they have something novel to add to the field. The skill lies in making a principle-based (and therefore an appropriate) choice of "move" in their lexical and grammatical choices as their argument develops. Further the skill involves the need to evaluate or appraise the arguments that others make in text with a view to improving our own argumentation (White, 2011).

In our course, we also refer briefly to our own characterization of ten principles of critical argumentation, a listing which is partially based on Paul and Elder (2006) and highlights self-direction as the guiding principle, alongside key principles that underline the importance of evidence and relevance. (see Nunn, Brandt, & Deveci, 2016, for a detailed explanation.)

A Four-Stage Academic Paper Analysis

As we are interested in holistic argumentation rather than just features of text in isolation, we have developed this course as a series of four stages: holistic generic structure, referencing, transitivity and modality. Each stage will be explained in detail below. It is intended to be a critical analysis. We believe therefore that there is value in using principles in combination to establish important generic features of academic texts to provide a principled justification of whatever template of specific sequential moves is adopted for particular sections of papers. Note that in the classroom, the approach described in this chapter is not delivered in the form of a lecture. The extracts form the basis for interactive discussion in class through which the underlying competence principles are evoked and critically debated.

We have used a variety of papers but most recently we have used papers from the journal *Nature* on subjects of cross-disciplinary interest such as climate change. We also provide students with a full written analysis of the paper as an example after the in-class interactive sessions. For reasons of length, we will illustrate here with some extracts rather than the full analysis using a text called "The carbon footprint of traditional woodfuels", (Bailis, Drigo, Ghilardi, & Masera, 2015). Students also select a paper from their own specialization and do a parallel four-stage analysis as four submitted assignments. Once a stage has been covered in class, students then submit their own analysis a week later. Once the four stages have been covered in this way, they submit a final copy with cover page, introduction, conclusion and reference list of their full analysis.

Stage 1: Holistic Generic Structure

At this stage, we emphasize the relationship between holistic generic structure and Grice's maxims of quantity and relation/relevance (Grice, 1989) and also the balance between different sections of the paper. In order to carry out the analysis, the text is first divided into sections according to actual or assigned headings.

Generic headings are those that are commonly found in academic papers such as "introduction" or "conclusion". As these are not systematically provided in the journal *Nature* we have sometimes assigned them using our own judgment. On the other hand, non-generic subheadings are specific to the paper and may be unique such as "Mitigation potential of efficient cookstoves". Some headings exhibit both "generic" and "non generic" characteristics. These are interpreted on a case by case basis.

The chosen article "The carbon footprint of traditional woodfuels" is a 3921-word 7-page document. The article contains five figures. Table 16.2 summarizes the generic structure in terms of quantity of words per section.

To indicate that generic structure cannot be seen as a predetermined or fixed sequential template to follow, we point out in class that this paper does not follow the traditional structure that many of our students assume to be a given. The methods section, which typically appears after a review of literature (often integrated into the introduction) and before a results section in a traditional science paper, comes last in this paper. The stated purpose in submission guidelines is to provide a scientific narrative that highlights the presentation and discussion of the novel and significant findings in the main body of the paper in relation to what is already known.

Based on our reading of *Nature*'s guidelines to authors, we also assume that the methods section does not appear in its traditional location before the results section as *Nature* caters for both specialists in the field or non-specialist scientific readers. The detailed methodology mainly targets specialized researchers who require detailed information about how the results were obtained. This extra information is therefore provided for specialists in a way that does not compromise the ability of the non-specialist to read the paper. Audience is therefore

TABLE 16.2 Generic text analysis

Heading	Word count	Type of heading or section
Abstract (assigned by us)	203	Generic
(Introduction) (assigned by us)	474	Generic
Pan-tropical woodfuel supply and demand	160	Non-Generic
Woodfuels and LCC	410	Non-Generic
Woodfuel sustainability	748	Non-Generic
GHG emissions	226	Non-Generic
Mitigation potential of efficient cookstoves	176	Non-Generic
Discussion and implications	641	Generic
Methods	865	Generic
Acknowledgements	18	Generic
Total	3921	

underlined as an essential part of the writing process. This ordering generates interesting in-class or online discussion because it does not follow the rather fixed pattern that many of our students have been used to.

Given that we are looking for accessible ways of discussing principles in a critical analysis, we refer to our adaptation of Grice's principle and four maxims of conversation for written argumentation (see Table 16.1). This covers *quantity* of information at different stages of argumentation, *quality* of evidence in relation to the truth value assigned to claims, the *relation* or relevance of statements at the stage where they occur in the argumentation and the *manner* of expressing the content such as intelligibility, clarity of expression, orderly organization and concision (Grice, 1989, pp. 26–27). To analyze an academic paper, what is "required" in terms of quantity in each section or "stage" depends partially on whether the information provided is relevant.

In Extract 2 below, the students are also able to determine that something important and relevant is missing. While we found the maxim of quantity was respected in our analysis, students used the same maxim to successfully critique other papers as exemplified in the extracts below, the first positive, the second identifying a quantitative imbalance in that something relevance is missing. The students are able to be quite specific about what would be required:

> Extract 1: Using the maxim of quantity
>
> In a nutshell, the generic structure in this paper makes it easy to understand and shows a "balance" between its sections. In my opinion, the paper obeys Grice's maxim of quantity and relevance.
>
> Extract 2: Critiquing quantity and balance
>
> These two sections together outweigh the rest of the section causing an imbalance in the general division of section lengths. In addition, the conclusion was too short (47 words), relatively, and lacking the elements of a professional technical conclusion. It's common in technical papers for the discussion section to be extensive and detailed, however, in this paper the discussion was abridged, dedicating more space to figures than explanatory text.

Stage 2: Referencing—Quantitative analysis

While we emphasize the importance of reporting the students' own contribution to knowledge in our course, this inevitably leads to a dual focus: references provide the "known" information upon which a new contribution is built. In other words, the referencing analysis highlights the relationship between knowledge taken from others and the authors' own thesis. We therefore try to generate data-based discussion on the role of referencing given that academic writing is one of the few genres to take such pains to identify where prior knowledge comes from. The references were divided into "non-integral" and "integral" (Thompson &

TABLE 16.3 Integral and non-integral references per section (quantitative analysis)

	Abstract	Intro.	Subdivisions (main body)		Discussion and implications	Methods	Total
Integral	0	2	0		0	0	2
Non-integral	0	23	11		2	19	55
			Pan-tropical woodfuel supply and demand	0–4			
			Woodfuels and LCC	0–2			
			Woodfuel sustainability	0–3			
			GHG emissions	0–0			
			Mitigation potential of efficient cookstoves	0–2			

Tribble, 2001). Integral references are those which are grammatically integrated into the sentence while non-integral references acknowledge the source but are not grammatically built into the sentence (see Extracts 3 and 4 below). In the carbon footprint paper, there were 48 references that were cited 57 times. 55 of the 57 uses were non-integral. Most of the references were located in the introduction and method sections.

Referencing—Qualitative Analysis

We do not assume that the numerical analysis has validity in itself, as we promote the view that authors select the appropriate choice depending on the needs of the assumed audience in a developing context. We also attempt to identify key aspects of referencing which illustrate underlying principles, such as the relationship between the self and the other in academic communication (White, 2011; Nunn, Brandt, & Deveci, 2016).

> Extract 3: (Integral referencing – introduction para. 3)
>
> The Intergovernmental Panel on Climate Change's Fourth Assessment claimed that 10% of global woodfuel is harvested unsustainably 19,20[1], and the Fifth Assessment stresses that net emissions from woodfuels are unknown 7.

For references 19, 20 in Extract 3 above, the Intergovernmental Panel on Climate Change Fourth Assessment itself is the author of the reference. In this case the authors of the *Nature* article are trying to highlight the impact of the unsustainable demand for woodfuel. The use of the reporting verbs "claim" and "stresses" that something is unknown, however, illustrates the *Nature* authors' intervention in the argumentation. The choice of reporting verbs, especially "claimed" here, can indicate that the authors are distancing themselves from and possibly minimizing the importance of the previously published knowledge. This is an interpretive intervention in the text.

A common argumentation effect of non-integral references is to provide authority for assumed facts, statistics and even mathematical calculations. In Extract 4, for example, the author is using non-integral referencing to provide factual scientific information. At the same time, the five non-integral uses help to build the authors' holistic background argument that the wood burning and harvesting issue is of global relevance.

> Extract 4: (Non-integral referencing to support holistic argumentation)
>
> Traditional woodfuels, which include both firewood and charcoal used for cooking and heating, represent approximately 55% of global wood harvest and 9% of primary energy supply 1,2. The current extent and future evolution of traditional woodfuel consumption is closely related to several key

challenges to sustainable development. Roughly 2.8 billion people worldwide 3, including the world's poorest and most marginalized, burn wood to satisfy their basic energy needs. Woodfuels can impact public health 4, cause deforestation or forest degradation 5, and contribute to climate change 6_8.

On the surface, the choice of non-integral references may appear to downplay the role of the author in building the argument. However, we would argue that the skilled selection of references and the way they are built into the developing research narrative provides opportunity to explore how arguments are created. Such a discussion with students demonstrates that our own holistic argument illustrates the critical writing skill of synthesis (Nunn, et al. 2016), through which the authors' intervention is still very apparent.

Stage 3: Transitivity Analysis

The transitivity analysis considers the way an author represents reality at different stages of the article, highlighting for example what is represented as a first-person contribution to knowledge by the authors and what is represented as scientific fact.

Transitivity Analysis—Quantitative Results

Authors have choices as to how to express or represent information (Halliday, & Matthiessen, 2004; Fowler, 1986). Taking advantage of transitivity analysis of "old" and "new" information in a sentence or clause, we look in particular at the way authors represent new information generated in their novel research in relation to what was already assumed to be known information established in their field. One way of analyzing transitivity is the two-way choice between active and passive. We also identify a third choice of choosing neither of those, by using "be" or "have" as the main verb (Nunn, 2010). These latter are termed relational verbs (or processes) and generally serve to identify a thing or its attributes (Halliday & Matthiessen, 2004). We exemplify this analysis:

- clauses in which the main verb is in the active voice ("...*we estimate that unsustainable harvesting...*")
- clauses in which the main verb is in the passive voice ("... *the woodshed is determined by the aggregate demand*")
- clauses in which the main verb is the verb "be", "have" or its equivalent ("*harvesting is sustainable*").

We also considered the use of first person and the distinction between a personal (with an active human agent) and impersonal voice (where the human agent is minimized or absent). (e.g. "I broke your favourite vase" represents an event very differently from "the vase just slipped out of my hand".) Table 16.4 shows the breakdown between active/passive and "be"/"have" clauses and first person usage in our model article.

A total of 355 clauses were identified, of which 107 (30%) were in the passive voice. 190 (54%) were active clauses, the remaining 58 (16%) used "be" or "have" as a main verb. However, we also found that distribution of different choices across sections also varied.

Transitivity Analysis—Qualitative Use of the Passive Voice

While transitivity is partially a question of grammar, we emphasize the way knowledge is represented differently when different choices are made. Giltrow (2002) identified a tendency to claim that the usage of agentless expressions in the passive is more "scientific" or "objective". Similarly, Pho (2013) claims that the agentless passive, which is frequently used in the method section, is preferable since it gives prominence to the subjects of the study or the instruments.

While *Nature* journal guidelines advise against the use of the passive voice at all, there is considerable use to be found in their published papers. Generally, the greatest proportional use of the passive voice is found in the method section of experimental papers (Swales, 1990), and this is evident in the analysis of the model article, as can be seen in Table 16.4. An example is provided in Extract 5 below in which a first person (we assume) is in contrast to the impersonal choices that follow it.

Extract 5: Impersonal transitivity (passive voice use)

We assume a threshold of 12-hour one-way travel. When several consumption sites are considered simultaneously, the woodshed is determined by the aggregate demand from all sites.

TABLE 16.4 Transitivity use: distribution across sections (main verbs only)

	Active voice	Passive voice	Verbs to be/have	First person
Abstract	9	3	6	6
Introduction	27	15	4	5
Pan-tropical woodfuel supply and demand	10	5	1	2
Woodfuels and LCC	25	15	3	11
Woodfuel sustainability	31	21	21	2
GHG emissions	11	2	6	0
Mitigation potential of efficient cookstoves	9	6	0	2
Discussion and implications	32	10	11	9
Methods	36	30	6	22
Total	*190*	*107*	*58*	*59*

The analysis of transitivity showed the greatest proportion of clauses used the active voice. However, most of the uses (69%) were impersonal uses rather than expressing the agency of the author. A personal and impersonal use is shown in Extract 6 below.

> Extract 6: Use of personal and impersonal active voice
>
> Using the best available data, we estimate that unsustainable harvesting and incomplete combustion contributed 1.9–2.3% of global emissions of well-mixed GHGs and SLCFs in 2009.

Use of First Person

First person usage reflects the authors' most direct or obvious intervention in the argumentation. It also makes sentences "more energetic, more persuasive, and easier to understand" (Sword, 2012, p. 37). We note in Extracts 5 and 6 above the uses of "we assume" and "we estimate". The former clearly indicates their willingness to state their assumptions ("we assume" appears six times in the paper) and the second illustrates their transparent acceptance of uncertainty. Different forms of the word "estimate" appear 17 times in the text, 13 of which are associated with a first person. "We define" appears five times in the paper. All of these represent the authors' conceptual interventions transparently.

Extract 7 further illustrates the multiple use of the first person to underline the novel contribution of the authors in relation to known knowledge. This paper is not an experimental research paper, but it does provide an original model to estimate woodfuel supply, demand and exploitation.

> Extract 7: Summarizing the authors' contribution in the introduction
>
> Here we present a spatially explicit snapshot of woodfuel supply and demand (Supplementary Section 1) throughout tropical regions where traditional woodfuel consumption is concentrated. Using 2009 as a base year, we quantify the extent to which woodfuel demand exceeds supply, [we] identify specific "hotspots" where harvesting rates are likely to cause degradation or deforestation, quantify the carbon emissions that result from current woodfuel exploitation, and [we] estimate the emission reductions that could be achieved from large-scale interventions 23.

In Extract 8, from the method section, we also observe the authors' clear representation of their own agency.

> Extract 8: Use of first person
>
> Woodfuel supply is defined by the productivity of woody biomass, which we model as a function of above-ground biomass (AGB) stock. We use recent

maps of land cover and ecological zones to define a broad system of land units, including cropland and crop mosaic (often neglected in assessments of woodfuel supply).

Stage 4: Epistemic Modality

Modality analysis is intended to indicate the degree of confidence expressed in the findings and views expressed in the article. We examine the relationship between claims and evidence by examining the levels of certainty or confidence attributed to statements, claims or conclusions. Appropriate use of epistemic modality reflects the level of confidence that we feel we can express in relation to the evidence available to support the wording of our claims. The degree to which we can claim something is true (Grice's maxim 2 of quality) (Grice, 1989; White, 2011) depends on our interpretation of the strength of the evidence that supports the claims (Fowler, 1986).

It is important to interpret the uses of modality in the context of the developing argumentation, as listing only tells half the story. In Extract 7 below it can be seen that the authors express caution in relation to their own contribution. The authors are interpreting potentially novel information or findings so this may explain the caution. Extract 9 illustrates the way mitigation can be very explicit in that it is expressed through common modal expressions such as "may" or "is likely". Importantly it can also be just implied in language not normally associated with "modality" such as "our assessment fills a critical gap" or "emerging" where we interpret this to mean that if it is novel or "emerging" or "filling a critical gap" it might be at a stage of less certain, developing knowledge.

> Extract 9: Implicit and explicit modality choices
>
> Moreover, by identifying areas where woodfuel-driven degradation or deforestation is likely to occur, our assessment fills a critical gap in knowledge about the extent to which woodfuel demand may contribute to deforestation or forest degradation and informs emerging REDD-based approaches to climate change mitigation.

Extract 10 below illustrates the way transitivity and modality operate in tandem integrated into a holistic argumentation. The authors' thinking and assumptions are expressed both with a first person and with an appropriate degree of confidence in the (perhaps limited) evidence currently available to support their assumptions expressed through modality choices. At the same time, they use metacommunication with a first person (we report) to point the reader towards further evidence in a supplementary section of the holistic generic structure of the paper. We also note that there is a balance between personal and impersonal transitivity and that impersonal transitivity can be expressed using either active or passive.

Extract 10: Transitivity and modality in tandem

Thus, minimum NRB indicates the degree to which a given region can sustainably meet woodfuel demand under ideal management. However, ideal management is unlikely. To simulate suboptimal harvesting, we assume that harvesting sometimes exceeds sustainable levels in some areas even if the sustainable supply in an adjacent accessible area has not been fully exploited. To estimate the extent of this deviation, we use a proxy defined by the fraction of each country's forested area under formal management plans (Methods). From this we derive an "expected" quantity of NRB, which we also express as a fraction of the total harvest (fNRB). Both minimum and expected NRB are expressed in absolute terms and as a fraction of the total harvest for a given region. We report expected NRB below; minimum NRB is given in Supplementary Information.

Conclusions From the Brief Analysis

We have just emphasized in relation to epistemic modality that each stage of analysis is not independent of the others. They all relate to each other, often in complex ways as an author builds a persuasive narrative that constitutes a holistic argumentation. As previously noted, one unusual feature of generic structure is the relegation of the methods section to the end of the paper. We have noted that this is a section in which the passive is more dominant, which is a feature in every paper we have analyzed. There is still extensive first person use in the method section, indicating a new approach to traditional woodfuel research. The analysis showed that non-integral references were used by the authors extensively in order to support their findings. These are often used with impersonal transitivity in contrast to the first-person uses expressing the authors' novel contribution. We have also indicated that these stages can be related to a critical analysis using Gricean maxims as a simple starting point. Novelty for example is closely related to the notion of "relevance" (Grice, 1989; Sperber & Wilson, 1995; Mackenzie, 2002). Sperber and Wilson emphasize that relevance is closely related to communicating something new to the reader or listener. If they already know it, it is not relevant. At the same time, referring to relevant literature is our way of demonstrating that what we are now proposing is relevant in relation to what is already known. Alongside relevance, we also focus on what constitutes "evidence", the strength of the evidence needing to be closely matched to the claims we make about it (epistemic modality). While referring to language philosophers may seem daunting for science students to outsiders, we have never experienced this. The basic message in relation to relevance and evidence is never beyond the reach of students and they express appreciation that there is a challenging, conceptual element to the course.

In course feedback students often referred to the skills learnt in relation to Grice's maxims. A typical comment being . . ."[i]t was not only about how to write but how to analyze the technical paper which strongly enhance our own writing and the way how to select our references", "[i]t focused in the skills student need to write their thesis and publications", hence avoiding the kind of purely instrumental uncreative sequential template short-cuts which evoke what Carter (1995, p. 55) has referred to as "narrow vocationalism".

Students Applying the Principles

The Analyses

Importantly, our experience over several years indicates that a majority of students in their analysis assignment do show the meta-communicative ability to apply the principles. In Extract 11 below for example, the student discusses the notion of transitivity and relates it to Grice's principle, especially the notion that what is "required" will vary according to the stage of communication. Results of our own and students' analyses consistently show transitivity being used very differently in different sections of the papers.

> Extract 11: A student applying the principles
>
> Transitivity of the text concerns how the language is describing or representing the events of the research rather than the time sense of the events. In other words, transitivity does not depend on the verb itself, but in fact it depends on the clause the verb is present in and the meaning behind it. This stage of the analysis is considered the hardest compared to the previous stages where major focus is required to make out and understand the language of the author/writer. Thus, transitivity links to the second maxim of communication which talks about clarity and to Grice's Principle which states that every stage of the paper has its own stage of communication (Grice 1989, pp. 26–27).

Although the student appears to wrongly assume that Grice's Cooperative Principle actually directly referred to written texts (rather than spoken interactions), in Extract 12, (having provided a distributional table and qualitative extracts from the text), he is able to provide a reasonable explanation as to why the passive dominates in just one section in a text in which the active voice dominates overall.

> Extract 12
>
> On the other hand, the passive verbs dominated the "Results and Discussion" section showing the comparison in performance of the ESS using different installations between the years of 2003 and 2016. As has been mentioned earlier, this analysis was performed by a computer software; hence, the excessive use of passive verbs.

The analyses regularly find that the passive is used mainly in the section where an experimental, step-by-step process is being described or with references to contrast with the authors' own (novel) contribution. Hence the important Grice-inspired principle of emphasizing the different requirements at different stages of communication.

Final Assignment

In an end of semester assignment introducing their own original research in their major area of study, we can also see the principles being applied. As we believe that holistic argumentation is important, we provide below just one extensive example in two consecutive extracts.

> Extract 13: Use of references
>
> The size of the elderly population is growing much faster than the overall population due to decreasing fertility and increasing life expectancy [2,3]. This increasing trend towards an elderly population is also reflected in the growing number of older office workers as retirement age is increasing globally [4]. In the USA one reason for the rise in older office workers can be contributed to the "Baby Boomer" generation reaching retirement age. The "Baby Boomers" are referred to as the demographic group born from mid-1946 to 1964. "Baby Boom" is distinguished by a dramatic increase in birth rates following World War II, and is one of the largest generations in US history [5]. Therefore, since "aging work force" forms a major part of the workplace environment, it is vital that the workplace environment addresses their needs in terms of their health, wellbeing and workplace ergonomics without discriminating against them by age or disabilities but as a positive reform in workplace ergonomics and design.

References are used in Extract 13 above with impersonal language, whether active or passive, to build up the student's summary of background information. More importantly, we note that she uses the references to build her own argumentation and to integrate her own generalization about the need to avoid discrimination.

> Extract 14: First person agency
>
> In our study, the designs in the facilities were compared to worldwide regulations and some violations were found and noted in this study to take immediate corrective actions. The scope of this study is focused on aging professionals aging from 55 years and above, who are in the academic domain such as professors. The scope was limited to The Petroleum Institute (PI), Abu Dhabi, United Arab Emirates, where assessment of the working areas and survey was conducted.

"Holistic Argumentation Creation" **281**

The objective of this study was to find out the gaps in the ergonomics and harmony of the workplace, which affected the aging knowledge workers working in the facilities [faculties] of the PI. The study further identifies the possible and probable improvements that could be made in order to meet the needs of the growing aging workforce.

While *Nature* journal, as studied in this course, suggests the use of "we" and an active verb, this student demonstrates in extract 14 that a first person argument is possible with a substitute first-person ("this study", "our study") and an impersonal, even passive construction. The student therefore adopts the principle, but applies it her own way. The student uses her own combination of modality (could be made, possible and probable), a substitute first person with impersonal active, passive or "be as main verb" constructions.

We also have many examples of students transferring their learning to future academic activity as illustrated briefly in Extract 15 below. In a post-course support activity, students writing a draft for conference proceedings used the first-person successfully as follows.

Extract 15

However, we are not aware of any studies that utilized the Kalman filter in studying and/or predicting the vibration of pipelines. Thus, this work focuses on the effect of tuning Q and R of a Kalman-based estimator, utilized for producing estimates of the vibration of a pipeline.

Conclusions

In this brief chapter, we have attempted to illustrate the way that discussing the merits of principles of communication (Grice, 1989) can be applied to writing (White, 2001; White, 2011; Nunn, et al., 2016), and in doing so, improves the long-term ability of students to transfer learning from a reading analysis study to their own research writing for publication. While fashions may change in writing, a critical awareness of principle-based maxims of competence helps prepare students to transfer their skills and abilities honed in one context to other as yet unpredicted genres and contexts that they may need in the future. We have provided a principled alternative approach to only following a given sequential "move-step" structure as a kind of template. We see the "move-step" structure as something that evolves as a paper develops based on the application of principles. We find no support for a predetermined "sequential template" pedagogical approach in the seminal literature on genre analysis (e.g., Swales 1990, 2004). Dudley-Evans (1994) for example refers rather to more fluid cyclical patterns and indicates that the early aims of genre analysis were to help demystify academic conventions rather than provide a fool-proof sequential formula. An awareness of moves and move sequences in relation to the application of principles allows the student to achieve a balance between developing an awareness of conventions and developing one's own voice.

We have attempted to share the way our students transfer their learning from a critical analysis to their own drafting, what we have called "holistic argumentation creation", with the emphasis on creation. However, one obvious limitation of our approach is the difficulty in one study of handling our desired focus on something as broad as holistic argumentation in relatively long pieces. In this brief chapter, we have therefore focused on one analysis in some detail and provided shorter extracts of students' work as illustrative examples of the work of many more students whose work we have not been able to show. Nonetheless, we feel emphasizing additional linguistic principles as outlined above contributes to the development of convincing holistic argumentation is an important long-term goal of critical academic literacy. We also wish to emphasize that this Writing for Publication course is one element of our university's holistic support system for graduate writers, which includes one-to-one support for students after the course to provide help with proposal, thesis or journal paper authoring. A small team of faculty have volunteered to provide this type of individualized support. We hope that what we have presented from our one context is translatable to other learning settings.

Note

1 Numbers in the extracts refer to in-text citations given according to IEEE.

References

Bailis, R. Drigo, R., Ghilardi, A., & Masera, O. (2015). The carbon footprint of traditional woodfuels. *Nature Climate Change*, 5(3), 266–272.

Carter, R. (1995). *Keywords in language and literacy*. London: Routledge.

Dudley-Evans, T. (1994). Genre analysis: An approach to text analysis for ESP. In M. Coulthard (Ed.). *Advances in discourse analysis* (pp. 2019–228). London: Routledge.

Fowler, R. (1986). *Linguistic criticism*. Oxford: Oxford University Press.

Giltrow, J. (2002). *Academic writing: Writing and reading across the disciplines* (3rd ed.). Peterborough, ON: Broadview Press.

Grice, P. (1989). *Studies in the way of words*. London: Harvard University Press.

Halliday, M. A. K., & Matthiessen, C. (2004). *An introduction to functional grammar* (3rd ed.). London: Arnold.

Mackenzie, I. (2002). *Paradigms of reading: Relevance theory and deconstruction*. Basingstoke, UK: Palgrave Macmillan.

Nunn, R. (2010). Aspects of a model for analyzing competent academic texts in ESP. *The Asian ESP Journal, Special Edition, the First Asian EFL Conference, Chongqing University, October 2009*, 20–42.

Nunn, R., Brandt, C., & Deveci, T. (2016). Project-based learning as a holistic learning framework: Integrating 10 principles of critical reasoning and argumentation. *Asian ESP Journal (Special Issue)*, 9–53.

Paul, R., & Elder, L. (2006). *Foundation for critical thinking*, Retrieved from http://www.criticalthinking.org/pages/universal-intellectual-standards/527.

Pho, P. D. (2013). *Authorial stance in research articles: Examples from Applied Linguistics and Educational Technology.* Basingstoke, UK: Palgrave Macmillan.

Sperber, D., & Wilson, D. (1995) *Relevance: Communication and cognition* (2nd ed.) Oxford: Blackwell Publishers, Inc.

Swales, J. (1990). *Genre analysis: English in academic and research settings.* Cambridge: Cambridge University Press.

Swales, J. M. (2004). *Research genres: Explorations and applications.* Cambridge: Cambridge University Press.

Sword, H. (2012). *Stylish academic writing.* Cambridge, Massachusetts, London: Harvard University Press.

Thompson, P., & Tribble, C. (2001). Looking at citations: Using corpora in English for academic purposes. *Language Learning and Technology, 5*(3), 91–105.

White, P. (2011). Appraisal. In J. Zienkowski, J. Ostman, & J. Vershueren (Eds.). *Discursive pragmatics* (pp. 14–31). Amsterdam, The Netherlands: John Benjamins.

White, R. (2001). Adapting Grice's maxims in the teaching of writing. *ELTJ, 55*(1), 62–69.

17
ENVOI

John M. Swales

PROFESSOR EMERITUS OF LINGUISTICS
UNIVERSITY OF MICHIGAN, USA

Envoi

This is the third recent volume devoted to the topic of producing acceptable research in English by speakers of English as an additional language, particularly by those in "off-network" locations. Its predecessors were *The Semi-periphery of Academic Writing* (2015) edited by Karen Bennett and *Publishing Research in English as an Additional Language* (2017) edited by Margaret Cargill and Sally Burgess. All three collections have interesting similarities and differences. All three, for example, have succeeded in creating a mix of chapters written by established figures and by newcomers or relative newcomers. All three have a combination of English L1 authors and EAL authors. All three aim for a geographical spread, but in somewhat different ways. The 2015 volume is largely restricted to eastern and southern Europe. The one which appeared in 2017 also largely deals with Europe (with a strong focus on Spain), but also includes contributions from Asia and Australia. This volume is even more enterprising since it covers, to a lesser or greater extent, almost all regions of the world. There are, for instance, three chapters from South America, three from the Persian Gulf, two from Africa, as well as single contributions from Iceland and Pakistan. It is particularly gratifying to hear from colleagues in such countries and of their efforts to help researchers and research students in their home institutions tackle the daunting task of getting their papers accepted by peer-reviewed English language international journals.

All three books contain many contributions that stress the tensions, dilemmas and conflicts that bedevil the academic lives of plurilingual people who are being pushed by over-ambitious national and institutional polices designed to reward publishing internationally in English. Meanwhile the plurilingual academics themselves are typically more comfortable—and likely successful—producing research in their local language that is relevant and useful to their local communities in such areas as education, public health or agricultural development. The Bennett volume emphasizes the semiperipheral status of these individuals, while the Cargill & Burgess collection stresses the complex set of factors that may impede international publication in English. In some contrast, the present volume is primarily concerned with what various enterprising individuals, often working in considerable isolation, have been able to do in order to mitigate the disadvantages experienced by these scholars in an increasingly Anglophone research world, and this thrust is nicely encapsulated in Corcoran, Englander and Muresan's title, *Pedagogies and Policies for Publishing Research in English*. It would appear that we are seeing here a movement that began by describing the problems and their causes, but has now moved on to searching for potential solutions.

But before proceeding further, it might be helpful to clear up some misapprehensions that may well be out there about higher education in the USA. Take the case of the State of Michigan, where I have lived for the past 30 years. There are in this state three major research universities: Wayne State in Detroit, Michigan State in the state capitol, Lansing, and the University of Michigan in Ann Arbor. The University of Michigan, for instance, has around 2000 post-doctoral fellows and nearly 5500 doctoral students; according to the latest statistics, 93% of the latter being fully funded. It produces several hundred PhDs every year. Requirements for hiring professorial faculty are demanding, as are the expectations for tenure and promotion. Numerous publications are expected, citational impact is taken into consideration, and, increasingly, grants are required. More and more fields are moving to "article compilation" doctoral dissertations, with at least one already published, one accepted, and a third perhaps under review. The library will basically buy any book faculty and doctoral students ask for, and complete access to electronic journals is available to all members of the university. Although I no longer teach the Writing for Publication classes (a role now ably filled by Christine Feak), I help her with some of the one-on-one tutorials, and so I see at first-hand how even University of Michigan students (both national and international) struggle with getting accepted by the leading journals in their fields. Further, these three large institutions are situated in urban areas with considerable cultural and recreational resources.

However, these three major research institutions are, as they say, "the tip of the iceberg", because there are more than 80 other institutions of higher education in the state; many are small, have no graduate programs, and have restricted financial and academic resources. Although many make claims about the importance of research and scholarship, these assertions are "more honoured in the breach than the observance". Teaching loads are double those at major research universities. Many have not jumped on the internationalization band-wagon. Library holdings and facilities are likely to be limited. Salaries are relatively low and the requirements for tenure and promotion will be primarily based on teaching performance. Publication of virtually any kind is thought of as being a bonus. One effect of this disparity between the major institutions and the minor ones has become increasingly apparent in my time in Michigan. When I arrived in Ann Arbor, the university still had considerable professorial strengths in what might be called the "field disciplines", with leading authorities on the trees, fishes, birds, plants, insects, etc, of the state and surrounding regions. These professors have practically all retired or have been persuaded to switch to molecular biology. So today the people who research natural life in the local habitats and who publish in small regional journals, like *The Great Lakes Entomologist*, are now found in the smaller universities. For example, the leading authority on bats in the region (a group of species in considerable trouble in recent years) works for Eastern Michigan University, which started life as the state's teacher-training college. I mention all this to point out that many professors in the state live in small towns and are, in many ways, in *semiperipheral* situations and, further, if they publish papers, these are more likely to appear in regional journals. While I accept the situation of scholars in some countries will be considerably more constraining (such as frequent power-outages) than in some of the struggling small liberal arts colleges in the USA, it still remains the case that the American universities people have heard of (e.g. Harvard, Berkeley, Stanford) form a very small minority.

One of the advantages of being invited to write an end-piece, whether it be an Afterword, Coda or Envoi, is that, unlike editors in the introduction, there is no strong imperative to deal even-handedly with all the preceding contributions. Instead, the outside composer of the end-piece can, if he or she wishes, opt to focus on particular aspects of particular chapters that would seem to warrant further commentary. In fact, most of the chapters were potential candidates for this further commentary, but in the end I decided to produce something more substantial on just three of them.

Let us first consider the situation of the typical EAP instructor or lecturer as she confronts new responsibilities in the emerging ERP/ERPP world. She probably has a first degree in English language and literature and a master's degree in Applied Linguistics/ESL. She has been teaching service English courses for undergraduates for several years, most likely in scientific or business English, with emphases on reading textbooks and writing reports of various kinds. Class sizes have been quite large and there has been little time for individual consultancies. She has probably attended a local conference or two and may have given a presentation based on her teaching experience. She has not yet published anything (with all that this entails) in the local ESL journal, nor has she ever reviewed a research paper for a journal. And yet she is now being expected to assist doctoral students to get their papers accepted by peer-reviewed international journals in some arcane sub-specialization. Her situation conjures up Dr Samuel Johnson's comment about a dog walking on two legs: "It is not surprising that it is not done well; it is surprising that it is done at all."

Many senior EAP practitioners have given lectures, workshops or short courses in China on various aspects of EAP and ERP to such teachers and graduate students. But in their chapter, Yongnan Li and Margaret Cargill take these kinds of initiative into new territory. As far as I am aware, this is the first time that the courageous step of offering an 18-hour "master class" for science graduate students on the topic of preparing to write an international science article has been undertaken. The EAP teachers observed Margaret Cargill's teaching from the back of the room with Dr Li acting as a participant observer. Further, the following seminar discussions on what they have observed and learned were video-taped and then analyzed. Dr Li also administered an end-of-course questionnaire and conducted group interviews with the teachers who took part.

Margaret's use of corpora plus a descriptive approach, subsumed under the mantra of "check your target journal", obviously came to the watching teachers as both a respite and a resource. The teachers were at the same time relieved of any expectation that they be omniscient about scientific writing and scientific publication and were now given the option of saying to their students: "Do your own research into what your target journals seem to expect and require." Another gain was a clearer sense of their scaffolding roles in enabling the students to better appreciate the macro as well as the micro features of research articles. Equally interesting to me were the teachers' perceptions of the challenges they face. I instance just three of these because I feel they have considerable resonance in many parts of the world. One was a lack of confidence arising from the fact they had not yet published articles themselves, plus a growing realization that if they at least attempted to do so, they would be in a better position to help their students. Another well-attested challenge is the indifference that low-status language teachers often meet when trying to establish working relations with content-area experts. Finally, there is the issue of a lack of understanding and appreciation on the part of the senior university administration, which may be committed in some general sense to internationalization and to rising up in the world university rankings, but does not readily perceive how lowly EAP/ERP instructors might play a useful part in realizing these ambitions. Indeed, as a couple of participants pointed out, there can be a sting in the tail here: the university administration is probably results-driven and if the new expansion into ERPP does not quickly produce increased numbers of international research articles, then ERPP teachers will be blamed. An impressive and original chapter.

The second chapter of the three I have selected is by Gerriet Janssen and Silvia Restrepo, who both work for one of the leading universities in Columbia. A first notable feature is the authorship itself; although the first author is expected since he is the ERPP program coordinator, the second is not—Dr Restrepo is her university's vice-chancellor for research! Those of us in EAP/ERP are often susceptible to what economists call "exogenous shocks" (such as reduced funding) when there are personnel changes in the senior levels of the university's administration. In fact, many years ago at a conference I heard an EAP director make the following astute comment: "Every time there is a change in the senior administration, there is an increase in the level of ignorance about what we do." So, mixed co-publications or co-presentations of this kind seem like a very promising strategy.

The chapter itself tells the interesting and instructive story of the evolution of an ERPP tutoring service. At its first iteration, it was set up as a writing lab class with a number of prerequisites. These pre-conditions included a guarantee that participants would attend for a minimum of ten hours, they would bring at the outset a draft of a completed empirical research paper, and disciplinary advisors would make themselves available to their students and their writing tutors. There were, I suspect, two motives for these strictures: first, these requirements might speed up the process of achieving successful results (as measured by Colombian papers being accepted by reputable English-language journals); and second, these arrangements would keep the activity more or less in line with other graduate offerings in the institution, such as graduate seminars. However, the comprehensive and well-structured "utilization-focused" program evaluation revealed that relatively few participants took up their full quota of hours, only about a third of the tutees actually had a complete draft of a paper at the outset, and by no means all advisors turned out to be helpful; further, some of the students wanted to work on other genres such as scholarship applications.

As a result, a number of changes were introduced for the 2016 and 2017 iterations, even if the actual tutoring processes (not described here) would remain largely the same. The program would no longer have a class setting, but services would be available as needed; a wider range of academic genres would be supported, such as grant proposals, conference posters, oral presentations, etc; assistance and support would be extended to professors; and additional tutors would be hired to meet the increased work load. This radical redirection is well documented and referenced and shows an impressive capacity to rethink an ERP service in the light of experience.

In this kind of service work, our immediate aim may be to produce better texts, but, of course, the longer-term aim is to produce better writers, and this is why this and many other chapters in this book place emphasis on rhetorical consciousness-raising not only about research genres, but also about aspects of their production and reception. And here it is once again the case that the "Center" has distinct advantages. For instance, most major disciplinary conferences have sessions in which groups of journal editors explain policies and respond to questions from the audience. (I was 50 before I learnt that there were occasions when it was possible to appeal a journal rejection.) It would seem that there is an increasing realization that it may not be a matter of identifying the greatest need, which in this case might well be increasing basic English proficiency, but in sensing where English specialist intervention is most crucial, opportune and beneficial.

My third choice is the chapter on ERP in Norway by Tom Muir and Kristen Solli. I have come to it last because in some ways it is the most challenging. It opens with a trenchant discussion of the "parallel language use" policy adopted by the higher education leadership in Nordic countries: English for international research communications and the local language for communicating with local audiences. They demonstrate, however, that in reality the authorities only pay lip-service to this open-handed policy because the reward systems those authorities have set up for academics (pay, promotion, status, etc.) are heavily skewed in favor of English language publication. (In fact, I was told a few years ago that the bonuses for publishing English language articles in Norway are five times higher than for those written in the local language.)

Muir and Solli then show that "tensions between 'internationalist' and 'culturalist' discourses are also crosscut by disciplinary concerns". More specifically, professional fields like law, education, nursing and social work are much impacted by local traditions, conventions and regulations, and yet as investigations in these areas become more aspirational, they experience what Muir and Solli call "academic drift", or a tendency to indulge in unwieldly theorizing. And we see this kind of drift also here at the University of Michigan. The relatively new doctorates in nursing struggle to establish their place within the medical research establishment and, in attempting to do so, often over-complicate nursing practices, while our professional masters-level degrees in social work have had to become at the doctoral level PhDs in "Social Work *and Social Science*". Meanwhile there is a recent book-length study of the travails of doctoral students—and their supervisors and external examiners—in the creative and performing arts in Australia as they attempt to come to terms with what might be appropriate written accounts of those creations and performances (Ravelli, Paltridge, & Starfield, 2014).

The authors then turn their attention to Karl Maton's Legitimation Code Theory (LCT) as a tool-kit for perceiving more clearly the dilemmas faced by Norwegian scholars and researchers. They focus particularly on his concept of waves that move up and down as the unfolding text oscillates between the "prosaic" and the "rarified". I had an inkling of the value of this kind of movement a number of years ago when a group of us was studying the spoken discourses of master's students in architecture as they defended their major project models and drawings before a "jury" of their teachers and invited prominent regional architects (Barks, Ostermann, Simpson, & Swales, 2001). This genre is traditionally highly combative and the students were frequently interrupted if they were too "prosaic" in their explanations (derisively known as "the janitor's tour") or too "rarified" (theory not well linked to their design or model). The few who did manage to hold the floor did so by moving adroitly between the levels. And in my own written feedback on doctoral student texts I often find myself writing comments like "a telling example would be helpful here" or making queries like "Can you link this finding back to the literature?" LCT may also be helpful in exploring how we might help those researchers who do good local research but cannot find a way to package or re-package their work so that it will escape the charge of "parochialism" when they submit internationally. However, I am beginning to wonder whether these kinds of juxtapositions are more a predeliction of English-language cultures rather than universals of effective argumentation. (My occasional reading of academic Italian suggests that there is less of it there.) So, in fact, it is not impossible that LCT may actually be working to validate and reify an Anglo-American style of rhetoric at the expense of others.

A final issue is whether there are aspects of the combined efforts as represented by the authors in this volume to help plurilinguals with EAL that might have been overlooked. There is at least one—that 21st century phenomenon known as "predatory publishing", which is only briefly discussed in the contribution from Nigeria (Omobowale, Akanle, & Akinsete, this volume). There has been a rapid rise in these journals, which take large fees without providing reviews or other decent editorial services for the manuscripts submitted to them. They solicit articles through aggressive marketing and spam emails. They offer extremely quick turn-around; some invitations I have seen offer publication of manuscripts within ten days! Their motive is purely financial gain and their websites are often designed to give the impression that they are based in an English-speaking country. Unfortunately, predatory publishing is often confused with open-access publishing, which when legitimate, has made many significant contributions to scholarly and scientific knowledge. Confusion is particularly likely with emerging open-access journals. However, Ana Bocanegra-Valle has recently published a very useful paper that establishes criteria for assessing the credibility of emerging journals in the language sciences (Bocanegra-Valle, 2017). Predatory journals offer especially dangerous and seductive temptations for novice researchers from less research-intensive institutions and/or for those who are not part of research networks. We need, therefore, to explore and explain the issue of predatory journals as part of our activities designed to assist our EAL participants in coping with the exigencies of navigating the process of getting published in international journals. Imagine the plight of a doctoral student now required to have at least one paper published in an international journal who finds, after handing over a large chunk of cash, that her paper has appeared in a totally spurious outlet.

References

Barks, D., Ostermann, A. C., Simpson, R. A., & Swales, J. M. (2001). Between critique and accommodation: Reflections on an EAP course for Masters of Architecture. *English for Specific Purposes, 20*, 439–458.

Bennett, K. (Ed.) (2014). *The semiperiphery of academic writing: Discourses, communities and practices.* London: Palgrave MacMillan.

Bocanegra-Valle, A. (2017). How credible are open-access emerging journals? A situational analysis in the humanities. In M. Cargill, & S. Burgess (Eds.). *Publishing research in English as an Additional language: Practices, pathways and potentials* (pp. 121–149). Adelaide: University of Adelaide Press.

Cargill, M., & Burgess, S. (Eds.) (2017). *Publishing research in English as an additional language: Practices, pathways and potentials.* Adelaide: University of Adelaide Press.

Ravelli, L., Paltridge, B., & Starfield, S. (2014). *Doctoral writing in the creative and performing arts.* Farringdon, UK: Libri Publishing.

CONTRIBUTOR BIOGRAPHIES

Editors

James N. Corcoran is an Assistant Professor of Applied Language Studies and English Language Studies at Renison University College/University of Waterloo, Canada.

Karen Englander is an applied linguist and former Professor at the Universidad Autónoma de Baja California, Mexico, and York University in Toronto, Canada.

Laura-Mihaela Muresan is Professor of English at the Bucharest University of Economic Studies, Romania.

Contributors

Georgina Aguilar-González is a full-time lecturer and researcher at the undergraduate degree program in ELT at Benemérita Universidad Autónoma de Puebla (BUAP), Mexico.

Olayinka Akanle is a lecturer in the Department of Sociology, University of Ibadan, Nigeria, and a Postdoctoral Fellow at the University of South Africa (UNISA), South Africa.

Charles Akinsete is a lecturer at the Department of English, University of Ibadan, Nigeria.

Birna Arnbjörnsdóttir is Professor of Second Languages Studies at the University of Iceland and Director of the Vigdís Finnbogadóttir Institute for Languages, Iceland.

Diana Balasanyan earned her PhD at the Universidad de La Laguna, Spain, in 2017 and she is currently involved in a number of educational projects, such as teaching an online course for university lecturers.

Sally Burgess is a lecturer in English at the University of La Laguna, Spain.

Yuan Cao is currently a lecturer in the College of English, Shanghai International Studies University, China.

Margaret Cargill holds an Adjunct Senior Lectureship in the School of Agriculture, Food and Wine at the University of Adelaide, Australia, and is Principal Consultant at SciWriting.

Gicela Cuatlapantzi-Pichón is a Professor at the undergraduate program in ELT at the Benemérita Universidad Autónoma de Puebla, Mexico.

Tanju Deveci is an Assistant Professor of English at Khalifa University of Science and Technology in Abu Dhabi, UAE.

Fátima Encinas-Prudencio has been an English teacher and teacher educator for more than 30 years. She is a former coordinator of the ELT BA and MA programs at the Benemérita Universidad Autónoma de Puebla, Mexico.

Behzad Ghonsooly is a Professor of English at Ferdowsi University of Mashhad, Iran.

Gerriet Janssen is Associate Professor in the Department of Languages and Culture at Universidad de los Andes, Colombia, where he was the principal developer of the TIPPs English-language tutoring program for professional purposes.

Yongyan Li is Associate Professor in the Faculty of Education, University of Hong Kong, China.

Raquel María Teresa Lothringer is an English Language and Literature teacher from Instituto del Profesorado (Paraná-Argentina) and former Head of the Modern Languages Department (Facultad de Ciencias de la Educación, Universidad Nacional de Entre Ríos-UNER).

Pedro Martín is a lecturer in English for academic purposes at the University of La Laguna, Spain.

Hayat Messekher is Associate Professor of English at the Ecole Normale Supérieure of Bouzaréah, Algiers. Algeria.

Mohamed Miliani is Professor of English at the University of Oran 2, Algeria.

Seyyed-Abdolhamid Mirhosseini is an Associate Professor at Alzahra University, Tehran, Iran.

Tom Muir is Associate Professor of English for Academic Purposes at Oslo Metropolitan University, Norway.

Sarwat Nauman is an Assistant Professor at the Department of Education, Institute of Business Management (IoBM), Karachi, Pakistan.

Alicia Noceti is a Professor of English and researcher at the Facultad de Ciencias de la Alimentación, Universidad Nacional de Entre Ríos, Argentina.

Roger Nunn is Professor and Head of the Department of Writing Studies at the American University of Sharjah, UAE. http://www.englishscholarsbeyondborders.org/members-profiles/roger-nunns-profile/

Ayokunle Olumuyiwa Omobowale is a Senior Lecturer in the Department of Sociology at the University of Ibadan, Nigeria.

Carmen Pérez-Llantada is Professor of English Linguistics at the University of Zaragoza, Spain.

Silvia Restrepo is Full Professor in the Department of Biological Sciences at Universidad de los Andes, Colombia, and is currently Vice-chancellor of Research and PhD programs.

Verónica Sánchez-Hernández has been an English teacher and teacher educator for 20 years, and was the Coordinator of the ELT MA program and the Research and Postgraduate Studies Secretary in the Language Department (2013–2016) at the Benemérita Universidad Autónoma de Puebla, Mexico.

Zahra Shafiee is currently a PhD student of Applied Linguistics at Alzahra University in Tehran, Iran.

Hesamoddin Shahriari is an Assistant Professor of Applied Linguistics at Ferdowsi University of Mashhad, Iran.

Kristin Solli is Associate Professor of English for Academic Purposes at Oslo Metropolitan University, Norway.

John M. Swales is Professor Emeritus of Linguistics and Co-Director of the Michigan Corpus of Academic Spoken English (MICASE) at University of Michigan.

Maria (Mia) Thomas-Ruzic is Senior Instructor and Director of the Program for TESOL Professionals at University of Colorado, Boulder.

Diana Waigandt is a Professor of English (ESP, EAP & ERPP) and a researcher at the Facultad de Ingeniería at Universidad Nacional de Entre Ríos, Argentina.

Yongyan Zheng is a Professor in the College of Foreign Languages and Literature, Fudan University, China.

INDEX

Page numbers in *italics* refer to figures. Page numbers in **bold** refer to tables.

academic drift 95–96, 289
academic literacy development 58
academic paper analysis, stages of 269–278
Achebe, C. 218, 224
activity theory 145–147, *149*
Adichie, C. 224
Africa: Nigeria 215–228; teaching the craft in 195–208
Afzal, M. T. 187–188
agency 50–51, 52
Alatas, S. 216
Aleixandre-Benavent, R. 130
Algeria 195–208
Amadi, E. 224
anxiety 50, 51
Argentina 56–70
Arnbjörnsdóttir, B. 84
Arnoux, E. 58
assessment activities 63
asymmetrical market of knowledge production 109
audience analysis 206–207
author-editing 226–227
authoring 38
authorship 36–53, **39**, **41**, **44–45**
Ávila-Reyes, N. 58
Awonusi, S. 220

Babajide, A. 224
Balasanyan, D. 136

Banjo, A. 217
Banta, T. 21
Barthomae 132
Barton, D. 110
Bazerman, C. 38
Belcher, D. 110, 112
Benesch, S. 132
Bennett, K. 93, 100, 102, 103, 131, 133, 284
Bernstein, B. 98
bias, perceptions of 244–246
bilingualism 110
biliteracy approach 161–173
Bocanegra-Valle, A. 169, 171, 253, 290
Brent, D. 26, 30
Buker, S. 132
Burgess, S. 284

Cadman, K. 132, 133
Canagarajah, A. S. 103, 219
Cao, Y. 46
Cargill, M. 86, 130, 147, 284, 286–287
Carlino, P. 58
Carrasco, A. 38
Casanave, C. 50
categorizations of linguistic factors 109–110
Central Committee of the Communist Party of China (CCCPC) 163
challenges: for Chinese students *149*, 151–156, 157; for EAP instructors

151–156, 287; for Iranian researchers 237–238, 244–246
Cheng, A. 122
China 161–173, 253
Christian, L. 243
citations, as indicator of quality 242
class size 155–156
co-authorship 202, 204, 246
code-switching 26, 103
cognitive dimension of learning to write 119
collaboration: difficulty achieving 153–154, 202; networking practices and 46–48
collective learning activity 145–146, *146*
Colombia 19–32, 287–288
colonization, effects of 215–228
communities of practice (CoP) 22, 26–28, 37–38, 50, 60, 86, 117, 119, 122, 132, 197–198, 205, 206, 208
Comprehensive Science Roadmap 255
conference presentations 26
Connor, U. 84, 110, 112
context awareness 42–46
cooperative principle 267–268, 279
Corcoran, J. N. 31, 59, 85, 86, 133, 137, 247, 285
corpus linguistics 7
Council of Europe 253
Craven 21
critical approaches 8
critical argumentation, principles of 269
critical-pragmatic approach 129, 131, 133–138
critical pragmatic pedagogy 128–138
cultural-historical activity theory (CHAT) 143, 145–147, 156–157, 158
culturalist discourses 91–92, 289
Cultural Revolution 163
Currey, J. 218
Curry, M. J. 46, 59, 110, 112, 238

Dalton, E. 243
Derrida, J. 92–93, 100, 101, 102
"descriptive" approach 150–151, 157
dialogic pedagogy 132
disciplinarity 94–96, 119
disciplinary enculturation 110, 119
discourse communities 27, 38, 47, 52, 60, 61, 82, 133
doctoral course in research writing 131–136, **134–135**
Dudley-Evans, T. 281
Duzak, A. 162
Dzul, M. 37

East Asia: Chinese scholars 161–173; "master class" in 143–158
Eastern and Southern Europe: Romanian academic ecosystem 109–123; Spain 128–138
editing: author 226–227; self- 207
editing services 247
editorial positioning 3
editors, working with 206–207
education system in Iran 236–237
Elder, L. 269
Encinas, F. 38, 52
enculturation processes 38, 50
Engeström, Y. 145
Englander, K. 31, 46, 59, 84, 85, 86, 133, 137, 247, 285
English Academic Discourse (EAD) 100–101
English for Academic Purposes (EAP): instructors of 143–158, 286–287; pedagogical responses and orientations 6–9; practitioners of 5
English for General Academic Purposes (EGAP) model 143
English for research publication purposes (ERPP) 2; tutoring service for 19–32
English Language Education and Research Communication for Business and Economics (EDU-RES) master's programme 111
English Language Teaching Reforms (ELTR) 179–180, 184–190, *185*
English Reformation 100
epistemicide 100–101, 131
epistemic modality 277–278
ethics 207
Evans, S. 242
Expediency Discernment Council (Iran) 235
experience, lack of 152–153

Fakoya, A. 221
Farooq, U. 180
Farsi 252, 254, 255–257, 258–259, 260–263
Feak, C. 26
Fenton-O'Creevy, M. 38
Ferguson, G. 26
Ferris, D. 24, 25
Ferris, D. R. 196
findings, application of 242
first person, use of 274–277, **275**, 278
Fish, A. 243
flexibility 26
Flowerdew, J. 157, 169, 237, 253

Fortes, J. 19
Fournier, D. 21
four-step assessment cycle 21
Freire, P. 59
Fullan, M. 52

Galloway, N. 216
Gao, X. 147
Gea-Valor, M. L. 29, 31
gender differences in confidence level 80, 82
generic structure, holistic 269–271, **270**, 278
genre analysis 152
genre-based approaches 7, 133, 136
genre expertise 120–121
Gentil, G. 110, 120–121, 162
Giltrow, J. 275
global contexts 4–5
global diglossia 162
González-Alcaide, G. 130
Gosden, H. 24, 25–26
graduate students, help for 266–282
grammar instruction 242
Grammarly 228
Grammar-Translation Method 203
Green, C. 242
Gregersen, F. 91–92
Grice, P. 267–268, **268**, 269, 271, 278–279
Grommes, P. 2
Gulden, A. T. 103
Gulzar, M. A. 180

Hadley, G. 133, 137
Hargreaves, A. 52
Harwood, N. 133, 137
Hedgcock, J. 24, 25
Hedgcock, J. S. 196
Hernandez-Zamora, G. 50
"hidden challenge" 81, 88
Higher Education Commission (HEC) Pakistan 179, 182–190
Higher Education Institute (HEI; Pakistan) 179
Higher Education Law (Argentina) 57
holistic argumentation creation 266–282
Hood, S. 98
Hu, A. 2
Hultgren, A. 91–92
Hutchinson, S. 38
Hyland, K. 30–31, 61, 157

Iceland 77–89
identity, language and 218, 261

Imagined Communities (ICs) 197–198
immersion 38
incomplete expression 223–224
indexing of journals 243–244, 253, 256, 262
indigenized Englishes 216
Ingvarsdóttir, H. 84
innovation, barriers to 153
institutional support, lack of 154–155
integral references 271–273, **272**
internationalist discourses 91–92, 289
internationalization policy 220
International Resource Person (IRP) training 184–185, 186, 190
interviews: on English language skills 80–81; in Iranian study 239–240, **239**, 251, 257, 259; modified subject-object (SO) 40; for Romanian study 112, 126–127; semi-structured protocol for 126–127, 240
Iran 235–248, 252–263
Islamic World Science Citation Database (ISC) 241

Janssen, Gerriet 20, 287–288
Johns, A. M. 110, 111
Joint Comprehensive Plan of Action 237
Jones, M. 243
Journal Citation Index (JCR) 241
journals: criteria for choosing 243–244; indexing of 243–244, 253, 256, 262; predatory 227, 290

Kachru, B. 237
Kachru, B. B. 220
Kaplan, R. 84
Kent, R. 38
Kirk S. 97
knowledge production, asymmetrical market of 109
Kubiak, C. 38
Kumari, R. 189–190

La Laguna, University of 128–138, **134–135**
language: functions of 217–218; identity and 218, 261
language-related difficulties in ERPP 169, *169*
language services 169, *170*
"languages of legitimation" 98
Lasky, S. 52
Latin America: Argentinian institutional initiatives 56–70; Colombian tutoring

service 19–32; Mexican authorship 36–53
Lave, J. 42
Legitimate Peripheral Participation (LPP) 37–38
Legitimation Code Theory (LCT) 93, 96–100, 103, 289
Leont'ev, A. N. 145
Leskes, A. 21
Lewkowicz, J. 162
Li, Y. 253, 286–287
Lillis, T. 46, 59, 110, 112, 238
linguistic factors, categorizations of 109–110
literacy: acquisition of 110; description of 57–58; sociocultural perspectives on 58–59
literacy brokering 3, 7, 22, 46–49, 60, 67–68, 69, 86, 248
literature, Derrida on 101
Ljosland, R. 93
LMD (License – Master – Doctorate) system 195
Lomnitz, L. 19
Luo, N. 30–31

MacDonald, S. 132
Malik, N. A. 186, 188
Mamoon, D. 188
Manchon, R. M. 197
Masrur, R. 187–188
"master class" 143–158, 287
Maton, K. 93, 96–97, 98–99, 289
maxims of conversation 267–268, **268**, 271, 278–279, 281
McGrath, L. 162, 172
McNamara, M. S. 97
Mediterranean Editors and Translators group 137
Mexico 36–53
Ministry of Health and Medical Education (Iran) 252, 255, 257
Ministry of Science, Research and Technology (Iran) 236, 238–239, 240–242, 248, 252, 255, 257
Mirza, M. S. 183
modality analysis 277–278
Mora, A. 38
Moreno, A. 29
morphological misrepresentations 225
"move-step" structure 281
Muir, T. 288–289
multiliteracies, theory of 59
multimodality 59
Muresan, L.-M. 285

narrative account format 112
Nasreen, A. 183
National Commission for University Evaluation and Accreditation (CONEAU) 57
National Education Policy (NEP; Pakistan) 180, 182, 189
national language domain loss 162
National Scientific and Technical Research Council (CONICET) 57
Nauman, S. 188
networking practices, collaboration and 46–48
Ngugi wa Thiong'o 217
Nigeria 215–228
non-integral references 271–274, **272**
Nordic Language Policy 77
North American New Rhetoric 59, 69
northern Europe: ERP in Norway 91–103, 288–289; supporting Nordic scholars 77–89
Norway 91–103, 288–289
Nwaubani, A. T. 221

Obi, M. 222
Obiahiagbon, P. 221–223
O'Connor, P. 86, 130, 147
"off-network" academics 162, 170, 237, 284
Okigbo, C. 218
Okri, B. 224
Olso Metropolitan University 91
online seminar for scholarly publication 61–65, *62*, *64*
onticide 101
Onwuzurukgbo, I. 216
open-access publishing 290

Pakistan 179–190
Palomba, C. 21
Paradis, J. 38
parallel language policy 77–78, 93, 162, 171, 288–289
"passion" 102
passive voice 274–275, **275**, 279–280
Patton, M. 20–22
Paul, R. 269
Pedagogies and Policies for Publishing Research in English (Corcoran, Englander, and Muresan) 285
peer editing 226
peer review 4, 32, 116, 117, 122, 197, 207, 243, 284, 286
Pennycook, A. 132
Pérez-Bustos, T. 136

Pérez-Llantada, C. 26
performance-based research funding policies 94
Perry, K. H. 59
Persian Gulf: graduate student help in 266–282; Iran 235–248, 252–263
Pho, P. D. 275
Phothongsunan, S. 112
Plo, R. 26
plurilingualism 2
plurilingual users of EAL 2, 5
points for publication 196
polishing 24
postgraduate online seminar 61–65, *62, 64*
pragmatic approaches 7–8
predatory journals 227, 290
"Preparing to Write an International Science Article (PWISA)" 147–158
Prior, P. A. 110
privileging of English 2–3
PRODEP 42
professionalization of EAP 157–158
program evaluation, theory of 21–22
proofreaders 81, 83, 84, 85, 246
publication practices, from Mexican study 48–50
Publishing Research in English as an Additional Language (Cargill and Burgess) 284–285
punctuation errors 224–225

qualitative analysis 273–274
quality articles, characteristics of 242–243
quantitative analysis 271–273, **272**
quantitative results 274–275
questionnaire: from Algerian study 198–202, 211–214; for China study 164–165; in Iranian study 257; self-reflective 112, 126

Raabi, A. 188
Rahman, A. 181
Ramírez, J. L. 37
referencing 271–274, **272**, 280–281
reflexive evaluation 204
Reform and Opening-up policy 163
relevance 278
research and teaching, linking 65–67
resentment 130
Restrepo, S. 20, 287–288
reviewers' feedback 117, 247
Reynolds, D. 24
Rey-Rocha, J. 29
Rezaeian, M. 254–255
rhetorical approaches 7

rhetorical machining 24
rhetorical strategies 242
Rice, C. 91–92, 102
Romania 109–123
Rose, H. 216
Rose, M. 201
Roux, R. 38
Royle, N. 101, 103
Ruzic, M. 38

Saleem, A. 187–188
Sánchez-Hernández, V. 52
Sandelin, B. 162–163, 172
Sarafogloiu, N. 162–163, 172
scaffolding 206, 287
scholarly publication seminar 61–65, *62, 64*
self-editing 207
self-reflective questionnaire 112, 126
semantic codes 98
semantic density 97–98
semantic gravity 97–98
semantic plane *99*
semantic waves 97–98, *98*
Semi-periphery of Academic Writing, The (Bennett) 284–285
sequential mixed methods approach 39
Séror, J. 110
Shamim, F. 187
Shay, S. 98
Shi, X. 216
Sivertsen, G. 94
Smith, M. 243
social practices 7
social theories of learning 22, 37–38
social writing practices 247–248
Solli, K. 288–289
South Asia, Pakistani scholars 179–190
Soyinka, W. 218, 224
Spain 128–138
Spanish for Research Publication Purposes (SRPP) 130
spell-check 207
Sperber, D. 278
staging 206
student motivation 156
subject-object protocol 40
Swales, J. M. 24, 26, 38, 59, 60, 65, 68, 69, 110, 132, 206

"talk around text" interviews 40, 48
target audience 116
teaching reforms, impact of 179–190
Tenopir, C. 243
Tenure Track System (TTS) 182
terminology 2–3

text level distribution **97**
think-aloud protocols 112, 206
Thøgersen, J. 91–92
Thomson Reuters report 186–187, 254
"threat of English" discourse 162, 168
traditional teaching approaches 203
transitivity analysis 274–277, 279
translation services 80, 81, 85
Trejo, N. P. 38
Trujeque, E. 38
tutoring service 19–32, **25**, **30**

undergraduate writing seminar 60
Universidad Nacional de Entre Rios (UNER) 56–70
University of Iceland 77–89
University Policies Secretariat (SPU) 57
Urdu 180–181, 188–189
utilization-focused program evaluation 19–32, 287–288
Uzuner-Smith, S. 84

Valderrama-Zurián, J. C. 130
Vandrick, S. 50

verbosity 221–223, 224
Virtual Education Program Pakistan (VEPP) 185
vulgar pragmatism 132
Vygotsky, L. 145

Wang, X. 147
Weissberg, R. 132
Wenger, E. 38, 42, 48
Wenger-Trayner, B. 38
Wenger-Trayner, E. 38
Wilson, D. 278
word cloud 113, *113*
Wright, B. D. 21
writing assistance: need for 82–84; program for 85–88, **87**; *see also* literacy brokering; "master class"
"Writing for Academic and Professional Purposes" (seminar) 60
"writing-for-publication" MA course 205–208, **206**

Zheng, Y. 46
Zhu, W. 28

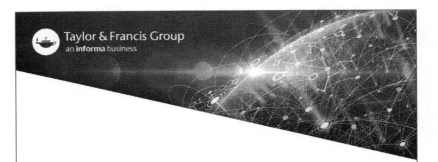